Organizational
Culture
and
Leadership

Edgar H. Schein

Organizational
Culture
and
Leadership

Second Edition

Jossey-Bass Publishers · San Francisco

FIRST PAPERBACK EDITION PUBLISHED IN 1997.

Substantial discounts on bulk quantities of Jossey-Bass books are available
to corporations, professional associations, and other organizations. For
details and discount information, contact the special sales department at
Jossey-Bass Inc., Publishers (415)433-1740; Fax (800) 605-2665.

For sales outside the United States, please contact your local Simon & Schuster
International Office.

 Manufactured in the United States of America on Lyons Falls Pathfinder
Tradebook. This paper is acid-free and 100 percent totally chlorine-free.

Library of Congress Cataloging-in-Publication Data

Schein, Edgar H.
 Organizational culture and leadership / Edgar H. Schein — 2nd
ed.
 p.   cm. — (A joint publication in the Jossey-Bass management
series and the Jossey-Bass social and behavioral science series)
 Includes bibliographical references and index.
 ISBN 1-55542-487-2 (alk. paper)
 ISBN 0-7879-0362-0 (paperback)
 1. Corporate culture.   2. Culture.   3. Leadership.   I. Title.
II. Series: Jossey-Bass management series.   III. Series: Jossey-Bass
social and behavioral science series.
HD58.7.S33   1992
302.3'5—dc20   92-23849

SECOND EDITION
HB Printing   10 9 8 7 6 5
PB Printing   10 9 8 7 6 5 4 3 2 1

Contents

Preface

I wrote the first edition of *Organizational Culture and Leadership* to clarify the concept of organizational culture and to show its relationship to leadership. In the mid eighties, when the book was published, there was great interest in understanding and managing culture because it was perceived to be not only a concept that could explain many organizational phenomena but also something that leaders could manipulate to create a more effective organization.

During the same time, many scholars and consultants wondered whether the use of culture as an explanation of various organizational phenomena was a fad that would wane once managers discovered that cultural manipulation was not as easy as they might have thought. But the faddish side of culture has not waned; in fact, an increasing number of researchers, practitioners, managers, and leaders have found the concept useful and necessary in analyzing and managing organizations. Leaders, especially, have become more aware of the critical role an understanding of culture plays in their efforts to stimulate learning and change and how intricately intertwined their own behavior is with culture creation and management.

During the past six years I have become involved in a number of these change efforts and have found leaders struggling with the concept of culture. The concept is hard to define, hard to analyze and measure, and hard to manage. But I perceived that the problems leaders were struggling with did indeed involve culture as I understood it, and they needed help in understanding both the concept itself and how to manage situations in which cultural assumptions were operating.

I undertook to revise this book to clarify and strengthen the culture concept to show more clearly what the content of culture is and how leadership was indeed intertwined with it. Much of what is in the first edition proved to be conceptually sound and has been retained and elaborated on. My experience of the last six years in dealing with cultural issues as a researcher and consultant has deepened my understanding and provided new examples, which appear in this edition. I also found that some of what I had written about earlier has proven to be less relevant and has therefore been dropped, in the hope of making this edition more coherent and better integrated. Finally, based on my recent experiences in working on those issues, I have added a number of practical suggestions for dealing with cultural issues in organizations.

Why Do We Need to Understand Culture?

Cultural analysis illuminates subcultural dynamics within organizations. One major reason for the increased interest in culture is, in my view, that the concept not only has become relevant to organizational level analysis, but also has aided understanding of what goes on inside organizations when different subcultures and occupational groups must work with each other. Many problems that were once viewed simply as "communication failures" or "lack of teamwork" are now being more properly understood as a breakdown of intercultural communications.

For example, most companies today are trying to speed up the process of designing, manufacturing, and delivering new products to customers. They are increasingly discovering that the coordination of the marketing, engineering, manufacturing, distribution, and sales groups will require more than goodwill, good intentions, and a few management incentives. To achieve the necessary integration requires understanding the subcultures of each of these functions and the design of intergroup processes that allow communication and collaboration across sometimes strong subcultural boundaries.

Cultural analysis is necessary if we are to understand how new technologies influence and are influenced by organizations. A new technology is usually a reflection of an occupational culture that is built around new core scientific or engineering concepts and tools. The occupational subculture reflecting these new concepts will often be partly inside the organization and partly outside in the form of vendors and academics.

For example, there is much discussion these days about information technology (IT) and its impact on transforming work and organizations. In order to understand how IT enters organizations and begins to transform some of the practices in the organization, we must recognize that in the implementation process the subculture of the occupational community of IT runs into various functional subcultures within the organization and that the interaction of those subcultures transforms the technology as well. We will fail to understand some of the phenomena that occur around the misadventures of implementing information technology unless we take a cultural perspective toward them.

Cultural analysis is necessary for management across national and ethnic boundaries. Just as the concept of culture has begun to help in the understanding of subcultural phenomena in organizations, so it has also become more relevant to the analysis of broader national and ethnic interrelationships as more organizations find themselves working with other nations and cultures in various joint ventures, strategic alliances, mergers, and acquisitions. Managers have always known that working across such borders was difficult, but only recently have researchers and consultants begun to develop concepts and perspectives that will enable us to analyze and solve these difficulties.

A severe problem we face in this broader intercultural arena is that cultural misunderstandings are usually considered undiscussable. To point out to a person of another culture some behavior we might find incomprehensible risks offending that person. So we tolerate rather than confront culturally based communication breakdowns, and this makes matters worse because we develop a mutual fiction that we understand each other when in fact we do not. The poor performance of many mergers, acquisitions, and joint ventures can often be explained by the failure to understand the depth of cultural misunderstanding that may be present.

Organizational learning, development, and planned change cannot be understood without considering culture as a primary source of resistance to change. Resistance to learning and change is a ubiquitous phenomenon often talked about but seldom understood. Consultants and managers know how frustrating it is when so much effort on the part of change agents yields so little change. But as change agents, we gain a much better perspective if we realize that most organizational change usually involves some changes in culture, often at the subcultural level. If we can better understand what is involved for members of a subculture when they have to change some of their basic assumptions, values, and behaviors, we become much more sympathetic to their resistance and much more realistic about how to manage change.

Organizational development is increasingly oriented around the notions of learning, innovation, adaptation, and perpetual change in response to the ever-increasing rates of technological, social, economic, and political change. As a stabilizing force in human systems, culture is one of the most difficult aspects to manage in a climate of perpetual change. The challenge lies in conceptualizing a culture of innovation in which learning, adaptation, innovation, and perpetual change are the stable elements.

Given these and related issues, it seems obvious that we must increase our study of culture and put this research on a solid conceptual foundation. Superficial concepts of culture will not be useful; we must come to understand fully what culture is all about in human groups, organizations, and nations so that we can have a much deeper understanding of what goes on, why it goes on, and what, if anything, we can do about it.

Who Should Read This Book?

This edition, as was the first, was written for several audiences. I have tried to continue to present an academically sound, balanced set of arguments based on empirical research and clinical experience. At the same time, I have tried to bring culture to life for the practitioner, consultant, and, most importantly, the operating manager. Managers live in cultures and often are instrumental in creating, developing, and destroying cultures. It is therefore mandatory that managers understand what they are dealing with and what they are doing when they attempt to manage culture. Leaders, in contrast, create and modify cultures. Culture creation, culture evolution, and culture management are what ultimately define leadership, so I am trying to reach both present and potential leaders as well.

Students who are trying to understand organizations are another prime audience for the book. Though it does not cover all of the research on organizational culture, the book attempts to provide a consistent perspective that allows students to observe and understand what is going on around them as they face organizational life. The book is not a popularized primer of culture, but it does explore issues in depth and present a range of representative research in language that is accessible to the interested layperson.

Overview of the Contents

The book is organized into six parts. Part One defines what organizational culture is, how leadership is related to culture, how one can think about culture, and how one would describe organizations as cultures. Chapter One introduces and defines the concept of culture. Chapter Two argues that the analysis of culture works best if one considers culture as *manifesting* itself at the level of behavior and espoused values, but that the *essence* of culture lies in the set of underlying assumptions that a group shares. Chapter Three illustrates this kind of analysis with two cases and argues for a clinical research point of view toward the study of culture.

Part Two presents a systematic review of some of the dimensions that researchers and/or leaders need to pay attention to as they attempt to describe a given culture. Chapter Four focuses on the issues of survival and the external problems of adaptation. Chapter Five shifts the focus to the internal problems of integration. Chapter Six examines some deeper dimensions of culture—shared assumptions about reality, truth, time, and space — and Chapter Seven explores the deeper assumptions about human nature, activity, and relationships.

Part Three then describes how one would go about deciphering a given culture, distinguishing two different processes: deciphering for purposes of making a culture visible to its members (Chapter Eight) and/or deciphering for purposes of explaining and writing about that culture to outsiders (Chapter Nine). This part closes with a discussion of the ethical problems of culture research (Chapter Ten).

Part Four focuses on how founders as leaders create and develop cultures. Chapter Eleven describes, using several cases, how the assumptions of leaders are gradually taught to new members and how culture is thereby created. In Chapter Twelve the various mechanisms that allow leaders to embed their assumptions in the organization's routines and processes are described. Chapter Thirteen analyzes the process by which organizations evolve into their own "midlife" and how the formation of subgroups and subcultures creates new forces and possibilities for culture change. The role of subcultures is then illustrated in Chapter Fourteen by contrasting some of the assumptions of the information technology subculture and the senior management subculture.

Part Five focuses on culture change and the critical role that leaders play in managing such change, with particular attention to how that role changes according to the developmental stage of the organization. Chapter Fifteen discusses the culture change mechanisms available to leaders in young organizations, and Chapter Sixteen continues the analysis by describing the leader's role in culture change processes in midlife, mature, and declining organizations. Chapter Seventeen provides a case study that illustrates these principles in action.

Finally, Part Six shifts to the concept of learning and the implications for leadership and culture of the growing rate of change we are all experiencing. Chapter Eighteen describes what would be the essential elements of an innovative or perpetually learning culture, the kind of culture that leaders would want to create to cope with perpetual change. Chapter Nineteen then pulls together the various implications for leaders if they are to become learners and culture managers.

The basic method of analyzing culture is the same in this second edition as in the original edition. The major changes are in dropping various materials that were peripheral to culture and in adding a number of chapters on subculture, culture deciphering, and the learning leader and culture. In each of the chapters that remain thematically the same, I have added new research findings and concepts to bring the book up to date and to deepen the analysis.

Acknowledgments

Since the first edition of this book was published, many colleagues, friends, reviewers, clients, and students have provided invaluable feedback. I cannot name them all, but I am especially indebted to the reviewers David Coghlan, Lyman Porter, Benjamin Schneider, and Robert Simerly, without whose feedback it would have been impossible to think clearly about how to improve this book. Special thanks go to my colleagues Deborah Ancona, Lotte Bailyn, Robert Thomas, John Van Maanen, and Eleanor Westney, whose continual input and stimulation have helped me learn. In the area of information technology and strategy, I have benefited greatly from discussions with Arnoldo Hax, Wanda Orlikowski, Jack Rockart, and Michael Scott-Morton. My former and recent students, particularly Stephen Barley, Deborah Dougherty, Gibb Dyer, Gideon Kunda, George Roth, Jane Salk, and Elaine Yakura, have strongly influenced my thinking through their seminal research.

As always, my wife, Mary, has been a steady support, suffering through the long hours while I was mentally "away" but always encouraging me.

Cambridge, Massachusetts   EDGAR H. SCHEIN
August 1992

To my children—
Louisa, who is an anthropologist,
and Elizabeth and Peter,
who have lived in organizations
and know the reality of cultures all too well

The Author

EDGAR H. SCHEIN is professor of management at the Sloan School of Management at the Massachusetts Institute of Technology. He received his B.A. degree (1947) from the University of Chicago in general education, his M.A. degree (1949) from Stanford University in social psychology, and his Ph.D. degree (1952) from Harvard University in social psychology.

Schein's main research activities have taken him through many subject areas: from a study of the brainwashing of Korean and Chinese POWs to a study of management development and organizational socialization, and on to a deeper look at managerial careers. His interest in culture grew primarily out of clinical work with organizations in which culture became highly visible. Schein is coeditor of the highly acclaimed Addison-Wesley series on organizational development (launched in 1969 with Richard Beckhard and Warren Bennis). His other recent books include *The Clinical Perspective in Field Work* (1987), *Organizational Psychology* (1980, 3rd ed.), and *Career Anchors* (1990, rev. ed.).

Schein was chair of the Organization Studies Group of the Sloan School of Management from 1972 to 1981 and has consulted with a range of organizations around the world on culture, organizational development, and careers. He is considered one of the founders of the field of organizational psychology.

Organizational
Culture
and
Leadership

PART ONE

What Culture
Is and Does

In this section of the book I define the concept of culture and show its relationship to leadership. Culture can be analyzed as a phenomenon that surrounds us at all times, being constantly enacted and created by our interactions with others. My perspective on culture is different. When one brings culture to the level of the organization and even down to groups within the organization, one can see more clearly how it is created, embedded, developed, and ultimately manipulated, managed, and changed. These dynamic processes of culture creation and management are the essence of leadership and make one realize that leadership and culture are two sides of the same coin.

Leadership has been studied in far greater detail than organizational culture, leading to a frustrating diffusion of concepts and ideas of what leadership is really all about, whether one is born or made a leader, whether one can train people to be leaders, and what the characteristics of successful leaders are. I will not review this literature but focus instead on what I consider to be uniquely associated with leadership — the creation and management of culture.

As we will see, this requires an evolutionary perspective. I believe that cultures begin with leaders who impose their own values and assumptions on a group. If that group is successful

1

and the assumptions come to be taken for granted, we have then a culture that will define for later generations of members what kinds of leadership are acceptable. The culture now defines leadership. But as the group encounters adaptive difficulties, as its environment changes to the point where some of its assumptions are no longer valid, leadership comes into play once more. Leadership now is the ability to step outside the culture that created the leader and to start evolutionary change processes that are more adaptive. This ability to perceive the limitations of one's own culture and to develop the culture adaptively is the essence and ultimate challenge of leadership.

If leaders are to fulfill this challenge, they must first understand the dynamics of culture. Our journey begins, then, with a focus on definitions, case illustrations, and a suggested way of thinking about organizational culture. Chapter One begins with some brief illustrations and a definition. Chapter Two expands the concept and argues for a multilevel conception of culture. Chapter Three examines in some detail two cases that illustrate the complexity of culture and are used throughout the rest of the book.

The most important message for leaders at this point is "Try to understand culture, give it its due, and ask yourself how well you can begin to understand the culture in which you are embedded."

CHAPTER ONE

Defining
Organizational Culture

Culture as a concept has had a long and checkered history. It has been used by the lay person as a word to indicate sophistication, as when we say that someone is very "cultured." It has been used by anthropologists to refer to the customs and rituals that societies develop over the course of their history. In the last decade or so it has been used by some organizational researchers and managers to indicate the climate and practices that organizations develop around their handling of people or to refer to the espoused values and credo of an organization.

In this context managers speak of developing the "right kind of culture" or a "culture of quality," suggesting that culture is concerned with certain values that managers are trying to inculcate in their organizations. Also implied in this usage is the assumption that there are better or worse cultures, stronger or weaker cultures, and that the "right" kind of culture will influence how effective organizations are.

If a new and abstract concept is to be useful to our thinking, it should refer to a set of events that are otherwise mysterious or not well understood. From this point of view, I will argue that we must avoid the superficial models of culture and build on the deeper, more complex anthropological models. Culture will be most useful as a concept if it helps us better understand

3

the hidden and complex aspects of organizational life. This understanding cannot be obtained if we use superficial definitions.

Most of us in our roles as students, employees, managers, researchers, or consultants work in and deal with organizations of all kinds. Yet we continue to find it amazingly difficult to understand and justify much of what we observe and experience in our organizational life. Too much seems to be bureaucratic, or political, or just plain irrational. People in positions of authority, especially our immediate bosses, often frustrate us or act incomprehensibly, and those we consider the leaders of our organizations often disappoint us.

If we are managers who are trying to change the behavior of subordinates, we often encounter resistance to change at a level that seems beyond reason. We observe departments in our organization that seem to be more interested in fighting with each other than getting the job done. We see communication problems and misunderstandings between group members that should not be occurring between "reasonable" people.

If we are leaders who are trying to get our organizations to become more effective in the face of severe environmental pressures, we are sometimes amazed at the degree to which individuals and groups in the organization will continue to behave in obviously ineffective ways, often threatening the very survival of the organization. As we try to get things done that involve other groups, we often discover that they do not communicate with each other and that the level of conflict between groups in organizations and in the community is often astonishingly high.

If we are teachers, we encounter the sometimes mysterious phenomenon that different classes behave completely differently from each other even though our material and teaching style remain the same. If we are employees considering a new job, we realize that companies differ greatly in their approach, even in the same industry and geographical area. We feel these differences even as we walk in the door of different organizations such as restaurants, banks, and stores.

The concept of culture helps explain all of these phenomena and to "normalize" them. If we understand the dynamics of culture, we will be less likely to be puzzled, irritated, and anxious when we encounter the unfamiliar and seemingly irrational behavior of people in organizations, and we will have a deeper understanding not only of why various groups of people or organizations can be so different but also why it is so hard to change them.

A deeper understanding of cultural issues in groups and organizations is necessary to decipher what goes on in them but, even more important, to identify what may be the priority issues for leaders and leadership. Organizational cultures are created in part by leaders, and one of the most decisive functions of leadership is the creation, the management, and sometimes even the destruction of culture.

Neither culture nor leadership, when one examines each closely, can really be understood by itself. In fact, one could argue that the only thing of real importance that leaders do is to create and manage culture and that the unique talent of leaders is their ability to understand and work with culture. If one wishes to distinguish leadership from management or administration, one can argue that leaders create and change cultures, while managers and administrators live within them.

By defining leadership in this manner, I am not implying that culture is easy to create or change or that leaders are the only determiners of culture. On the contrary, as we will see, culture refers to those elements of a group or organization that are most stable and least malleable. Culture is the result of a complex group learning process that is only partially influenced by leader behavior. But if the group's survival is threatened because elements of its culture have become maladapted, it is ultimately the function of leadership to recognize and do something about the situation. It is in this sense that leadership and culture are conceptually intertwined.

Two Brief Examples

To illustrate how "culture" helps illuminate organizational situations, I will describe two situations I encountered in my experience as a consultant. In the first case (the Action Company),

I was called in to help a management group improve its communication, interpersonal relationships, and decision making. After sitting in on a number of meetings, I observed among other things (1) high levels of interrupting, confrontation, and debate; (2) excessive emotionalism about proposed courses of action; (3) great frustration over the difficulty of getting a point of view across; and (4) a sense that every member of the group wanted to win all the time.

Over a period of several months, I made many suggestions about better listening, less interrupting, more orderly processing of the agenda, the potential negative effects of high emotionalism and conflict, and the need to reduce the frustration level. The group members said that the suggestions were helpful, and they modified certain aspects of their procedure, such as lengthening some of their meetings. However, the basic pattern did not change. No matter what kind of intervention I attempted, the group's basic style remained the same.

In the second case (the Multi Company), I was asked, as part of a broader consultation project, to help create a climate for innovation in an organization that felt a need to become more flexible in order to respond to its increasingly dynamic business environment. The organization consisted of many different business units, geographical units, and functional groups. As I got to know more about these units and their problems, I observed that some very innovative things were occurring in many places in the company. I wrote several memos describing these innovations, added other ideas from my own experience, and gave the memos to my contact person in the company with the request that he distribute them to the various business unit and geographical managers who needed to be made aware of these ideas.

After some months, I discovered that the managers to whom I had personally given a memo thought it was helpful and on target, but rarely if ever did they pass it on. Moreover, none of the memos were ever distributed by my contact person. I also suggested meetings of managers from different units to stimulate lateral communication but found no support at all for such meetings. No matter what I did, I could not seem to get information flowing, especially laterally across divisional, functional, or geographical boundaries. Yet everyone agreed in principle that innovation would be stimulated by more lateral communication and encouraged me to keep on "helping."

I did not really understand what happened in either of these cases until I began to examine *my own assumptions* about how things should work in these organizations and began to test whether my assumptions fitted those operating in my client systems. This step of examining the shared assumptions in the organization or group one is dealing with takes one into "cultural" analysis and will be the focus from here on.

It turned out that in the Action Company senior managers and most of the other members of the organization shared the assumption that one cannot determine whether or not something is true unless one subjects that idea or proposal to intensive debate. Only ideas that survive such debate are worth acting on, and only ideas that survive such scrutiny will be implemented. The group assumed that what they were doing was discovering truth, and in this context being polite to each other was relatively less important.

In the case of the Multi Company I eventually discovered that there was a strong shared assumption that each manager's job was his or her private turf, not to be infringed on. Articulated was the strong image that one's job is like one's home, and if someone gives one unsolicited information, it is like walking into one's home uninvited. Sending memos to people implies that they do not already know what is in the memo and that is potentially insulting. In this organization managers prided themselves on knowing whatever they needed to know to do their job.

In both of these cases I did not understand what was going on because my basic assumptions about truth and turf differed from the shared assumptions of the group members. Cultural analysis, then, is the encountering and deciphering of such shared basic assumptions.

Toward a Formal Definition of Culture

The word *culture* has many meanings and connotations. When we apply it to groups and organizations, we are almost certain to have conceptual and semantic confusion because groups and organizations are also difficult to define unambiguously. Most people have a connotative sense of what culture is but have difficulty defining it abstractly. In talking about organizational culture with colleagues and members of organizations, I often find that we agree "it" exists and that "it" is important in its effects but that we have completely different ideas of what "it" is. I have also had colleagues tell me pointedly that they do not use the concept of culture in their work, but when I ask them what it is they do not use, they cannot define "it" clearly.

To make matters worse, the concept of culture has been the subject of considerable academic debate in the last five years, and there are various approaches to defining and studying culture (for example, Barley, Meyer, and Gash, 1988; Martin, 1991; Ott, 1989; Smircich and Calas, 1987). This debate is a healthy sign in that it testifies to the importance of culture as a concept. At the same time, however, it creates difficulties for both the scholar and the practitioner if definitions are fuzzy and uses are inconsistent. For purposes of this introductory chapter, I will give only a brief overview of this range of uses and then try to give a precise and formal definition that makes the most sense from my point of view. Also, please note that from this point on I will use the term *group* to refer to social units of all sizes, including organizations and subunits of organizations except where it is necessary to distinguish type of social unit because of subgroups that exist within larger groups.

Commonly used words relating to culture emphasize one of its critical aspects — the idea that certain things in groups are *shared or held in common.* The major categories of such overt phenomena that are associated with culture in this sense are the following:

1. *Observed behavioral regularities when people interact:* the *language* they use, the *customs and traditions* that evolve, and the *rituals* they employ in a wide variety of situations (for example, Goffman, 1959, 1967; Jones, Moore, and Snyder, 1988; Trice and Beyer, 1984, 1985; Van Maanen, 1979b).
2. *Group norms:* the implicit standards and values that evolve in working groups, such as the particular norm of "a fair

day's work for a fair day's pay" that evolved among workers in the Bank Wiring Room in the Hawthorne studies
(for example, Homans, 1950; Kilmann and Saxton, 1983).

3. *Espoused values:* the articulated, publicly announced principles and values that the group claims to be trying to achieve,
such as "product quality" or "price leadership" (for example, Deal and Kennedy, 1982).

4. *Formal philosophy:* the broad policies and ideological principles that guide a group's actions toward stockholders, employees, customers, and other stakeholders, such as the
highly publicized "HP Way" of Hewlett-Packard (for example, Ouchi, 1981; Pascale and Athos, 1981).

5. *Rules of the game:* the implicit rules for getting along in the
organization, "the ropes" that a newcomer must learn to
become an accepted member, "the way we do things around
here" (for example, Schein, 1968, 1978; Van Maanen, 1976,
1979b; Ritti and Funkhouser, 1982).

6. *Climate:* the feeling that is conveyed in a group by the physical layout and the way in which members of the organization interact with each other, with customers, or with other
outsiders (for example, Schneider, 1990; Tagiuri and Litwin, 1968).

7. *Embedded skills:* the special competencies group members
display in accomplishing certain tasks, the ability to make
certain things that gets passed on from generation to generation without necessarily being articulated in writing
(for example, Argyris and Schön, 1978; Cook and Yanow,
1990; Henderson and Clark, 1990; Peters and Waterman,
1982).

8. *Habits of thinking, mental models, and/or linguistic paradigms:* the
shared cognitive frames that guide the perceptions, thought,
and language used by the members of a group and are
taught to new members in the early socialization process
(for example, Douglas, 1986; Hofstede, 1980; Van Maanen,
1979b).

9. *Shared meanings:* the emergent understandings that are created by group members as they interact with each other
(for example, Geertz, 1973; Smircich, 1983; Van Maanen
and Barley, 1984).

10. *"Root metaphors" or integrating symbols:* the ideas, feelings, and images groups develop to characterize themselves, that may or may not be appreciated consciously but that become embodied in buildings, office layout, and other material artifacts of the group. This level of the culture reflects group members' emotional and aesthetic responses as contrasted with their cognitive or evaluative response (for example, Gagliardi, 1990; Hatch, 1991; Pondy, Frost, Morgan, and Dandridge, 1983; Schultz, 1991).

All of these concepts relate to culture and/or reflect culture in that they deal with things that group members share or hold in common, but none of them are "the culture" of an organization or group. If one asks oneself why one needs the word *culture* at all when we have so many other words such as *norms, values, behavior patterns, rituals, traditions,* and so on, one recognizes that the word *culture* adds two other critical elements to the concept of sharing.

One of these elements is that culture implies some level of *structural stability* in the group. When we say that something is "cultural," we imply that it is not only shared but deep and stable. By deep I mean less conscious and therefore less tangible and less visible. The other element that lends stability is *patterning or integration* of the elements into a larger paradigm or gestalt that ties together the various elements and that lies at a deeper level. Culture somehow implies that rituals, climate, values, and behaviors bind together into a coherent whole. This patterning or integration is the *essence* of what we mean by "culture." How then do we think about this essence and formally define it?

The most useful way to think about culture is to view it as the accumulated shared learning of a given group, covering behavioral, emotional, and cognitive elements of the group members' total psychological functioning. For shared learning to occur, there must be a history of shared experience, which in turn implies some stability of membership in the group. Given such stability and a shared history, the human need for parsimony, consistency, and meaning will cause the various shared elements to form into patterns that eventually can be called a culture.

I am not arguing, however, that all groups develop integrated cultures in this sense. We all know of groups, organizations, and societies where cultural elements work at cross purposes with other elements, leading to situations full of conflict and ambiguity (Martin, 1991; Martin and Meyerson, 1988). This may result from insufficient stability of membership, insufficient shared history of experience, or the presence of many subgroups with different kinds of shared experiences. Ambiguity and conflict also result from the fact that each of us belongs to many groups so that what we bring to any given group is influenced by the assumptions that are appropriate to our other groups.

If the concept of culture is to have any utility, however, it should draw our attention to those things that are the product of our human need for stability, consistency, and meaning. Culture formation, therefore, is always, by definition, a *striving toward patterning and integration,* even though the actual history of experiences of many groups prevents them from ever achieving a clear-cut paradigm.

If a group's culture is that group's accumulated learning, how do we describe and catalogue the content of that learning? All group and organizational theories distinguish two major sets of problems that all groups, no matter what their size, must deal with: (1) survival, growth, and adaptation in their environment and (2) internal integration that permits daily functioning and the ability to adapt.

In conceptualizing group learning, we have to note that because of the human capacity to abstract and to be self-conscious, learning occurs not only at the behavioral level but also at an abstract level internally. Once people have a common system of communication and a language, learning can take place at a conceptual level and shared concepts become possible. Therefore, the deeper levels of learning that get us to the essence of culture must be thought of as concepts or, as I will define them, shared basic assumptions.

The process by which shared basic assumptions evolve is illustrated in detail in later chapters. For the present, I need only summarize that the learning process for the group starts

with one or more members taking a leadership role in proposing courses of action and as these continue to be successful in
solving the group's internal and external problems, they come
to be taken for granted and the assumptions underlying them
cease to be questioned or debated. A group has a culture when
it has had enough of a shared history to have formed such a
set of *shared* assumptions.

Shared assumptions derive their power from the fact that
they begin to operate outside of awareness. Furthermore, once
formed and taken for granted, they become a defining property
of the group that permits the group to differentiate itself from
other groups, and in that process, value is attached to such assumptions. They are not only "our" assumptions, but by virtue
of our history of success, they must be right and good. In fact,
as we will see, one of the main problems in resolving intercultural issues is that we take culture so much for granted and put
so much value on our own assumptions that we find it awkward
and inappropriate even to discuss our assumptions or to ask
others about their assumptions. We tend not to examine assumptions once we have made them but to take them for granted,
and we tend not to discuss them, which makes them seemingly
unconscious. If we are forced to discuss them, we tend not to
examine them but to defend them because we have emotionally invested in them (Bohm, 1990).

Culture Formally Defined

The *culture* of a group can now be defined as

*A pattern of shared basic assumptions that the group learned as
it solved its problems of external adaptation and internal integration, that
has worked well enough to be considered valid and, therefore, to be taught
to new members as the correct way to perceive, think, and feel in relation
to those problems.*

Note that this definition introduces three elements not
previously discussed.

1. *The problem of socialization.* It is my view that what we
think of as culture is primarily what is passed on to new generations of group members (Louis, 1980, 1990; Schein, 1968; Van

Maanen, 1976; Van Maanen and Schein, 1979). Studying what new members of groups are taught is, in fact, a good way to discover some of the elements of a culture, but one only learns about surface aspects of the culture by this means. This is especially so because much of what is at the heart of a culture will not be revealed in the rules of behavior taught to newcomers. It will only be revealed to members as they gain permanent status and are allowed to enter the inner circles of the group, where group secrets are shared.

On the other hand, *how* one learns and the socialization *processes* to which one is subjected may indeed reveal deeper assumptions. To get at those deeper levels one must try to understand the perceptions and feelings that arise in critical situations, and one must observe and interview regular members or old-timers to get an accurate sense of which deeper-level assumptions are shared.

Can culture be learned through anticipatory socialization or self-socialization? Can new members discover for themselves what the basic assumptions are? Yes and no. We certainly know that one of the major activities of any new member when she enters a new group is to decipher the norms and assumptions that are operating. But this deciphering can only be successful through the rewards and punishments that long-time members mete out to new members as they experiment with different kinds of behavior. In this sense, a teaching process is always going on, even though it may be quite implicit and unsystematic.

If the group does not have shared assumptions, as is sometimes the case, the new members' interaction with old members will be a more creative process of building a culture. Once shared assumptions exist, however, the culture survives through teaching them to newcomers. In this regard culture is a mechanism of social control and can be the basis of explicitly manipulating members into perceiving, thinking, and feeling in certain ways (Van Maanen and Kunda, 1989; Kunda, 1992). Whether or not we approve of this as a mechanism of social control is a separate question that will be addressed later.

2. *The problem of "behavior."* Note that the definition of culture that I have given does *not* include overt behavior patterns,

though some such behavior, especially formal rituals, would reflect cultural assumptions. Instead, the definition emphasizes that the critical assumptions deal with how we perceive, think about, and feel about things. Overt behavior is always determined both by the cultural predisposition (the perceptions, thoughts, and feelings that are patterned) and by the situational contingencies that arise from the immediate external environment.

Behavioral regularities could thus be as much a reflection of separate but similar individual experiences and/or common situational stimuli arising from the environment. For example, suppose we observe that all members of a group cower in the presence of a large and loud leader. Such cowering could be based on biological reflex reactions to sound and size, or individual learning, or shared learning. Such a behavioral regularity should not, therefore, be the basis for defining culture, though we might later discover that in a given group's experience, cowering is indeed a result of shared learning and therefore a manifestation of deeper shared assumptions. To put it another way, when we observe behavior regularities, we do not know whether we are dealing with a cultural manifestation. Only after we have discovered the deeper layers that I am defining as the essence of culture can we specify what is and what is not an "artifact" that reflects the culture.

3. *Can a large organization have one culture?* The definition provided does not specify the size of social unit to which it can legitimately be applied. Our experience with large organizations tells us that at a certain size, the variations among the subgroups are substantial, suggesting that it is not appropriate to talk of "the culture" of an IBM or a General Motors or a Shell Oil. My view is that this question should be handled empirically. If we find that certain assumptions are shared across all the units of an organization, then we can legitimately speak of an organizational culture, even though at the same time we may find a number of discrete subcultures that have their own integrity. In fact, as we will see, with time any social unit will produce subunits that will produce subcultures as a normal process of evolution. Some of these subcultures will typically be in conflict with each other, as is often the case with higher management

and unionized labor groups. Yet in spite of such conflict one will find that organizations have common assumptions that come into play when a crisis occurs or when a common enemy is found.

Summary and Conclusions

The concept of culture is most useful if it helps to explain some of the more seemingly incomprehensible and irrational aspects of groups and organizations. Analysts of culture have a wide variety of ways of looking at the concept. My formal definition brings many of these various concepts together, putting the emphasis on shared, taken-for-granted basic assumptions held by the members of the group or organization. In this sense, any group with a stable membership and a history of shared learning will have developed some level of culture, but a group having either a great deal of turnover of members and leaders or a history without any kind of challenging events may well lack any shared assumptions. Not every collection of people develops a culture; in fact, we tend to use the term *group* rather than *crowd* or *collection of people* only when there has been enough of a shared history so that some degree of culture formation has taken place.

Culture and leadership are two sides of the same coin in that leaders first create cultures when they create groups and organizations. Once cultures exist, they determine the criteria for leadership and thus determine who will or will not be a leader. But if cultures become dysfunctional, it is the unique function of leadership to perceive the functional and dysfunctional elements of the existing culture and to manage cultural evolution and change in such a way that the group can survive in a changing environment.

The bottom line for leaders is that if they do not become conscious of the cultures in which they are embedded, those cultures will manage them. Cultural understanding is desirable for all of us, but it is essential to leaders if they are to lead.

CHAPTER TWO

Uncovering
the Levels of Culture

The purpose of this chapter is to show that culture can be analyzed at several different levels, where the term *level* refers to the degree to which the cultural phenomenon is visible to the observer. Some of the confusion of definition of what culture really is results from not differentiating the levels at which it manifests itself. These levels range from the very tangible overt manifestations that one can see and feel to the deeply embedded, unconscious basic assumptions that I am defining as the essence of culture. In between we have various espoused values, norms, and rules of behavior that members of the culture use as a way of depicting the culture to themselves and others.

Many other culture researchers prefer the concept of "basic values" for describing the deepest levels. As I will try to show with later examples, my preference is for "basic assumptions" because these tend to be taken for granted and are treated as nonnegotiable. Values can be and are discussed, and people can agree to disagree about them. Basic assumptions are so taken for granted that someone who does not hold them is viewed as crazy and automatically dismissed. The levels at which culture can be analyzed are shown in Figure 2.1.

Figure 2.1. Levels of Culture.

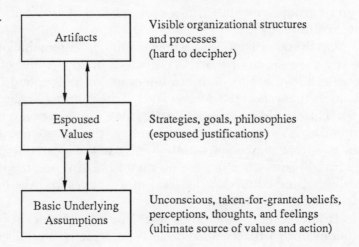

Artifacts — Visible organizational structures and processes (hard to decipher)

Espoused Values — Strategies, goals, philosophies (espoused justifications)

Basic Underlying Assumptions — Unconscious, taken-for-granted beliefs, perceptions, thoughts, and feelings (ultimate source of values and action)

Artifacts

At the surface we have the level of *artifacts,* which includes all the phenomena that one sees, hears, and feels when one encounters a new group with an unfamiliar culture. Artifacts would include the visible products of the group such as the architecture of its physical environment, its language, its technology and products, its artistic creations, and its style as embodied in clothing, manners of address, emotional displays, myths and stories told about the organization, published lists of values, observable rituals and ceremonies, and so on. For purposes of cultural analysis this level also includes the visible behavior of the group and the organizational processes into which such behavior is made routine.

The most important point about this level of the culture is that it is easy to observe and very difficult to decipher. The Egyptians and the Maya both built highly visible pyramids, but the meaning of pyramids in each culture was very different — tombs in one and temples as well as tombs in the other. In other words, the observer can describe what she sees and feels but cannot reconstruct from that alone what those things mean in the given group, or whether they even reflect important underlying assumptions.

On the other hand, one school of thought argues that one's own response to physical artifacts such as buildings and office layouts can lead to the identification of major images and root metaphors that reflect the deepest level of the culture (Gagliardi, 1990). This would be especially true if the organization one is deciphering is in the same larger culture as the researcher. The problem is that symbols are ambiguous, and one can only test one's insight into what something might mean if one has also experienced the culture at the level of its values and the level of its basic assumptions.

It is especially dangerous to try to infer the deeper assumptions from artifacts alone because one's interpretations will inevitably be projections of one's own feelings and reactions. For example, when one sees a very informal, loose organization, one may interpret that as inefficient if one's own background is based on the assumption that informality means playing around and not working. Alternatively, if one sees a very formal organization, one may interpret that to be a sign of lack of innovative capacity if one's own experience is based on the assumption that formality means bureaucracy and formalization.

Every facet of a group's life produces artifacts, creating the problem of classification. In reading cultural descriptions, one often notes that different observers choose to report on different sorts of artifacts, leading to noncomparable descriptions. Anthropologists have developed classification systems, but these tend to be so vast and detailed that cultural essence becomes difficult to discern.

If the observer lives in the group long enough, the meanings of artifacts gradually become clear. If, however, one wants to achieve this level of understanding more quickly, one can attempt to analyze the espoused values, norms, and rules that provide the day-to-day operating principles by which the members of the group guide their behavior. This kind of inquiry takes us to the next level of cultural analysis.

Espoused Values

All group learning ultimately reflects someone's original values, someone's sense of what ought to be as distinct from what is. When a group is first created or when it faces a new task, issue, or problem, the first solution proposed to deal with it reflects some individual's own assumptions about what is right or wrong, what will work or not work. Those individuals who prevail, who can influence the group to adopt a certain approach to the problem, will later be identified as "leaders" or founders, but the group as a group does not yet have any shared knowledge because it has not yet taken a common action in response to the new problem. Therefore, whatever is proposed can only have the status of a value from the point of view of the group, no matter how strongly the proponent may believe that he or she is uttering absolute proven truth. Until the group has taken some joint action and its members have together observed the outcome of that action, there is not as yet a shared basis for determining what is factual and real.

For example, in a young business if sales begin to decline, a manager may say, "We must increase advertising" because of her belief that advertising always increases sales. The group, never having experienced this situation before, will hear that assertion as a statement of that manager's values: "She believes that when one is in trouble it is a *good* thing to increase advertising." What the leader initially proposes, therefore, cannot have any status other than a value to be questioned, debated, challenged, and tested.

If the manager convinces the group to act on her belief and if the solution works and if the group has a shared perception of that success, then the perceived value that advertising is "good" gradually starts a process of *cognitive transformation*. First, it will be transformed into a *shared value or belief* and, ultimately, into a *shared assumption* (if action based on it continues to be successful). If this transformation process occurs — and it will occur only if the proposed solution continues to work, thus implying that it is in some larger sense "correct" and must reflect an accurate picture of reality—group members will tend to forget that originally they were not sure and that the proposed course of action was at an earlier time debated and confronted.

Not all values undergo such transformation. First of all, the solution based on a given value may not work reliably. Only values that are susceptible to physical or social validation and that continue to work reliably in solving the group's problems will become transformed into assumptions. Second, value domains dealing with the less controllable elements of the environment or with aesthetic or moral matters may not be testable at all. In such cases consensus through social validation is still possible, but it is not automatic.

By social validation I mean that certain values are confirmed only by the shared social experience of a group. Such values typically involve the group's internal relations, where the test of whether they work or not is how comfortable and anxiety free members are when they abide by them. Social validation also applies to those broader values that involve relationships to the environment but in a nontestable fashion, such as religion, ethics, and aesthetics.

In these realms the group learns that certain such values, as initially promulgated by prophets, founders, and leaders, work in the sense of reducing uncertainty in critical areas of the group's functioning. And as they continue to work, they gradually become transformed into nondiscussable assumptions supported by articulated sets of beliefs, norms, and operational rules of behavior. The derived beliefs and moral/ethical rules remain conscious and are explicitly articulated because they serve the normative or moral function of guiding members of the group in how to deal with certain key situations and in training new members in how to behave. A set of values that becomes embodied in an ideology or organizational philosophy thus can serve as a guide and as a way of dealing with the uncertainty of intrinsically uncontrollable or difficult events.

Values at this conscious level will predict much of the behavior that can be observed at the artifactual level. But if those values are not based on prior learning, they may also reflect only what Argyris and Schön (1978) have called espoused values, which predict well enough what people will *say* in a variety of situations but which may be out of line with what they will actually *do* in situations where those values should, in fact, be operating. Thus, a company may say that it values people and has high quality standards for its products, but its record in that regard may contradict what it says.

If the espoused values are reasonably congruent with the underlying assumptions, then the articulation of those values into a philosophy of operating can be helpful in bringing the group together, serving as a source of identity and core mission. But in analyzing values one must discriminate carefully between those that are congruent with underlying assumptions and those that are, in effect, either rationalizations or only aspirations for the future. Often such lists of values are not patterned, sometimes they are even mutually contradictory, and often they are inconsistent with observed behavior. Large areas of behavior are often left unexplained, leaving us with a feeling that we understand a piece of the culture but still do not have the culture as such in hand. To get at that deeper level of understanding, to decipher the pattern, and to predict future behavior correctly, we have to understand more fully the category of basic assumptions.

Basic Assumptions

When a solution to a problem works repeatedly, it comes to be taken for granted. What was once a hypothesis, supported only by a hunch or a value, comes gradually to be treated as a reality. We come to believe that nature really works this way. Basic assumptions, in this sense, are different from what some anthropologists call dominant value orientations in that such dominant orientations reflect the preferred solution among several basic alternatives, but all the alternatives are still visible in the culture, and any given member of the culture could, from time to time, behave according to variant as well as dominant orientations (Kluckhohn and Strodtbeck, 1961).

Basic assumptions, in the sense in which I want to define the concept, have become so taken for granted that one finds little variation within a cultural unit. In fact, if a basic assumption is strongly held in a group, members will find behavior based on any other premise inconceivable. For example, a group whose basic assumption is that the individual's rights supersede those of the group members will find it inconceivable that members would commit suicide or in some other way sacrifice themselves to the group even if they had dishonored the group. In a capitalist country, it is inconceivable that one might design a company to operate consistently at a financial loss or that it does not matter whether or not a product works. Basic assumptions, in this sense, are similar to what Argyris has identified as "theories-in-use," the implicit assumptions that actually guide behavior, that tell group members how to perceive, think about, and feel about things (Argyris, 1976; Argyris and Schön, 1974).

Basic assumptions, like theories-in-use, tend to be those we neither confront nor debate and hence are extremely difficult to change. To learn something new in this realm requires us to resurrect, reexamine, and possibly change some of the more stable portions of our cognitive structure, a process that Argyris and others have called double-loop learning or frame breaking (for example, Argyris, Putnam, and Smith, 1985; Bartunek and Moch, 1987). Such learning is intrinsically difficult because the reexamination of basic assumptions temporarily destabilizes our cognitive and interpersonal world, releasing large quantities of basic anxiety.

Rather than tolerating such anxiety levels we tend to want to perceive the events around us as congruent with our assumptions, even if that means distorting, denying, projecting, or in other ways falsifying to ourselves what may be going on around us. It is in this psychological process that culture has its ultimate power. Culture as a set of basic assumptions defines for us what to pay attention to, what things mean, how to react emotionally to what is going on, and what actions to take in various kinds of situations. Once we have developed an integrated set of such assumptions, which might be called a thought world or mental map, we will be maximally comfortable with others who share the same set of assumptions and very uncomfortable and vulnerable in situations where different assumptions operate either because we will not understand what is going on, or, worse, misperceive and misinterpret the actions of others (Douglas, 1986).

The human mind needs cognitive stability. Therefore, any challenge to or questioning of a basic assumption will release anxiety and defensiveness. In this sense, the shared basic assumptions that make up the culture of a group can be thought of at both the individual and group levels as psychological cognitive *defense mechanisms* that permit the group to continue to function. Recognizing this connection is important when one thinks about changing aspects of a group's culture, for it is no easier to do that than to change an individual's pattern of defense mechanisms. In either case the key is the management of the large amounts of anxiety that accompany any relearning at this level.

To understand how unconscious assumptions can distort data, consider the following example. If we assume, on the basis of past experience or education, that other people will take advantage of us whenever they have an opportunity, we expect to be taken advantage of and then interpret the behavior of others in a way that coincides with those expectations. We observe people sitting in a seemingly idle posture at their desks and interpret their behavior as loafing rather than thinking out an important problem. We perceive absence from work as shirking rather than doing work at home.

If this is not only a personal assumption but one that is shared and thus part of the organization's culture, we will discuss with others what to do about our "lazy" work force and institute tight controls to ensure that people are at their desks and busy. If employees suggest that they do some of their work at home, we will be uncomfortable and probably deny the request because we will assume that at home they would loaf (Bailyn, 1992; Perin, 1991).

In contrast, if we assume that everyone is highly motivated and competent, we will act in accordance with that assumption by encouraging people to work at their own pace and in their own way. If someone is discovered to be unproductive in the organization, we will assume that there is a mismatch between the person and the job assignment, not that the person is lazy or incompetent. If the employee wants to work at home, we will perceive that as evidence of wanting to be productive even if circumstances require him to be at home.

In both cases there is the potential for distortion. The cynical manager will not perceive how highly motivated some of the subordinates really are, and the idealistic manager will not perceive that there are subordinates who are lazy and who are taking advantage of the situation. As McGregor (1960) noted several decades ago, such assumption sets in the human area become the basis of whole management and control systems that perpetuate themselves because if people are treated consistently in terms of certain basic assumptions, they come eventually to behave according to those assumptions in order to make their world stable and predictable.

Unconscious assumptions sometimes lead to ridiculously tragic situations, as illustrated by a common problem experienced by American supervisors in some Asian countries. A manager who comes from an American pragmatic tradition takes it for granted that solving a problem always has the highest priority. When that manager encounters a subordinate who comes from a different cultural tradition, in which good relationships and protecting the superior's "face" are assumed to have top priority, the following scenario can easily result.

The manager proposes a solution to a given problem. The subordinate knows that the solution will not work, but his unconscious assumption requires that he remain silent because to tell the boss that the proposed solution is wrong is a threat to the boss's face. It would not even occur to the subordinate to do anything other than remain silent or even reassure the boss that they should go ahead and take the action if the boss were to inquire what the subordinate thought.

The action is taken, the results are negative, and the boss, somewhat surprised and puzzled, asks the subordinate what he would have done. When the subordinate reports that he would have done something different, the boss quite legitimately asks why the subordinate did not speak up sooner. This question puts the subordinate in an impossible bind because the answer itself is a threat to the boss's face. He cannot possibly explain his behavior without committing the very sin he is trying to avoid in the first place—namely, embarrassing the boss. He might even lie at this point and argue that what the boss did was right and only "bad luck" or uncontrollable circumstances prevented it from succeeding.

From the point of view of the subordinate, the boss's behavior is incomprehensible because it shows lack of self-pride, possibly causing the subordinate to lose respect for that boss. To the boss the subordinate's behavior is equally incomprehensible. The boss cannot develop any sensible explanation of the subordinate's behavior that is not cynically colored by the assumption that the subordinate at some level just does not care about effective performance and therefore must be gotten rid of. It never occurs to the boss that another assumption such as "one never embarrasses a superior" is operating and that to the subordinate that assumption is even more powerful than "one gets the job done."

If assumptions such as these operate only in an individual and represent her idiosyncratic experience, they can be corrected more easily because the person will detect that she is alone in holding a given assumption. The power of culture comes about through the fact that the assumptions are shared and therefore mutually reinforced. In these instances probably only a third party or some cross-cultural education could help to find common ground whereby both parties could bring their implicit assumptions to the surface. And even after they have surfaced, such assumptions would still operate, forcing the boss and the subordinate to invent a whole new communication mechanism that would permit each to remain congruent with her or his culture—for example, agreeing that before any decision is made and before the boss has stuck her neck out, the subordinate will be asked for suggestions and for factual data that will not be face threatening. Note that the solution must keep each cultural assumption intact. One cannot in these instances simply declare one or the other cultural assumption "wrong." One has to find a third assumption to allow them both to retain their integrity.

I have dwelled on this example to illustrate the potency of implicit, unconscious assumptions and to show that such assumptions often deal with fundamental aspects of life — the nature of time and space; human nature and human activities; the nature of truth and how one discovers it; the correct way for the individual and the group to relate to each other; the relative importance of work, family, and self-development; the proper role of men and women; and the nature of the family.

We do not develop new assumptions about each of these areas in every group or organization we join. Each member of a new group will bring her or his own cultural learning from prior groups, but as the new group develops its own shared history, it will develop modified or brand-new assumptions in critical areas of its experience. Those new assumptions make up the culture of that particular group.

Any group's culture can be studied at these three levels — the level of its artifacts, the level of its values, and the level of its basic assumptions. If one does not decipher the pattern of basic assumptions that may be operating, one will not know how to interpret the artifacts correctly or how much credence to give to the articulated values. In other words, the essence of a culture lies in the pattern of basic underlying assumptions, and once one understands those, one can easily understand the other more surface levels and deal appropriately with them.

Summary and Conclusions

Though the essence of a group's culture is its pattern of shared, taken-for-granted basic assumptions, the culture will manifest itself at the levels of observable artifacts and shared espoused values, norms, and rules of behavior. It is important to recognize in analyzing cultures that artifacts are easy to observe but difficult to decipher and that values may only reflect rationalizations or aspirations. To understand a group's culture, one must attempt to get at its shared basic assumptions and one must understand the learning process by which such basic assumptions come to be.

Leadership is originally the source of the beliefs and values that get a group moving in dealing with its internal and external problems. If what a leader proposes works and continues to work, what once was only the leader's assumption gradually comes to be a shared assumption. Once a set of shared basic assumptions is formed by this process, it can function as a cognitive defense mechanism both for the individual members and for the group as a whole. In other words, individuals and groups seek stability and meaning. Once these are achieved, it is easier to distort new data by denial, projection, rationalization, or various other defense mechanisms than to change the basic assumption. As we will see, culture change, in the sense of changing basic assumptions is, therefore, difficult, time consuming, and highly anxiety provoking. This point is especially relevant for the leader who sets out to change the culture of the organization.

The most central issue for leaders, therefore, is how to get at the deeper levels of a culture, how to assess the functionality of the assumptions made at each level, and how to deal with the anxiety that is unleashed when those levels are challenged.

CHAPTER THREE

Analyzing the Cultures
of Two Organizations

In Chapter Two I indicated in a rather abstract manner how one should think about the complex concept of culture as it applies to groups and organizations. I emphasized the need to go beyond the surface levels of artifacts and espoused values to the deeper shared assumptions that are taken for granted and create the pattern of cognitions, perceptions, and feelings displayed by the members of the group. I argued that unless one understands what is going on at this deeper level, one cannot really decipher the meaning of the more surface phenomena and, worse, might misinterpret them because of the likelihood that one will be projecting one's own cultural biases onto the observed phenomena.

In this chapter I would like to illustrate this multilevel analysis by describing two companies with which I have worked for some period of time, permitting me to begin to identify some key elements of their cultures. I say "elements" because it is not really possible to describe an entire culture. But one can get at enough elements to make some of the key phenomena in these companies comprehensible.

The Clinical Research Model

Most of the information I will provide about cultural assumptions in different kinds of companies was gathered by what I call clinical research (Schein, 1987a, 1991). To highlight what I mean by the clinical model, we can examine in Figure 3.1 several different kinds of approaches to organizational research.

The critical distinguishing feature of the clinical research model is that the data come voluntarily from the members of the organization because they initiated the process and have something to gain by revealing themselves to the clinician/consultant/researcher. The consultant/clinician is primarily in the organization to help with some problem that has been presented, but in the process of working on the problem, he or she uncovers culturally relevant information, particularly if the process consultation model, with its emphasis on inquiry and helping the organization to help itself, is used (Schein, 1969, 1987b, 1988). Furthermore, in the inquiry process the consultant/clinician is psychologically licensed by the client to ask relevant questions that can lead directly into cultural analysis and thereby allow the development of a research focus as well. Both the consultant and the client are fully involved in the problem-solving process, and the search for relevant data is therefore a joint responsibility.

Figure 3.1. Categories of Research on Organizations.

Level of Researcher Involvement →	Low to Medium *Quantitative*	High *Qualitative*
Level of Subject Involvement		
Minimal	Demographics; measurement of "distal" variables	Ethnography; participant observation; content analysis of stories, myths, rituals, symbols, other artifacts
Partial	Experimentation; questionnaires, ratings, objective tests, scales	Projective tests; assessment centers; interviews
Maximal	Total quality tools such as statistical quality control; action research	Clinical research; action research; organization development

The consultant/clinician is not, of course, limited to the data that are revealed in specific diagnostic activities such as individual or group interviews. In most consulting situations there are extensive opportunities to hang around and observe what is going on, allowing the researcher to combine some of the best elements of the clinical and the participant observer ethnographic models. The clinician can, as well, gather demographic information and measure various things unobtrusively, but if the subjects are to be involved at all, they must be involved on their own terms around problems they have identified.

It is in the middle row, where they are experimenting or giving various tests, that researchers are most at risk of getting invalid data and unwittingly harming the organization they are studying because they are typically working their own agenda and not paying enough attention to the consequences of their research interventions. In other words, if the subjects are to be involved at all, they must be involved in a way that is helpful *to them.*

The clinical model involves one other fundamental assumption — *one can understand a system best by trying to change it.* In this regard the clinical and the ethnographic models differ sharply in that the aim of the ethnographer is generally to leave the system as intact as possible. The ethnographic model thus implies that the culture can be deciphered if one spends sufficient time observing and interacting with it minimally. The clinical model assumes that culture will not reveal itself that easily and that one must actively intervene to determine where stable rituals, espoused values, and basic shared assumptions are located. My bias toward the clinical research model was frequently reinforced in my own dealings with companies because some of the most important things I learned about their cultures surfaced only as reactions to some of my intervention efforts. The cases that follow and other examples I will provide therefore reflect everything I learned about these companies through inquiry, observation, and intervention.

The Action Company

The data on the Action Company were primarily gathered in the 1970s and 1980s. The culture has obviously evolved since then, but many of the essential elements have remained the same. Discussion of how the culture has evolved or changed appears at various places throughout the book.

Artifacts: Encountering the Company

The Action Company is a very successful manufacturer of high-technology equipment. It is located primarily in the northeastern part of the United States but has branches throughout the world. To gain entry into any of its many buildings, one must sign in with a guard who sits behind a counter where several people are usually chatting, moving in and out, checking the badges of employees who are coming into the building, accepting mail, and answering phone calls. After signing in, one waits in a small, casually furnished lobby until the person one is visiting comes personally or sends a secretary to escort one to one's destination.

The things I recall most vividly from my first encounters with this organization some twenty-five years ago are the ubiquitous open-office landscape architecture, the extreme informality of dress and manners, a very dynamic environment in the sense of rapid pace, and a high rate of interaction among employees, seemingly reflecting enthusiasm, intensity, energy, and impatience. As we passed cubicles and conference rooms, I got the impression of openness. There were very few doors. The company cafeteria spread out into a big open area, where people sat at large tables, hopped from one table to another, and obviously were intensely involved in their work even at lunch. I also observed that many cubicles had coffee machines and refrigerators in them and that food seemed to be part of most meetings.

The physical layout and patterns of interaction made it very difficult to decipher who had what rank, and I was told that there were no status perquisites such as private dining rooms, special parking places, or offices with special views and the like. The furniture in the lobbies and offices was very inexpensive and functional, and the company was mostly headquartered in an old industrial building that had been converted for its use. The informal clothing most managers and employees wore reinforced this sense of economy and egalitarianism.

I had been brought into the Action Company to help the top-management team improve communication and group effectiveness. As I began to attend the regular staff meetings of the senior management group, I was struck by the high level of interpersonal confrontation, argumentativeness, and conflict. Group members easily became highly emotional and seemed to get angry at each other, though I also noticed that such anger did not extend outside the meeting.

With the exception of the president and founder, John Murphy, very few people had visible status in terms of how people deferred to them. Murphy himself, through his informal behavior, implied that he did not take his position of power all that seriously. Group members argued as much with him as with each other and even interrupted him from time to time. His status was evident, however, in the occasional lectures he delivered to the group when he felt that members were not understanding something or were wrong about something. At such times Murphy could become very emotionally excited in a way that other members of the group never did.

My own reactions to the company and these meetings must also be considered artifacts to be documented. It was exciting to be attending top-management meetings and surprising to observe so much behavior that seemed to me dysfunctional. I was made quite nervous by the level of confrontation I observed and had a sense of not knowing what this was all about. I learned from further observation that this style of running meetings was typical and that meetings were very common, to the point where people would complain about all the time spent in committees. At the same time, however, they would argue that without these committees they could not get their work done properly.

The company was organized in terms of functional units and product lines, but there was a sense of perpetual reorganization and a search for a structure that would "work better." Structure was almost viewed as something to tinker with until one got it right. Although there were many levels in the technical and managerial hierarchy, I got the sense that the hierarchy was just a convenience, not something one took seriously.

On the other hand, the communication structure was taken very seriously. Many committees were already in existence, new ones were constantly being formed, the company had an extensive electronic mail network that functioned worldwide, engineers and managers traveled frequently and were in constant telephone communication with each other, and Murphy would get upset if he observed any evidence of under- or miscommunication.

Many other artifacts from this organization will be described later, but for now the question is "What does any of this mean?" I knew what my emotional reactions were, but I did not really understand why these things were happening and what significance they had for members of the company. To gain some understanding one has to get to the next level, the level of espoused values.

Espoused Values

As I talked to people about my observations, especially those things that puzzled and scared me, I began to elicit some of the espoused values that drove the Action Company. Many of these were embodied in slogans or in parables that Murphy wrote from time to time and circulated throughout the company. For example, a high value was placed on personal responsibility. If one made a proposal to do something and it was approved, one had a clear obligation to do it or if it was not possible to do, to come back and renegotiate.

Employees at all levels were responsible for thinking about what they were doing and were enjoined at all times to "do the right thing," which in many instances meant being insubordinate. If the boss asks you to do something that you consider wrong or stupid, you are supposed to push back and attempt to change the boss's mind. If the boss insists and you still feel that it is not right, then you should not do it and take your chances on your own judgment. If you are wrong, you will get your wrist slapped but will gain respect for having stood up for your own convictions. Because bosses know these rules they are, of course, less likely to issue arbitrary orders, more likely to listen to you if you push back, and more likely to renegotiate the decision. So actual insubordination is rarely necessary, but the principle of thinking for yourself and doing the right thing is very strongly reinforced.

It is also a rule that you should not do things without getting "buy in" from others who have to implement the decision or who will be influenced by it. You must be very individualistic and, at the same time, very willing to be a team player, hence the simultaneous feeling that committees are a big drain on time but that you cannot do without them. To reach a decision and to get "buy in," you must convince others of the validity of your idea and be able to defend it against every conceivable argument. This causes the high levels of confrontation and fighting that I observed in groups, but once an idea has stood up to this level of debate and survived, it can then be moved forward and implemented because everyone is now convinced that it is the right thing to do. This takes longer to achieve, but once achieved, leads to more consistent and rapid action. If somewhere down the hierarchy the decision fails to stick because someone is not convinced that it is the right thing to do, that person has to push back, her arguments have to be heard, and she either has to be convinced or the decision has to be renegotiated up the hierarchy.

In asking people about their jobs, I discovered another strong value: one should figure out for oneself what the essence of one's job is and be very clear about it. Asking the boss what is expected is considered a sign of weakness. If one's own job definition is out of line with what the group or department requires, one will hear about it soon enough. The role of the boss is to set broad targets, but subordinates are expected to take initiative in figuring out how best to achieve them. This value requires a great deal of discussion and negotiation, often leading to complaints about time wasting; at the same time, however, everyone defends the value of doing things this way.

I also found out that people can fight bitterly in group meetings yet be very good friends. There is a feeling of being a tight-knit group and an acceptance of the norm that fighting does not mean that people dislike or disrespect each other. This norm seemed to extend even to "bad-mouthing" each other yet respecting each other in work situations. Murphy often criticized people in public, which made them feel embarrassed. It was explained to me that this only meant that those people should work on improving their area of operations, not that they were really in disfavor. Even if someone fell into disfavor, he or she was viewed merely as being in the penalty box, and stories were told of managers or engineers who had been in this kind of disfavor for long periods of time and then rebounded to become heroes in some other context.

When managers talked about their products they emphasized quality and elegance. The company was founded by engineers and dominated by an engineering mentality; that is, the value of a proposed new product was generally judged by whether the engineers themselves liked it and used it, not by external market surveys or test markets. In fact, customers were talked about in a rather disparaging way, especially those who might not be technically sophisticated enough to appreciate the elegance of the product that had been designed.

Murphy emphasized absolute integrity in designing, manufacturing, and selling. He viewed the company as highly ethical and strongly emphasized the work values associated with the Protestant ethic: hard work, high standards of personal morality, professionalism, personal responsibility, integrity, and honesty. Especially important were honesty and truthfulness in relations with each other and with customers. As this company grew and matured, it incorporated many of these values into formal statements and taught them to new employees. It viewed its culture as a great asset and felt that the culture itself had to be taught to all new employees (Kunda, 1992).

Basic Assumptions: The Action Company Paradigm

To understand the implications of the foregoing values and to show how they relate to overt behavior, one must seek the underlying assumptions and premises on which this organization is based (see Figure 3.2). The founding group, by virtue of its members' engineering background, was intensely individualistic and pragmatic in its orientation. The group developed a

Figure 3.2. The Action Company Paradigm.

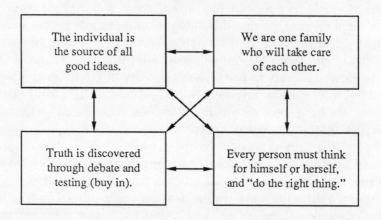

problem-solving and decision-making system that rests on three interlocking assumptions: (1) the individual is ultimately the source of ideas, (2) individuals are capable of taking responsibility and doing the right thing, and (3) no one individual is smart enough to evaluate his or her own ideas.

In effect the group was saying that truth cannot be found without debate, that there is no arbitrary way of figuring out what is true unless one subjects every idea to the crucible of debate among strong and intelligent individuals. Therefore, one must get others to agree before taking action.

Without understanding these assumptions, one cannot decipher most of the behavior observed, particularly the seeming incongruity between intense individualism and intense commitment to group work and consensus. Similarly, one cannot understand why there is intense conflict with authority figures, insubordination, and bad-mouthing of bosses and at the same time intense loyalty to the organization and personal affection across hierarchical boundaries unless one also understands a fourth interlocking assumption: "we are one family who will take care of each other." The implication is that no matter how much of a troublemaker one is in the decision process, one is valued in the family and cannot be kicked out of it.

Only when one grasps these assumptions, can one understand, for example, why my initial interventions of trying to get the group to be "nicer" to each other in the communication process were politely ignored. I was seeing the group's effectiveness in terms of my values and assumptions of how a good group should act. The Action Company's senior management committee was trying to reach "truth" and make valid decisions in the only way its members knew how and by a process that they believed in. The group was merely a means to an end; the real process going on in the group was a basic, deep search for solutions that it could have confidence in because they stood up even after intense debate.

Once I shifted my focus to helping the committee in this search for valid solutions, I figured out what kinds of interventions would be more relevant and found that the group accepted them more readily. For example, I began to focus more on agenda setting, time management, clarification of some of the debate, summarizing, consensus testing once debate was running dry, and in other ways focusing on the task process rather than the interpersonal process. The interrupting, the emotional conflicts, and the other behavior I observed initially continued, but the group became more effective in handling information and in reaching consensus. It was in this context that I gradually developed the philosophy of being a "process consultant" instead of trying to be an expert on how groups should work (Schein, 1969, 1988).

The four key assumptions can be thought of as the Action Company paradigm. What is important in showing these interconnections is the fact that single elements of the paradigm could not explain how this organization is able to function. Only by seeing the combination of assumptions concerning individual creativity, group conflict as the source of truth, individual responsibility, and commitment to each other as a family can one "explain" the day-to-day behavior one observes. It is this level of basic assumptions and their interconnections that defines some of the essence of the culture.

How general is this paradigm in the Action Company?

That is, if one were to study workers in the plants, salespeople in geographically remote units, engineers in technical enclaves, and so on, would one find the same assumptions operating? One of the interesting aspects of the Action Company is that at least for its first twenty or so years, this paradigm would have been observed in operation across all its rank levels, functions, and sites. But as we will see later, some elements of the Action culture have begun to change, and the paradigm no longer fits in some parts of the company.

It also needs to be noted that these four assumptions are not the whole Action Company culture. Assumptions about products, about customers, about quality, about how to run a business, about personnel policies, about how hard to work, about personal style, and on and on are also part of the culture and will be examined later. Finally, it should be noted that as the company grew and aged, subcultures formed, and some of the assumptions that grew up in those subcultures differed from the main assumptions in various ways. Even today, however, much of the essence of what I have described still operates, and the company is attempting to keep these assumptions alive in a rapidly changing environment that is testing some managers severely.

The Multi Company

My involvement with the Multi Company began in the mid 1970s and gradually lessened in the early 1980s. Again, a great many changes have occurred in this organization since then. Some of these changes are described in Chapter Seventeen.

Artifacts: Encountering the Multi Company

The Multi Company is a European multidivisional, geographically decentralized chemical company dealing in pharmaceuticals, agricultural chemicals, industrial chemicals, dyestuffs, and some technically based consumer products. The company is run by a board of directors and an internal executive committee of nine people who are legally accountable as a group for company decisions. The chairman of this executive committee functions as the chief executive officer, but the committee makes most decisions by consensus. Each member of the committee has oversight responsibility for a division, a function, and/or a geographical area, and these responsibilities rotate from time to time. The company has a long history of growth and was merged with another similar company a decade or more ago. The merger is considered to be a success, but there are still strong identifications with the original companies, according to many managers.

My original clients were the director of management development, Dr. Peter Stern, and his immediate boss, Richard Maier, the chairman of the executive committee. In this role Maier was clearly the chief executive of Multi and the originator of the project in which I became involved. Multi held annual three-day meetings of its top forty to fifty executives and had a tradition of inviting one or two outsiders to these meetings to lecture on some topic of interest to the company.

Dr. Stern contacted me by phone and asked me to give some lectures and lead some structured exercises to improve the group's understanding of creativity and to increase innovation and leadership in the company. Prior to the annual meeting I was to visit the company headquarters to be briefed, to meet some other key executives, especially Maier, and to review the material that was to be presented at the annual meeting. I got the impression that things were highly organized and carefully planned.

The Multi Company is headquartered in a small city in central Europe, and most of its managers are European. My first visit to the company revealed a sharp contrast to what I had encountered at the Action Company. I was immediately struck by Multi's formality as symbolized by large gray stone buildings and stiff uniformed guards in the main lobby. This spacious, opulent lobby was the main passageway for employees to enter the inner compound of office buildings and plants. It had high ceilings, large glass doors, and a few expensive pieces of modern furniture in one corner that served as a waiting area. (The reader will have detected that my own reactions to the Multi and Action environments were different. I liked the Action

environment more. In conducting a cultural analysis, those reactions are artifacts of the culture that must be acknowledged
and taken into account. It would be impossible and undesirable
to present any cultural analysis totally objectively because one's
emotional reactions and biases are primary data to be analyzed
and understood in the clinical research model.)

Upon entering the lobby I was asked by the uniformed
guard to check in with another guard, who sat in a glassed-in
office. I had to give my name and tell whom I was visiting and
where I was from. The guard then asked me to take a seat while
he did some telephoning and to wait until an escort could take
me to my appointed place. As I sat and waited, I noticed that
the guard seemed to know most of the employees who streamed
through the lobby or went to elevators and stairs leading from
it. I had the distinct feeling that any stranger would have been
spotted immediately and would have been asked to report as
I had been.

My client's secretary arrived in due course and took me
up in the elevator and down a long corridor of closed-door offices.
Each office had a tiny name plate that could be covered by a
hinged metal plate if the occupant wanted to remain anonymous.
Above each office door was a lightbulb; some lightbulbs showed
red and some green. I asked on a subsequent visit what this
meant and was told that if the light is green it is OK to knock,
whereas red means that the person does not want to be disturbed
under any circumstances.

We went around a corner and down another such corridor and never saw another soul during the entire time. When
we reached my client's office, the secretary knocked discreetly,
ushered me in when the door opened, and then went to her own
office and closed the door behind herself. I was offered tea or
coffee, which the secretary brought in on a large tray with a
small plate of cookies. Following our meeting, my client took
me to the executive dining room in another building, where we
again passed guards. This was the equivalent of a first-class restaurant, with a hostess who clearly knew everyone, reserved
tables, and provided discreet guidance on the day's specials.
Aperitifs and wine were offered with lunch, and the whole meal

took almost two hours. I was told that there was a less fancy dining room in still another building and an employee cafeteria as well but that this dining room clearly had the best food and was the right place for senior management to conduct business and to bring visitors. I got the impression that whereas at the Action Company kitchens and food were used as vehicles to get people to interact, at Multi, food, drink, and graciousness had some additional symbolic meaning, possibly having to do with status and rank. (I am inserting comparative statements into the case presentation because at the time of my encounters with Multi, my work with Action was well under way, and the contrast between the two companies was partly the basis for my reactions to Multi.)

Various senior officers of the company were pointed out to me, and I noticed that whenever anyone greeted someone else, it was always with a formal title, usually Dr. This or Dr. That. Observable differences in deference and demeanor made it fairly easy to determine who was superior to whom in the organization. It was also obvious that the tables in the room were assigned to executives on the basis of status and that the hostess knew exactly the relative status of all her guests.

In moving around the company I always felt a hushed atmosphere in the corridors, a slower, more deliberate pace, and much more emphasis on planning, schedules, and punctuality than I felt at Action, where I got the impression of frantic activity to make the most of what time there was. At Multi, time was carefully managed to maintain order. If I had an appointment with a manager at 2 P.M., the person I was with just prior to that meeting would stark walking down the hall with me at 1:58 so that we would arrive almost exactly on the dot. Only rarely was I kept waiting if I arrived on time, and if I was even a few minutes late, I had the strong sense that I had to apologize and explain.

Multi's managers impressed me as very serious, thoughtful, deliberate, well prepared, formal, and concerned about protocol. I learned later that whereas Action allocates rank and salary fairly strictly to the actual job an individual performs, Multi has a system of managerial ranks based on an individual's length of service, overall performance, and personal background rather than on the actual job the individual performs at a given time. Rank and status therefore have a much more permanent quality in Multi than in Action, where one's fortunes may rise and fall precipitously and frequently.

In meetings, I observed much less direct confrontation and much more respect for individual opinion at Multi. Recommendations made by managers in their specific area of accountability were generally respected and implemented. I never observed insubordination and got the impression that it would not be tolerated. Rank and status thus clearly have a higher value in Multi than in Action, whereas personal negotiating skill and the ability to get things done in an ambiguous social environment have a higher value in Action than in Multi.

Espoused Values

Values tend to be elicited when one asks about observed behavior or other artifacts that strike one as puzzling, anomalous, or inconsistent. If I asked managers at Multi why they always kept their doors closed, they would patiently and somewhat condescendingly explain to me that this was the only way they could get any work done and they valued work very highly. Meetings were a necessary evil, useful only for announcing decisions or gathering information. "Real work" was done by thinking things out and that required quiet and concentration. In contrast, at Action real work was done by debating things out in meetings!

It was also pointed out to me that discussion among peers was not of great value at Multi and that important information would come from the boss. Authority was highly respected, especially authority based on level of education, experience, and rank. The use of titles such as doctor or professor symbolized a respect for the knowledge that education bestows on people. Much of this had to do with Multi's great respect for science and the contributions of laboratory research to product development.

Both Multi and Action placed value on individual effort and contribution, but Multi gave the individual much more autonomy to make and implement decisions. On the other hand, one never went outside the chain of command and never did things that would be out of line with what one's boss had suggested. Multi also placed a high value on product elegance and quality and, as I discovered later, on what might be called product significance. Multi managers felt very proud of the fact that their chemicals and drugs were useful in protecting crops, in curing diseases, and in other ways helping to improve the world.

Basic Assumptions: The Multi Company Paradigm

Although many of the values that Multi employees articulated give a flavor of this company, without digging deeper to basic assumptions, one cannot fully understand how things worked. For example, the artifact that struck me most as I worked with this organization on the mandate to help it become more innovative was the anomalous behavior concerning my memos as noted in Chapter One. I realized that little lateral communication was occuring between units of the organization. Consequently, new ideas developed in one unit never seemed to get outside that unit. If I inquired about cross-divisional meetings, for example, I would get blank stares and questions such as "Why would we do that?" Because the divisions were facing similar problems, it would obviously be helpful to circulate some of the better ideas that came up in my interviews, supplemented with my own ideas based on my knowledge of what went on in other organizations.

Since Dr. Stern reported directly to the chairman of the executive committee, he seemed a natural conduit for communicating with all the divisional, functional, and geographic managers who needed the information I was gathering. Stern's failure to pass the information on was puzzling and irritating, but the consistency of this behavior clearly indicated that some strong underlying assumptions were at work. When I later asked one of my colleagues in the corporate staff unit that delivered training and other development programs to the organization why the information did not circulate freely, he revealed that he had similar problems. For example, he would develop a helpful intervention in one unit of the organization, but other units would seek help outside the organization before they would "discover" that he already had a solution. In other words, the common denominator seemed to be that unsolicited ideas were generally not well received.

We had a long exploratory conversation about this observed behavior and jointly figured out the explanation. At Multi, when a manager was given a job, that job became his private domain. Managers felt a strong sense of turf or ownership and made the assumption that each owner of a piece of the organization would be completely in charge and on top of it. The manager would be fully informed and make himself an expert in that area. Therefore, if someone provided unsolicited information pertaining to the job, this was potentially an invasion of privacy and possibly an insult in implying that the manager did not already have this information. One's superior could provide information, though even that was done only cautiously, but a peer would rarely do so, lest he unwittingly insult the recipient.

By not understanding this assumption I had unwittingly put Dr. Stern in the impossible position of risking insulting all his colleagues and peers if he circulated my memos as I had asked him to do. Interestingly enough, this kind of assumption is so tacit that even he could not articulate just why he had not followed my instructions. He was clearly uncomfortable and embarrassed about it but had no explanation until we brought the assumption about organizational turf and its symbolic meaning to the surface. (The reader should note that I am using exclusively male references in the Multi case because I did not encounter any senior women managers in this organization except in one subsidiary that will be referred to later.)

To further understand this and related behavior, it was necessary to consider some of the other underlying assumptions that had evolved in this company (see Figure 3.3). It had grown and achieved much of its success through fundamental discoveries made by a number of basic researchers in the company's central research laboratories. Whereas at Action truth has been discovered through conflict and debate, at Multi truth has come more from the wisdom of the scientist/researcher.

Figure 3.3. The Multi Company Paradigm.

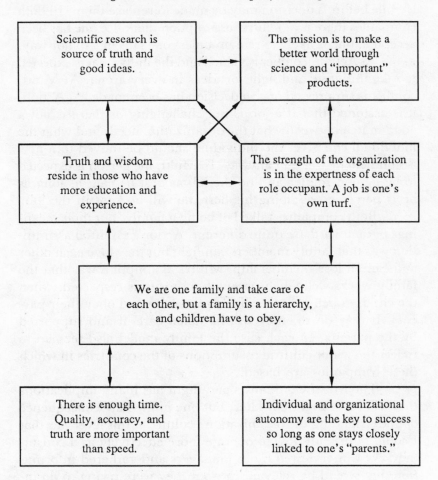

Scientific research is source of truth and good ideas.

The mission is to make a better world through science and "important" products.

Truth and wisdom reside in those who have more education and experience.

The strength of the organization is in the expertness of each role occupant. A job is one's own turf.

We are one family and take care of each other, but a family is a hierarchy, and children have to obey.

There is enough time. Quality, accuracy, and truth are more important than speed.

Individual and organizational autonomy are the key to success so long as one stays closely linked to one's "parents."

Both companies believe in the individual, but the differing assumptions about the nature of truth have led to completely different attitudes toward authority and the role of conflict. At Multi, authority is much more respected, and conflict tends to be avoided. As indicated above, the individual is given areas of freedom by the boss and then is totally respected in those areas. If role occupants are not well enough educated or skilled enough to make decisions, they are expected to train themselves. If they perform poorly in the meantime, that will be tolerated for quite a while before a decision may be made to replace them. In both companies there is a "tenure" assumption that once one has been accepted, one is likely to remain unless one fails in a major way.

At Action, conflict is valued and the individual is expected to take initiative and fight for ideas in every arena. At Multi, conflict is suppressed once a decision has been made. At Action, it is assumed that if a job is not challenging or there is not a good match between what the organization needs and what the individual can give, the individual should be moved to a new assignment or will quit anyway. In Multi, the person is expected to be a good soldier and do the job as best he can; as long as he is perceived as doing his best, he will be kept in the job.

Both companies talked of being a family, but their meanings of that word are quite different. Action's essential assumption was that family members can fight but they love each other and cannot lose membership. Multi's assumption was that the family works well when parental authority is respected, when the children behave according to the rules and obey their parents. If they do so, they will be taken care of and supported by the parents. In each case the family model also seemed to reflect the wider cultural assumptions of the countries in which these companies are based.

The Multi Company's paradigm has many implications that will be brought out later, but one immediate consequence of understanding the organization's culture at this level was that I could figure out how to operate more effectively as a consultant. As I interviewed more managers and gathered information that would be relevant to what they were trying to do instead of attempting to circulate memos to the various branches of the Multi organization through my contact client, I found that if I gave information directly, even if it was unsolicited, it was accepted because I was an "expert." If I wanted information to circulate, I sent it to the relevant parties on my own initiative; if I thought it needed to circulate down into the organization, I gave it to the boss and attempted to convince him that the information would be relevant lower down. If I really wanted to intervene by having managers do something different, I could accomplish this best by being an expert and formally recommending it to CEO Maier. If he liked the idea, he would then order "the troops" to do it.

Summary and Conclusions

Organizational culture can be analyzed at three levels: (1) visible artifacts; (2) espoused values, rules, and behavioral norms; and (3) tacit, basic underlying assumptions. As argued in this chapter, unless one digs down to the level of basic assumptions, one cannot really decipher the artifacts, values, and norms. On the other hand, if one finds some of those basic assumptions and explores their interrelationship, one is really getting at the essence of the culture and can then explain a great deal of what goes on in it. This essence can sometimes be analyzed as a paradigm in that some organizations function by virtue of an interlocking coordinated set of assumptions. Whereas each one alone might not make sense, their pattern explains the behavior and the success of the organization in overcoming its external and internal challenges.

Because I have only described certain elements of the cultures of two companies as they pertained to key goals that the organizations were trying to achieve, we should not assume that these paradigms describe the whole cultures, nor should we assume that we would find the same paradigm operating in every part of the same organization. The generality of the assumptions is itself something to be investigated and determined empirically.

I "discovered" these assumptions primarily through exploring with inside informants some of the anomalies that I experienced and observed between the visible artifacts and the espoused values. When we do not understand something, we need to pursue vigorously why we do not, and the best way to search is to use one's own ignorance and naïveté. This method of research, which I call clinical research, contrasts with various other research models that imply a lower level of involvement of the research subject. Although it is necessary to use all the research methods available when dealing with culture, the clinical method is central because only by involving the members of the group can one get at their deeper assumptions. The subjects must be motivated to reveal themselves, and this only occurs when they perceive themselves to be benefitting from the inquiry process itself.

What are some of the lessons to be learned from these cases, and what implications do they have for leadership? The most important lesson for me is the realization that culture is deep, pervasive, complex, patterned, and morally neutral. In both organizations described in this chapter I had to overcome my own cultural prejudices about the right and wrong way to do things and to learn that culture simply exists. Both companies are successful in their respective technological, political, economic, and broader cultural environments. Specific cultures may be maladapted to their environments, but the student/ observer should not trust his or her own emotional or aesthetic responses to guide that judgment. That is for careful analysis and for insiders to make.

In both cases the powerful influence of early leaders and historical circumstance was evident. Cultural assumptions have their roots in early group experience and in the pattern of success and failure experienced by each of the two companies. Current leaders strongly valued their cultures, were proud of them, and felt it important for members of their organizations to accept the basic assumptions. In both organizations stories were told of misfits who left because they did not like the way the company operated or who were not hired in the first place because they would either be disruptive or would not like it anyway.

As will be analyzed in more detail later, in both companies leaders were struggling with changing environmental demands and faced the issue of whether and how to develop or change their ways of operating. In each company, however, this was initially defined as *reaffirmation* of portions of the existing culture, not as *changes* in the culture. Though the companies were at different stages in their evolution, they both valued their cultures as important assets and were eager to preserve and enhance them.

PART TWO

The Dimensions
of Culture

Thus far I have defined and described culture as a structural concept. In this part of the book I describe what culture consists of, what an observer would view as the content of culture. If culture is shared basic assumptions, we still need to specify, assumptions about what? I argue that the content of organizational cultures reflects the ultimate problems that every group faces: dealing with its external environment (Chapter Four) and managing its internal integration (Chapter Five). Culture is pervasive and ultimately embraces everything that a group is concerned about and must deal with. Beyond these external and internal problems, cultural assumptions reflect deeper issues about the nature of truth, time, space, human nature, and human relationships. A way of thinking about and describing these deeper issues is spelled out in Chapters Six and Seven.

Part Two focuses more on the concept of culture and less on the concept of leadership. Nevertheless, the reader should remember that it is leadership in the history of the group that has created the particular culture content that the group ends up having. The categories of culture content that will be reviewed are therefore also categories of content that exist within the leader's head. *Every leader should be highly conscious of his or her own assumptions in each of those content areas.*

CHAPTER FOUR

Surviving in and Adapting to External Environments

A formal definition of organizational culture can tell us what culture is, but it does not tell us what cultural assumptions are about, why they form in the first place, and more important, why they survive. To understand the content and dynamics of culture, we must develop a model of how basic assumptions arise and why they persist. We need such a model because ultimately culture covers all aspects of group life. Along what dimensions, then, should we analyze it, and on what dimensions should we focus when we study a culture? For this purpose the most relevant model is one developed by sociology and group dynamics and based on the fundamental distinction between any group's problems of (1) survival in and adaptation to its external environment and (2) integration of its internal processes to ensure the capacity to continue to survive and adapt.

In other words, from an evolutionary perspective, we need to identify the issues that any group faces from the moment of its origin through to its state of maturity and decline. Although it may be difficult, sometimes even impossible, to study cultural origins and functions in ethnic units whose history is lost in antiquity, it is not at all impossible to study these matters in groups, organizations, or occupations whose history and evolution are available.

The process of culture formation is, in a sense, identical to the process of group formation in that the very essence of "groupness" or group identity, the shared patterns of thought, belief, feelings, and values that result from shared experience and common learning, results in the pattern of shared assumption that I am calling the culture of that group. Without a group there can be no culture, and without some shared assumptions, some minimal degree of culture, we are really talking only about an aggregate of people, not a group. So group growth and culture formation are inextricably intertwined, and both are the result of leadership activities and shared experiences.

What we need to understand, then, is how the individual intentions of the founders, leaders, or conveners of a new group or organization, their own definitions of the situation, their assumptions and values come to be a shared, consensually validated set of definitions that are passed on to new members as "the correct way to define the situation." And we need to understand along what dimensions leaders think in creating and managing groups. The issues or problems of external adaptation and survival basically specify the coping cycle that any system must be able to maintain in relation to its changing environment. The essential elements of that cycle are outlined below. Though each step in the cycle is presented in sequential order, any given organization probably works on most of the steps simultaneously once it is a going concern (Schein, 1980).

1. *Mission and strategy:* obtaining a shared understanding of core mission, primary task, manifest and latent functions
2. *Goals:* developing consensus on goals, as derived from the core mission
3. *Means:* developing consensus on the means to be used to attain the goals, such as the organization structure, division of labor, reward system, and authority system
4. *Measurement:* developing consensus on the criteria to be used in measuring how well the group is doing in fulfilling its goals, such as the information and control system
5. *Correction:* developing consensus on the appropriate remedial or repair strategies to be used if goals are not being met

Shared Assumptions About Mission and Strategy

Every new group or organization must develop a shared concept of its ultimate survival problem, from which it usually derives its most basic sense of core mission, primary task, or reason to be. In most business organizations, this shared definition revolves around the issue of economic survival and growth, which in turn involves the maintenance of good relationships with the major stakeholders of the organization: (1) the investors and stockholders, (2) the suppliers of the materials needed to produce, (3) the managers and employees, (4) the community and government, and last but not least, (5) the customers willing to pay for the good or service.

Several studies of organizations have shown that the key to long-range growth and survival is to keep the needs of these constituencies in some kind of balance and that the mission of the organization as a set of beliefs about its core competencies and basic functions in society is usually a reflection of this balance (Donaldson and Lorsch, 1983; Kotter and Heskett, 1992). It has been a mistake to think in terms of a total focus on any one of these constituencies because all of them together make up the environment in which the organization must succeed.

In religious, educational, social, and governmental organizations, the core mission or primary task is clearly different, but the logic that it ultimately derives from a balancing of the needs of different stakeholders is the same. Thus, for example, the mission of a university must balance the learning needs of the students, the needs of the faculty to conduct research and extend knowledge, the needs of the community to have a repository for knowledge and skill, the needs of the financial investors to have a viable institution, and ultimately even the needs of society to have an institution to facilitate the transition of late adolescents into the labor market and to sort them into skill groups.

Though core missions or primary tasks are usually stated in terms of a single constituency such as customers, a more useful way to think about ultimate or core mission is to change the question to "What is our function in the larger scheme of things?"

Posing the question this way reveals that most organizations have multiple functions reflecting the multiple stakeholders and that some of these functions are public justifications while others are latent and, in a sense, not spoken of (Merton, 1957). For example, the manifest function of a school system is to educate. But a close examination of what goes on in school systems suggests several latent functions as well: (1) to keep children off the streets and out of the labor market until there is room for them and they have some relevant skills, (2) to sort and group the next generation into talent and skill categories according to the needs of the society, and (3) to enable the various occupations associated with the school system to survive and maintain their professional autonomy. In examining the manifest and latent functions, members of the organization will recognize that to survive, the organization must to some degree fulfill all of these functions.

Core mission thus becomes a complex multifunctional issue, where some of the functions must remain latent in order to protect the organization's manifest identity. To announce publicly the baby-sitting, sorting, and professional autonomy functions would be embarrassing, but these functions often play an important role in determining the activities of school organizations. In business organizations the latent functions include, for instance, the provision of jobs in the community where the business is located, the provision of economic resources to that community in the form of goods and raw materials purchased, and the provision of managerial talent to be used in activities other than running the business. The importance of these latent functions is not apparent until an organization is forced to contemplate closing or moving. Then a number of interest groups that were in one way or another counting on that organization, even though implicitly, suddenly come forward to protest the decision to move or to close.

Internal debates start among members for whom the priorities among the different functions are different, forcing the organization to confront what collectively it has assumed to be at the top of this hierarchy. If no such overarching priority is found, the group may splinter and even dissolve. On the other hand, if the debate leads to an affirmation of what the group's ultimate mission and identity are, a strong cultural element has been formed, one that will carry forward through the beliefs and assumptions of senior management.

For example, at one stage in the evolution of the Multi Company, I heard lengthy debates among top managers on the question of whether Multi should design and produce any product provided it could be sold at a profit or whether designs and production should be limited to what some senior managers believed, on the basis of their conception of what the company had originally been built on and what their unique talents were, to be sound or valuable products. The debate focused on whether or not to keep an acquired company that was making money but whose products were clearly inconsistent with Multi's traditional products. After much soul searching, Multi sold the company and the senior managers affirmed the assumption that they should only be in businesses that had a clear scientific base.

The same issue came up in a different way in a large packaged-food company when it had to face the accusation from consumer groups and nutrition experts that some of its products, although they tasted good because they contained large amounts of sugar and artificial flavoring, had no nutritional value. For top management, the accusation raised not merely an economic question but also an identity question: Is this company a food company, or a consumer-oriented edibles company, or both, or neither?

At first the company responded by attempting to develop and sell more nutritious products, but it found that customers genuinely preferred the cheaper, less nutritious ones. An advertising campaign to sell nutrition did not overcome this customer resistance, nor did lowering the price. A debate ensued in the company about its basic mission beyond economic survival. In this debate the pragmatic market-oriented philosophy could be argued much more successfully by managers. The company discovered that its commitment to nutrition was not fundamental and that its identity rested much more on the assumption that it was in the consumer edibles business. The company would make and sell any kind of food for which people were willing to pay money.

In summary, one of the most central elements of any culture will be the assumptions the members of the organization share about their identity and ultimate mission or functions. These assumptions are not necessarily conscious but one can bring them to the surface by probing the organization's strategic decisions.

Shared Assumptions About Operational Goals Derived from the Mission

Consensus on the core mission does not automatically guarantee that the members of the group will have common goals. The mission is often understood but not well articulated. To achieve consensus on goals, the group needs a common language and shared assumptions about the basic logical operations by which one moves from something as abstract or general as a sense of mission to the concrete goals of designing, manufacturing, and selling an actual good or service within specified and agreed upon cost and time constraints.

For example, in the Action Company there was a clear consensus on the mission of bringing out a line of products that would win in the marketplace. However, this consensus did not solve senior management's problem of how to allocate resources among different product development groups, nor did it specify how best to market such products. Mission and strategy can be rather timeless, while goals must be formulated for what to do next year, next month, and tomorrow. Goals concretize the mission and facilitate the decisions on means. In that process goal formulation also often reveals unsolved issues or lack of consensus around deeper issues.

The Action Company debate around choice of products revealed a deep lack of semantic agreement on how to think about the marketing function. For example, one group thought that marketing meant better image advertising in national magazines so that more people would recognize the name of the company, one group was convinced that marketing meant better advertising in technical journals, one group thought it meant developing the next generation of products, while yet another group emphasized merchandising and sales support as the key elements of marketing. Senior management could not define clear goals because of a lack of consensus on the meaning of key functions and how those functions reflect the core mission of the organization. Senior management had to agree on whether it was better to develop the company by seeing that it was well known in the technical community or recognized nationally as a brand name in its industry.

At Multi there was a clear consensus on the mission to remain in the pharmaceutical business because it fitted senior management's broad self-concept and was profitable. However, there was considerable disagreement on what rate of return should be expected from that division and over what length of time its growth and performance should be measured.

Because operational goals have to be more precise, organizations typically work out their issues of mission and identity in the context of deciding annual or longer-range goals. If one really wants to understand cultural assumptions, one must be careful not to confuse assumptions about goals with assumptions about mission. Multi's concern with being only in businesses that make "useful" products did not become evident in their discussions about business goals until they hit a strategic issue like whether or not to buy another company. In fact, one way of looking at what we mean by strategy is to recognize that strategy concerns the evolution of the basic mission, while operational goals reflect the short-run tactical survival issues that the organization identifies. Thus, when a company embarks on basic strategy discussions, it is usually trying to assess in a more fundamental way the relationship between its sense of its mission and its operational goals.

In summary, goals can be defined at several levels of abstraction and in different time horizons. Is our goal to be profitable at the end of next quarter, or to make ten sales next month, or to call twelve potential customers tomorrow? Only as consensus is reached on such matters, leading to solutions that work repeatedly, can we begin to think of the goals of an organization as potential cultural elements. Once such consensus is reached, however, the assumptions about goals become very strong elements of that group's culture.

Shared Assumptions About Means to Achieve Goals

The group cannot achieve its goals and fulfill its mission unless there is clear consensus on the means by which goals will be met. The means to be used have to do with day-to-day behavior and therefore require a higher level of consensus. One can have ambiguous goals, but one must agree on how to design, finance, build, and sell the good or service if anything is to happen at all. From the particular pattern of these agreements will emerge not only the "style" of the organization but also the basic design of tasks, division of labor, organization structure, reward and incentive systems, control systems, and information systems.

The skills, technology, and knowledge that a group acquires in its effort to cope with its environment, then, also become part of its culture if there is consensus on what they are and how to use them. For example, in his study of several companies that make the world's best flutes, Cook (1992) shows that for generations the craftsmen were able to produce flutes that artists would recognize immediately as having been made by a particular company, but neither management nor the craftsmen could describe exactly what they had done to make it so. It was embedded in the processes of manufacturing and could be passed on for generations through an apprentice system, but it was not formally identifiable.

In the development of the means by which the group will accomplish its goals, many of the internal issues that the group must deal with get partially settled. The external problem of division of labor will structure who will get to know whom and who will be in authority. The work system of the group will define its boundaries and its rules for membership. The particular beliefs and talents of the group's founders and leaders will determine which functions become dominant as the group evolves. For example, engineers founding companies based on their inventions create very different kinds of internal structures than venture capitalists creating organizations by putting technical and marketing talent under the direction of financially or marketing-oriented leaders.

The founders of the Multi Company believed that solutions to problems result from hard thought, scientific research, and careful checking of that research in the marketplace. From the beginning this company had clearly defined research roles and distinguished them sharply from managerial roles. The norm had developed that one must become an expert in one's own area to the point where one knows more about that area than anyone else, a norm clearly derived from some of the assumptions of the scientific model on which the company operated. Historically, this link to the culture of science may have accounted, in part, for the assumption that one's area of expertise is one's own property or turf and the feeling that it might be considered insulting to be given advice in the area. The defined turf included one's subordinates, budget, physical space, and all other resources allocated to one. This level of felt autonomy and the formal relationships that developed among group members then became their means of getting work done.

At Action, on the other hand, a norm developed that the only turf one really owns is one's accountability for certain tasks and accomplishments. Budget, physical space, subordinates, and other resources were really seen as common organizational property over which one had only influence. Others in the organization could try to influence the accountable manager or his or her subordinates, but there were no boundaries or walls, physical space was viewed as common territory, and sharing knowledge was highly valued. Whereas at Multi to give ideas to another was considered threatening, at Action it was considered mandatory to survival.

Lack of consensus on who "owns" what can be a major source of difficulty. For example, at one time in Action's history, there was a lack of consensus on the rules for obtaining key engineering services, such as drafting and the use of the model-building shop. Some engineers believed that work would be done in the order in which it was submitted; others believed that it would be done according to the importance of the work, and they often persuaded the service manager to break into the queue to give their work priority. This aroused great anger on the part of those who were waiting their turn patiently and, as might be expected, made the service manager very anxious.

The total group eventually had to get together to establish a common set of policies; interestingly enough, this reinforced the existing pattern and legitimized it. Both engineering and service managers were to do the "sensible" thing, and if they could not figure out what that was, they were to refer the matter to the next higher level of management for resolution. The policy discussion ended up reinforcing the assumption that since no one is smart enough to have a formula for how to do things, people should use their intelligence and common sense at all times. Ambiguity was considered a reality that must be lived with and managed sensibly.

Feelings about territory, property, and turf also have a biological basis. Few things arouse as much aggression in animals as having their defined territory invaded. Few circumstances cause as much breakdown of normal behavior patterns as excessive crowding, rendering any private space a physical impossibility (Hall, 1966). In cultures where crowding is inevitable because of shortage of space, defensive cultural assumptions form to deal with the stress this creates. Butterfield (1982) notes in his description of China that when one bumps into someone in a crowded bus, one need not even say, "sorry," as Westerners would do routinely, because one has only bumped into a stranger, an impersonal object. The same kind of depersonalization operates in the Japanese subway and, for that matter, in any kind of intense crowding situation.

Division of labor, the allocations of various kinds of roles, can be seen as an extension of the allocation of physical and other kinds of property because various amounts of status, access to rewards, and certain privileges inevitably accompany the assigned roles. Therefore, how those roles are allocated and the consensus on criteria for allocation not only become the means by which tasks are accomplished but also resolve major internal group issues. Because the means by which things get done in the external environment become "property" in the internal environment, we often see the means controlling the ends. An efficient assembly line may mechanize behavior to such a degree that the organization begins to be perceived as caring more about efficiency and profit than the welfare of its employees. The production manager's turf can become sacred even though this may lead to organizational activities that violate other elements of the organization's identity and mission.

Changing an organization's structures and processes is therefore difficult because it involves not only considerations of efficiency and effectiveness vis-à-vis the external task but also the reallocation of internal "property." Similarly, changing reward systems and status allocation systems in the internal working of the organization may be difficult because such changes will affect how work is done and how well goals are achieved. For this reason organizational analysis is increasingly moving toward what has been termed *sociotechnical* system analysis, acknowledging the degree to which the formal technical means for task accomplishment are intrinsically intertwined with the internal status, turf, and role systems (Hanna, 1988; Pasmore and Sherwood, 1978; Rice, 1963; Trist and others, 1963).

In summary, as cultural assumptions form around the means by which goals are to be accomplished, they will inevitably involve the internal issues of status and identity, thus highlighting the complexity of both the analysis of means and the issues surrounding efforts to change the way an organization accomplishes its goals. Consensus on the means to be used creates the behavioral regularities and many of the artifacts that eventually come to be identified as the visible manifestations of the culture. Once these regularities and patterns are in place, they become a source of stability for members and are therefore strongly adhered to.

Shared Assumptions About Criteria for Measuring Results

Once the group is performing, it must have consensus on how to judge its own performance in order to know what kind of remedial action to take when things do not go as expected. For example, early in Action's history the evaluation of engineering projects hinged on whether certain key individuals in the company liked the product. The company assumed that internal acceptance was an acceptable surrogate for external acceptance. In another high-technology company, the criterion was completely different. Products had to be built and market tested before it was considered legitimate to mass produce them.

In the Wellmade flute company, evaluation was done at each node in the production process, so that by the time an instrument reached the end of the line, it was likely to pass inspection and to be acceptable to the artist. If a craftsman at a given position did not like what he felt or saw, he simply passed it back to the preceding craftsman, and the norm was that it would be reworked without resentment. Each person trusted the person in the next position (Cook, 1992).

Cook also found a similar process in a French brandy company, where not only was each step evaluated by an expert, but the ultimate role of taster, the person who makes the final determination of when a batch is ready, could only be assumed by a male son of the previous taster. In this company the last taster had no sons. Rather than pass the role on to the eldest daughter, it was passed on to a nephew on the assumption that female taste preferences were in some fundamental way different from male taste preferences!

Some companies teach their executives to trust their own judgment as a basis of decisions; others teach them to check with their bosses; still others teach them not to trust results unless they are based on hard data, such as test markets or at least market research; and still others teach them to rely on staff experts. If members of the group hold widely divergent concepts of what to look for and how to evaluate results, they cannot decide when and how to take remedial action.

For example, senior managers within companies often hold different views of how to assess financial performance — debt/equity ratio, return on sales, return on investment, stock price, and other indicators could all be used. If senior management cannot agree on which indicator to pay primary attention to, they cannot decide how well they are doing and what corrective action, if any, they need to take.

Debates can occur on whether financial criteria should override other criteria such as customer satisfaction, market share, or employee morale. These debates are complicated by potential disagreements on the correct time horizons to use in making evaluations—daily, monthly, quarterly, annually, or what? Even though the information systems may be very precise, such precision does not guarantee consensus on how to evaluate information.

The potential complexity of achieving consensus on measurement criteria was illustrated in an international refugee organization. Field workers measured themselves by the number of refugees processed, but senior management paid more attention to how favorable the attitudes of host governments were because those governments financed the organization through their contributions. Senior management therefore checked every decision that was to be made about refugees with virtually every other department and several layers of management to ensure that the decision would not offend one of the supporting governments. However, this process markedly slowed the making of decisions and often led to lowest-common-denominator conservative decisions. This, in turn, led to great irritation on the part of the field workers, who felt that they were usually dealing with crisis situations in which slowdowns might mean death for significant numbers of refugees. They perceived top management to be hopelessly mired in what they considered to be simply bureaucratic tangles, and they did not understand the caution that top management felt it had to exercise toward sponsoring governments.

Lack of agreement across the hierarchy on how to judge success—amount of money contributed or number of refugees processed—was the major source of difficulty in improving the overall performance and level of employee satisfaction in this organization. In addition, there may have been a basic lack of consensus even on the core mission. Whereas the field workers tended to think of the core mission as helping the survival of refugees, senior management was clearly more concerned with the survival of the total organization, which in its view depended on how it related to the United Nations and to the host governments. Senior management had to decide whether to indoctrinate field workers more effectively on what the core organizational survival problem really was or to live with the internal conflict that the lack of consensus seemed to generate. On the other hand, the younger idealistic field workers could well argue (and did) that to survive as an organization made no sense if the needs of refugees were not met. In this organization, then, one would have to speak of conflicting cultural assumptions or conflicting subcultures in that the headquarters and field each had consensus but that a total organizational consensus on mission and means was absent.

A comparable issue arose in evaluating the performance of different divisions of the Multi Company. The high-performing divisions chose to compare themselves internally to the low-performing divisions and were therefore complacent about pushing for even higher performance levels. Senior management chose to compare these same divisions to their external competitors in the same product/market space and found the former were underperforming by that criterion. Nonetheless, the tradition of being one family made it hard to convince division managers to accept tough external standards.

Many so-called culture change programs actually deal only with this one element of the culture—the measurements to be applied to future performance. Thus, new chief executives come in and announce that they will emphasize product quality, or bring costs under control, or get the organization to be more customer oriented. This sometimes sounds like a real change in mission but, on closer examination, turns out to be merely a new focus on how to measure success. From this perspective it is clear that such new signals will change only one element of the culture. If only the results signals are changed, without concern for mission, goals, and means, very little actual change may occur.

Consensus must be achieved both on the criteria and on the means by which information is to be gathered. There is a powerful assumption at Action that information and truth are the lifeblood of the organization.

In contrast, the Multi Company has a tightly structured reporting system, which involves weekly telephone calls, monthly reports to the financial control organization at headquarters, semiannual visits to every department by headquarters teams, and formal meetings and seminars where policy is communicated downward in the organization. The main assumption at Multi appears to be that information flows primarily in designated channels and informal systems are to be avoided because they can be unreliable.

In summary, how an organization decides to measure its own activities and accomplishments — the criteria it uses and the information system it develops to measure itself — become central elements of its culture as consensus develops around these issues. If consensus fails to develop and strong subcultures form around different assumptions, the organization will find itself in serious conflict that can potentially undermine its ability to cope with its external environment.

Shared Assumptions About
Remedial and Repair Strategies

The final area of consensus crucial for external adaptation concerns what to do if a change in course is required and how to do it. If information indicates that the group is not on target — sales are off, market share is down, profits are down, product introductions are late, key customers complain about product quality, or the like — what is the process by which the problem is diagnosed and remedied?

For example, if a product fails in the marketplace, does the organization fire the product manager, reexamine the marketing strategy, reassess the quality of the research and development process, convene a diagnostic team from many functions to see what can be learned from the failure, or brush the failure under the rug and quietly move the good people into different jobs?

At Action the diagnosis and remedy are likely to result from widespread open discussion and debate among members at all levels of the organization. After the discussion and debate, self-corrective action often is taken because people now recognize problems about which they can so something. Thus, by the time top management ratifies a course of action and announces it, most of the problem has already been dealt with. On the other hand, if the discussion leads to proposals that violate some of the founder's assumptions or intuitions, he will step into the debate and attempt to influence thinking. Or he will empower different groups to proceed along different paths in order to play it safe.

At Multi remedial action is taken locally, if possible, to minimize the upward delegation of bad news. However, if companywide problems arise, top management will go through a formal period of diagnosis, often with the help of task forces and other specific processes. Once a diagnosis has been made and remedial action decided on, the decision is formally disseminated through systematic meetings, memos, phone calls, and other formal means.

Another company found that one of the most difficult remedial actions was for the product development function to stop working on a product that was not successful. Even though market test data consistently showed that customers would not buy a particular product, the development team would rationalize the data away and assume that sooner or later the product would sell. Management had to develop tough rules and time limits that, in effect, forced the abandonment of projects over the objections of the development team when market test data revealed negative customer responses.

"Corrective" processes are not limited to problem areas. If a company is getting signals of success, it may decide to grow faster, or develop a careful strategy of controlled growth, or take a quick profit and risk staying small. Consensus on these matters becomes crucial to effectiveness, and the kind of consensus achieved is one of the determinants of the company's style. Organizations that have not had periodic survival problems may not have a style of responding to such problems. On the other hand, organizations that have had survival crises have often discovered in their responses to such crises what some of their deeper assumptions really are. In this sense an important piece of an organization's culture can be genuinely latent. No one really knows what response it will make to a severe crisis, yet the nature of that response will reflect deep elements of the culture, particularly those sociotechnical elements that reflect internal integration.

For example, many organizations about to go out of business have discovered, to their surprise, high levels of motivation and commitment among their employees. One also hears the opposite kinds of stories, often from wartime, of military units that were counting on high levels of commitment only to find individuals losing their will to fight, seeking excuses to get out of combat, and even shooting their own officers in the back. Crisis situations reveal whether worker subcultures have developed around restriction of output and hiding ideas for improvement from management or whether these subcultures support productivity goals.

In a first-generation company, crises will reveal some of the deeper assumptions of the founder, and as these become manifested, the culture of the group may be elaborated around them. In one company the founder reacted to poor economic circumstances by ordering massive layoffs of even his closest colleagues. In contrast, in another company, the founder in a similar situation put everyone on a part-time schedule and suggested that everyone take a percentage pay cut. He made it clear that he valued his employees and wanted to retain as many of them as possible. "Neurotic" organizations, whose culture becomes chronically dysfunctional, often arise from a series of such crisis resolutions, which produce a systematic bias in how problems are responded to (Kets de Vries and Miller, 1984, 1987; Miller, 1990). Responses to crises thus provide opportunities for culture building and reveal aspects of the culture that have already been built. From that point of view, this area of organizational adaptation is one of the most important to analyze, understand, and if possible, manage.

The remedial or corrective strategies that an organization employs in response to the information it gathers about its performance represent an important area around which cultural assumptions form. These assumptions are likely to reveal other assumptions about mission and identity and are likely to be closely connected to the assumptions that the organization makes about its internal functioning.

Summary and Conclusions

Cultural assumptions evolve around all aspects of a group's relationship to its external environment. The group's ultimate mission, goals, means used to achieve goals, measurement of its performance, and remedial strategies all require consensus if the group is to perform effectively. If there is conflict between subgroups that form subcultures, such conflict can undermine group performance. On the other hand, if the environmental context is changing, such conflict can be a potential source of adaptation and new learning. As we will see, degree of consensus is more functional in the early growth of the group and can become dysfunctional in later stages.

How these external survival issues are worked out strongly influences the internal integration of the group. Ultimately, all organizations are sociotechnical systems in which the manner of external adaptation and the solution of internal integration problems are interdependent. Although we are examining the internal and external processes in serial order for purposes of exposition, they are, of course, actually occurring simultaneously.

The most important conclusion to be derived from this analysis is that culture is a multidimensional, multifaceted phenomenon, not easily reduced to a few major dimensions. Culture ultimately reflects the group's effort to cope and learn and is the residue of the learning process. Culture thus fulfills not only the function of providing stability, meaning, and predictability in the present but is the result of functionally effective decisions in the group's past.

The implications for leadership are several. First of all, the external issues described in this chapter are usually the leader's primary concern because it is the leader who creates the group and wants it to succeed. Even if the group precedes the leader historically, it will generally put one of its members into the leadership role to worry about external boundary management, survival, and growth. Second, the successful management of these several functions is usually the basis on which leaders are assessed. If they cannot create a group that succeeds, they are considered to have failed as leaders. Internal dissent can be forgiven, but a leader who fails in the external functions is usually abandoned, voted out, or gotten rid of in a more dramatic way. The steps of the coping cycle and the issues groups face thus make a useful checklist against which leaders can assess their own performance.

CHAPTER FIVE

Managing
Internal Integration

If a group is to accomplish tasks that enable it to adapt to its external environment, it must be able to develop and maintain a set of internal relationships among its members. The processes that build and develop the group occur at the same time as the processes of problem solving and task accomplishment. What we ultimately find to be the culture of the group will reflect both externally and internally oriented processes. The processes that allow a group to internally integrate itself reflect the major internal issues that any group must deal with, as summarized below.

1. *Creating a common language and conceptual categories:* If members cannot communicate with and understand each other, a group is impossible by definition.
2. *Defining group boundaries and criteria for inclusion and exclusion:* The group must be able to define itself. Who is in and who is out, and by what criteria does one determine membership?
3. *Distributing power and status:* Every group must work out its pecking order, its criteria and rules for how members get, maintain, and lose power. Consensus in this area is crucial to help members manage feelings of aggression.

4. *Developing norms of intimacy, friendship, and love:* Every group must work out its rules of the game for peer relationships, for relationships between the sexes, and for the manner in which openness and intimacy are to be handled in the context of managing the organization's tasks. Consensus in this area is crucial to help members manage feelings of affection and love.

5. *Defining and allocating rewards and punishments:* Every group must know what its heroic and sinful behaviors are and must achieve consensus on what is a reward and what is a punishment.

6. *Explaining the unexplainable — ideology and religion:* Every group, like every society, faces unexplainable events that must be given meaning so that members can respond to them and avoid the anxiety of dealing with the unexplainable and uncontrollable.

Creating a Common Language and Conceptual Categories

To function as a group, the individuals who come together must establish a system of communication and a language that permits interpretation of what is going on. The human organism cannot tolerate too much uncertainty and/or stimulus overload. Categories of meaning that organize perceptions and thought, thereby filtering out what is unimportant while focusing on what is important, become not only a major means of reducing overload and anxiety but also a necessary precondition for any coordinated action.

Two children on a seesaw not only need to be able to signal each other that they want to operate the seesaw together. They also need some verbal or nonverbal means of signaling when to push and when to relax, or how far back to sit if their weight is different, or how fast to move. Members of a founding group coming together to create a new organization need to learn about each other's semantic space (even if they start with a common basic language, such as English) in order to determine what they mean by such abstractions as "a good product," of "high quality," produced at "low cost," to get into the "market" "as rapidly as possible."

If several members of a group are using different category systems, they not only cannot agree on what to do but will not even agree on their definition of what is real, what is a fact, when something is true or false, what is important, what needs attention, and so on. Most communication breakdowns between people result from their lack of awareness that in the first place they are making basically different assumptions about meaning categories.

For example, in my role as a consultant to a small family-owned food company, I asked some managers whether they experienced any conflicts with subordinates, peers, or superiors in their daily work. Unless I happened to be talking to a particularly disgruntled person, I usually elicited an immediate and flat denial of any conflict whatsoever. This response puzzled me because I had been called in by the president to help figure out what to do about "severe conflicts" that members of the organization were perceiving and/or experiencing. I finally realized that I was making two assumptions not shared by the managers I was questioning: (1) *conflict* is a general term referring to any degree of disagreement between two or more people, and (2) conflict is a normal human condition that is always present to some degree.

My interviewees, on the other hand, held two quite different assumptions: (1) the word *conflict* refers to a severe disagreement that is difficult if not impossible to reconcile (a different semantic interpretation of the word itself), and (2) conflict is bad in the sense that a person who has conflicts is not managing well. Once I realized that different assumptions were at the root of the communication problem, I could change my question to "Tell me about the things that make it easy or hard for you to get your job done." If any evidence of interpersonal "disagreements" began to surface, I made my own assumption explicit, that is, that such disagreements are, in my view, completely normal in organizations. I then often got vivid and detailed stories of severe "conflicts" and, in subsequent discussions, found that the word itself could be used without further misunderstanding or defensiveness. In this example my clients and I were building a common language for our own work.

In this same organization I observed in group meetings that the president often got angry with a member who was not contributing actively and began to draw conclusions about the competence of that member. The chairman assumed (as I learned later by asking about the situation) that the silence meant ignorance, incompetence, or lack of motivation. The silent member, it turned out, was usually ready to make a presentation and was very frustrated because he was never called on to give it. He assumed that he was not supposed to volunteer, and he began to believe that his boss did not value him because he was not called on. If their different assumptions about the meaning of silence were not brought into the open, the danger was that both would validate their own incorrect assumption, thus setting up a classic case of a self-fulfilling prophecy. In this group the absence of a consensually validated communication system undermined effective action. A total group culture had not yet formed, though various subgroups might already have been operating on shared assumptions, such as "Our boss does not value our contributions."

It is often the creators of groups who build the common category system. For example, the founder of a small high-technology company whose own sense of his mission was to give the world a cheaper yet technically better product had to teach his engineers how to design an optimal level of elegance and quality into the product. He had to point out in detail what to look for and pay special attention to in the myriad details involved in design, in how to analyze customer responses, in how to think about costs, and in how to react to feedback from manufacturing and marketing. One might label such teaching as getting across certain values, but in fact the process went much deeper than that. The values were embedded in the conceptual categories themselves, and what was being taught was really a category system, along with the values embedded in the rules of how to respond.

How powerful such categories can become is illustrated in the Action Company, where the shared assumption developed early in the history of the company that the best model of a customer was the design engineer himself because he was a prototype of the user of the product being designed. If the engineer liked his own product, he assumed that others would also like it; and this concept of how to measure product "goodness" was accepted in many other parts of the company. The term *marketing* came to be associated with taking these "good" products and ensuring that they would get out to the customers efficiently. It was assumed that customers would automatically appreciate the products, and this assumption was sufficiently confirmed in the marketplace to validate the original concept.

The idea that marketing might involve finding out what potential customers would want in the future and building such criteria into the initial product designs did not surface until years later, when the technology made it possible to reach a less sophisticated user. Real communication problems then developed between those groups who were continuing to build sophisticated products, in accordance with one marketing concept, and other groups who were trying to develop completely different products based on different cognitive definitions of what a good product was and what marketing meant in relation to product development. The important lesson to learn is that the disagreement was not about business judgment but reflected a lack of a common language and shared categories that would make judgment possible.

Critical conceptual categories are usually built into the basic language a group uses. Thus, English speakers learn through English words the major cultural categories of the Anglo-Saxon cultural tradition. For example, the word *management* reflects the proactive, optimistic, pragmatic approach that characterizes the U.S. culture. It is a surprise to many people who speak only English that a comparable word does not exist in other languages, such as German. Even more important, if the word does not exist, the concept also may not exist in the same sense. For example, in German there are words for leadership, leading, and directing; but *managing,* as English speakers mean it, does not readily transpose either as a word or as a concept.

Because new groups always emerge from a host culture,

it is often difficult to distinguish what is culturally new in a new group. Does the new company simply reflect its members' culture of origin? The founders will, of course, bring their own prior cultural assumptions to the new situation. But as the new group begins to experience its own issues of survival and growth and begins to develop its own history, it will develop, in addition, its own language and conceptual categories that refine and elaborate the basic language.

In summary, a common language and common conceptual categories are clearly necessary for any other kind of consensus to be established and for any communication to occur at all. This common understanding begins with the categories of action, gesture, and speech that are often provided by the person who brought the group together or the more active members of the group once it is together. Because the members are usually all from the same host culture, a common language is initially available; as the group matures, however, it invests common words with special meanings, and the assumptions of what certain words really mean ultimately become one of the deepest layers of that group's culture.

Defining Group Boundaries

If a group is to function and develop, one of the most important areas for clear consensus is the perception of who is in the new group and who is out, or not in, and by what criteria the decisions are made. New members cannot really function and concentrate on their primary task if they are insecure about their membership, and the group cannot really maintain a good sense of itself if it does not have a way of defining itself and its boundaries.

Initially, the criteria for inclusion are usually set by the leader, founder, or convener, but as the group members interact, those criteria are tested and a group consensus arises around the criteria that survive the test. In a young company, there is often intense debate over who should be an owner or a partner, who should have stock options, who should be hired for key functions or be an officer, and who should be ejected because he or she does not fit. In this debate real personnel decisions are being made, and at the same time the criteria of inclusion are themselves being forged, tested, and articulated so that they become clear to everyone. Such debate also provides opportunities for testing mission statements, goal clarity, and means clarity, illustrating how several cultural elements are simultaneously being created, tested, articulated, and reinforced.

One way of determining a group's core assumptions is to ask present members what they really look for in new members and to examine carefully the career histories of present members in order to detect what accounts for their inclusion in the group. For example, when one inquires about the Action Company's hiring process, the answer is that every potential new member of the technical or managerial staff must be interviewed by at least five to ten people, and only if that individual is acceptable to the entire set, is he or she offered a job. If one asks what the interviewers look for, one finds that intelligence, self-reliance, the ability to articulate clearly, tolerance for ambiguity, and high motivation are all central criteria used in selection, though most of them operate implicitly. What interviewers tend to say when they are questioned is more vague: "We want someone who will fit in."

Once the Action Company hires people, they are provisionally accepted as permanent members. If they fail in an initial job assignment, the assumption is that they are competent but were put in the wrong job. In other words, once a person is "in," it is difficult to lose that status. In an economic crisis, the company tended to slow down its rate of hiring but was typically reluctant to lay off anybody. And when pressures for staff reduction mounted, the organization redefined layoffs as "transitions" in which employees were given a great deal of latitude and choice. Thus, it was important to preserve the assumption that no one is so bad that he or she deserves to be laid off but that economic and technological changes can create conditions where it is in the person's own best interest to make a transition to a new job inside the company, if it is available, or to another company.

In the Multi Company, prior education is a key criterion for membership. Most of the young technical and managerial staff members come from a scientific background, highlighting the assumption that if one is to succeed in the company, one must understand the scientific base on which it was built. Having an advanced degree, such as a doctorate, is a distinct advantage even if one is being hired into a marketing or managerial job.

Both Action and Multi have difficulty hiring and absorbing what they called MBAs, by which they mean all-purpose generalists who do not have a solid technical or scientific background and who might be more concerned with personal ambition than contributing to the technical work of the organization. Behind these perceptions lies the further assumption in both of these companies that general management, though necessary, is not the key to success. These assumptions have had a powerful impact on Action Company's ability to develop in different directions because there has always been a shortage of experienced general managers.

Who is in and who is out applies not only to the initial hiring decision but continues to have important symbolic meaning as one progresses in the group. One of the immediate consequences of defining who is in and who is out is that differential treatment rules begin to be applied. Insiders get special benefits, are trusted more, get higher basic rewards, and most important, get a sense of identity from belonging to a defined organization. Outsiders not only get fewer of the various benefits and rewards but, more important, lose specific identity. They become part of a mass that is simply labeled "outsiders" and are more likely to be stereotyped and treated with indifference or hostility.

Organizations can be thought of, then, as involving three dimensions of human movement: (1) lateral movement from one task or function to another, (2) vertical movement from one rank to another, and (3) inclusionary movement from outsider to insider (Schein, 1978, 1990a). Consensus forms around criteria not only for promotion but also for inclusionary movement; as one moves farther in, one becomes privy to some of the more secret assumptions of the group. One learns the special meanings attached to certain words and the special rituals that define membership, such as the secret fraternity handshake, and discovers that one of the most important bases for status in the group is to be entrusted with group secrets.

As organizations age and become more complex, the problem of defining clear external and inclusionary internal boundaries becomes more complex. More people — such as salespeople, purchasing agents, distributors, franchisees, board members, and consultants — come to occupy boundary-spanning roles. In some industries economic circumstances have made it necessary for companies to reduce the size of their work force, causing an increase in the hiring of temporaries or contract workers, who can be laid off more easily if necessary. Cultural assumptions then come into bold relief when certain questions are raised from a policy perspective: what is a temporary, for how long can one keep people in that status, to what benefits if any are they entitled, and how does one deal with the threat that temporaries pose to more permanent members of the organization (Kunda, 1992)?

In a complex society, individuals belong to many organizations, so their identity is not tied up exclusively with any one organization. Locating and defining what a cultural unit is then becomes more difficult because a given organization may really be a complex set of overlapping subcultures (Louis, 1983). But consensus on criteria for membership is always one means of determining whether a cultural unit exists in any given group, and seeking such consensus will always be a preoccupation of any given group in order to differentiate itself from other groups. From the point of view of the individual moving through the organization during her or his career, frequent rotational movement from one functional or geographic group to another can result in failure to absorb any of the deeper assumptions operating in any of the groups. The person may continue to feel marginal and experience intrapsychic conflict if the assumptions of different groups are different. This suggests that if an individual is to be socialized into a complex multiunit organization, each assignment must be long enough for that individual to absorb some key assumptions but not so long as to cause oversocialization into any one subculture.

In summary, defining the criteria for deciding who is in

and who is out of an organization or any of its subunits is one of the best ways of beginning to analyze a culture. Moreover, the very process by which a group makes those judgments and acts on them is a process of culture formation that forces some integration of the external survival issues, such as what the mission is, and the internal integration issues being discussed in this chapter.

Distributing Power and Status

A critical issue in any new group is how influence, power, and authority will be allocated. The process of stratification in human systems is typically not as blatant as the dominance establishing rituals of animal societies, but it is functionally equivalent in that it concerns the evolution of workable rules for managing aggression and mastery needs. Human societies develop pecking orders just as chickens do, but both the process and the outcome are, of course, far more complex.

The easiest way to observe this process is to watch a new group, such as a committee or a training group, in the early hours of its life. Much of the behavior of the new members can be explained only if we assume that they are insecure, unsure of their role or position, and in effect "testing the social waters." Everyone comes into the new situation with some need to have influence, but that need will vary greatly from person to person. Each person will also come into the situation with very different prior or assumed status and have varying degrees of power and authority attributed to him or her (Schein, 1988).

The process of group formation will involve a complex mutual testing of who will grant how much influence to whom, and who will seek how much influence from whom. The founders of the group will, of course, influence this process by initially applying their own criteria and attempting to grant power to the members of their choice. Some members will be given formal positions associated with power or authority, and some rules about how to make decisions will be specified—for example, do we vote, seek consensus, do what the chairman wants, or debate everything until we are unanimous? Yet the process of group formation always involves a certain amount of testing of what the founder may attempt to impose, so that the assumptions that eventually come to be shared are usually a negotiated outcome, not an initially imposed set of rules or guidelines. And, in fact, every time a new member enters the group, some degree of renegotiation must take place to determine where the new member fits into the stratification scheme.

The core issue of power distribution derives from the underlying biological nature of the human organism. Culture eventually covers over with a veneer of civilization the underlying biological roots of human behavior. However, we cannot ignore the fact that all human beings have to learn to deal with their biologically based aggressive feelings, their needs to dominate, control, and master others and the environment. Only when we recognize that cultural norms regarding the handling of aggression help us deal with feelings that might run out of control, endangering us and others, can we understand why those norms are not easily changed. The very process of change may invite a period of instability during which we may fear loss of control, and that fear may keep us committed to whatever cultural assumptions we have, even if another set of assumptions might be more desirable from an objective point of view.

We discover how thin the cultural veneer is when we see in television newscasts the aggression that we are capable of, especially as members of groups. In a report of a strike in a midwestern meat packing plant, the visual coverage showed a group of adult male strikers heaving baseball-sized rocks with all their might at the windshields of the cars of fellow workers who had decided to cross the picket lines. In the recent Rodney King case of alleged police brutality, we not only saw on videotape three policemen in Los Angeles repeatedly beating a person who was lying on the ground trying to defend himself, but also, subsequent to the acquittal of the policemen, massive rioting, looting, arson, and even murder. One of the reasons why control of handguns is so important is that anyone can suddenly find himself or herself angry enough to start shooting at another human being. Because our aggressive impulses are easily tapped, the cultural restraints must be very strong to keep our environment more or less safe for ourselves.

Action and Multi differ dramatically in their methods of allocating power and channeling aggression. At Action power is derived from personal success and the building of a network of support. Formal rank, seniority, and job description have relatively less influence than personal characteristics and track record. Personal characteristics such as the ability to negotiate, to convince, and to be proved right by circumstance are emphasized. The formal system of status is deliberately de-emphasized in favor of an assumption that everyone has a right to participate, to voice an opinion, and to be heard since it is assumed that good ideas can come from anyone. As previously mentioned, however, because no one is smart enough to evaluate the quality of his or her own idea, anyone has a right to challenge and debate and, in fact, is obligated to do so. Aggression is thus channeled into the daily working routines but directed at ideas, not people. A further assumption—that once one is in the organization, one is a member of "the family" and cannot really lose membership—protects people from feeling personally threatened if their ideas are challenged.

Multi, on the other hand, has a very formal system of allocating power, a system based on personal background, educational credentials, seniority, loyalty, and successful performance of whatever jobs were allocated to the person by higher authority. After a certain number of years, an employee acquires a rank similar to the kind of rank one acquires with promotion in military service or the civil service, and this rank is independent of particular job assignments. Status and privileges go with the rank and cannot be lost even if the employee is given reduced job responsibilities. The working climate emphasizes politeness, formality, and reason. Displays of aggression are taboo, but behind-the-scenes complaining, bad-mouthing, and politicking are the inevitable consequences of suppressing overt aggression.

Both organizations could be labeled "paternalistic" from some points of view in that they generate strong family feelings and a degree of emotional dependence on leaders or formal authorities. However, the drastic difference in how the rules of power allocation actually work in these two organizations serves to remind us how vague and potentially unhelpful broad labels such as "autocratic" or "paternalistic" are in characterizing organizational cultures. One should also note once again the tight interrelationship between the external issues of mission and task, on the one hand, and the internal issues of power distribution. The kind of technology and task involved in each organization had a direct effect on the kind of power distribution that eventually arose. The more autocratic assumptions of the science of chemistry and the more egalitarian assumptions of the engineering community of an emerging technology could be seen as powerful influences through the assumptions brought into the organizations by the founders and new members.

Developing Rules for Intimacy, Friendship, and Love

Every new group must decide simultaneously how to deal with authority problems and how to establish workable peer relationships. Whereas authority issues derive ultimately from the necessity to deal with feelings of aggression, peer relationship and intimacy problems derive ultimately from the necessity to deal with feelings of affection, love, and sexuality. Thus, societies develop clear sex roles, kinship systems, and rules for friendship and sex that serve to stabilize current relationships while ensuring procreation mechanisms and thereby the survival of the society.

For the new group or organization, the deeper issues of sex and procreation are typically irrelevant unless we are talking about a family firm that is specifically concerned with keeping succession in the family. Then who marries whom and which children come into the firm are indeed major problems, and the emerging norms of the organization will reflect the assumptions of the founding family about succession (Beckhard and Dyer, 1983a, 1983b; Dyer, 1986). Recall Cook's (1992) finding that the role of chief taster in the French brandy company could only pass to another male so the succession went to a nephew instead of a daughter.

One of the most salient features of family firms is that certain levels of intimacy and trust appear to be reserved for family members, creating a kind of dual intimacy system in the organization. In the Jones Food Company, a large supermarket chain (to be described in Chapter Eleven), the founder hired another person who became virtually a partner in all business affairs, but the owner would never allow this person to own any stock. The two were very intimate in all business relations and were close friends, but ownership had a special meaning to the founder and could only be shared with blood relatives.

As Freud pointed out long ago, one of the models we bring to any new group situation is our own family model, the group in which we spent most of our early life. Thus, the rules that we learned from our own parents for dealing with them and with our siblings are often our initial model for dealing with authority and peer relationships in a new group. Because the different members of a new group are likely to have had widely varying experiences in their families of origin, they may start with very different models of what those relationships should be, leading to potential disagreement and conflict over the right way to relate to others in the new group.

If the group's founder is a very dominant person with a very clear model of how these relationships should function, he or she may, over time, be able to impose that model on the other new members (Kets de Vries and Miller, 1984). Yet even with a strong founder, the outcome is, in the end, a negotiated one, and the norms that gradually evolve in the group will reflect the initial underlying assumptions of a number of the influential members as well as the group's actual experiences.

The leaders of the Action Company believed strongly that good decisions can be made only if everyone is encouraged to challenge authority and if peers are encouraged to debate every issue. The consequence of this belief was that passive and/or dependent behavior by a subordinate was always severely punished, while insubordination was tolerated, even encouraged, as long as the subordinate was dealing with a task issue. If two peers were having a debate and one of them backed down under an aggressive onslaught, the boss usually would punish the one who backed down rather than the one who behaved aggressively.

Needless to say, there developed a climate of high conflict, high competition among peers, and relatively low levels of intimacy among those peers. Needs for closeness, affection, and intimacy were met off the job, usually with the same people who were being argued with on the job. But if close friendships led to less confrontation at work this became problematic. The possibility that peers were colluding or making private deals was extremely threatening, leading to intense challenges and probing to ensure that it was not happening. From the point of view of fulfilling its primary task, this organization operated very effectively during its growth phase, but the culture was not one in which people felt particularly comfortable, and as the organization matured, the norms of openness and confrontation became harder to maintain (Van Maanen and Kunda, 1989; Kunda, 1992). We see here again how the assumptions about how one discovers truth influenced the assumptions about appropriate relationships.

This pattern of assumptions inhibited certain kinds of change. As a consultant, I became involved in trying to build teamwork among a group of project managers and found surprisingly little support for or skill in working as a team. Early efforts to develop teamwork were based on arguments by top management that the business now needed it, and I, as the consultant, marshaled arguments for why teamwork was theoretically desirable in the situation. There was ample surface agreement; but whenever an important issue came up, group members always lapsed into highly individualized debating, withheld emotional support, and showed in their behavior a visible lack of support for the idea that teams could be useful and productive.

No progress was made until we began collectively to decipher the sources of resistance — the unconsciously held assumptions about peer relationships, truth, and conflict. Once the underlying cultural pattern had been identified, we could see why the individuals found it difficult to behave as a team. The group members then entered a difficult period of reexamining their original assumptions and in this process discovered that certain members were unwilling to adapt to new norms because the old norms, built on individualistic assumptions, were more congruent with their own personal style.

The outcome of the whole team-building program, which lasted more than a year, was a very selective and limited attempt to build teamwork only for those projects where external requirements for such teamwork were overwhelmingly clear. An insightful internal organization consultant told me recently that he had finally achieved some insight by noting that the word *team* itself is semantically very ambiguous at Action and that the only kind of team that made sense to him was a track team or a gymnastics team in which individual interdependence is limited only to some events like the relay race.

At the Multi Company, relationships were much more aloof and formal, reflecting the larger culture in which Multi was embedded and the personalities of most of the current leaders of the group. However, Multi formalized informality and closeness by a particular ritual that occurred at each annual management meeting of the top forty or fifty people. One afternoon and evening of the three-day meeting were always devoted to an event that was planned by the meeting organizer but kept secret until the group actually boarded buses. The event always involved some sport at which everyone would be relatively incompetent and would therefore look foolish in everyone else's eyes. Rank and status were thus deliberately equilibrated and a level of kidding and teasing replaced the work-a-day formality. Following the sports event everyone went to an informal dinner at which humorous speeches laced with more teasing and jibes at each other were given. With the consumption of much alcohol people really let down their hair and interacted in a way that would never have been possible at work. The secrecy surrounding what would be done each year heightened the emotionality associated with the event and made the ritual comparable to a group of children anticipating what their Christmas gifts would be. One could almost say that in this organization intimacy was achieved through periodic regression rituals.

Allocating Rewards and Punishment

To function, every group must develop a system of sanctions for obeying or disobeying the rules. There must evolve some consensus on what symbolically and actually is defined as a reward or punishment and on the manner in which they are administered. The shared assumptions concerning this issue constitute some of the most important elements of an emerging culture in a new organization.

Let us look at some examples. In the market-oriented food company previously mentioned, the norm developed that a product manager who did his job competently could expect to be moved to a bigger and better product within approximately eighteen months. Managers who did not move every eighteen months began to feel that they were failing. By way of contrast, in the Action Company the assumption developed that the designer of a product should see it through from cradle to grave, so a reward was defined as being allowed to stay with one's product through manufacturing and marketing all the way to sales. Being pulled off a project would have been perceived as a punishment.

At Multi the key short-run rewards were the personal approval of senior management and public recognition in the company newspaper. Longer-range rewards were promotion to a higher rank or movement to a clearly more important job assignment. Length of assignment to a given job could mean that the person was either dead-ended or doing such a good job that he or she was irreplaceable. Action used bonuses, stock options, and raises as signals of good performance, whereas Multi relied much more heavily on symbolic nonmonetary rewards. Salary was tied more to rank and length of service.

The degree to which the allocation of rewards and punishments is culturally specific was illustrated by my misunderstanding some of the events at an annual meeting of a large British multinational company. The company had been reorganized from a geographically decentralized form into a series of businesses that would operate worldwide and be run from a single world headquarters. This meant that the geography managers would have less power and the business unit managers would have more power. At this annual meeting of the top fifty people, the chairman was discussing with his subordinates some of the implications of the new form of organization.

What I observed was a very gentle, caring man giving the disempowered country managers some advice on how their roles might be restructured in the future. When I mentioned to a colleague in the company how impressed I was with the chairman's gentleness, he burst out laughing and said: "Are you kidding? That was one of the most aggressive punishing meetings we have ever had. What you saw was a real bloodbath, the likes of which we have never before witnessed." So much for my interpretation of the signals!

Punishments, like rewards, will have local meanings in different organizations. In several high-tech companies that have clear espoused values about not laying people off, people can lose the particular task they are working on and become "boat people" or "wander the halls" while looking for another job within the organization. They will be carried on the payroll indefinitely, but it is clear that they have been punished. Often the signals are subtle, but colleagues know that someone is in the doghouse or in the penalty box. Actual loss of bonuses or the failure to get a raise may follow, but the initial punishment is clear enough already.

In fact, deciphering when one has been rewarded and when one has been punished is one of the most difficult tasks for newcomers in organizations because the signals are so often ambiguous from an outsider's point of view. Being yelled at by the boss may be a reward while being ignored may be a punishment, and only someone farther along in the understanding of the culture could reassure the yelled at newcomer that she or he was, in fact, doing well. In many companies, teamwork is espoused as a major characteristic of how work gets done, but only after some time does a newcomer learn what teamwork in a given company means. Being open and confrontive in meetings can be rewarded or punished, depending on such meanings.

The system of rewards and punishments usually reflects other important cultural themes. For example, acquired rewards can be treated as acquired social "property" and serve as a basis for increased status and power. Thus, just as a bonus or a stock option can be translated into acquired material property, approval on the part of the boss or a formal promotion can be translated into social property or status. Rewards and punishments from more senior or higher-status members of the organization are the key signals by which the person measures his or her progress along the inclusionary dimension that highlights the importance of what one is told or not told as a key organizational reward. Being told company secrets is a major reward, while being frozen out by not being told can be a major punishment that signals ultimate excommunication. Being no longer in the loop is a clear signal that one has done something wrong.

The reward system, viewed as a dynamic process, usually has both short- and long-range implications. Many of the short-range aspects concern the organization's performance in its defined external environment—getting a product out, reducing inventory, cutting costs, and so on. Ultimately, such organizational performance must be translated into the individual performances of different people in their different roles. A system of short-run incentives and rewards usually develops to maximize the performance of the actors in those roles. Longer-range aspects of the reward system relate to track records, potential, and other aspects of contribution that are assumed to be a cumulation of continued high performance. In most organizations, short-run rewards and longer-range rewards are different (for example, an annual bonus versus a promotion).

When studying the culture of an organization, one must investigate the reward and punishment system because it reveals fairly quickly some of the important rules and underlying assumptions in that culture. Once one has identified what kinds of behavior are "heroic" and what kinds of behavior are "sinful," one can begin to infer the assumptions that lie behind those evaluations. The manner in which heroic and sinful behaviors are rewarded and punished, then, provides further evidence about those underlying assumptions.

Managing the Unmanageable
and Explaining the Unexplainable

Every group inevitably faces some issues not under its control, events that are intrinsically mysterious and unpredictable and hence frightening. At the physical level, such events as natural disasters and the weather require explanation. At the biological level, such events as birth, growth, puberty, illness, and death require one to have a theory of what is happening and why.

In a culture heavily committed to reason and science, there is a tendency to treat everything as explainable; the mysterious is only as yet unexplained. But until science has demystified an event that we cannot control or understand, we need an alternative basis for putting what has happened into a meaningful context. Religious beliefs can provide such a context and can also offer justification for events that might otherwise seem unfair and meaningless. Religion explains the unexplainable and provides guidelines for what to do in ambiguous, uncertain, and threatening situations. Those guidelines usually specify and reinforce what is considered heroic and desirable and what is considered sinful and undesirable, thus creating an ideology that unites into a coherent whole the various assumptions about the nature of human nature, the nature of relationships, and the nature of society itself.

Ideology can be seen as a set of overarching values that can serve as a prescription for action vis-à-vis other groups and the broader environment, especially in areas that are difficult to explain and manage. In a society that is dominated by religion, ideology merges with religion. The more the society is based on reason, logic, and science, the more ideology has a secular base and comes to be clearly distinguishable from religion.

The organizational equivalent of this general cultural process tends to occur around critical events in the organization's history, especially ones that are difficult to explain or justify because they were not under organizational control. Organizations are capable of developing the equivalent of religion and/or ideology on the basis of the manner in which such critical events were managed. Myths and stories develop around the founding of the company, times when the company had particular difficulty surviving or an unusual growth spurt, times when a challenge to core assumptions brought about a rearticulation of those assumptions, and times of transformation and change.

For example, certain individual contributors and managers at the Action Company are associated with getting the company out of trouble whenever a severe crisis occurs. Also, certain processes are viewed almost superstitiously as "the way" to get out of trouble. One such process is to bring together a task force under the leadership of one of these heroic managers and give that task force complete freedom for a period of time to work on the problem. Sometimes consultants are brought in with the same kind of faith that something constructive will happen as a result of the presence of the outsider.

In a study of the introduction of computerized tomography into hospital radiology departments, Barley (1984a, 1984b) observed that if the computer went down at an awkward time, such as when a patient was in the middle of a scan, the technicians tried all kinds of remedial measures, including the proverbial kicking of the machine. If the computer resumed operating, as it did occasionally, the technician carefully documented what he or she had just done and passed on this "knowledge" to colleagues, even though there was no technical or logical basis for it. In a real sense, this was superstitious behavior, even in a realm where logical explanation was possible.

An organization's ideology in this context can be any of several things. Sometimes it is the conscious component of the total set of assumptions that make up the culture. Sometimes it is a set of rationalizations for essentially unexplained or superstitious behavior. Sometimes ideology reflects ideals and future aspirations as well as current realities and thereby functions as a guide and incentive system to members. Ideologies often involve statements about the core mission, the goals, the preferred means for accomplishing them, and the preferred set of relationships among organizational members.

Ideologies often are partially stated in formal company documents as the organization's key values. They are likely to be embodied in company charters, annual reports, and orientation and training materials, but in this form they are often merely a list of espoused values and may not even make up a coherent ideology. Only where there are stories supporting the values and when the underlying assumptions behind the values are articulated can one determine what the substance of the ideology really is.

Stories and myths about how the organization dealt with

key competitors in the past, how it survived a downturn in the economy, how it developed a new and exciting product, how it dealt with a valued employee, and so on not only spell out the basic mission and specific goals (and thereby reaffirm them) but also reaffirm the organization's picture of itself, its own theory of how to get things done and how to handle internal relationships (Dandridge, Mitroff, and Joyce, 1980; Koprowski, 1983; Martin, 1982; Mitroff and Kilmann, 1975, 1976; Ouchi, 1981; Pettigrew, 1979; Wilkins, 1983).

For example, a story widely circulated in one high-technology company is that during a severe recession no one was laid off because management and hourly people alike were willing to work shorter hours for less pay, thus enabling the company to cut its costs without cutting people. The lesson to be derived is the affirmation of strong values around people (Ouchi, 1981). A similar story is told at Action about the "rehabilitation" of a key engineer who was associated with several important projects, all of which failed. Instead of firing him, the company, reaffirming its core assumption that if someone fails, it is because he or she is mismatched with the job, found an assignment for him in which he could succeed and once again become a hero. Buried in this story is also the assumption that individuals count and any person whom the company has hired is by definition competent.

A story from Action's early history concerns an engineer who was sent to the West Coast to repair some equipment. He caught the midnight plane but did not have time to pack any clothing. The work took a week, requiring the engineer to buy clothing, which he duly charged to the company. When the accounting department refused to approve the charge, the engineer threatened to quit. Murphy, the founder, heard about it and severely punished the accounting department, thereby reaffirming the company's dedication to technical values and to its highly motivated technical employees.

Through stories, parables, and other forms of oral or written history, an organization can communicate its ideology and basic assumptions — especially to newcomers, who need to know what is important not only in abstract terms but by means of concrete examples that can be emulated. Even in this domain, however, the point of a story or parable may not be clear until insiders in the culture explain the meaning to the newcomer. Published ideologies and philosophies are, therefore, little more than cultural artifacts that are easy to see but hard to decipher.

Summary and Conclusions

Every group must learn how to become a group. The process is not automatic. In fact, it is complex and multifaceted. Humans, being what they are, must deal with a finite and describable set of issues in any new group situation. At the most basic level they must develop a common language and category system that clearly define what things mean. Formal languages do not specify with enough precision what work, teamwork, respect, quality, and so on mean. Groups must reach consensus on the boundaries of the group, who is in and who is not in. They must develop consensus on how to distribute influence and power so that aggression can be constructively channeled and formal status accurately determined. They must develop rules that define peer relationships and intimacy so that love and affection can be appropriately channeled.

Groups must develop clear assumptions about what is a reward and what is a punishment so that group members can decipher how they are doing. And, finally, groups must develop explanations that help members deal with unpredictable and unexplainable events, the functional equivalents of religion, mythology, and ideology.

The assumptions that develop around these issues constitute along with the assumptions about mission, goals, means, results detection, and correction mechanisms a set of dimensions along which one can study and describe a culture. These are not necessarily the only dimensions one could use, but they have the advantage of being tied to a large body of research on groups and permit one to begin to get a sense of the dynamics of culture—how cultural assumptions begin and evolve. They also represent a conceptual grid into which one can sort cultural data that one observes.

Ultimately, what makes it possible for people to function

comfortably with each other and to concentrate on their primary task is a high degree of consensus on the management of the issues discussed in this chapter. If internal issues are not settled, if people are preoccupied with their position and identity, if they are insecure, if they do not know the rules of the game and therefore cannot predict or understand what is going on, they cannot concentrate on the important survival issues the organization may face. On the other hand, the confrontation of survival issues most often stimulates rapid consensus around the internal integration issues.

The internal integration and external adaptation issues are thus interdependent. The environment sets limits on what the organization can do, but within those limits not all solutions will work equally well. Feasible solutions are also limited by the characteristics of the members of the group.

The culture that eventually evolves in a particular organization is thus a complex outcome of external pressures, internal potentials, responses to critical events, and probably to some unknown degree, chance factors that could not be predicted from a knowledge of either the environment or the members. What I have tried to do is to identify the common issues that every new group faces, recognizing that the manner in which those issues are dealt with will result in a unique outcome.

Leadership comes into play once again as the original source of ideas or the original behavioral models that are then tested against the internal and external environments. Norms, rules, languages, reward systems, and so on do not come out of thin air, nor is it sufficient to say, as some sociologists argue, that such things are enacted and result from the interaction of members. That is true but insufficient. In any group situation, some members will be more active than others and will propose verbally or by example how things should be. These acts of leadership can come from different members at different times, but they are always there in some form or another. As we will see in Chapter Eleven on culture formation, leader behavior by group founders plays a major role in how the group evolves. In the meantime, the culture categories identified so far can again serve as a kind of checklist to enable leaders to assess their own behavior.

CHAPTER SIX

Assumptions About
Reality, Truth, Time, and Space

As groups and organizations evolve, they develop shared assumptions about more abstract, more general, and deeper issues. Most of the dimensions underlying such issues are derived from the wider cultural context in which the group is located, so their existence as assumptions can be quite invisible and taken for granted in homogeneous cultural contexts. But when one examines the formation of groups that are initially multicultural, one sees how disagreement on this higher level of abstraction can make group formation extremely difficult.

The dimensions to be reviewed in this and the next chapter are originally based on Kluckhohn and Strodtbeck's (1961) classic comparative study of cultures in the U.S. Southwest, but they have been added to and elaborated upon on the basis of my own experience in working in different countries. To the extent that such dimensions are interrelated, they form the basis for cultural paradigms around which some efforts to build cultural typologies have been made. As we will see, such typologies have some heuristic value, but they usually fail to capture what is ultimately important in any given organization.

The dimensions I will review are shown below and underlie the various issues dealt with in Chapters Four and Five. For example, organizational missions, primary tasks, and goals

94

reflect basic assumptions about the nature of human activity and the ultimate relationship between the organization and its environment. The means chosen to achieve the goals will reflect assumptions about truth, time, space, and human relationships in the sense that the kind of organization that is designed will automatically reflect those deeper assumptions. Similarly, the measurement system and assumptions about how to take corrective action will reflect assumptions about the nature of truth and the appropriate psychological contract for employees.

The internal integration issues also tie in closely with these more abstract categories. Language and conceptual systems certainly reflect directly fundamental assumptions about time, space, and truth. Status systems, reward systems, rules for intimacy and for the channeling of aggression all reflect deeper assumptions about the nature of human nature, human activity, and human relationships. Moreover, religion and ideology can certainly be seen as directly connected to deeper assumptions about truth, time, and space and, especially, about human nature. Here, then, are the deeper dimensions around which shared basic assumptions form.

1. *The nature of reality and truth:* The shared assumptions that define what is real and what is not, what is a fact in the physical realm and the social realm, how truth is ultimately to be determined, and whether truth is revealed or discovered.
2. *The nature of time:* The shared assumptions that define the basic concept of time in the group, how time is defined and measured, how many kinds of time there are, and the importance of time in the culture.
3. *The nature of space:* The shared assumptions about space and its distribution, how space is allocated and owned, the symbolic meaning of space around the person, the role of space in defining aspects of relationships such as degree of intimacy or definitions of privacy.
4. *The nature of human nature:* The shared assumptions that define what it means to be human and what human attributes are considered intrinsic or ultimate. Is human nature good, evil, or neutral? Are human beings perfectible or not?

5. *The nature of human activity:* The shared assumptions that
   define what is the right thing for human beings to do in
   relating to their environment on the basis of the foregoing
   assumptions about reality and the nature of human nature.
   In one's basic orientation to life, what is the appropriate
   level of activity or passivity? At the organizational level,
   what is the relationship of the organization to its environment? What is work and what is play?

6. *The nature of human relationships:* The shared assumptions that
   define what is the ultimate right way for people to relate
   to each other, to distribute power and love. Is life cooperative or competitive; individualistic, group collaborative,
   or communal? What is the appropriate psychological contract between employers and employees? Is authority ultimately based on traditional lineal authority, moral consensus, law, or charisma? What are the basic assumptions
   about how conflict should be resolved and how decisions
   should be made?

What the connections between the internal issues and these
more abstract categories imply is that when any new group
forms, its members will bring with them cultural assumptions
at this deeper level. If the members of the group come from
different ethnic or occupational cultures, they are likely to have
different assumptions on this level. These differences will cause
initial difficulty in the group's efforts to work and to make life
safe for itself. As members get to know each other, they will
gradually develop some common assumptions at this fundamental level, and such new assumptions may, in the end, differ somewhat from any given member's original assumptions. As we will
see, however, some recent data on joint ventures between parent companies from different countries show that sometimes the
new group forms because one culture comes to dominate the
other or a new group fails to form because neither set of cultural assumptions gives way (Salk, 1992).

An example from the Action Company will make some
aspects of this dynamic clear. Action's French subsidiary was
managed by a Frenchman who knew the Action culture very
well and implemented it. He hired a young Parisian to be the

manager of human resources and told him, "Define your own job; figure out how you can best help." When I talked to this personnel manager about a year after he had been hired, he said that the first six months were absolutely traumatic because he had been brought up in the best French tradition of expecting a strong boss who would tell a person what to do. The manager kept searching for guidance and for someone to lean on, but he found neither.

As he tells the story, one day he finally decided to take some initiative and try out some of his own ideas. He found immediate support and positive reinforcement for this behavior. So he took the individual initiative route again and again and found that it was always successful. He was learning how to work at Action. In describing this socialization process, he said: "I had to give up my 'Frenchness' to work in this company. I like it, but I don't think I could ever work in a traditional French company after this experience." As an aside, some listeners to this tale note that the Action Company culture is so unusual that once one has learned to work in it, one probably could not work in any other company again! In any case, the Action assumptions about human nature, human activity, and human relationships ended up modifying some of the assumptions this man had brought with him from his culture of origin.

Because of the ultimate importance of these assumptions, we must understand them at some level of detail so that we can compare organizations and subunits within them and also begin to compare national and ethnic cultures on a broader scale. In the remainder of this chapter we will take up the first three dimensions, those dealing with reality and truth, time, and space; in Chapter Seven we will examine the other three dimensions, those dealing with human nature, human activity, and human relationships.

Shared Assumptions About the Nature of Reality and Truth

A fundamental part of every culture is a set of assumptions about what is real and how one determines or discovers what is real. These assumptions do, of course, relate to other assumptions about human nature and relationships, but the focus now is on how members of a group determine what is relevant information, how they interpret information, how they determine when they have enough of it to decide whether or not to act, and what action to take.

For example, as I have already pointed out several times, in the Action Company, reality and truth are defined by debate and by pragmatic criteria of whether things work. If an objective test is impossible or too difficult to construct, the idea is debated to see whether it stands the test of being subjected to severe critical analysis. In the Multi Company, much more emphasis is given to research results from the laboratory and to the opinions of those considered wise and experienced. Both companies exist in broader Western cultures dominated by concepts of science and rationally based knowledge. To analyze this further, we need to look at different levels at which reality can be defined.

Levels of Reality

External physical reality refers to those things that can be determined empirically by objective or, in our Western tradition, "scientific" tests. For example, if two people are arguing about whether or not a piece of glass will break, they can hit it with a hammer and find out (Festinger, 1957). If two managers are arguing over which product to introduce, they can agree to define a test market and establish criteria by which to resolve the issue. On the other hand, if two managers are arguing over whether or not to give corporate funds to a political campaign, both would have to agree that the conflict cannot be resolved at the external physical level of reality.

Different cultures have different assumptions about what constitutes external physical reality. In many cultures what we would regard as the spirit world, which is not real to us, would be regarded as externally real. Vivid examples of how ambiguous the borderline can be are provided in Castaneda's (1968, 1972) descriptions of his experiences with the Indian shaman Don Juan and in the controversies that surround research on extrasensory perception. At its core physical reality is obvious; at its boundaries it becomes very much a matter of cultural consensus, raising the issue of social reality.

Social reality refers to those things that members of a group agree are matters of consensus, not externally, empirically testable. The most obvious domains of social reality concern the nature of relationships, the distribution of power and the entire political process, and assumptions about the meaning of life, ideology, religion, group boundaries, and culture itself. How a group defines itself, the values it chooses to live by, obviously cannot be tested in terms of our traditional notions of empirical scientific test but certainly can be tested in terms of achieved consensus. If people believe in something and define it as real, it becomes real for that group, as sociologists pointed out long ago.

In the international context, there is no way to test who is right about a territorial conflict or a belief system, as the 1991 war in the Middle East amply demonstrated. Hence, negotiation becomes very difficult and nations resort to the use of economic and military power. The bad joke about the naive diplomat who tells the Arabs and the Israelis to settle their differences in a good Christian manner makes the point well.

One of the reasons why business decisions are often difficult to make and why management is an intrinsically complex activity is the lack of consensus on whether a given decision area belongs in the realm of physical or social reality. If an organization is to have coherent action, there must be shared assumptions about which decisions can be scientifically resolved and which ones are based on consensual criteria such as "Let the most experienced person decide" or "Let's decide by majority vote." Notice that the consensus must be on the criteria and on the process to be used, not necessarily on the ultimate substance of the decision.

Individual reality refers to what a given person has learned from her or his own experience and that therefore has a quality of absolute truth to that person. However, that truth may not be shared with anyone else. When we disagree at this level, it becomes very hard to move forward until we can clearly articulate what our actual experience base is. We must also have some kind of consensus on whose experience we are willing to trust. In a traditional, lineal society, based on hierarchical authority, if so-called elder statesmen speak, we take their experience as valid and act as if what they say is objectively true. In a pragmatic, individualistic society, on the other hand, the attitude might well be "prove it to me," and beyond that, what is accepted as proof might be all over the map.

What is defined as physical, social, or individual reality is itself the product of social learning and hence, by definition, a part of a given culture (Van Maanen, 1979b; Michael, 1985). But cultural assumptions are assumed to have relatively less importance in the area of physical reality, which in Western society is assumed to operate according to natural laws as discovered by the scientific method. Cultural assumptions become relatively more important in the area of social reality, or what Louis (1981) calls intersubjective reality, as distinct from universal objective reality or individual subjective reality. In fact, the bulk of the content of a given culture will concern itself primarily with those areas of life where objective verification is assumed not to be possible and where, therefore, a social definition becomes the only sound basis for judgment. It is in this area that we are most susceptible to discomfort and anxiety if we do not have a common way of deciphering what is happening and how to feel about it.

High Context and Low Context

A useful distinction can be found in Hall's (1977) differentiation between what he calls high-context and low-context cultures and Maruyama's (1974) contrast between unidirectional and mutual causal cultural paradigms. In the low-context, unidirectional culture, events have clear universal meanings; in the high-context, mutual causality culture, events can be understood only in context, meanings can vary, categories can change, and causality cannot be unambiguously established.

Though this distinction has more meaning when one compares countries or large ethnic units, it has utility for organizations as well. For example, Action has a high-context culture in which the meaning of words and actions depends on who is speaking and under what conditions. Managers know each other well and always take into account who the actors are. When a senior manager is observed publicly punishing a subordinate for doing something "dumb," this may mean simply that the subordinate should have consulted a few more people before going off on his own. If the manager doing the punishing is a newcomer to the company, the observers may judge that the subordinate is in deep trouble. Multi, by contrast, has a low-context culture in which messages tend to have the same meaning no matter whom they are coming from.

When we refer to "language," we often overlook the role of context. We assume that when one has learned the language of another country, one will be able to understand what is going on and take action. But as we know all too well from our own cross-cultural travel experiences, language is embedded in a wider context where nonverbal cues, tone of voice, body language, and other signals determine the true meaning of what is said. A vivid example from my own experience was the previously cited senior management meeting of the British multinational company at which I thought I observed polite explanations from the chairman, only to be told later that he had never been more brutal than he was at that meeting.

Moralism-Pragmatism

A useful dimension for comparing groups on their approach to reality testing is an adaptation of England's (1975) moralism-pragmatism scale. In his study of managerial values, England found that managers in different countries tended to be either pragmatic, seeking validation in their own experience, or moralistic, seeking validation in a general philosophy, moral system, or tradition. For example, he found that Europeans tended to be more moralistic while Americans tended to be more pragmatic. If we apply this dimension to the basic underlying assumptions that a group makes, we can specify different bases for defining what is true.

1. *Pure dogma, based on tradition and/or religion:* It has always been done this way; it is God's will; it is written in the Scriptures.
2. *Revealed dogma, that is, wisdom based on trust in the authority of wise men, formal leaders, prophets, or kings:* Our president wants to do it this way; our consultants have recommended that we do it this way; she has had the most experience, so we should do what she says.
3. *Truth derived by a "rational-legal" process,* as when we establish the guilt or innocence of an individual by means of a legal process that acknowledges from the outset that there is no absolute truth, only socially determined truth: We have to take this decision to the marketing committee and do what they decide; the boss will have to decide this one because it is his area of responsibility; we will have to vote on it and go by majority rule; we agreed that this decision belongs to the production department head.
4. *Truth as that which survives conflict and debate:* We thrashed it out in three different committees, tested it on the sales force, and the idea is still sound, so we will do it; does anyone see any problems with doing it this way . . . if not, that's what we'll do.
5. *Truth as that which works, the purely pragmatic criterion:* Let's try it out this way and evaluate how we are doing.
6. *Truth as established by the scientific method, which becomes, once again, a kind of dogma:* Our research shows that this is the right way to do it; we've done three surveys and they all show the same thing, so let's act on them.

This dimension not only highlights the basis on which truth is determined but also can be related to uncertainty avoidance (Hofstede, 1980) and tolerance for ambiguity (Adorno and others, 1950), dimensions that have been found useful in cultural analysis. Managers and employees in different countries and in different companies vary in the degree to which they are comfortable with and can tolerate uncertainty and ambiguity. Some researchers argue that higher tolerance levels in certain managerial areas are associated with more effectiveness (Davis and Davidson, 1991; Pascale and Athos, 1981; Peters, 1987).

Analysts concerned about planning and adapting to an uncertain and uncontrollable future would argue that as environments become more turbulent, the ability to tolerate uncertainty becomes more necessary for survival and learning, suggesting that organizational and national cultures that can embrace uncertainty more easily will be inherently more adaptive (Michael, 1985).

From the point of view of this analysis, one needs to determine not which position along any of these dimensions is the "correct" one but whether or not there is consensus on the underlying assumptions that the members of a group hold. If such consensus does not exist, the collection of people will not evolve as a group in the first place.

This discussion can be summarized best by showing how it applies to our two organizations. Action has high consensus that reality is defined by pragmatic criteria and debate. In my consultation work with Action, for instance, I was never asked for a recommendation. If I gave one, it was usually overridden immediately by various ideas from the client, which were then debated among the members. The company is comfortable with ambiguity and has its own system of pragmatically moving toward action alternatives.

At Multi I was always treated as an authority and asked what I knew from my research and other consulting experience and what I would recommend. I was treated as a scientist who was bringing some knowledge to the organization, and I often found that my recommendations were implemented exactly. On the other hand, if what I recommended conflicted with another cultural element, as when I suggested more lateral communication, the recommendation was dismissed outright. Multi does not tolerate ambiguity well and operates much closer to the moralistic end of the dimension.

What Is "Information"?

How a group tests for reality and makes decisions also involves consensus on what constitutes data, what is information, and what is knowledge. As information technology has grown, the issue has become sharpened because of debates about the role of computers in providing information. Information technology "professionals" often hold shared assumptions that differ in substantial ways from the assumptions of senior managers, an issue we will explore in greater depth in Chapter Fourteen. For example, many company presidents will point out that all you get on a computer screen is data and what they really need is information, which implies a level of analysis of the data that is typically not available unless a sophisticated decision support system or expert system has been programmed in (Rockart and DeLong, 1988). For a group to be able to make realistic decisions, there must be a degree of consensus that is relevant to the task at hand on what information is.

Dougherty's research on new product development teams shows that when such groups do not develop a common definition of relevant information, they are more likely to come up with products that do not make it in the marketplace (Dougherty, 1990). She identifies five separate "thought worlds" that operate in the functional specialists who are usually brought together in product development teams. Each member of the team believes that he or she "knows a lot" about the team's customers, but what these members know turns out to be very different kinds of things. The engineers know just how big the product should be, what its technical specifications should be, where the power plug should go, and so on. The manufacturing people know what the potential volumes are and how many models might be needed. Marketers/business planners know in general whether or not a market exists, the size of the potential market, what price and volume would produce appropriate profit levels, what the market trends are, and so on. The field salespeople know what the potential customers will use the product for, what the users' specific needs are, and how important the product is to customers relative to competitor's products. And the distribution people know how the product will be sold, what the merchandising plans are, and how many sales channels there will be. Each of these groups, by virtue of its members' occupational background and functional experience, has built up concepts and language that are common to the group members but not necessarily understood clearly by others.

When members of these subcultures are brought together into a product development team, their ability to discover the others' realities is, according to Dougherty, a major determinant of whether or not the product that is developed will succeed in the marketplace. All organizations advocate teamwork at this level and have formal processes that are supposed to be followed. However, Dougherty's data indicate that only if the team goes outside the formally defined process is there a chance that enough mutual understanding will arise to permit real coordination of relevant information. Apparently, when the process is formalized, groups get only the illusion that they are communicating relevant information to each other and never discover that what they define as information is itself different from subgroup to subgroup. If they go outside the formal channel, they are more likely to feel the need to become a real group, to get to know each other at a more personal level, thus providing opportunities to discover where they agree and disagree and how their information sets differ in content.

In summary, one of the most important dimensions of culture is the nature of how reality, truth, and information are defined. Reality can exist at physical, group, and individual levels, and the test for what is real will differ according to the level — overt tests, social consensus, or individual experience. Groups develop assumptions about information that determine when they feel they have enough to make a decision, and those assumptions reflect deeper assumptions about the ultimate source of truth. What is a fact, what is information, and what is truth each depends not only on shared knowledge of formal language but also on context.

Shared Assumptions About the Nature of Time

The perception and experience of time are among the most central aspects of how any group functions; when people differ in their experience of time, tremendous communication and relationship problems typically emerge. Consider how anxious and/or irritated we get when someone is "late," or when we feel our time has been "wasted," or when we feel that we did not get "enough time" to make our point, or when we feel "out of phase" with someone, or someone is taking on "too much at one time," or when we can never get our subordinate to do things "on time" or to show up "at the right time."

In an analysis of time, Dubinskas (1988, p. 14) points out its central role in human affairs: "Time is a fundamental symbolic category that we use for talking about the orderliness of social life. In a modern organization, just as in an agrarian society, time appears to impose a structure of work days, calendars, careers, and life-cycles that we learn and live in as part of our cultures. This temporal order has an 'already made' character of naturalness to it, a model of the way things are."

But time itself is not a unidimensional, clear construct. It has been analyzed from many perspectives, and a number of these are particularly relevant to cultural analysis.

Basic Time Orientation

Anthropologists have noted that every culture makes assumptions about the nature of time and has a basic orientation toward the past, present, or future (Kluckhohn and Strodtbeck, 1961; Redding and Martyn-Johns, 1979). For example, in their study of multiple cultures in the U.S. Southwest, Kluckhohn and Strodtbeck noted that some of the Indian tribes lived mostly in the past, the Spanish-Americans were oriented primarily toward the present, and the Anglo-Americans were oriented primarily toward the near future. At the level of the organization, one can distinguish companies that are primarily oriented to the past, thinking mostly about how things used to be; the present, worrying only how to get the immediate task done; the near future, worrying mostly about quarterly results; and the distant future, investing heavily in research and development or in building market share at the expense of immediate profits.

One high-tech company I have worked with made the assumption that only the present counts. Employees worked extremely hard on the immediate tasks that challenged them, but they had little sense of past history and did not care much about the future. People in the planning department complained that plans were made in a ritual way, planning books were filled with things to do, but nothing ever got implemented.

One can also find many organizations that live in the past, reflecting on their past glories and successes while ignoring present and future challenges. They make the basic assumption that if things worked in the past, they must be good enough to work in the present and future and therefore do not need to be reexamined. That assumption can indeed be valid if the technology and the environment have remained stable, but it can lead an organization to destruction if new environmental demands require real changes in how the organization defines its mission, its goals, and the means by which to accomplish them.

How future oriented an organization should be is the subject of much debate, with many arguing that one of the problems of U.S. companies is that the financial context in which they operate (the stock market) forces a near-future orientation at the expense of longer-range planning. From an anthropological point of view, it is, of course not clear what is cause and what is effect. Is the United States, culturally speaking, a near-future-oriented pragmatic society that has therefore created certain economic institutions to reflect our need for quick and constant feedback, or have our economic institutions created the short-run pragmatism?

Monochronic and Polychronic Time

Edward Hall in several very insightful books about culture (1959, 1966, 1977) points out that in the United States most managers view time as monochronic, an infinitely divisible linear ribbon that can be divided into appointments and other compartments but within which only one thing can be done at a time. If more than one thing must be done within, say, an hour, we divide the hour into as many units as we need and then do "one thing at a time." When we get disorganized or have a feeling of being overloaded, we are advised to "do one thing at a time." Time is viewed as a valuable commodity that can be spent, wasted, killed, or made good use of; but once a unit of time is over, it is gone forever.

In contrast, some cultures in southern Europe, Africa, and the Middle East regard time as polychronic, a kind of medium defined more by what is accomplished than by a clock and within which several things can be done simultaneously. Even more extreme is the Asian cyclical concept of time "as phases, rather circular in form. One season follows the next, one life leads into another" (Sithi-Amnuai, 1968, p. 82). The manager operating according to this kind of time holds court in the sense that she or he deals simultaneously with a number of subordinates, colleagues, and even bosses, keeping each matter in suspension until it is finished.

Because relationships may be more important than short-run efficiency in such cultures, the rapid completion of a task or punctuality may not be valued as highly as it is in the United States. A monochronically oriented U.S. manager can become very impatient and frustrated in a polychronic culture when, for no discernible reason, he or she must wait outside someone's office for an unknown length of time. Yet polychronic time concepts do exist in U.S. organizations. A doctor or dentist, for example, may simultaneously see several patients in adjacent offices, and a supervisor is usually totally available at all times to all his or her machine operators. Parents and homemakers may simultaneously cook, clean house, and deal with each of several children. As individuals we may have preferences for which kind of time we find most comfortable, but we all know how to function in both monochronic and polychronic situations. What is important in groups is the degree of consensus among group members on which concept is appropriate to use at a given time.

Monochronic time controls human behavior and is therefore well suited to situations that require highly coordinated actions ("Synchronize your watches!"). Because this form of time facilitates coordination, it is well suited to the management of large systems and is the form of time taken for granted in most organizations as the only way to get things done efficiently. Polychronic time assumptions are more effective for building relationships and for solving complex problems where information is widely scattered and highly interactive so that all channels must be kept open at all times. Polychronic time is therefore more suitable for the early stages of an organization, for smaller systems, and for organizations where one person is the central point of coordination.

Time concepts such as these also define in a subtle way how status is displayed, as illustrated by the frustrating experiences that Americans and northern Europeans have in Latin cultures, where "lining up" and "doing things one at a time" are less common. I have stood in line at a small post office in Southern France only to discover that some people barge to the head of the line and actually get service from the clerk. My friends have pointed out to me in this situation that not only does the clerk have a more polychronic view of the world, leading her to respond to whoever seems to shout loudest, but that a higher-status person considers it legitimate to break into the line and get service first as a legitimate display of his status. If others live in the same status system, they do not get offended by being kept waiting. In fact, it was pointed out to me that by staying in line and fulminating, I was displaying a low sense of my own status; ortherwise, I would be up at the head of the line demanding service as well.

Planning Time and Development Time

In a study of biotechnology companies, Dubinskas (1988) found that when biologists who had become entrepreneurs worked with managers who came from an economics or business background, subtle misunderstandings would occur over how long things took, how one viewed milestones, and how one perceived the future in general during the planning process. The managers viewed time in a linear, monochronic way, with targets and milestones tied to external objective realities like market opportunities and the stock market. Dubinskas labeled this form of time "planning time."

In contrast, the biologists seemed to operate from something he called "development time," best characterized as "things will take as long as they will take," referring to natural biological processes that have their own internal time cycles. To caricature the distinction, a manager might say we need the baby in six months to meet a business target, while the biologist would say sorry but it takes at least nine months to make one. The person operating from planning time sees herself more in a world of objects that can be manipulated and as a "finished adult" operating on an external world. The person operating from development time sees herself more in a process world, where her own development and that of other things in her world are more oriented to natural processes that cannot be easily speeded up or slowed down and where development is a never-ending, open-ended process. Planning time seeks closure; development time is open ended and can extend far into the future. Managers and scientists operating in terms of these two types of time can work together and even influence each other's concepts, but they must first understand the differences in each other's assumptions.

Discretionary Time Horizons

Another dimension of time on which group members need consensus has to do with the size of relevant units in relation to given tasks (Jaques, 1982). Do we measure and plan for things annually, quarterly, monthly, daily, hourly, or by the minute? What is considered accurate in the realm of time? How many minutes after an appointed time can one show up and still be considered "on time"? What are the timetables for certain events, such as promotions? How much time should be spent on a given task, and what is the length of a feedback loop? What is our planning horizon in days, months, or years?

As Lawrence and Lorsch (1967) noted years ago, one of the reasons why sales and R & D people have trouble communicating is that they work with totally different time horizons. In their comparative study of several types of organizations, Lawrence and Lorsch observed that the length of the time horizon depended on the kind of work one was doing. For salesmen the time horizon involved the completion of a sale, which could take minutes, hours, days, or weeks. In general, however, even their longer time horizons were much shorter than those of the research people, for whom a one- or two-year horizon was normal. In other words, research people would not get closure, in the sense of knowing that they had a good product, until a much longer period of time had elapsed, partly because they operated more in terms of "development time," as described above, and partly because in many industries it is not known whether the new product or process will work when it is scaled up to greater volume production. Particularly in the chemical industry, a reseacher does not know whether he has been successful until his product has passed the pilot plant and full production facility hurdles. At each step the larger scale can change the process and reveal things that will require new research and development.

If we now consider the communication process between the researcher and the salesperson/marketer, when the latter says that she wants a product "soon" and the researcher agrees that the product will be ready "soon," they might be talking about completely different things and not realize it. For example, at Action I constantly heard complaints from the sales department that engineering was not getting the products out on time. If I talked to engineering, I was told that the product was on schedule and doing just fine. Each function got angry at the other. Neither recognized that the judgments being made about what "on time" is differed because different assumptions about time units were being used. The researcher viewed a six-month delay as within the promised time limit on a project that took three years to complete, while the salesperson saw that same delay as much too long because a three-month market window was missed.

Action and Multi differ in their overall time horizons, probably because of their underlying technologies and markets. The slow deliberateness of the research process at Multi seems to have spilled over into the management process. Things are done slowly, deliberately, and thoroughly. If a project is going to take several years, so be it. Time is expressed in spatial terms in a commonly heard phrase around the company: "The first thousand miles don't count." In other words be patient and persistent. Things will eventually work out.

Time horizons differ not only by function and occupation but by rank. The higher the rank, the longer the time horizon over which a manager has discretion (Jaques, 1982), or what Bailyn (1985) has called operational autonomy. This period of time is usually defined as the time between formal reviews of whether or not one is doing one's basic job. Production workers may get reviewed every few minutes or hours, supervisors may get reviewed daily or weekly, middle managers may get reviewed monthly or annually, and top executives may get reviewed only once every several years, depending upon the nature of their industry. Different norms about time arise, therefore, at different rank levels. Senior managers assume that one must plan in cycles of several years, whereas such an assumption may not make sense to the middle manager or the worker, whose time cycle is daily, weekly, or monthly.

Differing assumptions about discretionary periods can cause difficulty in managing. Bailyn (1985) found that senior managers in one large R & D organization believed that their scientists wanted to set their own research goals (they were given goal autonomy), but because those scientists were perceived to be undisciplined in their management of budgets and time, they were reveiwed frequently (they were not given operational autonomy). When Bailyn talked to the scientists, she discovered that two of the main reasons why they felt demoralized was that management was "not allowing them to get involved in helping to set goals" (because they were in industry, they wanted to work on relevant problems as specified by management) and that "they were constantly being reviewed and never allowed to get any work done." In other words, the scientists wanted just the opposite of what management was providing—they wanted less goal autonomy and more operational autonomy.

Jaques (1982) takes the argument about discretionary time horizons even further by noting that managerial competence can be judged by whether or not a given manager is functioning in terms of the time horizons appropriate to the level of his or her job. A production worker thinking in terms of years and a senior manager thinking in terms of hours and days would be equally likely to be ineffective in terms of what their jobs demand of them. As one moves up the hierarchy of jobs that require longer-range planning, one can assess the manager's potential for promotion partly in terms of his or her ability to take longer-range points of view. When senior managers operate with too short a time horizon, they are likely to overmanage.

Temporal Symmetry and Pacing

A subtle but critical aspect of time is the way activities are paced. In a study of the introduction of computerized equipment into radiology departments, Barley (1988) discovered that one of the major impacts of the technology was the degree to which the pacing of the activities of the technicians and the radiologists became more or less symmetrical. In the traditional X-ray department the technicians worked monochronically as far as scheduling patients and making films. But if they needed to consult a radiologist, the technicians became frustrated by the polychronic world of the radiologists. For example, if a technician needed the services of a radiologist to give an injection to a patient, to conduct a fluoroscopy, or to review preliminary films, the technician would often have to wait because the radiologist was simultaneously dealing with other doctors on the phone, other technicians doing things, and reading films. The following quotation captures the asymmetry well.

> To locate a radiologist, a technologist often has to search several offices and ask other technologists about the radiologist's last known whereabouts. Even after the tech found a radiologist, there was no guarantee that he would be immediately available. At the time of the tech's arrival, the radiologist could be talking on the telephone, discussing a film with a physician, consulting a colleague, or about to assist with another examination. In each instance the technologist would have to wait. But even if the technologist successfully engaged the radiologist's attention, he or she still had no firm claim on the radiologist's time. The radiologist could always be diverted by a number of events, including a telephone call, a consultation, or even another technologist with a request that the radiologist deemed more important. [Barley, 1988, p. 145]

When computerized tomography, magnetic resonance, and ultrasound came into the departments, the temporal orders of the two sets of people became more symmetrical because of the greater duration of each test, the technicians' greater level of expertise in reading the results, and the degree to which the special procedures involved in the new technologies often required the radiologists and technicians to work side by side throughout. In the case of working in ultrasound, because the diagnostic procedure could not be done in the first place unless the technicians knew how to read results as they were forthcoming, the technicians acquired, de facto, more operational autonomy. They did not need the help or counsel of a radiologist to complete the procedure. This greater operational autonomy gave them more status, as did the reality that they often knew better than the radiologist how to read the results because of their greater amount of experience. The new technologies created a world in which both technician and radiologist work in a monochronic manner, making it easier to coordinate their efforts and achieve efficiency for the patient and in the use of the equipment.

Polychronically driven work always has the potential for frustrating the person who is working monochronically, as exemplified in the interaction between an air traffic controller (polychronic) and the pilot of a single aircraft waiting for landing clearance (monochronic). Similar issues arise when a patient gets frustrated waiting in the emergency room because she is not aware of the fact that the physician is treating a large number of cases at once. Because the monochronically driven person typically does not understand the multiple demands being placed on the polychronically driven person, the potential is very high for misunderstanding and the attribution of inappropriate motivations, such as perceiving the polychronically driven one as lazy or inefficient.

In summary, there is probably no more important category for cultural analysis than the study of how time is conceived and used in a group or organization. Time imposes a social order, and how things are handled in time conveys status and intention. The pacing of events, the rhythms of life, the sequence in which things are done, and the duration of events all become subject to symbolic interpretation. Misinterpretations of what things mean in a temporal context are therefore extremely likely unless group members are operating from the same sets of assumptions. Some of the main aspects of time reviewed, such as (1) past, present, near-, or far-future orientation; (2) monochronicity or polychronicity; (3) planning or developmental time; (4) time horizons; and (5) symmetry of temporal activities, can form an initial diagnostic grid to help one begin to understand how time is viewed in a given organization.

Ultimately, time is so critical because it is, in a sense, so invisible, so taken for granted, and so difficult to speak about. When we are late or early, for example, we mumble apologies and possibly provide explanations, but rarely do we ask, "When did you expect me?" or "What does it mean to you when I am late?" One of the most important contributions of Forrester's systems dynamics models is that they deal explicitly with the dynamics of time and invite managers who are learning to develop these models to think through their own assumptions about time and to study the effects on a total system of time delays at various stages in a production process (Senge, 1990).

Shared Assumptions About the Nature of Space

The meaning and use of space are among the most subtle aspects of organizational culture because assumptions about space, like those about time, are likely to be taken for granted totally and therefore to operate outside of awareness. At the same time, when those assumptions are violated, as when members of different cultures confront each other, very strong emotional reactions occur. The basic reason for this is that space comes to have very powerful symbolic meanings, as expressed in the current phrase, "Don't get into my 'space.'" Hall (1966) points out that in some cultures, if one is walking in a certain direction, the space ahead of one is perceived to be one's own, so that if someone crosses in front of one, that person is violating one's space. In office design it is obvious that designers consider both the location and amount of space allocated to be a direct correlate of organizational position and status. Space, therefore, requires some close analysis. Space, like time, can be analyzed from a number of different points of view.

Distance and Relative Placement

Space has both a physical and a social meaning (Van Maanen, 1977). For coordinated social action to occur, one must share assumptions about the meaning of the placement of physical objects in an environment and also know how to orient oneself spatially in relation to other members of one's group. Placement of oneself in relation to others symbolizes status, social distance, and membership. For example, Hall (1966) points out that in the United States there is high consensus on four kinds of "normal distance" and that within each of these there is consensus on what it means to be "very near" or "very far."

1. *Intimacy distance.* Among those who consider themselves to be intimate with each other, contact and touching are defined as being very near; six to eighteen inches is the range for being far. This is what sociologists call the ideal sphere around each of us that defines the space we only allow to be entered by people with whom we feel we have an intimate relationship.

2. *Personal distance.* Eighteen to thirty inches is being near, two to four feet is being far. This is the range within which we have personal conversations with another individual even if we are in a crowd or at a party. This distance permits a normal or soft tone of voice to be used and is usually accompanied by intense eye contact. The easiest way to appreciate the power of this distance norm is to recall what happens at parties when someone from another culture in which personal distance is defined as closer than it is in the United States moves in "too close." We find ourselves backing up only to discover that the other person is pursuing us, trying to make the distance seem right to him or her. Eventually we feel cornered, and all kinds of irrelevant motives or personality attributes get called into play, when in fact the only thing operating is the fact that in two different cultures, the norm of what is appropriate personal distance varies.

3. *Social distance.* Four to seven feet is near; seven to twelve feet is far. Social distance defines how we talk to several people at once, as at a dinner party or a seminar; it usually involves some raising of the voice and less personal focus on any given individual. Our eyes will scan the group or be focused on floor or ceiling. Designers of seminar rooms or tables for committee meetings have to work around these kinds of norms if they are concerned about making the room feel appropriate for what kind of meeting is supposed to go on there. The more we want to meet informally and really get to know each other, the more the room has to be scaled down to allow that to happen.

4. *Public distance.* Twelve to twenty-five feet is near; more than twenty-five feet is far. At this distance the audience is defined as undifferentiated, and we raise our voice even more or use a microphone. Our eyes rove systematically or do not focus on anyone, as when we read a speech to an audience.

Feelings about distance have biological roots. Animals have clearly defined flight distance (the distance that will elicit fleeing if the animal is intruded upon) and critical distance (the distance that will elicit attacking behavior if the animal is intruded upon). Conditions of crowding not only elicit pathological behavior in subhuman species but are one of the most reliable ways of eliciting aggression in humans. Hence, most cultures have fairly clear rules about how to define personal and intimate space through the use of a variety of cues to permit what Hall calls sensory screening. We use partitions, walls, sound barriers, and other physical devices, and we use eye contact, body position, and other personal devices to signal respect for the privacy of others (Goffman, 1959; Hatch, 1990; Steele, 1973, 1981).

We also learn how to manage what Hall calls intrusion distance, that is, how far away to remain from others who are in personal conversation without interrupting the conversation yet making it known that one wants attention when appropriate. In some cultures, including ours, intrusion occurs only when one interrupts with speech (one can stand close by without "interrupting"), whereas in other cultures even entering the visual field of another person constitutes a bid for attention and hence is seen as an interruption. In these cultural settings, the use of physical barriers such as closed offices has an important symbolic meaning—it is the only way to get a feeling of privacy (Hall, 1966).

At the organizational level, one can clearly see that Action and Multi have contrasting assumptions about space. Action has opted for completely open office landscaping, with partitions low enough to permit everyone to see over the tops. At Multi the offices are arranged along corridors and have heavy doors that are kept shut.

The Symbolics of Space

Organizations develop different norms of who should have how much and what kind of space. They also hold different implicit assumptions about the role of space utilization in getting work accomplished. In most organizations the best views and locations are reserved for the highest-status people. Some organizations use space allocation as a direct status symbol. Size of office, quality of furniture in the office, and even quality of wall decoration are determined on the basis of rank. In contrast, Action, which aggressively tries to reduce status and privileges, reserves the good locations, such as corners, for conference rooms. High-status people are expected to take inside offices so that clerical and secretarial people can work on the outside, next to windows. How employees decorate their own work space is left entirely to their own discretion.

Where things are located, how they are built, the kind of architecture involved, the decorations encouraged or allowed, the furnishings—all the things that provide the visual environment—will vary from one organization to the next and may well reflect deeper values and assumptions held in the larger culture and by the key leaders. Because buildings and the environment around them are highly visible and relatively permanent, organizations attempt to symbolize important values and assumptions through the design. The physical layout not only has this symbolic function but is often used to guide and channel the behavior of members of the organization, thereby becoming a powerful builder and reinforcer of norms (Berg and Kreiner, 1990; Gagliardi, 1990; Steele, 1973, 1981).

For example, the Action Company is highly decentralized geographically and has always opted for inexpensive, unobtrusive, low buildings. The interior open office layout is designed to stimulate high levels of communication and to symbolize efficiency and cost consciousness. The need for communication in the company is reinforced by a transportation system that similarly symbolizes the importance of meetings and getting together. Specifically, Action runs bus shuttles between all of its buildings and has regular helicopter flights between facilities that are farther apart. In contrast, Multi, with its greater emphasis on work as a private activity, encloses areas as much as possible, is comfortable with private dining rooms for different levels of executives, and encloses its buildings in an almost fortress like manner.

Body Language

One of the more subtle uses of space is how we use gestures, body position, and other physical cues to communicate our sense of what is going on in a given situation and how we relate to the other people in the situation. On the gross level, whom we sit next to, whom we physically avoid, whom we touch, whom we bow to, and so on convey our perceptions of relative status and intimacy. As sociologists have observed, however, there are many more subtle cues that convey our deeper sense of what is going on and our assumptions about the right and proper way to behave in any given situation (Goffman, 1967; Van Maanen, 1979b).

Rituals of deference and demeanor that reinforce hierarchical relationship are played out in the physical and temporal positioning of behavior as when a subordinate knows just where to stand at a meeting relative to the boss and how to time his questions or comments when he is disagreeing with the boss. The boss, for her part, knows that she must sit at the head of the table in the board room and time her remarks to the group appropriately. But only insiders know the full meaning of all these time/space cues, reminding us forcefully that what we observe around spatial arrangements and the behavioral use of time are only cultural artifacts, difficult to decipher if we do not have additional data obtained from insiders through interview, observation, and joint inquiry. It would be highly dangerous to use our own cultural lenses to interpret what we observe, as when I misjudged the feeling tone of the meeting at the British company mentioned earlier.

Time, Space, and Activity Interaction

Orienting oneself in both time and space is fundamental in any new situation. Thus far we have analyzed time and space as separate dimensions, but in reality they interact in complex ways around the activity that is basically supposed to occur. It is easiest to see this in relation to the basic forms of time. Monochronic time assumptions have specific implications for how space is organized. If one has to have individual appointments and privacy, one needs areas in which they can be held, thus requiring desks that are far enough apart, cubicles, or offices with doors. Because monochronic time is linked with efficiency, one also requires a space layout that allows a minimum of wasted time. Thus it must be easy for people to contact each other, distances between important departments must be minimal, and amenities such as toilets and eating areas must be placed in such a way as to save time. In fact, at Action the frequent placement of watercoolers, coffee machines, and small kitchens around the organization clearly signals the importance of continuing to work even as one satisfies bodily needs.

Polychronic time, in contrast, requires spatial arrangements that make it easy for simultaneous events to occur, where privacy is achieved by being near someone and whispering rather than by retreating behind closed doors. Thus one finds large rooms built more like amphitheaters that permit a senior person to hold court or sets of offices or cubicles built around a central core that permit easy access to each one. One might also expect more visually open environments such as office bullpens that permit supervisors to survey the entire department so that they can easily see who might need help or who is not working.

When buildings and offices are designed in terms of certain intended work patterns, both distance and time are usually considered in the physical layout. These design issues get very complex, however, because information and communication technology is increasingly able to shrink time and space in ways that may not have been considered. For example, a group of people in private offices can communicate by telephone, electronic mail, fax, and videophone and even be a virtual team by using conference calls enhanced by various kinds of computer software, now called groupware (for example, Grenier and Metes, 1992; Johansen and others, 1991).

The difficulty of introducing some of these technologies points up the interaction of assumptions in that some managers become conscious of the fact that they need face-to-face interaction to gauge whether or not their message is getting through and how the other person is reacting. At Action, for example, electronic mail is widely used by certain sets of engineers who feel comfortable solving problems with each other by this means even if they do not know each other personally; senior executives, on the other hand, insist on meetings and face-to-face communication. As we will see later in the discussion of culture change, the introduction of new technologies such as information technology sometimes forces to the surface assumptions that had been taken for granted, and this is most likely to occur around concepts of how time, space, and activities interact.

Summary and Conclusions

Anthropologists and sociologists have conceptualized the roles that time, space, and the perception of reality play in cultural analysis. Underneath the previously analyzed group dimensions lie cognitive dimensions that affect the fundamental way that group members come to deal with their physical, social, and personal reality. It is important to recognize that how we conceptualize reality, what concepts and dimensions guide our perception of time, and how we construct and utilize our physical spatial environment are very much a matter of prior cultural learning and that in any given new organization shared assumptions arise only over the course of time and common experience. The analyst of culture must be careful not to project his or her own conceptions of reality, time, and space onto groups and must remember that the visible artifacts surrounding these conceptions are easy to misinterpret.

What are the implications of all this for leaders and managers? The most obvious implication has already been stated — they must learn to decipher cultural cues so that the normal flow of work is not interrupted by cultural misunderstandings. More important than this point, however, is the implication that how leaders act out their own assumptions about time and space comes to train their subordinates and ultimately their entire organization to accept those assumptions. Most leaders are not aware of how much the assumptions they take for granted are passed on in day-to-day behavior by the way they manage the decision-making process, time, and space. If the external context then changes, requiring new kinds of responses, it will not only be difficult for the leader to learn new things but even more difficult to retrain members of the organization who have become used to the way the leader structured things in the past. How we define reality, time, and space represents the deepest level of assumptions and, hence, is the level we will most cling to in order to avoid uncertainty and anxiety.

CHAPTER SEVEN

Assumptions About Human Nature, Activity, and Relationships

This chapter will explore what it means to be human, what a culture's basic assumptions are about the appropriate kinds of action for humans to take with respect to their environment, and most important, what a culture's basic assumptions are about the right and proper forms of human relationships. It is this last category that frequently receives all the attention and defines for many people what the word *culture* is all about. However, it is important to recognize that assumptions about human relationships are deeply connected not only to assumptions about human nature and activity but also to assumptions about time, space, and the nature of truth, as discussed in Chapter Six.

Shared Assumptions About the Nature of Human Nature

In every culture there are shared assumptions about what it means to be human, what our basic instincts are, and what kinds of behavior are considered inhuman and therefore grounds for ejection from the group. Kluckhohn and Strodtbeck (1961) note that in some societies humans are seen as basically evil, in others as basically good, and in still others as mixed or neutral, capable of being either good or bad. Closely related are assumptions about how perfectible human nature is. Is our goodness or badness intrinsic and do we simply accept what we are, or can we, through hard work or faith, overcome our badness and earn our salvation?

In every culture there are also shared assumptions about the relationship of the individual to the group that ultimately reflect the concept of self. For example, Redding and Martyn-Johns (1979) point out that Western and Asian societies have strikingly different core concepts of the self. Asians are less focused on differentiating the individual from the group and therefore put less emphasis on self-actualization as a core personality process, whereas Westerners have developed strong concepts of the individual and the self as something potentially quite distinct from the group and something to be developed in its own right.

In some cultures the self is compartmentalized, so that work, family, and leisure involve different aspects of the self; in other cultures the self is more of a whole, and even the idea of separating work from family does not make any sense. Hofstede's (1980) comparative study reinforces this point in identifying individualism as one of the core dimensions along which countries differ. For example, countries such as the United States, Australia, and the United Kingdom come out highest on this dimension, while Pakistan, Colombia, and Venezuela come out lowest.

At the organizational level, the basic assumptions about the nature of human nature—that is, how workers and managers are viewed—will, no doubt, reflect the more basic assumptions of the host culture. However, each organization will also build up its own elaborations of such assumptions. And the broader cultural assumptions may leave a great deal of latitude in that human nature may be considered highly variable. In our Western tradition, human nature is generally regarded as proactive. Humans are seen (except by some religious groups) as intrinsically neither good nor bad; more important, humans are assumed to be perfectible if they do the right things (such as work hard). In any case, the individual is ultimately responsible and is assumed to be the basic and ultimate unit of society.

Within the Western tradition we have seen an evolution

of assumptions about human nature from a classical notion of humans as rational-economic actors to humans as social animals with primarily social needs to humans as problem solvers and self-actualizers with primary needs to be challenged and to use their talents (Schein, 1980, first published 1965). Early theories of employee motivation were almost completely dominated by the assumption that the only incentives available to managers are monetary ones because the only essential motivation of employees was assumed to be economic self-interest. The Hawthorne studies (Roethlisberger and Dickson, 1939; Homans, 1950) launched a new series of "social" assumptions, postulating that employees are motivated by the need to relate well to their peer and membership groups and that such motivation often overrides economic self-interest. The main evidence for these assumptions came from studies of restriction of output, which showed clearly that workers will reduce their take-home pay rather than break the norm of a fair day's work for a fair day's pay.

Subsequent studies of work, particularly on the effects of the assembly line, introduced another set of assumptions: employees are self-actualizers who need challenge and interesting work to provide self-confirmation and valid outlets for the full use of their talents (Argyris, 1964). Motivation theorists, such as Maslow (1954), organized these vying assumptions into a hierarchy: if the individual is in a survival mode, economic motives will dominate; if survival needs are met, social needs come to the fore; if social needs are met, self-actualization needs are released.

McGregor (1960) observed that within this broad framework an important second layer of assumptions was held by managers vis-à-vis employees. Ineffective managers tended to hold an interlocked set of assumptions that McGregor labelled Theory X. Theory X managers assumed that people are lazy and must therefore be motivated and controlled. In contrast, effective managers held a different set of assumptions that he labeled Theory Y. These managers assumed that people are basically self-motivated and therefore need to be challenged and channeled, not controlled. Whereas Theory X assumes that employees are intrinsically in conflict with their employing organization, Theory Y assumes that it is possible to design organizations that make it possible for employee needs to be congruent with organizational needs.

Most current theories are built on still another set of assumptions, namely, that human nature is complex and malleable and that one cannot make a universal statement about human nature; instead, one must be prepared for human variability. Such variability will reflect (1) changes in the life cycle in that motives may change and grow as humans mature and (2) changes in social conditions in that humans are capable of learning new motives as may be required by new situations. Such variability makes it essential for organizations to develop some consensus on what their own assumptions are because management strategies reflect those assumptions. Both the incentive and control systems in most organizations are built on assumptions about human nature, and if those assumptions are not shared by the managers of the organization, inconsistent practices and confusion will result.

McGregor (1960) also noted that because humans are malleable, they will often respond adaptively to the assumptions that are held about them. This is particularly a problem in organizations that are run by managers who share a Theory X set of assumptions because the more that employees are controlled and treated as untrustworthy, the more they are likely to behave in terms of those expectations. The cynical manager then feels vindicated but fails to note that the employee behavior was learned and does not reflect intrinsic human nature.

The initial assumptions that members of a new group adopt may well reflect the personal biases of the founders/owners of an organization because they will tend to select associates who share assumptions similar to their own. These assumptions then become embedded in the incentive, reward, and control systems of the organization so that new members are motivated to share those assumptions or, if they cannot share them, to leave the organization.

As noted previously, the core assumption about human nature at the Action Company is that individuals are self-motivated and capable of responsible and creative decision making. The core assumption at Multi is more difficult to decipher, but there are strong indications that individuals are viewed ultimately as good soldiers, who will perform responsibly and loyally and whose loyalty the organization will reward. Individuals are expected to do their best in whatever is asked of them, but loyalty is ultimately assumed to be more important than individual creativity. One gets the sense that at Action the individual is ultimately more important than the organization and that at Multi the organization is ultimately more important than the individual.

Shared Assumptions About Appropriate Human Activity

Closely connected to assumptions about human nature are assumptions about the appropriate way for humans to act in relation to their environment. Such assumptions then also translate at the group level into how the group should relate itself as a collectivity to its environment. Several basically different orientations have been identified in cross-cultural studies.

The Doing Orientation

Kluckhohn and Strodtbeck (1961) note in their comparative study that at one extreme one can identify a "doing" orientation, which correlates closely with (1) the assumption that nature can be controlled and manipulated, (2) a pragmatic orientation toward the nature of reality, and (3) a belief in human perfectibility. In other words, it is taken for granted that the proper thing for people to do is to take charge and actively control their environment. This is the predominant orientation of the United States and is certainly a key assumption of managers in the United States, reflected in the World War II phrase "Can do" and in the stock American phrases "getting things *done*" and "let's *do* something about it." The notion that the impossible just takes a little longer is central to United States business ideology. I chose the pseudonym Action for the organization I have repeatedly referred to because this assumption is one of the most deeply held in that organization. When there is a difficulty, do something about it, solve the problem, involve other people, get help, but do something; don't let it fester.

The doing orientation focuses on the task, on efficiency, and on discovery, what some authors have identified with the Greek god Prometheus (Morris, 1956). Handy (1978) describes two types of organizations that assume a basic activity orientation. The first type is linked to Athena and focuses on the task activity; the other is linked to Zeus and focuses on the building of useful relationships, on enhancing one's position of influence through actively building political alliances and developing personal charisma. These typologies help us focus on some variations in orientation, but they are not very helpful in categorizing the cultures of particular organizations because they tend to be too general. Each organization I have dealt with has developed its own particular mix of assumptions, and these generally do not fit into the broad theoretically derived typologies.

The Being Orientation

At the other extreme from doing is a "being" orientation, which correlates closely with the assumption that nature is powerful and humanity is subservient to it. This orientation implies a kind of fatalism: since one cannot influence nature, one must become accepting and enjoy what one has. Handy (1978) describes this kind of organization as Dionysian. It has an existential orientation that focuses more on the here and now, on individual enjoyment, and on acceptance of whatever comes. Organizations operating according to this orientation would look for a niche in their environment that would allow them to survive and would always think in terms of adapting to external realities rather than trying to create markets or dominate some portion of the environment.

The Being-in-Becoming Orientation

A third orientation, which lies between the two extremes of doing and being, is "being in becoming," referring to the idea that the individual must achieve harmony with nature by fully developing his or her own capacities and thereby achieve a perfect union with the environment. Through detachment, meditation, and control of those things that can be controlled (for instance, feelings and bodily functions), one achieves full self-development and self-actualization. The focus is on what the person *is* rather than what the person can *accomplish,* on achieving a certain state of development rather than doing and accomplishing. In short, "the being-in-becoming orientation emphasizes that kind of activity which has as its goal the development of all aspects of the self as an integrated whole" (Kluckhohn and Strodtbeck, 1961, p. 17).

In Handy's (1978) typology this orientation would come closest to the kind of organization that he has identified with Apollo. An Apollonian organization is one that emphasizes hierarchy, rules, clearly defined roles, and other means to help people curb and control their "natural" impulses and desires and thereby makes it possible to reach a state of developmental perfection. Implicit in this view is, of course, the assumption that basic impulses are dangerous and must be controlled. Another version of this same orientation might start with the assumptions that all human functions, feelings, and impulses are natural and that true development must involve accepting all of them instead of suppressing some of them in the service of others.

The relevance of this dimension can be seen most clearly in organizational attitudes and norms about the expression of emotions. In a European subsidiary of a U.S. multinational company, senior managers complained that they could not find any competent managers to put on their internal board of directors. In observing their meetings devoted to succession planning and management development, I noted that French and Italian managers were frequently labeled as too emotional and that this disqualified them from further consideration for higher-level jobs. Apparently, the assumption in this organization was that good management involves being unemotional, an assumption that I later found out was very dominant in the U.S. headquarters organization.

Activity Orientation and Role Definition

One element of activity orientation that is increasingly important today relates to underlying assumptions about the nature of work and the relationships between work, family, and personal concerns. One assumption would be that work is primary; another, that the family is primary; another, that self-interest is primary; and still another, that some form of integrated lifestyle is possible and desirable both for men and for women (Bailyn, 1978, 1982; Schein, 1978, 1990a). If members of a given organization have different assumptions about the nature of work activity and its relative importance to other activities, those differences will manifest themselves in frustration and communication breakdowns.

How activity orientation is linked to sex roles also must be examined. Hofstede (1980) found in his survey a basic dimension labeled masculinity, reflecting the degree to which, in a given country, male and female roles are clearly distinguished. Countries that come out highest on his combined index are Japan, Austria, and Venezuela; countries at the lowest end are Denmark, Norway, Sweden, and the Netherlands. The United States is near the middle of the distribution on this measure.

As was noted in the discussion of assumptions about human nature, the validity of all of these typologies is marginal in that they are based on fundamentally Western assumptions about the separation of self from other aspects of society and nature. In particular, the way we categorize sex roles and differentiate work from family and self is clearly not the way some other cultures conceive of human nature, and it is difficult for Westerners even to imagine how human nature and human activity are conceptualized in non-Western cultures.

In the United States we are also discovering through a painful process of consciousness raising how gender- and race-related assumptions come to be so taken for granted that they function to create de facto kinds of discrimination through stereotyping and the creation of various kinds of barriers such as "glass ceilings." In these areas many culture researchers have found the best evidence of culture conflict and genuine ambiguities

about roles, influencing even the kinds of problems that researchers have identified and studied (Martin, 1991).

Organization/Environment Relations

In every group there will evolve a deeply held view of whether
nature, the perceived total environment, can be subjugated and
controlled (the Western tradition), whether nature must be har-
monized with (the assumption of many Oriental religions and
societies), or whether one must subjugate oneself to nature (the
assumption of some Southeast Asian religions and societies).
The organizational counterpart of this core assumption is the
group's view of its relationship to its defined and perceived environment within the larger host culture. Does the group view
itself as capable of dominating and changing its environment;
does it assume that it must coexist in and harmonize with its
environment by developing its proper niche; or does it assume
that it must subjugate itself to its environment and accept whatever niche is possible?

At this level we are talking about the assumption underlying an organization's primary task, core mission, or basic functions, whether manifest or latent. If the organization's assumption about itself at this level is out of line with environmental
realities, it may sooner or later face a survival problem. Therefore, when organizations examine their strategy, they should
focus heavily on initial assumptions about the environment and
attempt, as much as possible, to validate those assumptions before deciding on goals and means.

Shared Assumptions About the
Nature of Human Relationships

At the core of every culture are assumptions about the proper
way for individuals to relate to each other in order to make the
group safe, comfortable, and productive. When such assumptions are not widely shared, we speak of anarchy and anomie.
Whereas the previous assumption areas deal with the group's
relationship to the external environment, this set of assumptions

deals more with the nature of the group itself and the kind of internal environment it creates for itself.

Assumptions about relationships must solve the problems of (1) power, influence, and hierarchy and (2) intimacy, love, and peer relationships. Such assumptions will, of course, reflect the even more basic assumptions about the nature of human nature. For example, if we assume that humans are inherently aggressive, we will develop a society built around controls of such aggression and relationship assumptions such as "One must take care of oneself" or "One must compete, but compete fairly." If we assume that humans are inherently cooperative, the assumptions about relationships might well emphasize how to cooperate to accomplish external goals. Assumptions about relationships, therefore, will directly reflect or be coordinated with assumptions about human nature, the nature of the external environment, and the nature of truth and reality.

Individualism and Groupism

If one looks at cultures around the world, obvious differences appear in assumptions about how people relate to each other and what the basic relational units are. Some cultures are what Kluckhohn and Strodtbeck (1961) call individualistic and Havry-lyshyn (1980) calls individual competitive (the United States, for example); other cultures are said to be collateral or group cooperative in emphasizing that the group is more important than the individual (Japan, for example); still other cultures are called lineal in that they emphasize hierarchy and tradition as bases of authority (some Latin countries, for example).

Hofstede's (1980) dimension of "power distance" identifies a related variable. He notes that countries vary in the degree to which people in a hierarchical situation perceive greater or lesser ability to control each other's behavior. People in high power distance countries, such as the Philippines, Mexico, and Venezuela, perceive more inequality between superiors and subordinates than do people in low power distance countries, such as Denmark, Israel, and Austria. If one looks at the same index by occupation, one finds higher power distance among unskilled and semiskilled workers than among professional and managerial workers, as would be expected.

At the organizational level, assumptions about relationships will, of course, reflect the assumptions of the wider culture, but they become elaborated and differentiated. The founder/leader may believe that the only way to run an organization is to assign individual tasks, hold individuals accountable for performance, and minimize group/cooperative work because that would only lead to lowest-common-denominator group solutions or, worse, diffusion of responsibility. Another leader might emphasize cooperation and communication among subordinates as the best means of solving problems and implementing solutions because that would lead to the level of teamwork that task accomplishment requires. These two leaders would develop quite different working styles, which would be reflected ultimately in the organization's processes, reward systems, and control systems.

Action and Multi differ dramatically in this regard. Action reduces power distance between superiors and subordinates as much as possible, building on the assumption that good ideas can come from anyone at any time. Senior managers are always available and willing to talk to anyone about any issue, constrained only by the practicalities of time and space. A senior manager in R & D recently left the organization for a bigger and better job, only to return three months later with the following comment: "In the new company I had an idea for a new product and was told that I would have to talk first to my boss, then to the director of R & D, and then to the senior vice president. In Action if I have an idea, I go straight to Murphy (the CEO) and we kick it around. This is the kind of place in which I want to work." To overcome time and space barriers Action has a worldwide electronic mail network that is frequently used.

In contrast, Multi values hierarchy, formality, and protocol. One does not approach people informally. Meetings and conferences must be well defined, have a clear purpose accepted by all, and be planned with rank and appropriate deference in mind. During my consulting visits, I saw only people who had specifically requested some of my time concerning some specific problems that they were concerned about. It would not have been appropriate for me to drop in on people or to strike up conversations beyond the minimal cordialities in the executive dining room.

At Action there is a great effort to make individuals accountable because Murphy believes that if groups make decisions, no one will feel responsible and nothing will get done. Multi is run by an executive committee that is by law accountable as a group. Job assignments are highly individual and people feel that they have their own turf, but at the same time there is a strong sense of collective responsibility.

Participation and Involvement

Most of the typologies proposed in this area focus on the degree of participation considered appropriate in the basically hierarchical system of organizations. Perhaps the most general theory here is Etzioni's (1975), which distinguishes among (1) coercive systems, (2) utilitarian systems, and (3) systems based on goal consensus between leaders and followers. In the coercive system, members are assumed to be alienated and will exit if possible; in the utilitarian system, they are assumed to be rationally economic calculative and will participate according to the norm of a fair day's work for a fair day's pay; and in the normative consensus system, they are assumed to be morally involved and to identify with the organization.

Assumptions about peer relationships can be derived from these systems. In the coercive system, peer relationships develop as a defense against authority, leading to unions and other forms of self-protective groups. In the utilitarian system, they evolve around the work group and typically reflect the kind of incentive system that management uses. In the normative system, they evolve naturally around tasks and in support of the organization.

At a more specific level than Etzioni's are a number of typologies that focus specifically on how authority is used and what level of participation is expected in the organization: (1) autocratic, (2) paternalistic, (3) consultative or democratic, (4)

participative and power sharing, (5) delegative, and (6) abdica-
tive, which implies delegating not only tasks and responsibilities but power and controls as well (Bass, 1981; Harbison and
Myers, 1959; Likert, 1967; Tannenbaum and Schmidt, 1958;
Vroom and Yetton, 1973). Some typologies add a dimension
of "professional" or collegial relationships in an organization
where individuals have broad vested rights and a "moral" orientation toward organizational goals, such as in professional part-
nerships in law or medicine (Jones, 1983; Shrivastava, 1983).

These organizational typologies deal much more with aggression, power, and control than with love, intimacy, and peer
relationships. In that regard they are always built on underlying
assumptions about human nature and activity. The arguments
that managers get into about the "correct" level of participation
and use of authority usually reflect the different assumptions
they are making about the nature of the subordinates they are
dealing with. Building a viable organization then becomes much
more a matter of locating assumptions on which group members can agree than on deciding what the ultimate truth about
human nature is. Looking at participation and involvement as
a matter of cultural assumptions also makes clear that the debate about whether leaders should be more autocratic or participative is ultimately highly colored by the assumptions of a
particular group in a particular context. The search for the
universally correct leadership style is doomed to failure because
of cultural variation by country, by industry, by occupation,
and by the particular history of a given organization.

Characteristics of Role Relationships

Human relationships can also be usefully analyzed with the aid
of Parsons's (1951) original pattern variables. He enumerated
the following role relationships that will exist in any social
system.

1. *Emotionally charged or emotionally neutral.* Are relationships in the system emotionally charged, as in a friendship, or
is an attempt made to minimize emotionality, as in a purely

professional relationship or a business relationship? How does a given culture define the degree of emotionality that is appropriate in any given type of relationship? For example, in the United States, as previously noted, we tend to define business relationships as emotionally neutral and view managers who are too emotional as not being competent. U.S. managers are impatient with managers from other countries who want to build informal relationships before they even begin to discuss business, and we tend to assume that if feelings enter the relationship they will undermine rationality and clear thinking.

2. *Diffuse or specific.* Do individuals relate to one another along many dimensions, as with family members, or are the relationships limited to a single dimension, as with a salesperson-customer relationship? In the United States we tend to distinguish clearly between the diffuse relationships of friendship and family and the more specific relationships we maintain at work and in business. In some other cultures it is considered impossible to conduct business unless the relationship is allowed to become more diffuse and multidimensional.

3. *Universalistic or particularistic.* Are the same broad criteria applied to all members of a given role or status (for example, to all sales managers), or are specific criteria applied to given individuals on the basis of their individual situation (for example, "Jones should get a special bonus because she has had a tough territory" or "Smith gets let off the hook for something he messed up because he has a physical handicap")? Stereotyping is an example of applying universalistic criteria to a given person or role, something one tends to do more, the greater the psychological distance between roles. In the United States we tend to define personal relationships as particularistic (each friend is a unique individual to us) and business relationships as universalistic (all salespeople are equivalent).

4. *Ascription or achievement oriented.* Are social rewards, such as status and rank, assigned on the basis of (a) what the person is by birth or family membership or (b) what the person has actually accomplished? The United States differs from most other countries in being more explicitly achievement oriented, as expressed in the value of equality of opportunity and giving re-

wards for achievement regardless of one's origin, as in the Horatio Alger myth. We find it difficult to understand societies where status and position are ascribed primarily on the basis of birth, family, particular school attended, and other criteria that may have nothing to do with the individual's actual accomplishments.

5. *Self or collectivity oriented.* Are an individual's actions ultimately related to individual self-interest or to a larger collective unit? This reflects the previously mentioned dimension of individual competitive versus group collaborative assumptions.

Using these variables, we would say that relationships in the Action Company are emotionally charged, specific, particularistic, highly achievement oriented, and self-oriented; in the Multi Company they are emotionally neutral, specific, somewhat though not totally universalistic, somewhat mixed on ascription versus achievement, and also mixed on self versus collectivity orientation. Achievement clearly counts at Multi, but ascriptive criteria such as the right family background and the right level of education also are considered. One of the high-potential division managers who was a widower was strongly encouraged to remarry as a prerequisite to being promoted to the internal board of the company. People at Multi are assumed to be ambitious, but the good of the company is taken into account more than it is at Action, where the assumption seems to be that if everyone does the correct thing — that is, makes her or his best individual effort — that will turn out to be best for the company as a whole.

These and other dimensions identify the specific areas where consensus is needed if the organization is to function smoothly. Consensus in these areas then becomes a deep layer of the culture and surfaces only when someone challenges or violates one of the assumptions. For example, an American manager brought up with strong beliefs in achievement as the basis for status could not cope with the fact that a Canadian family firm into which he had moved as a general manager was completely dominated by assumptions of ascription, particularism, and emotional diffuseness. Tasks were assigned on the basis of who was who, decisions were made on the basis of who liked whom, and promotions were clearly reserved for family members. After a year or more of turmoil and conflict he left the organization, but in that process it became clearer to everyone what the assumptions on which the company was operating were.

Rules of Interaction — The Joint Effect of Time, Space, and Relationship Assumptions

In the section on space we saw how intimacy is defined by distance and position. If we combine such assumptions with assumptions about timing and assumptions about the appropriate way for people to relate to each other, we have, in effect, the assumption set that specifies what in most cultures would be thought of as the rules of interaction (Goffman, 1967; Van Maanen, 1979b). What we think of as tact, poise, good manners, and etiquette can be deconstructed into a set of rules that preserve the social order, what Goffman and others have called face work. In other words, in every human group, the members sooner or later learn that in order to survive as a group, they must develop rules and norms that make the environment safe for each other. Members must learn to preserve each other's face and self-esteem, lest the social environment become dangerous. If I humiliate you, I license you to humiliate me.

This area was previously discussed in Chapter Five in regard to internal integration mechanisms, but we need to note now how the articulation of such mechanisms, the rules of interaction, draw on a combination of assumptions about time, space, and what are thought to be proper human relationships. The content of these rules will differ from group to group, but the existence of some set of such rules can be safely predicted for any group that has had some stability and joint history.

For example, both Action and another company, we will call it Twin Tech, strongly espouse teamwork as a necessary condition for successful performance, and in both companies it is considered bad not to be a team player. But when one examines the actual rules of interaction in operation, one discovers almost diametrically opposed assumptions. At Action to be a team player means to be open and truthful and trustworthy.

If you agree to do something, you do it. If you do not agree, you do not promise to do something that you do not intend to do.

At Twin Tech, on the other hand, the assumption has grown up that groups should reach consensus, that being nice to each other and being cooperative are important in reaching consensus, and that arguing too much or sticking to your own point of view too much is equivalent to not being a team player. Consequently, decisions are reached much more quickly, but they do not stick. People agree in public to uphold the norms but then in private fail to follow through, forcing the decision process to start all over again.

At Action it is considered timely to speak up right away if you don't agree; at Twin Tech it is considered timely to agree right away even if you don't intend to follow up on your own words or if you have reservations about the decision. Action puts more ultimate weight on truth, while Twin Tech puts more ultimate weight on the creation of a certain kind of work climate. The important point to note is that the new member of either of these organizations must acquire knowledge of how to manage spatial relationship vis-à-vis others, must learn how time is perceived and allocated and how fast one is supposed to do something, and must develop a sense of what is an appropriate relationship between people in the organization. And all of these assumption sets are interrelated in the day-to-day working out of behavior among the group members.

Cultural Paradigms as Interrelated Sets of Assumptions

Chapters Four through Seven have reviewed areas of group functioning that generate assumptions on the basis of which group members will come to perceive, think, and emotionally react. I have argued that culture is not only deep but wide. Culture in a mature group comes to cover all aspects of life, which makes it very difficult to analyze because it is so extensive. The final and, perhaps, most difficult aspect of the analysis of such a wide set of assumptions deals with the degree to which they come to be interlocked into paradigms or coherent patterns.

Not all assumptions are mutually compatible or consistent with each other. If there is a cognitive drive for order and consistency in the human brain, we can assume that human groups will gradually learn sets of assumptions that are compatible and consistent. If we observe inconsistency and lack of order, we can assume that we are dealing with an as yet unformed culture or that we are observing a conflict among several cultures or subcultures.

To illustrate what I mean by consistency, if we believe or assume that problems are ultimately solved through individual effort and that individuals are the ultimate source of ideas and creativity, we cannot simultaneously hold the assumption that the best kinds of relationships between members of an organization are collaborative consensual ones. If we believe that ultimately relationships between workers and organizations are either coercive or utilitarian and that there can never be a common interest between them, then we cannot simultaneously believe in participative management theories because these theories assume that workers want to contribute to the welfare of the organization. If a group assumes that the correct way to survive is to conquer nature (that is, to manage its environment aggressively), it cannot simultaneously assume that the best way for members to relate to each other is by passively seeking harmonious relationships.

One of the major dilemmas that leaders encounter when they attempt to change the way organizations function is how to get something going that is basically countercultural, that does not fit the paradigm. For example, the use of quality circles, self-managed teams, autonomous work groups, and other kinds of organizational devices that rely heavily on commitment to groups may be so countercultural in the typical U.S. individualistic competitive organization as to be virtually impossible to make work unless they are presented pragmatically as the only way to get something done. By invoking the higher-order assumption of pragmatism, it is possible to put group work into a positive perspective.

Furthermore, if we think of cultures as interlocking sets of assumptions, what often goes wrong in organizational change programs is that we manipulate some assumptions while leaving others untouched. We create tasks that are group tasks, but we leave the reward system, the control system, the accountability system, and the career system alone. If those other systems are built on individualistic assumptions, leaders should not be surprised to discover that teamwork is undermined and subverted.

Kluckhohn and Strodtbeck (1961) illustrate the paradigm notion at a higher level in asserting that Western culture is oriented toward the mastery of nature, holds an active and optimistic view of man as perfectible, views society as built on individualistic competitive relationships, and has an optimistic future orientation built on a notion of progress. To this we could add a pragmatic scientific view of truth and reality, a basically monochronic view of time, a view of space and resources as being infinitely available, and a view of authority relationships as rational-legal in the sense that power should go to those who have the expertise and are elected or appointed by a process that rests on the democratic principle of the consent of the governed. In the business realm, we expect relationships to be emotionally neutral, specific, universalistic, achievement oriented, and self-oriented (Newman, 1972). Attempts to characterize other cultures in such paradigm terms are probably not feasible, however, because the very notion of paradigm and the kinds of dimensions we use are culturally specific to Western cultures.

Organizational cultures may not develop to the point of fully articulated paradigms, but when we speak of strong cultures, what we probably have in mind is some degree of such articulation. In this sense both Action and Multi are strong cultures, and it was possible in describing them to articulate some interlocking sets of assumptions (see Chapter Three). These examples indicate that cultural paradigms are far more complex than some of the typologies of organizations that one finds in our literature. Many of these typologies take a single assumption dimension, develop several types along that dimension, and then call the types archetypes. In fact, those archetypes often ignore other assumptions and therefore fail to test whether or not coherent paradigms are operating. Two so-called autocratic companies may differ dramatically in their view of time, space, truth, relationships to nature, and activity, just as two so-called bureaucratic organizations may differ dramatically from each other on these dimensions. In fact, one of the reasons why organization theory may not have progressed farther than it has is that most of the typologies that are published tend to be unidimensional.

On the other hand, evidence is mounting that if one can conceptualize the complex interrelationships among assumptions, one can much better understand why and how organizations function the way they do. Lorsch (1985) in his study of twelve successful companies has shown how the leadership in each of those companies holds a complex set of interconnecting beliefs about financial goals, what businesses the firm could succeed in, how marketing should be done, what types of risks are acceptable, and so on, all based on a central assumption about the distinctive competence of the firm and its history of success. Once one understands that leaders operate with belief *systems,* not just individual assumptions and beliefs, it becomes clearer why culture has the strength that it does, and why it takes so long for culture change to occur. In Lorsch's sample, changes that the companies described took ten to fifteen years to accomplish.

Kotter and Heskett (1992), in their extensive study of strong and weak corporate cultures, found that those strong cultures that were able to adapt to their changing environments had a set of interlocked core beliefs about the importance of people, the importance of meeting the needs of all stakeholders, and the importance of perceptual learning and change. Although these core values themselves did not change, they fueled changes in the more peripheral parts of each culture.

Unless we have searched for the pattern among the different underlying assumptions of a group and have attempted to identify the paradigm by which the members of a group perceive, think about, feel about, and judge situations and relationships, we cannot claim that we have described or understood the group's culture. At minimum, we should take each of the assumption areas described in Chapters Four through Seven and attempt to answer systematically whether or not real consensus exists in that area among group members. We can then decide that there is no culture, or a weak culture, or culture conflict among several groups. Unless we achieve this level of analysis, however, we should not make any statement at all about culture. Superficial statements run the risk of losing the very meaning of the concept of culture or trivializing it to a point at which the concept becomes redundant with other concepts such as climate, values, or norms.

Summary and Conclusions

This chapter has reviewed the deeper cultural dimensions that deal with human nature, human activity, and human relationships. The set of issues and dimensions reviewed in Part Two of this book constitutes a kind of grid against which to map a given culture, should that be one's purpose. From the researcher's point of view, this can be a useful starting point, but it should be remembered that in any given group, the relative importance and salience of these different dimensions will vary. If one wants an accurate feeling for a culture, therefore, one should not start with these dimensions except as a general checklist to guide one's listening.

Leaders should note that culture is deep, wide, and complex. They should avoid the temptation to stereotype organizational phenomena in terms of one or two salient dimensions, and they should be sensitive to the power they have to influence the groups with which they work. The set of functional categories provided in the last four chapters can be used by a leader who wants to study the culture of her organization to think through systematically what assumptions are operating in each of the categories of analysis that has been provided, and especially to conduct a self-study to increase self-insight.

PART THREE

How to Study
and Interpret Culture

This part of the book deals with the practical issue of how one can decipher cultural assumptions. Chapter Eight focuses on helping organizations decipher their own assumptions if and when a cultural analysis becomes relevant for some problem that the organization is trying to solve. This chapter provides a number of minicases that illustrate not only the method of deciphering by means of a clinical research paradigm but also some additional cultural variants in different types of organizations. In Chapter Nine the focus is on deciphering cultural assumptions when an outsider needs to understand a culture better for purposes of generating new knowledge for others outside the organization. The analysis does not advocate the traditional ethnographic paradigm but suggests instead some methods of getting at cultural assumptions that are much faster because they involve insiders to a greater degree. The ethical problems involved in these cases are explored in Chapter Ten.

The reader will note that the emphasis in Part Three is practical and oriented toward what leaders, researchers, and consultants can actually do about deciphering culture. Although the conceptual categories presented here are a necessary background to help figure out what sorts of things to look for, the process of deciphering can proceed without that content knowledge. Readers who are not interested in these practical steps can go to Parts Four and Five on leadership in relation to culture building, embedding, and changing.

CHAPTER EIGHT

Deciphering Culture
for Insiders

There are basically two reasons for wanting to study and decipher an organization's culture: (1) scientific reasons that pertain to the building of theory and (2) action research reasons that relate to helping leaders manage cultural issues in their organizations. In the first case it is essential that the *outsider,* the person inquiring about the culture, learn what is really going on; in the latter case it is only essential that the *insiders* learn what is really going on. This distinction leads to two different approaches to how to study culture, approaches that are described in this chapter and Chapter Nine. We will start with the action research approach because it typically reveals enough about the culture to make further, more formal study easier and richer.

Deciphering Cultural Assumptions
in Order to Manage Them

This section describes a process for working with organizations on cultural issues that enables members of the organization to identify important cultural assumptions and to evaluate the degree to which those assumptions aid or hinder some strategic purpose that the group is concerned about. The process involves the commitment of one or more key groups in the organization, the identification of some clear reasons for conducting the cultural analysis, and anywhere from half a day to a full day of work, depending on the nature of the problem being addressed.

The following important assumptions lie behind this approach:

1. Culture is a set of *shared* assumptions; hence obtaining the initial data in a group setting is appropriate and valid.

2. The contextual meaning of cultural assumptions can only be fully understood by members of the culture; hence creating a vehicle for *their understanding* is more important than for the researcher or consultant to obtain that understanding.

3. Not all parts of a culture are relevant to any given issue the organization may be facing; hence attempting to study an entire culture in all of its facets is not only impractical but also usually inappropriate.

4. Insiders are capable of understanding and making explicit the tacit assumptions that make up the culture, but they need outsider help in this process. The helper/consultant should therefore operate primarily from a process consulting model and avoid as much as possible being an expert on the content of any given group's culture (Schein, 1987b, 1988).

5. Some cultural assumptions will be perceived as helping the organization to achieve its strategic goals or resolving its current issues, while others will be perceived as constraints; hence it is important for the group members to have a process that allows them to sort cultural assumptions into these categories.

6. Changes in organizational practices to solve the problems that initiated the culture analysis can often be achieved by building on existing assumptions. That is, the culture deciphering process often reveals that new practices can be derived from the existing culture.

7. Change in cultural assumptions, if necessary, will rarely, if ever, involve the whole culture. This will always be a mat-

ter of changing one or two assumptions in a broader cultural context. Only rarely does the basic paradigm have
to change, but if it does, the group faces a multi-year major
change process.

The implementation of a culture-deciphering process
based on these assumptions can be described in terms of a number of steps. Case illustrations are provided at the end of the
chapter.

Step 1. Obtaining Leadership Commitment

Deciphering cultural assumptions and evaluating their relevance
to some group purpose must be viewed as a major intervention
in the group's life and must, therefore, only be undertaken with
the full understanding and consent of the leaders of the organization. In practical terms this means that if someone from an
organization calls or writes me to ask if I will help her or him
figure out culture, my first question is always some form of "Why
do you want to do this?" or "What problem are you having that
makes you think a cultural analysis is relevant?" The only times
I have tried to help a group analyze its own culture without a
problem or issue to motivate the process, the analysis has essentially failed for lack of interest on the part of the group.

If there is a reason, usually a desired change in goals,
values, or priorities, we proceed to a meeting to decide first
whether the "client" wants to proceed once he or she understands
what the total process will be and second what group of people
should be involved. The latter will depend on the nature of the
problem and who the key "culture carriers" are perceived to be.
The group can be as small as three and as large as fifty. If important subcultures are believed to be operating, one can repeat
the process in different groups or deliberately bring in samples
of members from different groups in order to test in the meeting whether the assumed differences exist.

The composition of the group is further determined by
the client's perception of the level of trust and openness in the
group, especially in regard to the decision of whether senior

people who might inhibit the discussion should be present. On the one hand, it is desirable to have a fairly open discussion, which might mean keeping higher levels out. On the other hand, it is critical to determine to what extent the assumptions that eventually come out in the group meetings are shared by the leaders, which argues for their presence. Because level of trust and openness across various boundaries is itself likely to be a cultural issue, it is best to start with a heterogeneous group and let the group experience the extent to which certain areas of communication are or are not inhibited by the presence of others.

Next, we must decide on an appropriate locale and setting for doing the exercise (needed are a large comfortable room with lots of wall space for hanging flip chart pages and a set of break-out rooms in which subgroups can meet) and how best to involve the group. The point here is to put the focus on the problem or issue to be worked, not on the culture analysis. This analysis is a means to facilitate progress in solving the problem or resolving the issue, not something that is done for its own sake. Leaders can simply call the meeting with a statement of their purpose and say that part of the working session will involve examining the group's culture and subcultures.

Step 2. Conducting the Large Group Meeting

The large group meeting should start with a restatement by someone perceived to be in a leadership or authority role of the problem or issue that motivated the meeting in the first place. The process consultant is then introduced as being the outsider who will help the group conduct an analysis of how the group's culture is an aid or a constraint to solving the problem or resolving the issue. The process consultant can be an outsider or a member of the organization who is part of a staff group devoted to providing internal consulting services.

Substep 2a. Giving a Short Lecture on How to Think About Culture. In thirty minutes or so, I try to get across to the group that culture is a learned set of assumptions based on a group's shared history that come to be shared and unconscious, but that these assumptions manifest themselves at different levels: (1) the level of artifacts, (2) the level of espoused values, or (3) the level of shared underlying assumptions. I then provide some examples for each level and describe how the group will spend the remainder of the time allotted.

Substep 2b. Eliciting Descriptions of the Artifacts. I tell the group we are going to start by describing the culture through its artifacts. A useful way to begin is to find out who has joined the group most recently and ask that person what it felt like to enter the group (organization) and what he or she noticed most upon entering it. Everything that is mentioned I write down on a flip chart, and as the pages are filled, I tear them off and hang them on the wall so that everything remains visible.

If group members are active in supplying information, I stay relatively quiet, but if they need priming I will suggest categories such as dress codes, desired modes of behavior in addressing the boss, the physical layout of the workplace, how time and space are used, what kinds of emotions one would notice, and so forth. The process consultant can use the content chapters outlined in this book to ensure that many different categories of artifacts are covered, but it is important not to give out such a list before spontaneous group discussion because it may bias the group's perception of what is important. The outsider does not know initially what areas of the culture are especially salient and relevant and so should not bias the process of deciphering.

This process should continue for about one hour or until the group clearly runs dry, and it should produce a long list of artifacts covering all sorts of areas of the group's life. Being visually surrounded by the description of their own artifacts is a necessary condition for the group to begin to stimulate its own deeper layers of thinking about what assumptions its members share.

Substep 2c. Identifying Espoused Values. The question that elicits artifacts is "What is going on here?" By contrast, the question that elicits espoused values is "Why are you doing what you are doing?" Typically, I pick an artifactual area that is clearly

of interest to the group and ask people to articulate the reasons
why they do what they do. For example, if they have said that
the place is very informal and that there are few status symbols, I ask why. This usually elicits value statements such as
"We value problem solving more than formal authority" or "We
think that a lot of communication is a good thing" or even "We
don't believe that bosses should have more rights than subordinates."

As values or beliefs are stated, I check to see whether the
other group members agree and if they do, I write down the
values or beliefs on a new chart pad. If they disagree, I explore
why by asking whether this is a matter of different subgroups
having different values or there is genuine lack of consensus,
in which case the item goes on the list with a question mark
to remind us to revisit it. I encourage the group to look at all
the artifacts they have identified and to seek for themselves what
values seem to be implied. If I see some obvious ones that they
have not named, I will suggest them as possibilities, but in a
spirit of joint inquiry, *not* as an expert conducting a content analysis of their data. Once we have a list of values to look at, which
usually occurs within another hour or so, we are ready to push
on to underlying assumptions. On the other hand, if the group
starts to come up with assumptions sooner, I certainly go along
with that and write them down on still another flip chart.

*Substep 2d. Making a First Cut at Shared Underlying As-
sumptions.* The key to getting at the underlying assumptions
is to check whether the espoused values that have been identified really explain all of the artifacts or whether things that
have been described as going on have clearly not been explained
or are in actual conflict with some of the values articulated. For
example, the members of a group from the Contempo Company noted that they spend a great deal of time in planning activities but that the plans usually get overridden by the needs
of a here-and-now crisis. They even put planning on their list of
values and felt genuinely puzzled and ashamed that they followed through so little on the plans they had made. This raised
the whole issue of how time was perceived, and after some dis-

cussion, the group members agreed that they operated from a deeper assumption that can best be stated as "Only the present counts." Once they stated the assumption in this form, they immediately saw on their own artifact list other items that confirmed this and thought of several new artifacts that further reinforced their orientation toward the present.

As another example of how assumption identification operates, the same group identified many different informal activities that members engage in, including parties at the end of work day, celebrations when products are launched, birthday parties for employees, joint travel to recreational areas such as ski lodges, and so on. The value they espoused was that they liked each other. But as we pondered the data, it became clear that a deeper assumption was involved, namely, "Business can and should be more than making money; it can and should be fun as well." Once this assumption was articulated, it immediately led the group to realize that a further one was operating— "Business can and should be more than just making money; it can and should be socially significant."

The latter assumption reminded the group members of a whole series of artifacts concerning the value they put on certain of their products, why they liked some products better than others, why they valued some of their engineers more than others, how their founders had articulated their original values, and so on. Important and salient assumptions are ones that trigger a whole new set of insights and new data, that begin to make sense of a whole range of things that they do and espouse.

Often these salient assumptions reconcile what the group may have perceived as value conflicts. A group of human resource professionals at an insurance company doing this exercise identified as an important value becoming more innovative and taking more risks as the environment changed; but the members could not reconcile the fact that very little actual innovation was taking place. In pushing to the assumption level they realized that throughout its history the company had operated on two very central assumptions about human behavior: (1) people work best when they are given clear rules to cover all situations (among the artifacts the group had listed was a "mile-long shelf of procedure manuals"), and (2) people like immediate feedback and will not obey rules unless rule violation is immediately punished. Once the human resource professionals stated these assumptions, they realized that the assumptions were driving the behavior far more than the espoused value of innovation and risk taking.

This phase of the exercise is finished when the group and the process consultant feel that they have identified most of the critical assumption areas and participants are now clear on what an assumption is. At this point I have found that if the group is larger than ten or so people, it is necessary to proceed in subgroups.

Step 3. Identifying Cultural Aids and Hindrances in Subgroups

The task for subgroups depends in part on what the presenting problems were, whether or not subcultures were identified in the large group exercise, and how much time is available. For example, if there was evidence in the large group meeting that there are functional, geographical, occupational, or hierarchical subcultures, the consultant may wish to send off subgroups that reflect those presumed differences and have each subgroup further explore its own assumption set. Or, if the consultant finds that there is reasonable consensus in the large group on the assumptions identified, he or she can compose the subgroups randomly, by business unit, or by any other criterion that makes sense given the larger problem or issue that is being addressed.

In any case, the task for the subgroups consists of two parts: (1) spending some time (an hour or so) refining assumptions and identifying other assumptions that may have been missed in the large group meeting and (2) categorizing the assumptions according to whether they will aid or hinder the solution of the problem that is being addressed. This problem or issue is usually stated in the form of some new strategic direction in which the organization wishes to go, so the assumptions can then be analyzed in terms of which ones will help and which ones will hinder in the achievement of the new objective. I ask the subgroups to list the two or three main assumptions that will aid and the two or three that will hinder and to be prepared to report these to the total group.

It is very important to require the participants to look at assumptions from this dual point of view because of a tendency to see culture only as a constraint and thus put too much emphasis on the assumptions that will hinder. In fact, culture change probably arises more from identifying assumptions that will aid than from changing assumptions that will hinder, but groups have a harder time seeing how the culture can be a source of positive help.

Step 4. Reporting Assumptions and Joint Analysis

The purpose of the fourth step of the exercise is to reach some kind of consensus on what the important shared assumptions are and what the implications of those assumptions are for what the organization wants to do. The process starts when the subgroups report their own separate analyses to the full group. If there is a high degree of consensus, the process consultant can go straight into a discussion of implications. More likely there will be some variations, possibly disagreements, which will require some further inquiry by the total group with the help of the process consultant. At this point the group may agree that there are strong subculture differences that must be taken into account. Or some of the assumptions may have to be reexamined to determine whether they reflect a deeper level that would resolve disagreements. Or the group may come to recognize that for various reasons it does not have many shared assumptions. In each case, the role of the outside process consultant is to raise questions, force clarification, test perceptions, and in other ways help the group achieve as clear a picture as possible of the assumption set that is driving the group's day-to-day perceptions, feelings, thoughts, and ultimately, behavior.

Once there is some consensus on what the shared assumptions are, the discussion proceeds to the role of those assumptions in aiding or hindering what the group wants to do. At this point the consultant must be careful to ensure a balanced discussion because of the tendency to quickly identify a constraining assumption and put all the energy on figuring out what to do about it. As previously stated, one of the biggest insights for the group comes from seeing how some of the assumptions will aid them, creating the possibility that their energy should go into strengthening those positive assumptions instead of worrying about overcoming the constraining ones.

If, however, real constraints are identified, the group discussion then shifts to an analysis of how culture can be managed and what it would take to overcome the identified constraints. At this point a brief lecture may be needed to review some of the culture change mechanisms that are implied and a new set of subgroups may be formed to develop a change strategy. Typically, this would require an additional half-day at the minimum. Thus, if culture change is to be undertaken, additional time beyond the original one-day meeting is required. This whole process is best illustrated in the context of the following case examples.

Case Examples

Decentro Tech

The recently appointed CEO of a high-tech company that consisted of ten or more divisions asked me to help him figure out how the organization could develop a "common culture." He felt that its history of decentralized autonomous divisions was now dysfunctional and that the company should work toward a common set of values and assumptions. The CEO, the director of human resources, and I were the planning group to decide how to approach the problem. We reached the conclusion that all of the division directors, all of the heads of corporate staff units, and various other individuals who were considered to be relevant to the discussion would be invited to an all-day meeting whose purpose was to identify the elements of a common culture for the future. Thirty people attended the meeting.

We began with the CEO stating his goals and why he had asked the group to come together. He introduced me as the person who would stage manage the day but made it clear that we were working on his agenda. I then gave a thirty-minute lecture on how to think about culture and launched into the process described above by asking some of the less senior people in the group to share what it was like to enter this company. As people brought out various artifacts and norms, I wrote them down on flip charts and hung up the filled pages around the room. This was symbolically important to immerse the group in its own culture. It appeared clear that there were powerful divisional subcultures, but it was also clear that there were many common artifacts across the group. My role, in addition to writing things down, was to ask for clarification or elaboration as seemed appropriate to me.

As we worked into our second and third hours, some central value conflicts began to emerge. The various divisional units really favored the traditional assumption that high degrees of decentralization and divisional autonomy were the right way to run the overall business, but at the same time they longed for strong centralized leadership and a set of core values that they could rally around as a total company. My role at this point was to help the group confront the conflict and to try to understand both its roots and its consequences. We broke at lunchtime and instructed randomly selected subgroups of seven to eight members to continue the analysis of values and assumptions for a couple of hours after lunch and then met at around three o'clock for a final two-hour analysis and wrap-up session.

To start off the final session each group gave a brief report of the assumptions that it felt aided and those it felt hindered achievement of a common corporate culture. In these presentations the same divisional versus corporate conflict kept emerging, so when the reports were done, I encouraged the group to dig into this a little more. Because some mention had been made of strong founders, I asked the group to talk further about how the divisions had been acquired. This discussion led to a major insight. It turned out that almost every division had been acquired with its founder still in place and that the early policy of granting autonomy had encouraged those founders to remain as CEOs even though they had given up ownership.

Most of the managers in the room had grown up under those strong leaders and had enjoyed that period of their history very much. Now, however, all the founders had either retired, left, or died, and the divisions were led by general managers who did not have the same charisma the founders had. What the group longed for was the *sense of unity and security they each had had in their respective divisions under their founders.* They did not in fact want a strong *corporate* culture and leadership because the businesses of the divisions were really quite different. What they wanted was stronger leadership at the divisional level but the same degree of divisional autonomy as they had always had. They realized that their desire for a stronger corporate culture was misplaced.

These insights based on historical reconstruction led to a very different set of proposals for the future. The group, with the blessing of corporate leadership, agreed that they only needed a few common corporate policies in areas such as public relations, human resources, and research and development. They did not need common values or assumptions, though if such developed naturally over time that would be fine. On the other hand, they wanted stronger leadership at the divisional level and a development program that would maximize their chances to obtain such leadership. Finally, they wanted to strongly reaffirm the value of divisional autonomy to enable them to do the best possible job in each of their various businesses.

Lessons. This case illustrates the following important points about deciphering culture and managing cultural assumptions:

1. A senior management group with the help of an outside facilitator is able to decipher key assumptions that pertain to a particular business problem, in this case, whether or not to push for a more centralized common set of values and assumptions.

2. The cultural analysis revealed several assumptions that were centrally related to the business problem, as judged by the participants. However, other elements of the culture that were

clearly revealed in the artifacts were not judged to be relevant. Inasmuch as every culture includes assumptions about virtually everything, it is important to have a deciphering technique that permits one to set priorities.

3. The resolution of the business problem did not require any culture change. In fact, the group reaffirmed one of its most central assumptions. In this context the group did, however, define some new priorities for future action — to develop common policies and practices in certain business areas. Often what is needed is a change in business practices within the context of the given culture, not necessarily a change in the culture.

Contempo Computers

Contempo Computers decided to conduct a cultural analysis as part of a long-range planning exercise focused on human resource issues. How big would the company be in five years, what kind of people would it need, and where should it locate itself geographically under different size scenarios? A ten-person working group consisting of several line managers and several members of the human resource function were assigned the task of figuring out how Contempo's culture would influence growth and what impact it might have on the kinds of people who would be attracted to it in the future. The vice president for human resources knew of my work on culture and asked me to be a consultant to this working group. He functioned as its chairman.

The original plan was to sort out various planning tasks and to delegate these to other committees for more detailed work since the presentation to the company meeting was six months off. One of these other groups was charged with analyzing Contempo's culture on the basis of preliminary work that our committee would do. My role was to help organize the study, teach the group how best to study culture, and consult with the culture subcommittee down the line.

The first meeting of the group was scheduled for a full day and involved the planning of several different kinds of activities of which the culture study was just one. When it came to deciding how to study the Contempo culture, I asked for twenty minutes to describe the model of artifacts, espoused values, and basic underlying assumptions. I also described in general terms how I had used the model with other organizations to help them decipher their culture. The group was intrigued enough to accept my next suggestion, which was to try the process out in this group if we were willing to commit a couple of hours to it. The group agreed so after the twenty-minute lecture, we launched directly into uncovering artifacts and values.

Because this group was used to thinking in these terms, it was easy for them to mix the analysis of assumptions, values, and artifacts so we ended up rather quickly with a provisional set of underlying assumptions backed by various kinds of data that the group generated. These were written down in draft form on flip charts and organized by me that evening into a more ordered set of what we ended up calling governing assumptions.

1. We are not in the business for the business alone but for some higher purpose — change society and world, create something lasting, solve important problems, have fun.

> One of the major products was designed to help children learn.
>
> Another major product was designed to make computing easier and more fun.
>
> It was alleged that many people at Contempo would object if the company went after the broad business market and if it sold products to selected groups who would misuse the product (for example, the Department of Defense).
>
> Contempo engaged in many rituals designed to be fun — for example, after-hours parties, playfulness at work, magic shows at executive-training events.
>
> Only what is fun and what is unique get the big rewards.
>
> Creativity and innovativeness are highly rewarded.

2. Task accomplishment is more important than the process used or the relationships formed.

> When you fail in Contempo, you are alone and abandoned; you become a "boat person."

Seniority/loyalty/past experience don't count relative to present task achievements.

When you trip, no one picks you up.

Out of sight, out of mind; you are only as good as your latest hit; relationships formed at work do not last.

People are so intent on their mission that they don't have time for you or to form relationships.

Bonding occurs only around tasks and is temporary.

Groups are security blankets.

Contempo views itself as a club or a community, not a family.

3. The individual has the right and obligation to be a total person.

Individuals are powerful, can be self-sufficient, and can create their own destiny.

A group of individuals motivated by a shared dream can do great things.

People have an inherent desire to be their best and will go for it.

Contempo neither expects company loyalty from individuals nor expects to guarantee employment security to individuals.

Individuals have the right to be fully themselves at work, to express their own personality and uniqueness, to be different.

There is no dress code and no restriction on how personal space is decorated.

Children or pets can be brought to work.

Individuals have the right to have fun, to play, to be whimsical.

Individuals have the right to be materialistic, to make lots of money, to drive fancy cars no matter what their formal status.

4. Only the present counts.

Contempo has no sense of history or concern for the future.

Seize the moment; the early bird gets the worm.

Contempo does not see itself as a lifetime employer.

Longer-range plans and tasks get discussed but not done.

People do not build long-range cross-functional relationships.

Nomadic existence inside Contempo is normal; people don't have "offices," only "campsites" and "tents."

The physical environment is constantly rearranged.

It is easier to fix things than to plan for perfection; flexibility is our greatest skill.

People are forgotten quickly if they leave a project or the company.

"We learn by doing."

These governing assumptions and the supporting data were passed on to the subcommittee dealing with the Contempo culture, where they were tested and refined with further interviews. Interestingly enough, no substantial changes were made on the basis of several more months of work, suggesting that a group can get at the essentials of its culture very rapidly.

Lessons. This case illustrates the following important points:

1. If a motivated insider group is provided with a process for deciphering its culture, members can rather quickly come up with some of their most central driving assumptions. I revisited Contempo several years after this event and was shown a recent report on the company's culture. The same set of assumptions was written down in this report as still being the essence of the culture, though the various assumptions were stated in somewhat different order and with some additional comments about areas that needed to change.

2. Stating these governing assumptions allowed the company managers to assess where their strategy might run into cultural constraints. In particular, they realized that if they were to grow rapidly and enter the broad business market, they would have to deal with members of their organization who grew up under the assumption that business should involve more than just making money. They also realized that they lived too much

in the present and would have to develop longer-range planning and implementation skills.

3. Contempo reaffirmed its assumptions about task primacy and individual responsibility by starting to articulate explicitly a philosophy of no mutual obligation between the company and its employees. When layoffs became necessary, the company simply announced them without apology and carried them out.

Twin Tech

The third case example is intended to show that a group of insiders working off this model of culture can quickly reveal to themselves and to the outsider where some of the strains and stresses are in a given culture. Twin Tech is a fifty-year-old company that grew up in a high-tech field that did not require computers in its early days but then found that by adding computers it could greatly enhance its original technology. As it developed its computer business, it found itself with essentially two cultures and the uncomfortable feeling that the two were not entirely compatible. More specifically, a number of managers from Twin Tech whom I met in various executive development courses over the past decade told me that the original culture found the computer types to be more rough and tumble, something I did not fully understand until recently, when I was invited by an organization development consultant from the company to meet with ten of the managers of one of the computing divisions to help them analyze their culture and, specifically, some of the sources of their frustration in carrying out projects in the company.

The working day began with a restatement of the business problem that the managers faced, specifically, the difficulty of getting high-quality decisions that would be reliably implemented. They complained that too often decisions that were made in groups did not get implemented, causing great loss of time and frustration. I then gave my thirty-minute lecture on the model and invited the group to start off with artifacts. We quickly proceeded to values as the group began to see connections between the various artifacts. This led almost immediately to a more holistic description of some of the critical elements of the Twin Tech culture that affected decision making. The following assumptions, values, and artifacts were identified.

Central Assumption — The Individual Is a Sacred Cow. The group pointed out that all the company's incentive and reward systems were geared to individual performance, that the founders had often referred to the importance of individual creativity and performance, and that individuals could and often did veto decisions without getting punished for it. However, as noted below, the veto was usually not public; rather, it was in the form of failure to implement something that others thought had been agreed on.

The group noted that teamwork and consensus were strongly espoused but that no visible team or group incentives existed to reinforce them. On the other hand, the next assumption explained some of the anomalies that were observed.

Central Assumption — It Is Possible to Run a Profitable Business in a "Gentlemanly" Fashion. Twin Tech prided itself on its explicit value system concerning human relations and teamwork. The company was perceived to be very paternalistic and caring for its people, but in a parent to child mode, not in an adult to adult mode. The importance of teamwork and consensus was explicitly espoused, articulated in many company documents, and touted as one of the reasons why it was pleasant to work there.

Group discussion revealed that teamwork had a special meaning in this organization — that in group or interpersonal contacts one should always be nice and agreeable to others and that one should not hold onto one's own point of view too tenaciously if the group was clearly leaning in a different direction. Consensus was thus achieved by a process of encouraging conformity rather than battling things out to some resolution (as they would have been at Action).

This was the issue that particularly troubled the managers because they felt that people would agree in public but then not implement what had been agreed to, thus subverting the whole decision process. I asked what would happen if someone did continue to argue in the group for his or her point of view and was told that after the meeting the boss would tell that person that he or she was not a team player. The strength of this mode of operating was further made visible quite accidentally when I recently met a young female MBA who had been hired six months earlier by a Twin Tech manufacturing division at a geographically different location (the original project had been done over a year before). She spontaneously told me that she had recently disagreed with her peers on some issue and stuck to her point of view. Right after the meeting, the boss of the group said, "Martha, I've never seen you like this before; what is the matter?"

In other words, in Twin Tech one must always be agreeable and nice, one must never hurt others, and one must seek consensus at all times. If one fights and is labeled not a team player, one is gradually ostracized. The strength of these norms is attributed by insiders to the fact that the founder held these values very strongly and that they worked effectively for the kind of technology that existed when the company started. At that time, high-quality products could be designed by creative individuals, and there was not much reason for disagreement and controversy. The introduction of the "computing culture" was the source of discomfort, yet the computing managers did not see how they could get timely high-quality decisions unless they fought things out. They therefore found themselves in a difficult situation, especially since senior management mostly came from the original culture that espoused the norms and values of teamwork and being nice.

It seemed to most of the managers in this group that the only solution in this privately individualistic and publicly conformist environment was to learn how to be a superb politician and to build credibility on a track record of individual success. Unfortunately, as they pointed out, the projects were generally complicated team efforts that depended upon everyone's cooperation. Since that cooperation could not be counted on, they felt frustrated and discouraged. In this case, the cultural analysis identified the problem but revealed very little in the way of possible remedies. Most of the senior managers were from the other technical culture so the foregoing assumptions were thoroughly entrenched.

Lessons. Once again it was evident that central assumptions in a culture can be identified rapidly and efficiently in a group context. However, the identification of key assumptions does not necessarily provide solutions to the business problem. In this case the day's activity reinforced the discouragement that the participating managers already felt.

U.S. Army Corps of Engineers

The final case example illustrates the culture-deciphering process in a different type of organization. As part of a long-range strategy-planning process, I was asked to conduct an analysis of the culture of the U.S. Corps of Engineers. In attendance were the twenty-five or so senior managers, both military and civilian, with the avowed purpose of analyzing their culture in order to (1) remain adaptive in a rapidly changing environment, (2) conserve those elements of the culture that are a source of strength and pride, and (3) manage the evolution of the organization realistically. The managers knew that the corps' fundamental mission had changed over the last several decades and that the survival of the organization hinged on getting an accurate self-assessment of its strengths and weaknesses.

The usual procedure was followed, and the discussion developed the following themes, stated as either values or assumptions, depending on how the group itself experienced that element.

1. Our mission is to solve pragmatically (river control, dams, bridges, and so forth), not aesthetically, but our responsiveness to our environment leads to aesthetic concerns within the context of any given project.
2. We always respond to crisis and are organized to do so.
3. We are conservative and protect our turf but value some adventurism.
4. We are decentralized and expect decisions to be made in

the field but control the field tightly through the role of the district engineer.

5. We are numbers driven and always operate in terms of cost/benefit analyses, partly because quality is hard to measure.
6. We minimize risk because we must not fail; hence things are overdesigned, and we use only safe, well-established technologies.
7. We exercise professional integrity and say no when we should.
8. We try to minimize public criticism.
9. We are responsive to externalities but attempt to maintain our independence and professional integrity.
10. We are often an instrument of foreign policy through our non-U.S. projects.

The problem the group identified was that the traditional mission of flood control was largely accomplished, and with changing patterns in Congress, it was not easy to tell what kinds of projects would continue to justify the budget. Financial pressures were seen to cause more projects to be cost shared with local authorities, requiring degrees of collaboration that the corps was not sure it could handle. The culture discussion provided useful perspectives on what was ahead but did not provide clues as to the specific strategy to pursue in the future.

Lessons. This case like the others illustrates that one can get a group to decipher major elements of its culture and that this can be a useful exercise in clarifying what is strategically possible.

Summary and Conclusions

The most efficient and possibly valid way to decipher cultural assumptions is for an outsider to work directly with a group of motivated insiders on a model of artifacts, values, and assumptions. This works best when the group has some purpose for conducting the cultural analysis and when there are no special communication barriers in the group that would prevent a free flow of communication. A prerequisite for this kind of deciphering is that the leaders of the group have a specific purpose in mind and understand the process well enough to know what they are committing their group to.

The main purpose of the resulting cultural description is to provide insight to the organization so that it can figure out how different cultural assumptions aid or hinder what members are trying to do. It does not matter whether the outsider who facilitates the process fully understands the culture or not. The purpose is not to get a description to publish but to provide the group a useful mirror on itself. To this end it should be noted that the group process described here is extremely fast. Within a few hours one can get a good approximation of what some of the major assumptions are. Individual interviews or questionnaires are less useful and also less desirable because they take much more time and are less valid inasmuch as the outsider does not know initially what questions to ask and the individual often does not know how to answer.

If it is important for the outsider/researcher to be able to describe the culture in more detailed terms, the method suggested in Chapter Nine is probably more relevant. In terms of implications for leadership, I would argue that in most situations in which leaders need to manage some element of their culture, this internal deciphering process is the most likely to be useful.

Reporting About Culture to Outsiders

Suppose it is the intention of clinician/reseacher to decipher the culture in order to make it visible not only to group members but to scientific colleagues. How does the researcher get enough data to understand at least elements of the organization's culture? The traditional way, of course, would be to become a participant observer and to proceed as an ethnographer. This is time consuming and, I believe, not necessary unless one wants to study the culture in great detail. An alternative is to adopt a clinical perspective, attempt to be helpful to the organization, and conduct a series of interviews with individuals and groups geared to discovering shared underlying assumptions.

The Iterative Clinical Interview

The basic approach I propose here is best described as an iterative clinical interview, a series of encounters and joint explorations between the investigator and various motivated informants who live in the organization and embody its culture. My assumption is that only a joint effort between an insider and an outsider can decipher the essential assumptions and their patterns of interrelationships (Evered and Louis, 1981; Schein, 1987a). This joint effort may involve relatively elaborate and extensive data-gathering activities and may include some of the more formal methods that anthropologists propose. But the final determination of the cultural "essence" must be a joint effort, for two basic reasons: *to avoid the subjectivity bias* and *to overcome the insider's lack of awareness.*

The outsider cannot experience the categories of meaning that the insider uses because she or he has not lived long enough in the culture to learn the semantic nuances, how one set of categories relates to other sets of categories, how means are translated into behavior, and how such behavioral rules apply situationally. What the newcomer learns at entry reveals surface layers of the culture; only when inner boundaries are crossed is the member told what really goes on and how to think about it (Schein, 1978; Van Maanen and Schein, 1979). Furthermore, the outsider inevitably imposes her or his own categories of meaning on observed events, and these interpretations are incorrect to an unknown degree. Only if the insider and the outsider talk things out explicitly can the insider correct misperceptions or misinterpretations that the outsider may be making.

The insider cannot tell the outsider what the basic assumptions are and how they are patterned because they have dropped out of awareness and are taken for granted. The insider can become aware of them only by trying to explain to the outsider why certain things that puzzle the outsider happen the way they do or by correcting interpretations that the outsider is making. This process requires work on the part of both the insider and outsider over a period of time. The nature of this work can be likened to trying to bring to the surface something that is hidden but not concealed deliberately. It is so taken for granted that it escapes notice, but it is perfectly visible once it has been brought into consciousness, as shown in Chapter Eight.

Notice that this process requires considerable investment of time and energy on the part of the insider and hence is more likely to be successful if insiders are also attempting to solve their problems and have asked the outsider for help. As a result this is defined as a clinical situation in which the outsider is providing help in a consulting role. If the deciphering is done purely as a research process where the outsider attempts to get permission to observe and talk to insiders, she or he will not get the level of cooperation and motivation needed to really decipher what is going on. On the other hand, if the researcher has enough time to become an accepted *and helpful* part of the group, the process can work because the insiders will then become motivated to help the researcher.

The steps involved in the method proposed here are listed and described in the following paragraphs. They differ from many of the methods advocated by other corporate culture analysts (for example, Schwartz and Davis, 1981; Kilmann, 1984; Peters, 1980; Pettigrew, 1979; Silverzweig and Allen, 1976; Tichy, 1983) in that they do not assume that if one just asks the "right" questions initially or gives the right sort of questionnaire, one can decipher the culture. In the model suggested here there are no initial magic questions or correct things to observe. The theoretical categories discussed in the preceding chapters can alert the investigator to the areas where observations should be made, but such categories should not be used as a guide to questioning prior to exposing oneself to the culture in a natural way.

Step 1. Entering and Focusing on Surprises

The interested outsider enters the organization or group to be deciphered and begins to experience the culture, both actively through systematic observation and passively through encountering surprises, or things that are different from what the outsider expected (Louis, 1980). At Action, I was most surprised by the high level of interpersonal conflict, which seemed to be immune to my interventions. At Multi, I was most surprised by the fact that my communications did not circulate freely. Both of these proved to be important symptoms or artifacts of deep cultural assumptions.

Step 2. Systematically Observing and Checking

The outsider engages in systematic observation to calibrate the surprising experiences as best he or she can and to verify that the surprising events are indeed repeatable experiences and thus likely to be a reflection of the culture, not merely random or idiosyncratic events.

Step 3. Locating a Motivated Insider

The outsider must now find someone in the organization who is analytically capable of deciphering what is going on and who is motivated to do so. It is the insider's motivation to obtain some kind of help or clarity that makes this a clinical rather than an ethnographic approach. Often the insider initiates the project by seeking help of some kind and then becomes involved as a participant in unraveling aspects of the culture. At Action and Multi, such people were initially the clients who brought me into their system. Subsequently, additional resources for mutual exploration came from the personnel and training departments. It turned out that some of the internal consultants and some of the people in the training department themselves wanted to discuss my observations with me, so they provided a natural vehicle for further deciphering.

Step 4. Revealing the Surprises, Puzzlements, and Hunches

Once a relationship has been established with the insider, the outsider can reveal his or her observations, surprises, reactions, and even projections, theories, and hunches about what is going on in the culture. Often such revelations are "set up" by the insider with routine questions such as "What do you think of our company, now that you have been here for a while?" If the insider does not provide a natural setting for revelation of reactions, the outsider must be able to create such a setting. Specifically, the outsider must assess the insider's readiness to hear observations that may sound judgmental and to deal with them in a nondefensive manner.

How the outsider reveals his or her observations is crucial. I generally avoid abstractions and generalizations; instead, I stick very closely to my own personal reactions to events, thereby allowing the insider to consider the possibility that my idiosyncrasies rather than cultural forces are operating. This form of communicating minimizes the risk of the insider's becoming defensive if the observation hits a sensitive spot.

Step 5. Jointly Exploring to Find Explanation

The insider then attempts to explain to the outsider what the surprising event means, or if the outsider has a hunch, the insider elaborates on or corrects the outsider's interpretation. Both parties now have to probe systematically for the underlying assumptions and the patterns among them. At this point the theoretical categories, the issues that every group must face, and the categories of basic assumptions (as outlined in Chapters Four through Seven) become relevant as a mental checklist to ensure that all of the cultural terrain is being covered. That is, both people must relate the observations to the various theoretical categories to see where there is most clearly a connection and where the data clearly reveal an underlying assumption.

In this process the outsider must assume the role of a clinical interviewer who is helping the insider search in his or her own mind for the deeper levels of explanation that can help both people decipher the basic assumptions of the culture. Since the essential data are in the insider's head, the process must be designed to bring out things that the insider takes for granted. The outsider must be sensitive to how best to probe without arousing defensiveness, inducing superficial explanations, or exhausting the insider to the point of wanting to terminate the relationship. In practice this activity usually takes place when both parties are relaxed, maybe at the end of a consulting day or over a meal, or at a session deliberately designed to be diagnostic.

At Multi I spent countless hours with a young professional internal consultant and trainer, talking out my own frustrations in working with the company and having him provide a necessary cultural framework for understanding what was going on, adding data where relevant from his own experience. Where our experiences were identical, we knew we were dealing with a real cultural issue. At Action, much of the clarification came from another process that happened to be available. The company was using other consultants in various parts of the organization, and we all met periodically with several internal organization development consultants to compare notes on what was happening and to decipher assumptions in a group context. With five or six of us sharing our experiences at Action, we could calibrate more accurately what the major cultural assumptions seemed to be.

Step 6. Formalizing Hypotheses

The output of step five is explanations that make sense, stated in the form of underlying assumptions, but these assumptions can be taken only as hunches about the culture at this point and must be formalized into hypotheses. Both the insider and the outsider must determine what additional data would constitute a valid test of whether such an assumption is operating. Such data might be in the form of operational values that should be derivable from the assumptions or actual behavior that one should be able to observe if the assumption holds. For example, in the Twin Tech case described earlier, the key assumption that business can be run with people always being nice to each other and agreeable in group meetings was tested by my spontaneously interviewing the new employee and discovering that she had been questioned by her boss about why she had refused to back down at a meeting.

Step 7. Systematically Checking and Consolidating

Through new interviews or observations, the interested insider and the outsider now search for new evidence. At this point systematic interviewing of informants may be in order because the outsider now has some idea of what questions to ask. In the initial stages of encountering the culture, the outsider would have such a vast array of possible things to ask about that he or she would hardly know where to begin. At this point in the process, the outsider knows enough to know where to look, what to look for, and whom to ask. Questionnaires; content analysis of documents, stories, and other artifacts; formal interviews; systematic observations; and all the other techniques of gathering social data now may become relevant.

Step 8. Searching for Shared Assumptions

One of the most difficult steps in the deciphering process comes when one must go beyond the articulated values and attempt to understand the shared tacit assumptions behind them. The essence of this step is to take the confirmed hypothesis and attempt to state clearly what assumption is operating and how that assumption affects behavior. At Action, as I began to understand what it means to fight over an idea in the search for truth in an uncertain world, it no longer made me uncomfortable. Once I understood the assumptions, I could understand the rules of the game. At Multi I now understand what it means to want to solve one's own problem, to be the expert and to seek help only from other experts, so I am no longer surprised at the kinds of questions I am asked and the kinds of problems in which I am involved. I now know when my own behavior fits the culture and when it is countercultural.

Step 9. Perpetually Recalibrating

As new data surface and as the outsider becomes better acquainted with the culture, the outsider can refine and modify the model of the culture that he or she has begun to construct and can test that model on other interested insiders. But they must be interested and analytical; otherwise, they may not recognize some of the assumptions by which they operate. Worse, they may get defensive if they feel that a judgment is being made or embarrassed that their behavior has been "exposed." In other words, a correct view of the culture is not necessarily readily accepted by the uncritical members of that culture because they may not like the assumptions by which they operate or because the assumptions are simply too complicated to comprehend.

I had counterproductive experiences both at Action and at Multi when I attempted to lecture to insiders about their culture, even if they requested the lecture. Clearly, they were sometimes not ready to have their culture analyzed. On the other hand, culture discussions of this sort provide important new data that permit recalibration. Just as in group training or therapy, resistance to interpretations provides important data, so in cultural analysis, the reaction of people to cultural descriptions provides important further data on what the culture is all about.

Step 10. Writing a Formal Description

As a final test of our understanding of the assumptions of a given organizational culture, it is necessary to write down the assumptions and to show how they relate to each other in a meaningful pattern to articulate the paradigm. It is very easy to assume that we understand and have an intuitive feel for what is going on, but unless we can clearly write out what we think we feel, we cannot tell whether we really understand and whether anyone else could understand. The written analysis may undergo perpetual modification as new data arise, but some description is an essential step in the process of deciphering.

The interested insider can go over the written description as a further test of accuracy, but it is not at all clear that making such a written description generally available is helpful. The whole issue of when and how one reveals a culture to the group members requires further clinical diagnosis and raises some ethical questions discussed in Chapter Ten. Ultimately, how the cultural data are used is a function of what problems the client system wishes to address and what audience the researcher is trying to reach. At Multi the cultural description became relevant when we were diagnosing forces that would aid or hinder the change project (described in Chapter Seventeen), but until then it remained only an interesting bit of data, which I shared with the internal consultants and the director of management development.

At Action there was so much internal preoccupation with the culture already that my role was more that of a clarifier, sharpener, and implications tester. For example, I once asked, "If your culture really assumes that every individual must think for himself, how is that consistent with your wish to have senior management make decisions and push them down the system?" This question provoked a thoughtful silence and a new insight that the group longed for greater certainty but did not really want answers from top management, thus reinforcing the assumption of autonomy and self-determination ("Do the right thing").

The Inquiry Interview Methodology

If one has established helping relationships with insiders and has opportunities to conduct systematic interviews, how does one interview a willing informant to begin to get at cultural assumptions? Such interview information is a useful supplement to the immediate data that the outsider obtains from his or her own encounters with the organization, and of course, each interview is itself an encounter to be deciphered in accordance with the preceding steps.

The basic principle of interviewing is *not* to ask about values or assumptions. Not only are such questions likely to produce what the informant thinks is socially desirable and acceptable, but even if she or he is not motivated just by social desirability, the informant is unlikely to be able to focus on those categories. Instead, the outsider should ask questions that produce a natural story, that access the informant's thoughts and memories in a way that they are naturally organized, that is, chronologically. The best way to do this is to get a historical reconstruction of how the group solved its major problems of external adaptation and internal integration and to focus on which kinds of solutions worked repeatedly and became embedded. One can ask about critical incidents in the history of the group, again using the categories discussed in Chapters Four through Seven as a private mental checklist to make sure that everything has been covered. In other words, the interview should take the informant through the history of the unit being studied to discover what problems the group encountered and how they were handled. For example:

1. "Let's go back over the history of your organization.

Can you tell me when it was founded and describe the events that occurred at that time?"

a. "Who was involved?" (Try to locate the important founding figures or leaders who might have been the real culture creators, and find out what their values, biases, assumptions, and goals were.)

b. "What were the critical problems in getting started?" (Try to find out what the survival issues were and how they were handled.)

c. "What was the basic mission of the group at that time?" (Try to get a sense of the organization's ultimate "reason to be.")

d. "Were there specific goals and ways of working that emerged early?" (Probe for goal conflicts and priorities.)

2. "Were there any critical incidents that occurred early in your history?" (A critical incident is any major event that threatened survival, or caused reexamination or reformulation of goals or ways of working, or involved membership or inclusion issues. To discover a critical incident, the interviewer might ask the respondent to recall events that caused problems for which the organization had no ready solutions, or events that challenged existing norms and solutions, such as an act of insubordination, or anything interpersonal that was unusual or tension provoking and required some kind of response.)

a. "Tell me how people were feeling about what was happening. Were they anxious or angry or delighted or what?"

b. "What was done? Who did anything?" (Here the interviewer tries to elicit in detail the nature of the response and the key actors who were responsible for the response. If an informant says, for example, "We were faced with a cutback, but instead of laying people off, we all worked fewer hours and took a pay cut," the interviewer might ask: "Who thought of this idea? How was it implemented?")

c. "What happened? Did the response work? How did people feel subsequently? Did the response continue?" (The interviewer then asks about the next crisis or critical event, using the same series of questions again.)

As one elicits incidents, feelings, what was done, and how it worked, one should try to elicit or imagine the underlying values and assumptions that may be involved in the responses and begin to look for patterns in them. This is the analytical activity that accompanies steps five and six in the sequence described at the beginning of this chapter. We cannot argue that we are dealing with a cultural element until we see some repetition of response, some behaviors, values, and assumptions that clearly are shared and continue to be used in new situations. One needs to elicit enough history to begin to see the pattern.

Group Interviews to Elicit Positions on Specific Dimensions

The group interview can be used in addition to individual interviews or as the primary data-gathering activity if motivated and interested people are available and willing to discuss their organization in a group context. In the group situation one can get at shared assumptions more directly by the methodology described in Chapter Eight, and one can attempt to get at specific dimensions of the culture with more focused questions if one has reason to believe that those dimensions are relevant.

This technique is useful because the group provides the stimulus to bring out what is ordinarily hidden, and the interviewer can observe the behavior of group members from the point of view of the very assumption being analyzed. In other words, where opportunities to make unobtrusive ethnographic observations do not exist, one can still observe a great deal of the culture in action by creating and observing group meetings at which cultural issues are discussed. An incident that occurred at Multi will make this clear. A group of internal consultants and I were discussing Multi's impact on new members of the company. One of the consultants had been with Multi six months, so he took the lead in observing that "In Multi it is hard for a newcomer to be listened to. People seem to value only someone who has been around for a long time." At this point the senior member of the group shot back: "How can you make a statement like that when you have only been around for six months?" A very pregnant, shocked silence followed.

If the interviewer has hypotheses about specific dimensions

of the sort identified in Chapters Four through Seven, questions can be designed to focus on those areas. For example, if it appears that important cultural assumptions are governing how the organization defines its mission and goals, the interviewer can ask the group to talk about the mission, ask how it was derived, whether or not it is associated with specific individuals, how much consensus there is on the mission, how much it actually determines behavior, and so on.

If a deeper dimension is to be investigated, such as the nature of truth, the interviewer can ask the group to identify several strategic decisions that have been made in recent times and explore just how those decisions were made. Who was involved, what kind of information was utilized, and what decision process was used? The conceptual material such as the moralism-pragmatism dimension (page 102) can be shared with the group and the group members can be asked where they would place their organization in terms of how decisions are made and so on. Each cultural dimension shown in Chapters Four through Seven can be shared with the group, and members can be asked where they would place themselves and why.

Other Sources of Cultural Data

How much can one infer from an analysis of artifacts, such as the structure of the organization, its information and control system, and its announced goals, charters, mission statements, myths, legends, and stories? Because such data are often used, their strengths and weaknesses must be briefly discussed here (for example, Gagliardi, 1990).

Organizational Structure

The problem with inferring culture from an existing structure is that one cannot decipher what underlying assumptions initially led to that structure. The same structure could result from different sets of underlying assumptions. For example, a highly centralized structure in an organization could result from any of the following assumptions: (1) this is the right way to organize for the primary task, or (2) the leaders believe they have a monopoly on truth, or (3) key positions have to be protected for the leader's friends and relatives, or (4) people cannot really be trusted (Theory X) and therefore must be tightly controlled, or (5) only hierarchical relationships and clear lines of authority make it possible to run any organization. Such a structure could also result from earlier leaders' assumptions that have simply become a historical tradition. The structure is a clear, visible artifact, but its meaning and significance cannot be deciphered without additional data. Such data can, of course, be gathered in individual or group interviews by asking respondents how their structure came to be and why they think it exists.

Information, Control, and Reward Systems

One can examine as artifacts the formal processes of budgeting, accounting, performance appraisal, compensation, and other systems in use, but one cannot determine from that examination alone whether key managers actually attend to what is highlighted in these systems. I have seen organizations where the formal system and the informal processes of management bear little relationship to each other. In fact, in some organizations managers actively ridicule their control system as something that the accountants or "financial types" have cooked up but that is largely irrelevant to really managing the place. Similarly, I have encountered organizations that proudly tout their formal performance appraisal system only to discover that line managers treat it as a paper factory dreamed up by the personnel department and not to be taken too seriously.

On the other hand, the formal systems are clearly an artifact of the culture and therefore reflect something. At the minimum, they may reflect the fact that one of the subcultures within the organization is working at cross-purposes with other parts of the culture, as in the examples just cited. The nature of this conflict can serve as a useful starting point for diagnosing the strains within the larger culture, but in any case, one must supplement what one observes in the formal system with interview data.

As with structure, unless one examines the historical origins and the intentions of the creators of the systems and procedures, one does not really know what the underlying assumptions are. For example, Multi operates worldwide and therefore has clearly formulated central policies and procedures covering travel from headquarters to various regional units. To take a trip, a member of the headquarters personnel organization must get approval from his own boss and from his boss's boss. When I first learned about this, it struck me as the kind of artifact that clearly supported the strong hierarchical assumptions of the organization, and I further assumed that it reflected a lack of willingness to delegate. Why not give people a travel budget and make them live within it?

When I raised this question with several senior managers, I uncovered a totally different set of reasons for the existence of the policy. Apparently, the company had for years given complete freedom to its headquarters personnel. As a result, travel to the regional units was so frequent that the regional line managers felt as if they were doing nothing but entertaining headquarters visitors. Attempts to impose budgets did not curb the amount of visiting of the regions. It was in reaction to the strong frustration of the regional managers that higher management imposed what amounted to a travel ban, which really signaled to the organization that the regions were more important as organizational units than the staffs in the central headquarters organizations. To ensure that the regions were properly supported, the headquarters staffs had to be curbed.

What seemed a repressive policy on travel proved to be a cultural artifact rich in information about headquarters-field relationships, attitudes toward delegation, and changing priorities as the company evolved. But only after investigation was I able to decipher what the artifact actually reflected and how it should be interpreted. My suspicion is that most organizational procedures have rich cultural histories of this sort, but one will not understand the meaning of those procedures until their histories have been analyzed and deciphered.

Myths, Legends, Stories, and Charters

Many of the published analyses of culture limit themselves to the analysis of explicit artifacts, such as stories and organizational credos. While it may be possible to determine how stories about founders and the charters and credos of their companies reinforce leader assumptions, one cannot infer those assumptions from such data alone. One cannot assume that what is in the stories and charters is anything more than the espoused values, which may or may not match with actual assumptions that operate. The same caution must be applied to the content of materials that are to be transmitted to newcomers and to the myths and legends that arise in every organization to help everyone remember important values (Martin, 1982; Mitroff and Kilmann, 1975, 1976; Smith and Simmons, 1983).

The origins and functions of organizational "stories" are not at all clear, but some themes have been identified. Stories often communicate the values and beliefs of founders or other central characters in the organization who have become symbolic role models. The stories are often prescriptive and can thus become direct vehicles of indoctrination. On the other hand, in an organization with many subcultures or conflicting coalitions, stories can become a means of spreading a counterculture or of revealing inconsistencies or absurdities in the main culture. In an illuminating paper, Martin and Siehl (1983) analyze the key values of General Motors as seen in an official history and as seen by the disenchanted John DeLorean (Wright, 1979). The point of most of DeLorean's stories is to make the company look ridiculous and ineffective.

Sometimes stories are used to idealize former leaders, even though the idealized behavior is no longer relevant. For example, in Kodak it is said that "the ghost of George Eastman still walks the halls." In this case the point of the story is not only to communicate a value but also to give employees a sense of pride and something with which to identify. In a large European company, it was said that an employee went to one of the important past leaders who built the company into its leadership position, and opened the conversation with "Herr Doctor Schmitt." Schmitt immediately interrupted the employee and said, "I am not a doctor," at which point the employee excused himself and said, "Herr Director Schmitt." Schmitt again interrupted and said, "I am not a director; I am an entrepreneur, and I employ directors." What comes through in the story is not only the personality of this early leader but the prestige hierarchy that one must learn if one works in this organization. Entrepreneurial behavior is assumed to be the key to success.

Published statements of creeds, philosophies, and charters make the espoused message explicit, reflecting the leader's intentions to get across a certain message. But we cannot assume that these consciously articulated messages necessarily reflect what may be more implicit cultural themes either because the leader is not aware of them, or is conflicted about them, or is deliberately trying to displace some implicit themes with more consciously explicit ones that fit her or his intentions better. I have often wondered whether the claims made in credos and published value statements actually revealed precisely where the organization felt vulnerable because the operating assumptions were the *opposite* of what was claimed.

Closely related to published philosophies and creeds are published recruiting brochures, employee orientation handbooks, initial indoctrination and training materials, videotapes, and other artifacts that attempt to get across to newcomers what some key elements of the culture of the organization are. Such materials are more likely to exist in companies that are past their youth, that have developed enough of an espoused value system to be able to articulate it, but such materials also exist in first-generation companies in the form of letters from the founder, videotapes of the founder, and other materials that bring founding principles and values to the newcomers. All such organizational artifacts are better used to check one's hypotheses about basic assumptions than to decipher what those assumptions are in the first place. And when one interviews newcomers, one often discovers that they pay far more attention to what behavior they observe in the senior members of the organization than what the printed materials or training courses portray.

Data from Surveys and Questionnaires

A number of culture researchers have designed survey instruments that purport to measure culture (for example, Hofstede,

1980; Hofstede and Bond, 1988; Kilmann and Saxton, 1983; Schneider, 1990; Tucker and McCoy, 1988, 1989). Such surveys imply that one can give a questionnaire to employees in an organization and from the resulting data infer cultural assumptions. There are several problems with such a claim.

First, the survey labels itself as a culture survey but is, in fact, measuring aspects of the organization's climate or its norms. In that regard the data are perfectly valid artifacts, but they are artifacts that have to be interpreted and deciphered in the same way as other artifacts. One cannot decipher the culture from them alone.

Second, if the questionnaire is designed to get at cultural assumptions, how is the designer to know which of the many dimensions of a culture to build into the questionnaire? Culture ultimately covers all aspects of a group's internal and external life, so one would have to design a very large number of questions to cover the areas described in Chapters Four through Seven. Even if one only investigated the basic underlying dimensions of truth, time, space, activity, human nature, and human relationships, one would have a long and elaborate survey.

Third, not all cultural dimensions are equally salient or relevant to a given group's functioning. If one were to design a questionnaire covering many dimensions, one might still not know which of those dimensions are important to the group in regard to any given issue. For example, Hofstede's (1980) dimensions may be reliable and valid as indicators of what he is measuring, but how do we know whether tolerance for ambiguity, masculinity, individualism, and power distance are relevant in any given group or organization as components of its culture? Once again, without observational or interview data, one can treat the questionnaire results only as an artifact from which to proceed further.

Fourth, questionnaires given to individual members of the organization assume that the responses will be responsible and accurate. There is no way of knowing whether a given group member is answering in terms of what she thinks someone is looking for, or whether she is doing her best to answer how she really perceives things. Furthermore, how do we know when we ask a question about something as complex as assumptions about truth or time, whether the individual respondent in the middle of a questionnaire can figure out what is really going on in her organization? Because cultural assumptions are tacit and have dropped out of awareness, it may be difficult for an individual to bring relevant data to the surface. She may answer to the best of her ability but still be unable to access what may really be going on. In contrast, in a group setting one can see how individuals working their way through artifacts and values begin to stimulate in each other the perceptions that allow assumptions to surface. There is no way a questionnaire can do that.

In summary, questionnaires can be a very useful tool for getting at norms of behavior and at organizational climate, but such data should not be confused with cultural assumptions as I am defining them. At best the survey results are an artifact of the culture, subject to the same interpretation problems as other artifacts.

Writing About Culture

As Van Maanen (1979a, 1988) has argued, how one presents in writing the insights one has obtained raises a whole separate set of issues. Such issues are particularly acute when there is disagreement about the legitimacy of different research styles for the study of culture. If one operates from a classical ethnographic paradigm, one can identify the several "correct" ways to present ethnographic data. However, it has become increasingly clear that this classical paradigm is less and less tenable even as a research model. It is not possible to remain objective or to leave the culture as one found it. One's very presence is an intervention; therefore, one's own role as an agent of change must become part of the analysis and written description.

If one operates from a traditional social psychological paradigm and relies on operational definitions, questionnaires, and other forms of objective data, the written description tends to be fairly formalized by the criteria used by the main journals.

The problem with this model is that it leads to more of an illusion of objectivity than actual objectivity. It feels safe to argue that culture is simply that which has been operationally defined as culture, but that approach may lead to conclusions that have very little to do with what actually goes on in organizations. To satisfy certain canons of "normal science," we end up sacrificing credibility and validity.

If one takes the clinical perspective that has been argued in this book, one's main concern must be the discovery and accurate depiction of the phenomenological reality as experienced by both the outsider and the insider. The accuracy of the depiction is then judged by the credibility of that description to insiders who live in the culture and, at the same time, to outsiders who are trying to understand it. Accurate description is the key, with full recognition of the biases that are brought to the situation both by the insider and by the outsider. And such accurate description requires one to be very objective in describing artifacts and espoused values and very empathic in describing basic shared assumptions as they are experienced by insiders.

There is as yet no formula for doing this, but it is clear that one must intervene to bring certain categories of data to the surface. Pure aloof observation will not do the trick. One must also find situations where the members of the culture are motivated to reveal themselves because they have problems to solve. If the outsider is there only as a favor, too much will remain concealed. Therefore, the written descriptions will often be analyses of how the problems were solved, not simply pure descriptions of cultures. Better taxonomies of cultural phenomena will then eventually develop as we build more of a file of clinical cases of working with culture.

Case Example: Stevens Pharmaceuticals

As part of an ongoing consultation I was asked to help analyze a management succession problem that had, from the point of view of senior management, some cultural implications. Specifically, the current director of sales, Hanly, had been with Stevens for twenty-five years and had built a highly successful sales force that was making money for the organization in spite of the fact that there were very few products to sell. The success of the organization was perceived to be the result of the talent, dedication, single-mindedness, and autocratic and paternalistic style of the sales director.

The division general manager and the corporate VP of human resources wanted to know whether it would be better to break up the culture by bringing in someone from the outside to replace Hanly or to promote from within and thereby reinforce the culture. This issue had arisen because Hanly was close to retirement and corporate management wanted to ameliorate the conflict that had developed between marketing and sales. Hanly's retirement was announced, but at the same meeting, the division general manager (my client) announced that a study would be done of the sales department culture to decide how best to replace Hanly. I was asked to interview Hanly, his immediate staff, and the regional and district sales managers to find out what kind of a culture had been built in the sales department.

This request posed an immediate tactical problem inasmuch as I knew that I could not adequately decipher the culture from individual interviews and there was not enough time to become a participant observer in it. I did, however, feel that if I could partially employ the self-diagnostic methods described in Chapter Eight, the insiders and I could learn enough about the culture to get some sense of what might be the right next step. This case is, therefore, not a pure case of scientific deciphering but falls somewhere between insider and outsider deciphering.

My data consisted of individual interviews of the sales director, his counterpart marketing director, the division general manager, and several headquarters staffers in marketing and sales. I followed the process consultation principle of always involving the client in each intervention. For example, after interviewing the three top people, I asked them individually what they thought of bringing the regional managers and the headquarters staff together as a group. They thought this would work well with the regional managers because they were used to meeting as a group and trusted each other. However, the three cautioned against bringing the headquarters staff together as a group because there was so much tension between marketing and sales that people would clam up.

After interviewing the regional sales managers, I asked them how best to get to the district level and learned that there was to be a national sales meeting followed by regional sales meetings, which would be highly representative of how sales worked and would afford me the opportunity of meeting lots of the people. I attended the meetings and held individual and group interviews at meals and at free times. The senior managers introduced me as a consultant who had been hired to find out what the culture of the sales department was. This produced some initial awkwardness and a tendency to say just nice things, but it soon became evident that openness and the ability to be critical were both strong values, resulting in fairly frank and open discussions. At the district meeting I met individual sales reps and other research and marketing staff members, so I had a fairly representative view of the whole sales organization.

Because the data were highly consistent throughout, I wrote a preliminary report for the sales director, the regional managers, and the district managers, asking for amendments and corrections. As it turned out these people gave the report to the general manager, who followed up with a three-hour private conversation with me to see whether he understood the report and to clarify his own thinking about it. The content of the report was as follows:

Comments and Questions
About Stevens Sales Culture

Based on group interviews of headquarters, regional, and district sales managers, interviews of marketing, and observations of the one regional meeting at which reps were present, I have the following observations about the situation in the sales department.

1. There is a very strong sales culture that goes back to pre-Stevens days and precedes Hanly in many of its elements, though Hanly is credited

as having been the leader who created the organization and its values as it exists today.

2. The present culture (as will be described below) is credited with the success that Stevens has had so far, especially in view of the small number of products that have been available.

3. The present sales culture is also perceived to be the best hope for Stevens in the future. In other words, the sales organization is the strength of the organization and should not therefore be tampered with.

4. The key elements of that strength are the following:

   a. The high morale, dedication, and loyalty of the reps.

   b. The degree of flexibility of the reps in response to the changing management demands in the marketing of the existing products.

   c. The high degree of openness of communication that permits rapid problem solving, collaboration, and shifting of strategy when needed. Communication with marketing appears to be excellent at the district level with district managers feeling that their point of view and that of the reps gets listened to and understood by marketing.

   d. The strong family feeling.

   e. The development program and the opportunity structure that allow sales reps multiple career options according to their talents and needs.

   f. The high professional and ethical standards relative to their competitors; the commitment to educating doctors.

5. There is very strong feeling at all levels that only an insider would understand and preserve these strengths even as changes were made to com-

pensate for present weaknesses. Therefore, the
risk in bringing in an outsider is that the very
things that have made the sales force successful
may be undermined and destroyed.

6. The weaknesses that have to be addressed are
to further train and professionalize the sales
force, to further improve the relationship between sales and marketing, especially to get sales
more involved with and understanding of the
future marketing issues facing the company. It
appears that the sales organization is familiar
with the new marketing issues, but it is not clear
whether they have the skills to respond to them.

7. A further weakness may be the assumption held
in sales that some disagreement and difference
in point of view between sales and marketing
is a good thing. This assumption could inter-
fere with the building of more integrated sales-
marketing teams.

Though I encouraged people to comment on and correct
the report, none chose to do so, and the project ended three
months later, when the general manager called me to tell me
that the company had promoted the primary inside candidate.
In other words, it chose to preserve the culture.

As the reader will note, the report is not couched as an
analysis of the culture content as such but rather as an aid to
the organization in trying to solve its succession dilemma. I could
have attempted a diagram such as those portraying the Action
Company and Multi Company paradigms, but my data were
insufficient and I decided in any case that this would not be helpful to the client system.

Case Example: Three Danish Computer Companies

In an effort to test the levels model of culture and the specific
categories of inquiry I have proposed, two Danish researchers
undertook to describe three computer companies on the basis

of observations and interviews conducted in those companies (Pedersen and Sorensen, 1989). They systematically observed artifacts in four categories: (1) physical symbols, (2) language, (3) traditions, and (4) stories. They conducted interviews to evaluate both espoused values and values-in-use and were able to deduce the shared basic underlying assumptions operating in each company.

One of these companies is a start-up consulting firm founded by three consultants who were dissatisfied with the way their original company had treated them. They set up their company on the academic assumptions of equality in decision making, minimalization of hierarchy, and helpfulness in business practice. They assumed they had a small niche and were very optimistic about their ability to fill it. The researchers noted that given its youth, this company's culture was in the process of being created by the founders and that difficulties would arise, especially around the issue of individualism and groupism, both of which were strongly espoused.

The second company studied is a fifteen-year-old rapidly growing software concern that is primarily installing a particular product in various client systems. The firm has grown to sixty people but is still owned by the founders, one of whom left but kept his stock. The essence of this culture can be characterized by a set of value statements that seems to operate as basic assumptions, namely:

1. Treat people with consideration.
2. Do not lay people off; give them a chance to find another job in the company. (Both 1 and 2 basically reflect Theory Y optimistic assumptions about people.)
3. Do not brag or play Mr. Know It All.
4. Promote yourself but do it in the right way. (Be efficient, roll up your sleeves, get going.)
5. Ask before you do anything. (This reflects an underlying assumption that senior management is wiser and should be consulted before action is taken.)
6. Get things done; results count.

The authors also noted that there were growing differences between the information technology (IT) specialists and the administrative and sales functions that reflected the evolution of two subcultures potentially in conflict with each other.

The third company studied is a forty-year-old partnership between the Danish state and the municipal and county organization whose primary function is the administration of various IT functions for the government agencies. This company employs about 1,500 people and is organized around its various client systems. The authors describe this organization in quite different terms from the other two companies, emphasizing its high value on rules, control, and doing things right, which reflects the assumption that centralization is the way to organize. The company believes that there is virtue in size, in the importance of craftsmanship, and in company loyalty. This latter is reflected in strong pressures to join the union, for which, in exchange, one gets job security. Relative to the other two, this company appears to be much less individualistic, reflecting instead the values of group collaboration.

These brief summaries do not do justice to the descriptions provided by the authors but are presented to illustrate that it is possible to go into an organization with a framework such as has been presented and, to a considerable degree, decipher the culture. Enough of the major themes can be identified to allow one to draw some inferences about potential difficulties that these companies will have or how they would fare if they were merged or acquired.

Summary and Conclusions

This chapter has reviewed how one might go about deciphering a group's culture if one's intention is to understand it well enough to present it to outsiders. The importance of working with a motivated insider, the establishment of a joint inquiry model based on individual and group interview data, and the testing of hypotheses based on initial deciphering of puzzles and anomalies were all emphasized.

There is no reliable, quick way to identify cultural assumptions. Sometimes such assumptions are obvious at the outset. Sometimes they are highly elusive, even after months of study. And sometimes one must conclude that there are no shared assumptions working across the organization because of a lack of shared history. What may be very clear to insiders and satisfy their need to understand their own culture (as explored in Chapter Eight and as illustrated in the Stevens case) may be quite unsatisfactory from the point of view of trying to describe that culture to someone outside the organization.

The only safe approach to such external deciphering is cross checking each bit of information obtained against other bits of information until a pattern finally begins to reveal itself. In this process the dialogue between the insider and outsider is crucial. An important part of such cross checking is to test one's insights by seeing how members of the organization respond to one's own behavior and interventions. As Lewin (1947) noted long ago, if one wants to understand a system, one should try to change it. The spirit of that dictum underlies action research and diagnostic activities in all human systems and is especially relevant to the diagnosis of cultural elements.

The major implication for leaders is to be cautious in how they interpret other people's descriptions of the culture of their organization or any part thereof. What may seem very obvious to an outsider may make no sense and actually be incorrect. If it is important for the leader to understand her or his own culture, it is essential that she or he participate in deciphering it.

CHAPTER TEN

Ethical Problems in Studying Organizational Cultures

The deciphering of culture has some inherent risks that both the insider and the outsider must assess before proceeding. The risks differ, depending on the purpose of the analysis, and the risks are often subtle and unknown. As a result, the desire to go ahead and the organization's permission to do so may not be enough to warrant proceeding. The outside professional, whether consultant or ethnographer, must make a separate assessment and sometimes limit his or her own interventions to protect the organization. In this chapter I will try to describe these risks in terms of deciphering for insider use only and in terms of deciphering to make the culture known to others.

Risks of an Internal Analysis

If an organization is to understand its own strengths and weaknesses and if it is to make informed strategic choices based on realistic assessments of external and internal factors, it must study and understand its own culture. This process is not without its problems, risks, and potential costs, however. Basically, two kinds of risks must be assessed: (1) the analysis of the culture could be incorrect and (2) the organization might not be ready to receive feedback about its culture.

The analysis of what the basic assumptions are and how they fit into a pattern and paradigm may be wrong and, if so, may give the decision maker incorrect data on which to base decisions. If decisions are made on the basis of incorrect assumptions about the culture, serious harm could be done to the organization. Such errors are most likely to occur if culture is defined at too superficial a level, if espoused values or data based on questionnaires are taken to be an accurate representation of the underlying assumptions without group and individual interviews that specifically dig for assumptions as proposed in Chapters Eight and Nine.

On the other hand, the analysis may be correct, but insiders other than those who made the analysis may not be prepared to digest what has been learned about them. If culture is like character and functions in part as a set of defense mechanisms to help avoid anxiety and to provide positive direction, self-esteem, and pride, then various conditions might make an organization reluctant to accept the cultural truth about itself. Psychotherapists and counselors constantly must deal with resistance or denial on the part of patients and clients. Similarly, unless an organization's personnel recognize a real need to change and feel psychologically safe enough to examine data about the organization, they will not be able to hear the cultural truths that inquiry may have revealed or, worse, may lose self-esteem because some of their myths or ideals about themselves may be destroyed by the analysis.

A potentially even more dangerous risk is that the group will achieve instant insight and automatically and thoughtlessly attempt to produce changes in the culture that (1) some other members of the organization may not want, (2) some other members may not be prepared for and therefore may not be able to implement, and/or (3) may not solve the problem.

One reason people avoid therapy is that they are not ready for the insights that therapy inevitably brings. Insight produces change automatically because certain illusions and defenses can no longer be used. If culture is to the organization what character is to the individual, then insight into one's own culture may remove defenses that had been operating and on which the organization had been relying. To study a culture and reveal that culture to the insiders, then, can be likened to an invasion of privacy, which under many conditions is not welcome. Therefore, the student of culture should make the client system fully aware that there are consequences to having elements of one's culture laid bare, so to speak.

One company, for example, discovered through self-study and with the aid of outside consultants that it assumed that people are motivated and will put in a fair day's work for a fair day's pay. The company measured output, not number of hours on the job, and generally held an idealistic view of human nature. During a period of economic decline, it was confronted with its idealistic assumptions about employees and, because productivity had become a problem, was ready to make a change. Its managers decided that idealism was no longer tenable and that they had better get control of the situation. They installed time clocks and had industrial engineers study the behavior of the workers to make sure that productivity could be controlled and maximized. Once the new procedures were installed, the workers concluded that the company had really changed for the worse, lost some of their motivation, began to resent the time clocks, tried to figure out how to cheat them, and generally kept their productive effort to the minimum that they could get away with.

This kind of sad tale is usually associated with the advent of hard-nosed managers who come in with different styles. In this case, however, the only intervention was the clear exposure to the members of the company of how idealistic their cultural assumption about human nature really was. Because top management was frightened of the economic downturn, they were not able to perceive accurately that their culture still represented a viable way of dealing with economic diversity and that they did not need to institute radical changes. They might have been better off not uncovering this aspect of their culture.

Risks of an External Analysis

However the basic cultural data are gathered, the organization could be made vulnerable through having its culture revealed to outsiders. If a correct analysis of an organization's culture becomes known to outsiders because it either is published or is simply discussed among interested parties, the organization may become vulnerable or put at a disadvantage because data that would ordinarily remain private now may become public. For various reasons the members of the organization may not want their culture laid bare for others' viewing. If the information is inaccurate, potential employees, customers, suppliers, and any other categories of outsiders who deal with the organization may be adversely influenced.

Here again the analogy to character is useful in that we clearly would not publish an accurate personality profile of a living individual unless that person, for reasons of his or her own, wanted such a publication. If it is important to the scientific community to have such material published or if psychiatrists or clinical psychologists want to inform their colleagues about the cases they have treated, the cases must be sufficiently disguised to ensure the absolute anonymity of the individuals involved. Paradoxically, business organization cases are rarely disguised, even though they often include revealing details about an organization's culture. If the organization fully understands what it is revealing and if the information is accurate, no harm is done. But if the case reveals material that the organization is not aware of, such publication can produce undesirable insight or tension on the part of members and can create undesirable impressions on the part of outsiders. If the information is not accurate, then both insiders and outsiders may get wrong impressions and may base decisions on incorrect information.

Obligations of the Culture Analyst

If the foregoing risks are real, then who should worry about them? Is it enough to say to an organization that we will study your culture and let you know what we find and that nothing will be published without your permission? If we are dealing with surface manifestations, artifacts, and publicly espoused values, then the guideline of letting members clear the material seems sufficient. If we are dealing with the deeper levels of the culture, the assumptions and the patterns among them, however, then the insiders clearly may not know what they are getting into and the obligation shifts to the outsider as a professional, in the same way that it would be the psychiatrist's or counselor's job to make the client genuinely aware of what the consequences are of proceeding in an investigation of personality or character. The principle of informed consent does not sufficiently protect the client or research subject if he or she cannot initially appreciate what will be revealed.

The analyst of a culture undertakes a professional obligation to understand fully what the potential consequences of an investigation are. Such consequences should be carefully spelled out before the relationship reaches a level where there is an implied psychological contract that the outsider will give feedback to the insiders on what has been discovered about the culture, either for inside purposes of gaining insight or for clearing what may eventually be published.

Examples to Illustrate Ethical Issues

Thus far I have identified risks and indicated who must be responsible for assessing those risks. But do we have any evidence on potential costs, on what might actually happen if we investigate organizational cultures, give feedback, and/or publish results? We know what can happen in the individual realm, and we have plenty of experience from action research projects undertaken under the broad label of "organizational development" of the effects of giving back to a system data about itself, but we have relatively limited experience in the culture realm. The following examples, drawn from my own experiences, illustrate some of the potential costs involved.

Case 1. Projecting Incorrect Assumptions

A clear example of projecting wrong assumptions occurred at a meeting of managers of a company that prided itself on taking into account the feelings and preferences of its personnel and their families. A group of senior managers were discussing succession in several key jobs, including the job of president. At one point in the discussion, a person was nominated to become head of the international division—a job that could lead eventually to the position of executive vice president and ultimately president.

The personnel vice president and one other group member had talked to this individual and reported that he did not want to move to the overseas headquarters because of the critical age of his children. At this point the president entered the discussion and said, "Let me talk to him. Maybe I can explain the situation to him more clearly." My own reaction at this moment was one of dismay because this apparent attempt at persuasion seemed to me a clear violation of the company's principle that personal feelings should weigh heavily in such decisions. Others in the group felt the same way and challenged the wisdom of the president's intervening on the grounds that it would put too much pressure on the individual. We were all perceiving that the president was operating from the assumption that this candidate was corporate property and that it would be legitimate to persuade him to do his duty for the corporation. This assumption would clearly be in violation of the espoused assumption that family issues are taken seriously in the company.

The president then explained his logic, and it was at this point that a deeper assumption emerged. The president said: "I understand that we should not pressure him to take the job if he does not want it and if he understands fully what he is giving up. I want to explain to him that we consider the international VP job a crucial stepping stone, that we consider him the logical candidate to move up the ladder, and that we will be forced to move him off the ladder if he does not take this job. We don't have time to develop him in an alternate fashion, and he may not realize the consequences of rejecting the offer. But if he understands what he would be giving up and still feels that he should reject it, we will respect that decision and look for another candidate."

The deeper assumption, then, was that a key executive must be given full organizational information and allowed to make a choice. If the person knew that he was in line for the presidency, he might want to reassess the family priorities and consider other options — he could move, he could commute, he could leave his family behind, he could leave the children in their school but have them live with someone else, and so on. The implied assumption was that the individual is the only one who can ultimately make the choice. Had the group simply moved this person off the ladder, it would have made the choice for him. Once we dug into the issue in this way, it became clear to everyone that the deeper assumption was the one they really lived by and it would have been a mistake to jump to the conclusion that "explanation" would automatically be inappropriate "pressure." Everyone acknowledged that it would certainly put pressure on the individual, but that was less damaging to the total culture than not to give people a choice.

Case 2. Providing Unwelcome Cultural Data in Multi

In the change project I will describe in Chapter Seventeen, I was asked to present my analysis of the Multi Company's culture to its top management. From my point of view I had clear data and I attempted to be objective and neutral in my analysis. At one point, however, I likened certain aspects of Multi's culture to a military model. Several members of the executive committee who were themselves former military men and who loved the army took offense at what they viewed as a derogatory depiction of the army (though I believed I had been neutral in my statements). Their perception that I misunderstood and had challenged one of their values led to an unproductive argument about the validity of the cultural description and to some degree discredited me as a consultant in their eyes. Ever since this event, I have felt that my relationship with these individuals is strained and that they did not want to use me as a consultant from that point on.

There are several possible lessons here. The most obvious one is that the outsider should never lecture insiders on their own culture because one cannot know where the sensitivities will lie and one cannot overcome one's own subtle biases. Perhaps if I had stated each of my points carefully as hypotheses or questions for them to react to, I might have avoided this trap.

Second, I learned that my analysis plunged the group members into an internal debate that they were not prepared for and that had multiple unanticipated consequences. The people who objected to my analogy revealed some of their own biases at the meeting in ways they might not have intended, and comments made later suggested that some people were shocked because so-and-so had revealed himself to be a such-and-such kind of person.

The analogy itself, likening aspects of the organization's functioning to the military, unleashed feelings that had more to do with the larger culture in which the organization operated and introduced a whole set of irrelevant feelings and issues. Many people in the group were made very uncomfortable by the insight that they were indeed operating like the military because they had either forgotten this aspect or had illusions about it. My comments stripped away those illusions.

Third, and perhaps this is the most important lesson, I learned that giving feedback to an individual is different from giving feedback to a group because the group very likely is not homogeneous in its reactions. My "lecture" on the culture was well received by some members of the group, who went out of their way to assure me that my depiction was totally accurate. Obviously, this segment of the group was not threatened by what I had to say. But with others I lost credibility, and with still others I created enough threat to unleash defensiveness, plunging the group into an uncomfortable new agenda that then had to be managed.

Case 3. Creating External Vulnerability

Whereas the preceding example focuses on internal consequences, this example focuses on external ones. I was teaching in a management school as a visiting faculty member and accidentally discovered that a case a colleague was using in his course dealt with the Action Company. I read the case and found that it created a totally wrong impression of the company along several important cultural dimensions, but no one was aware of this or, for that matter, cared. Unfortunately, the areas where wrong impressions were created made the company seem an unattractive place to work, and the students who were using the case were potential recruits to that company. I did some informal checking among students and found that their attitudes were indeed subtly influenced and that several had sentiments along the line of "I would never work at a place like that." Such a reaction is perfectly reasonable if the data on which it is based are accurate. But the data were not accurate, the faculty member using the case did not know that they were not accurate, and the company did not know that the case was being used.

The only way to prevent undesirable consequences in this case would have been to disguise the company name and data sufficiently to make it impossible for students to get impressions of an actual company from the case.

Case 4. Getting Permission to Publish Research

A student with whom I am acquainted interviewed a large number of managers and observed the behavior of a subgroup in a company for nine months in order to decipher and describe its culture. The study was carefully done, and in the final write-up the organization was fairly well disguised. Insiders in the group studied pronounced the description accurate but asked, "Couldn't you say it in a way that would not make us look so bad?" It should be noted that the evaluation of looking bad was entirely, as in Case Two, the reaction of only some insiders. The write-up attempted to report objectively without evaluating.

One of the managers who did not like the report discovered, long after the project had been launched with complete insider approval, that a company policy formulated within the preceding year prohibited the publication of case studies about the company — probably for reasons of avoiding inaccurate impressions, along the lines of the events of Case Three. Several insiders who felt that they had an obligation to the student fought to have the description released; but several other insiders were sufficiently nervous about the description, even though it was completely disguised, that it took several months and many rewrites before they felt relatively comfortable about the paper.

When the insiders initially approved this project, they did not know what the cultural description would actually look like; they had no way of assessing whether they should approve it. Since they did not have a particular need to gain insight into their own culture at this point in their history, the actual confrontation with the data was for some members of the company uncomfortable. Truths were spelled out that were better left implicit or buried; and the fact that outsiders probably would not recognize the company was small comfort because everyone knew that other insiders would immediately recognize it. The availability of the description in written form became a de facto intervention in this company's functioning because it articulated many thoughts, values, and assumptions in ways that they had never been articulated before, and the company had not contracted for anything other than giving a student permission to interview and observe. Whether, on balance, the intervention will prove to be helpful or harmful remains to be seen. What is clear, however, is that a good description of the culture, made available in written form, is an intervention even before it is externally published.

Some Implications

Several implications suggest themselves. First of all, since organizations have high visibility in society today, a description of an organization's culture makes public the deeper underlying aspects of that organization at a time when it is still very much part of the scene. We should not do this lightly, and we should have a clear picture of what our motivation is when we do it. Organizational research of any sort is an intervention, and the ethics of research should first of all be the ethics of intervention. We should be guided by the values of the clinician and recognize that organizational research, particularly on such a sensitive issue as organizational culture, requires a clear understanding between the client and the researcher that satisfies ethical principles of intervention, such as protection of the client's welfare (Schein, 1980, 1987b, 1991).

The researcher/interventionist should know as much as

possible about the potential consequences of the project and ensure that those consequences are communicated to the client. Where the consequences are better understood by the researcher than the client, the researcher should make a highly responsible decision not to engage in projects that could be harmful to the client.

What if we want to analyze a culture in order to reveal some of its *undesirable* consequences? Here the principle of fully disguising the organization seems to solve the problem. But suppose we want a given organization to be embarrassed or want to show up some malevolent aspects of an organization to which we are opposed? Here the analogy would be to the psychiatrist who wants to publish a character analysis of a person considered evil or reveal to the authorities some criminal intent on the part of a patient. Under what conditions can we name the company and describe the undesirable consequences of its culture? For scientists/interventionists the answer would probably be never unless clear illegal actions flowed from some of the cultural assumptions. Nevertheless, we know that we develop passions and sometimes act as political animals. In such instances we should at least not hide our political activities under the umbrella of science. In fact, we would have to be very careful not to let our initial feelings about "good" or "bad" aspects of a given organizational culture destroy our objectivity in analyzing that culture. In the current fad of trying to figure out why some Japanese companies are seemingly outproducing their American counterparts, I get the feeling that I am reading more about evaluations of their organizational cultures than I am about the facts of those cultures.

To give but one example, the debate about the supposed benefits of Ouchi's (1981) Theory Z type of company has completely obscured the fact that the current descriptions of the culture of a Theory Z clan type of organization have not gone beyond the artifactual and value levels. We know that such companies have lifetime employment and that they care about people, but we do not know, in the company examples cited, the underlying assumptions on which the policies, practices, and values are built. Should this make us nervous? Yes, because one can build lifetime employment on the assumption that employees are "owned" by the company, to be done with whatever the company pleases to do with them — an assumption that was not uncommon in strongly paternalistic companies in the early part of this century. The consequence sometimes was that employees became, in effect, prisoners because leaving meant disloyalty and would lead to their being blackballed from the company forever (or even blacklisted so that others in the industry might not hire them). The very thing we are praising at artifact and value levels might turn out to be something we would condemn if we understood the assumptions behind it.

This issue comes up repeatedly when we talk about strong cultures that use culture as a device to control employees. If one can teach everyone the same values and assumptions, then everyone automatically will behave appropriately from that organization's point of view. It then becomes very difficult to assess what is good or bad, what is appropriate or not. I do not have any answers to these dilemmas, but it is important to raise them as we move more deeply into cultural analyses of various sorts.

One thing can be concluded. To evaluate an organization, it is important to spell out the underlying assumptions accurately and not to settle for surface manifestations that could reflect very different assumption sets. And if one is against certain practices, one must be careful not to attribute to the organization assumptions that fit one's biases but may be completely wrong. Analyses of secondary data about organizations are therefore probably useless as anything but cultural artifacts. Yet one frequently sees evaluations of organizations based on what journalists or casual observers attribute to the particular organization. Careful deciphering that involves both insiders and outsiders would seem to be a bare-bones minimum to avoid such premature evaluation.

Summary and Conclusions

Deciphering a culture for purposes of an insider or for purposes of describing that culture to outsiders each has a set of associated risks and potential costs. These risks are internal in the sense that the members of the organization may not want to know or be able to handle the insights into their own culture, and they are external in that the members of the organization may not be aware of the manner in which they become vulnerable once information about their culture is made available to others. In either case, there is the danger that the interpretation is incorrect or so superficial that the deeper layers remain unknown.

In our effort to define a culture, we may discover that no single set of assumptions has formed as a deep-down paradigm for operating or that the subgroups of an organization have different paradigms, which may or may not conflict with each other. Furthermore, culture is perpetually evolving; the cultural researcher must be willing to do perpetual searching and revising. To present "data" about that organization to either an insider or an outsider is inherently risky.

Even if we begin to have an intuitive understanding of an organization's culture, we may find it extraordinarily difficult to write down that understanding in such a way that the essence of the culture can be communicated to someone else. We have so few examples in our literature that it is even hard to point to models of how it should be done. But when we see the essence of a culture, the paradigm by which people operate, we are struck by how powerful our insight into that organization now is, and we can see instantly why certain things work the way they do, why certain proposals are never bought, why change is so difficult, why certain people leave, and so on. Few concepts are so powerful in the degree to which they help us decipher what may be a very opaque area. It is the search for and the occasional finding of this central insight that make it all worthwhile. Suddenly we understand an organization; suddenly we see what makes it tick. That level of insight is worth working for, even if in the end we can share it only with colleagues.

The implication for leaders is "Be careful." Cultural analysis can be very helpful if the leader knows what she or he is doing and why. By that I mean that there must be some valid purpose to a cultural analysis. If it is done for its own sake, the risks of either wasting time or doing harm increase. However, the potential for insight and constructive action is tremendous if the leader works with a responsible outsider to analyze and decipher culture in the service of legitimate organizational ends.

PART FOUR

The Role of Leadership
in Building Culture

Parts Two and Three examined the content of culture and the process of deciphering cultural assumptions. The primary focus was on culture. The focus now shifts to leadership, especially the role that leadership plays in creating and embedding culture in a group. As I have argued throughout, the unique function of leadership that distinguishes it from management and administration is this concern for culture. Leaders create culture and, as we will see in Part Five, must manage and sometimes change culture.

　　To understand fully the relationship of leadership to culture we also have to take a developmental view of organizational growth. The role of leadership in the formation of an organization is covered in Chapter Eleven. Chapter Twelve describes how leaders of a young and successful organization can systematically embed their own assumptions in the daily workings of the organization, thereby creating a stable culture. In Chapter Thirteen the growth and evolution of the organization into subunits is described, and the growth of subcultures is noted. An example of a particular kind of subculture, the shared assumptions of the information technology occupational community, is described and its relationship to some of the assumptions of the subculture of top management is examined in Chapter Fourteen.

These chapters are especially relevant for leaders because they describe in detail what kind of leadership behavior causes cultural assumptions to develop, evolve, and ultimately change.

CHAPTER ELEVEN

How Leaders Create Organizational Cultures

One of the most mysterious aspects of organizational culture is how it originates. How do two companies with similar external environments and founders of similar origins come to have entirely different ways of operating over the years? Equally mysterious are the evolution of culture and the degree to which culture at times seems to resist change. Why do some cultural elements survive even though they seem to serve no useful purpose, and why do they sometimes survive in the face of intense efforts by leaders and/or group members to change them?

Culture Beginnings and the Impact of Founders as Leaders

Cultures basically spring from three sources; (1) the beliefs, values, and assumptions of founders of organizations; (2) the learning experiences of group members as their organization evolves; and (3) new beliefs, values, and assumptions brought in by new members and leaders.

Though each of these mechanisms plays a crucial role, by far the most important for cultural beginnings is the impact of founders. Founders not only choose the basic mission and the environmental context in which the new group will operate, but they choose the group members and bias the original responses that the group makes in its efforts to succeed in its environment and to integrate itself. Organizations do not form accidentally or spontaneously. Instead, they are goal oriented, have a specific purpose, and are created because one or more individuals perceive that the coordinated and concerted action of a number of people can accomplish something that individual action cannot. Social movements or new religions begin with prophets, messiahs, or other kinds of charismatic leaders. Political groups are initiated by leaders who sell new visions and new solutions to problems. Firms are created by entrepreneurs who have a vision of how the concerted effort of the right group of people can create a new good or service in the marketplace.

The process of culture formation is, in each case, first a process of creating a small group. In the business organization, this process will usually involve some version of the following steps:

1. A single person (founder) has an idea for a new enterprise.
2. The founder brings in one or more other people and creates a core group that shares a common goal and vision with the founder. That is, they all believe that the idea is a good one, is workable, is worth running some risks for, and is worth the investment of time, money, and energy that will be required.
3. The founding group begins to act in concert to create an organization by raising funds, obtaining patents, incorporating, locating work space, and so on.
4. Others are brought into the organization, and a common history begins to be built. If the group remains fairly stable and has significant shared learning experiences, it will gradually develop assumptions about itself, its environment, and how to do things to survive and grow.

Founders usually have a major impact on how the group initially defines and solves its external adaptation and internal integration problems. Because they had the original idea, they will typically have their own notion, based on their own cultural history and personality, of how to fulfill the idea. Founders not only have a high level of self-confidence and determination, but they typically have strong assumptions about the nature of the world, the role that organizations play in that world, the nature of human nature and relationships, how truth is arrived at, and how to manage time and space (Schein, 1978, 1983). They will, therefore, be quite comfortable in imposing those views on their partners and employees as the fledgling organization copes, and they will cling to them until such time as they become unworkable or the group fails and breaks up (Donaldson and Lorsch, 1983).

The Jones Food Company

Founder Jones was an immigrant whose parents had started a corner grocery store in a large urban area. His parents, particularly his mother, taught him some basic attitudes toward customers and helped him form the vision that he could succeed in building a successful enterprise. He assumed from the beginning that if he did things right, he would succeed and could build a major organization that would bring him and his family a fortune. Ultimately, he built a large chain of supermarkets, department stores, and related businesses that became for many decades the dominant force in its market area.

Jones was the major ideological force in his company throughout its history and continued to impose his assumptions on the company until his death in his late seventies. He assumed that his primary mission was to supply a high-quality, reliable product to customers in clean, attractive surroundings and that his customers' needs were the primary consideration in all major decisions. There are many stories about how Jones, as a young man operating the corner grocery store with his wife, gave customers credit and thus displayed trust in them. He always took products back if there was the slightest complaint, and he kept his store absolutely spotless to inspire customer confidence in his products. Each of these attitudes later became a major policy in his chain of stores and was taught and reinforced by close personal supervision.

Jones believed that only personal examples and close supervision would ensure adequate performance by subordinates. He would show up at his stores unexpectedly, inspect even minor details, and then — by personal example, by stories of how other stores were solving the problems identified, by articulating rules, and by exhortation — would "teach" the staff what they should be doing. He often lost his temper and berated subordinates who did not follow the rules or principles laid down.

Jones expected his store managers to be highly visible, to be very much on top of their own jobs, and to supervise closely in the same way he did, reflecting deep assumptions about the nature of good management. These assumptions became a major theme in later years in his concept of "visible management," the assumption that a good manager always has to be around to set a good example and to teach subordinates the right way to do things.

Most of the founding group in this company consisted of Jones's three brothers, but one "lieutenant" who was not a family member was recruited early and became, in addition to the founder, the main culture creator and carrier. He shared the founder's basic assumptions about how to run a business and set up formal systems to ensure that those assumptions became the basis for operating realities. After Jones's death this man continued to articulate the theory of visible management and tried to set a personal example of how to perpetuate this by continuing the same close supervision policies that Jones had used.

Jones assumed that one could win in the marketplace only by being highly innovative and technically in the forefront. He always encouraged his managers to try new approaches, brought in a variety of consultants who advocated new approaches to human resource management, started selection and development programs through assessment centers long before other companies tried this approach, and traveled to conventions and other businesses where new technological innovations were displayed with the result that his company was one of the first to introduce the bar code technology and one of the first to use assessment centers in selecting store managers. He was always willing to experiment in order to improve the business. Jones's view of truth and reality was that one has to find them wherever one can; therefore, one must be open to one's environment and never take it for granted that one has all the answers.

If things worked, Jones encouraged their adoption; if they did not, he ordered them to be dropped. Measuring results and solving problems were, for Jones, intensely personal matters, deriving from his theory of visible management. In addition to using a variety of traditional business measures, he always made it a point to visit all his stores personally; if he saw things not to his liking, he corrected them immediately and decisively even if that meant going around his own authority chain. He trusted only those managers who operated by assumptions similar to his own and clearly had favorites to whom he delegated more authority.

Power and authority in this organization remained very centralized in that everyone knew that Jones or his chief lieutenant could and would override decisions made by division or other unit managers without consultation and often in a very peremptory fashion. The ultimate source of power, the voting shares of stock, were owned entirely by Jones and his wife, so that after his death his wife was in total control of the company.

Jones was interested in developing good managers throughout the organization, but he never assumed that sharing ownership through granting stock options would contribute to that process. He paid his key managers very well, but his assumption was that ownership was strictly a family matter, to the point that he was not even willing to share stock with his chief lieutenant, close friend, and virtual cobuilder of the company.

Jones introduced several members of his own family into the firm and gave them key managerial positions and favored treatment in the form of good developmental jobs that would test them early for ultimate management potential. As the firm diversified, family members were made heads of divisions, often with relatively little management experience. If a family member performed poorly, he would be bolstered by having a good manager introduced under him. If the operation then improved, the family member would likely be given the credit. If things continued badly, he would be moved out, but with various face-saving excuses.

My introduction to the company occurred around this issue. Jones had only daughters and had moved the husband of his oldest daughter into the presidency of his company. This man was very congenial but not trained for his general management position, so Jones authorized the creation of a management development program for the top twenty-five people in the organization, with the hidden agenda of teaching his son-in-law something about management. I was brought in as a consultant and trainer as part of this management development program by Jones's chief lieutenant and was told at the outset that part of the goal was to educate the son-in-law.

Peer relationships among nonfamily members inevitably became highly politicized. They were officially defined as competitive, and Jones believed firmly in the value of interpersonal competition. Winners would be rewarded and losers discarded. However, since family members were in positions of power, one had to know how to stay on the good side of those family members without losing the trust of one's peers, on whom one was dependent.

Jones wanted open communication and a high level of trust among all members of the organization, but his own assumptions about the role of the family and the correct way to manage were, to a large degree, in conflict with each other. Therefore, many members of the organization banded together in a kind of mutual protection society that developed a culture of its own. They were more loyal to each other than to the company and had a high rate of interaction with each other, which bred assumptions and norms that became to some degree countercultural to the founder's.

Several points should be noted about the description given thus far. By definition, something can become part of the culture only if it works in the sense of making the organization successful and reducing the anxiety of the members, including Jones. Jones's assumptions about how things should be done were congruent with the kind of environment in which he operated, so he and the founding group received strong reinforcement for those assumptions. As the company grew and prospered, Jones felt more and more confirmation of his assumptions and thus more and more confidence that they were correct. Throughout his lifetime he steadfastly adhered to those assumptions and did everything in his power to get others to accept them. However, as already noted, some of those assumptions made nonfamily managers anxious and led to the formation of a counterculture.

Jones also learned that he had to share some concepts and assumptions with a great many other people. As a result, as his company grew and learned from its own experience, he gradually had to modify his assumptions in some areas or withdraw from those areas as an active manager. For example, in its diversification efforts, the company bought several production units that would enable it to integrate vertically in certain food and clothing areas where that was economically advantageous. But because Jones learned that he knew relatively little about production, he brought in strong managers and gave them a great deal of autonomy in those areas. Some of those production divisions never acquired the culture of the main organization, and the heads of those divisions never enjoyed the status and security that insiders had.

Jones eventually also had to learn somewhat painfully that he did not send as clear and consistent signals as he thought he did. He did not perceive his own conflicts and inconsistencies and hence could not understand why some of his best young managers failed to respond to his competitive incentives and even left the company. He thought he was adequately motivating them and could not see that for some of them the political climate, the absence of stock options, and the arbitrary rewarding of family members made their own career progress too uncertain. Jones was perplexed and angry about much of this, blaming the young managers while holding onto his own assumptions and conflicts.

Following Jones's death the company experienced a long period of cultural turmoil because of the vacuum created by his absence and the retirement of several other key culture carriers, but the basic philosophy of how to run stores was thoroughly embedded and remained. Various family members continued to run the company, though none of them had the business skills that Jones had. With the retirement of Jones's chief lieutenant, a period of instability set in; it was marked by the discovery that some of the managers who had been developed under Jones were not as strong and capable as had been assumed. Because none of Jones's children or their spouses were able to take over the business decisively, an outside person was brought in to run the company. This person predictably failed because he could not adapt to the culture and to the family.

After two more failures with CEOs drawn from other companies, the family turned to a manager who had originally been with the company and had subsequently made a fortune outside the company in various real estate enterprises. This manager stabilized the business because he had more credibility by virtue of his prior history and his knowledge of how to handle family members. Under his leadership some of the original assumptions began to evolve in new directions. Eventually, the family decided to sell the Jones company, and this manager and one of Jones's cousins started a company of their own, which ended up competing with the Jones company.

One clear lesson from this example is that a culture does not survive if the main culture carriers depart and if the bulk of the members of the organization are experiencing some degree of conflict because of a mixed message that emanates from the leaders during the growth period. The Jones Food Company had a strong culture, but Jones's own conflicts became embedded in that culture, creating conflict and ultimately lack of stability.

Smithfield Enterprises

Smithfield built a chain of financial service organizations, using sophisticated financial analysis techniques in an area of the country where insurance companies, mutual funds, and banks were only beginning to use such techniques. He was the conceptualizer and salesman, but once he had the idea for a new kind of service organization, he got others to invest in, build, and manage it.

Smithfield believed that he should put only a very small amount of his own money into each enterprise because if he could not convince others to put up money, may be there was something wrong with the idea. He made the initial assumption that he did not know enough about the market to gamble with his own money, and he reinforced this assumption publicly by telling a story about the one enterprise in which he failed. He had opened a retail store in a midwestern city to sell ocean fish because he loved it, assumed others felt as he did, trusted his own judgment about what the marketplace would want, and failed. Had he tried to get many others to invest in the enterprise, he would have learned that his own tastes were not necessarily a good predictor of what others would want.

Because Smithfield saw himself as a creative conceptualizer but not as a manager, he not only kept his financial investment minimal but also did not get very personally involved with his enterprises. Once he put together the package, he found people whom he could trust to manage the new organization. These were usually people like himself who were fairly open in their approach to business and not too concerned with imposing their own assumptions about how things should be done.

One can infer that Smithfield's assumptions about concrete goals, the best means to achieve them, how to measure results, and how to repair things when they were going wrong were essentially pragmatic. Whereas Jones had a strong need to be involved in everything, Smithfield seemed to lose interest once the new organization was on its feet and functioning. His theory seemed to be to have a clear concept of the basic mission, test it by selling it to investors, bring in good people who understand what the mission is, and then leave them alone to implement and run the organization, using only financial criteria as ultimate performance measures.

If Smithfield had assumptions about how an organization should be run internally, he kept them to himself. The cultures that each of his enterprises developed therefore had more to do with the assumptions of the people he brought in to manage them. As it turned out, those assumptions varied a good deal. And if one analyzed Smithfield Enterprises as a total organization, one would find little evidence of a corporate culture because there was no group that had a shared history and shared learning experiences.

This brief case illustrates that there is nothing automatic about founder leaders imposing themselves on their organizations. It depends on their personal needs to externalize their various assumptions. For Smithfield the ultimate personal validation lay in having each of his enterprises become financially successful and in his ability to continue to form creative new ones. His creative needs were such that after a decade or so of founding financial service organizations, he turned his attention to real estate ventures, then became a lobbyist on behalf of an environmental organization, tried his hand at politics for a while, then went back into business, first with an oil company and later with diamond mining company. Eventually, he became interested in teaching, ending up in a midwestern business school developing a curriculum on entrepreneurship.

The Action Company

Action's founder, Murphy, is a very dominant, strong personality who began with a clear theory of how things should be. He and four others founded the company because they believed they could build a particular new high-tech product for which there would eventually be a very large market. They were able to convince investors because of their own credibility and the unanimity of their basic vision of the company's core mission. However, after some years they found that they did not share a vision of how to build an organization, and all except Murphy left the organization.

Murphy's assumptions about the nature of the world and how one discovers truth and solves problems were very strong at this stage of Action's growth and were reflected in his management style. He believed that good ideas can come from anyone, regardless of rank or background, but that neither he nor any other individual is smart enough to determine whether a given idea is correct. Murphy felt that open discussion in a group is the only way to test ideas and that one should not take action until the idea has survived the crucible of an active debate. One may have intuitions, but one should not act on them until they have been tested in the intellectual marketplace. Hence, Murphy set up a number of committees and groups and insisted that all ideas be discussed and debated before they were acted on.

Murphy bolstered his assumptions with a story that he told frequently to justify his thrusting issues onto groups. He said that he would often *not make a decision* because, "I'm not that smart; if I really knew what to do I would say so. But when I get into a group of smart people and listen to them discuss the idea, I get smart very fast." For Murphy, groups were a kind of extension of his own intelligence and he often used them to think out loud and get his own ideas straight in his head.

Murphy also believed that one cannot get good implementation of ideas if people do not fully support them and that the best way to get support is to let people debate the issue and convince themselves. Therefore, on any important decision, Murphy insisted on a wide debate, with many group meetings to test the idea and sell it down the organization and laterally. Only when it appeared that everyone wanted to do it and fully understood it would he "ratify" it. He even delayed important decisions if others were not on board, though he was personally already convinced of the course of action to take. He said that he did not want to be out there leading all by himself and run the risk that the troops were not committed and might disown the decision if it did not work out. Past experiences of this kind had taught him to ensure commitment before going ahead on anything even if the consensus-building procedure was time consuming and frustrating.

While Murphy's assumptions about decision making and implementation led to a very group-oriented organization, his theory about how to organize and manage work led to a strong individuation process, which reinforced his assumption that individuals are ultimately the source of creativity. His theory was that one must give clear and simple individual responsibility and then measure the person strictly on that area of responsibility. Groups can help to make decisions and obtain commitment, but they cannot under any circumstances be responsible or accountable.

Murphy believed completely in a proactive model of human nature and in people's capacity to master nature, a set of assumptions that appear to correlate closely with his own engineering background. Hence, he always expected people to be on top of their jobs and was very critical of them, both in public and in private, if he felt that they were not completely in control. Recognizing that circumstances might change the outcome of even the best laid plans, Murphy expected his managers to renegotiate those plans as soon as they observed a deviation. Thus, for example, if an annual budget had been set at a certain level and the responsible manager noticed after six months that he would overrun it, he was expected to get the situation under control according to the original assumptions or to come back to Murphy and senior management to renegotiate. It was absolutely unacceptable either not to know what was happening or to let it happen without informing senior management and renegotiating.

Murphy believed completely in open communications and the ability of people to reach reasonable decisions and make appropriate compromises if they openly confront the problems and issues, figure out what they want to do, and are willing to argue for their solution and honor any commitments they make. He assumed that people have "constructive intent," a rational loyalty to organizational goals and shared commitments. Withholding information, playing power games, competitively trying to win out over another member of the organization on a personal level, blaming others for one's failures, undermining or sabotaging decisions one has agreed to, and going off on one's own without getting other's agreement were all defined as sins and brought public censure.

As previously noted, even today the architecture and office layout of Action reflect Murphy's assumptions about creativity and decision making. He insisted on open-office landscaping, preferred cubicles instead of offices with doors for engineers, encouraged individualism in dress and behavior, and minimized the use of status symbols, such as private offices, special dining rooms for executives, and personal parking spaces. Instead, there were many conference rooms and attached kitchens to encourage people to interact comfortably.

This "model" of how to run an organization to maximize individual creativity and decision quality worked very successfully in that the company experienced dramatic growth and had exceptionally high morale. However, as the company grew larger, people found that they had less time to negotiate with each other and did not know each other as well personally, making these processes more frustrating. Some of the paradoxes and inconsistencies among the various assumptions came to the surface. For example, to encourage individuals to think for themselves and do what they believed to be the best course of action, even if it meant insubordination, clearly ran counter to the dictum that one must honor one's commitments and support decisions that have been made. In practice the rule of honoring commitments was superseded by the rule of doing only what one believes is right, which meant that sometimes decisions would not stick.

Action had increasing difficulty in imposing any kind of discipline on its organizational processes. If a given manager decided that for organizational reasons a more disciplined autocratic approach was necessary, he ran the risk of Murphy's displeasure because freedom was being taken away from subordinates and that would undermine their entrepreneurial spirit. Murphy felt he was giving his immediate subordinates great freedom, so why would they take it away from the levels below them? At the same time, Murphy recognized that at certain levels of the organization, discipline was essential to get anything done; the difficulty was in deciding just which areas required discipline and which areas required freedom.

When the company was small and everyone knew everyone else, there was always time to renegotiate, and basic consensus and trust were high enough to ensure that if time pressure forced people to make their own decisions and to be insubordinate, others would, after the fact, mostly agree with the decisions that had been made locally. In other words, if initial decisions made at higher levels did not stick, this did not bother anyone until the organization became larger and more complex. What was initially a highly adaptive system began to be regarded by more and more members of the organization as disorganization and chaos. Murphy believed that those processes that could be simplified

should be routinized and high discipline imposed in enforcing
them, but as the company became more complex it became more
difficult to agree on which processes could and should be simplified and subjected to arbitrary discipline.

Murphy also believed in the necessity of organization and
hierarchy, but he did not trust the authority of position nearly
as much as the authority of reason. Hence, managers were
granted authority de facto only to the extent that they could sell
their decisions, and as indicated above, insubordination was not
only tolerated but positively rewarded if it made sense and led
to better outcomes. Managers often complained that they could
not control any of the things for which they were responsible;
yet at the same time, they believed in the system and shared
Murphy's assumptions because of the kinds of people they were,
the degree to which they had been socialized into the system,
and the obvious success of this way of managing in building
a company.

Murphy also believed that the intellectual testing of ideas,
which he encouraged among individuals in group settings, can
be profitably extended to organizational units if it is not clear
what products or markets should be pursued. He was willing
to create overlapping product/market units and to let them compete with each other, not realizing, however, that such internal
competition undermined openness of communication and made
it more difficult for groups to negotiate decisions. Yet this way
of doing things had enough success in the marketplace that Action managers came to believe in it as a way of operating in
a rapidly shifting market environment.

The company thrived on intelligent, assertive, individualistic people who were willing and able to argue for and sell
their ideas. The hiring practices of the company reflected this
bias clearly in that each new applicant had to undergo a large
number of interviews and be convincing in each one of them
to be viewed as a positive candidate. So over the course of its
first decade, the organization tended to hire and keep only those
kinds of people who fitted the assumptions and were willing to
live in the system even though it might at times be frustrating.
The people who were comfortable in this environment and en-

joyed the excitement of building a successful organization found themselves increasingly feeling like members of a family and were emotionally treated as such. Strong bonds of mutual support grew up at an interpersonal level, and Murphy functioned symbolically as a brilliant, demanding, but supportive and charismatic father figure. These familial feelings were implicit but important because they provided subordinates with a feeling of security that made it possible for them to challenge each other's ideas. When a proposed course of action did not make sense, the proposer might be severely challenged and even accused of having dumb ideas, but he could not lose his membership in the family. Frustration and insecurity grew, however, as the size of the company made it more difficult to maintain the level of personal acquaintance that would make familial feelings possible.

Murphy represents an entrepreneur with a clear set of assumptions about how things should be, both at the level of how to relate externally to the environment and how to arrange things internally in the organization. His willingness to be open about his theory and his rewarding and punishing behavior in support of it led both to the selection of others who shared the theory and to strong socialization practices that reinforced and perpetuated it. Consequently, the founder's assumptions are reflected in how the organization operates today. However, as noted above, Action also illustrates how a set of assumptions that works under one set of circumstances may become dysfunctional under other sets of circumstances. The growing frustration that resulted from trying to maintain such assumptions on a large scale in a more competitive environment has led to a number of efforts to reassess the organizational model and to figure out how to continue to be adaptive with the kind of culture that Action has developed.

Murphy's role in this process has been to reassert his basic beliefs in giving people freedom to propose and sell ideas, and, once approved, to hold them accountable. He has steadfastly resisted formulating centralized top-down strategies, even though the organization has increasingly needed them to maintain coordination among the many business units it now has. He clearly believes that entrepreneurial behavior at lower levels is the key to success and that strategy comes out of the integration of these entrepreneurial efforts throughout the organization. One of the things that frustrates him most is that he sees managers to whom he has given the freedom to propose and be accountable taking that freedom away from their own subordinates. However, according to his own logic, he cannot simply fire them but must rely instead on persuasion and the clear articulation of his philosophy in the hope that they will learn from their own experience that giving freedom works better.

Summary and Conclusions

The three cases presented in this chapter illustrate how organizations begin to create cultures through the actions of founders who operate as strong leaders. It is important to recognize that even in mature companies one can trace many of their assumptions to the beliefs and values of founders and early leaders. The special role that these leaders play is to propose the initial answers to the questions that the young group has about how to operate internally and externally. The group cannot test potential solutions if nothing is proposed. Once a leader has activated the group, it can determine whether its actions solve the problems of working effectively in its environment and create a stable internal system. Other solutions can then be proposed by strong group members, and the cultural learning process becomes broadened. Nevertheless, we cannot overlook the tremendous importance of leadership at the very beginning of any group process.

I am not suggesting that leaders consciously set out to teach their new group certain ways of perceiving, thinking, and feeling. Rather, it is in the nature of entrepeneurial thinking to have strong ideas about what to do and how to do it. Founders of groups tend to have well-articulated theories of their own about how groups should work, and they tend to select as colleagues and subordinates others who they sense think like them. Both founders and the new group members will be anxious in the process of group formation and will look for solutions. The leader's proposal, therefore, will always receive special attention in this phase of group formation.

Early group life also will tend toward intolerance of ambiguity and dissent. In the early life of any new organization one can see many examples of how partners or cofounders who do not think alike end up in conflicts that result in some people leaving, thus creating a more homogeneous climate for those who remain. If the original founders do not have proposals to solve the problems that make the group anxious, other strong members will step in and leaders other than the founders will emerge. I did not observe this in the three cases reviewed in this chapter, but I have seen it happen in many other organizations. The important point to recognize is that the anxiety of group formation is typically so high and covers so many areas of group functioning that leadership is highly sought by group members. If the founder does not succeed in reducing the group's anxiety, other leaders will be empowered by the group.

Because founder leaders tend to have strong theories of how to do things, their theories get tested early. If their assumptions are wrong, the group fails early in its history. If their assumptions are correct, they create a powerful organization whose culture comes to reflect their original assumptions. If the environment changes and those assumptions come to be incorrect, the organization must find a way to change its culture, a process that is exceptionally difficult if the founder is still in control of the organization. Such change is difficult particularly because over time founder leaders have multiple opportunities to embed their assumptions in the various routines of the organization. How this process occurs is detailed in Chapter Twelve.

How Founders and Leaders Embed and Transmit Culture

Socialization from a Leadership Perspective

In Chapter Eleven we saw how leaders in their role as founders of organizations initially start the culture formation process by imposing their own assumptions on a new group. In this chapter I want to explore this process further by detailing the many mechanisms that become involved as leader assumptions are "taught" to the group. I deliberately put the emphasis on teaching instead of learning because cultural analysis has too often viewed culture acquisition from the passive learning point of view. It is true that the group learns from its external experience in terms of how things work out. However, the things that the group tries out are the result of leader-imposed teaching, and it is important to understand in detail how this teaching occurs.

How do founders and other powerful figures in an emerging group get their proposed solutions implemented? How do they see to it that the assumptions underlying those solutions are communicated and embedded in the thinking, feeling, and behavior of the group? The focus here is not on the beginnings but on the early growth and development of the organization. Once the organization has some stability by virtue of a series of successes, the dynamics change, but in its building stage the major impact on culture formation is still the founder leader.

At this point socialization, the process by which new members acquire the core elements of a new culture, is also more of an active process by which the organization through its layers of management teaches the various rules of behavior and the assumptions that lie behind them.

The simplest explanation of how leaders get their message across is through charisma in that one of the main elements of that mysterious quality undoubtedly is a leader's ability to communicate major assumptions and values in a vivid and clear manner (Bennis and Nanus, 1985; Conger, 1989; Leavitt, 1986). The problem with charismatic vision as an embedding mechanism is that leaders who have it are rare and their impact is hard to predict. Historians can look back and say that certain people had charisma or had a great vision. It is not always clear at the time, however, how they transmitted the vision. For clues to that process we must look to more mundane organizational phenomena.

Some of the mechanisms that leaders use to communicate their beliefs, values, and assumptions are conscious, deliberate actions; others are unconscious and may even be unintended (Kunda, 1992). The leader may be conflicted and may be sending mutually contradictory messages (Kets de Vries and Miller, 1987). Among the leaders described in Chapter Eleven Jones officially stated a philosophy of delegation and decentralization but retained tight centralized control, intervened frequently on very detailed issues, and felt free to go around the hierarchy. Murphy sent inconsistent signals concerning simplicity and complexity. He always advocated simple structures in which accountability was clearly visible, yet his decision-making style forced high degrees of complexity as various managers worked their proposed solutions through various committees. Managers who grew up in the company understood that one could simultaneously advocate both, but newcomers often had difficulty with what seemed to be obvious inconsistencies. On the one hand, Murphy wanted simplicity, clarity, and high levels of cooperation, but on the other hand, he often supported and even encouraged overlaps, ambiguity, and competitiveness.

Subordinates will tolerate and accommodate contradictory

messages because, in a sense, founders, owners, and others at higher levels are always granted the right to be inconsistent or, in any case, are too powerful to be confronted. The emerging culture will then reflect not only the leader's assumptions but the complex internal accommodations created by subordinates to run the organization in spite of or around the leader. The group, sometimes acting on the assumption that the leader is a creative genius who has idiosyncrasies, may develop compensatory mechanisms, such as buffering layers of managers, to protect the organization from the dysfunctional aspects of the leader's behavior. In those cases the culture may become a defense mechanism against the anxieties unleashed by inconsistent leader behavior. In other cases the organization's style of operating will reflect the very biases and unconscious conflicts that the founder experiences, thus causing some scholars to call such organizations neurotic (Kets de Vries and Miller, 1984). In the extreme, subordinates or the board of directors may have to find ways to move the founder out altogether, as has happened in a number of first-generation companies.

Because the initiative tends always to be with the founder, however, we will examine the process of cultural embedding from the point of view of how the power of the founder can be used to inculcate assumptions. The mechanisms, as shown in Exhibit 12.1, vary along several dimensions: (1) how powerful their effects are, (2) how implicit or explicit the messages conveyed are, and (3) how intentional they are.

Primary Embedding Mechanisms

Taken together, the six primary embedding mechanisms shown in Exhibit 12.1 create what would typically be called the "climate" of the organization (Schneider, 1990). At this stage the climate created by founder leaders precedes the existence of a group culture. At a later stage climate will be a reflection and manifestation of cultural assumptions, but early in the life of a group it reflects only the assumptions of leaders.

Exhibit 12.1. Culture-Embedding Mechanisms.

Primary Embedding Mechanisms	Secondary Articulation and Reinforcement Mechanisms
What leaders pay attention to, measure, and control on a regular basis	Organization design and structure
	Organizational systems and procedures
How leaders react to critical incidents and organizational crises	
	Organizational rites and rituals
Observed criteria by which leaders allocate scarce resources	Design of physical space, facades, and buildings
Deliberate role modeling, teaching, and coaching	Stories, legends, and myths about people and events
Observed criteria by which leaders allocate rewards and status	Formal statements of organizational philosophy, values, and creed
Observed criteria by which leaders recruit, select, promote, retire, and excommunicate organizational members	

What Leaders Pay Attention to, Measure, and Control

One of the most powerful mechanisms that founders, leaders, managers, or even colleagues have available for communicating what they believe in or care about is what they systematically pay attention to. This can mean anything from what they notice and comment on to what they measure, control, reward, and in other ways *systematically deal with*. Even casual remarks and questions that are consistently geared to a certain area can be as potent as formal control mechanisms and measurements.

If leaders are aware of this process, then being systematic in paying attention to certain things becomes a powerful way of communicating a message, especially if the leaders are totally consistent in their own behavior. On the other hand, if leaders are not aware of the power of this process or they are inconsistent in what they pay attention to, subordinates and colleagues will spend inordinate time and energy trying to decipher what a leader's behavior really reflects and even project motives where none may exist.

As a consultant I have learned that my own consistency in what I ask questions about sends clear signals to my audience about my priorities, values, and beliefs. It is the consistency that is important, not the intensity of the attention. To illustrate, McGregor (1960) tells of a company that wanted him to help install a management development program. The president hoped that McGregor would propose exactly what to do and how to do it. Instead, McGregor asked the president whether he really cared about identifying and developing managers. On being assured that he did, McGregor proposed that he should build his concern into the reward system and set up a consistent way of monitoring progress; in other words, start to pay attention to it.

The president agreed and announced that henceforth 50 percent of each senior manager's annual bonus would be contingent on what he had done to develop his own immediate subordinates during the past year. He added that he himself had no specific program in mind, but that each quarter he would ask each senior manager what had been done. The senior managers launched a whole series of different activities, many of them pulled together from work that was already going on piecemeal in the organization. A coherent program was forged over a two-year period and has continued to serve this company well. The president continued his quarterly questions and once a year evaluated how much each manager had done for development. He never imposed any program, but by paying consistent attention to management development, he clearly signaled to the organization that he considered management development to be important.

At the other extreme, some Action Company managers illustrate how inconsistent and shifting attention causes subordinates to pay less and less attention to what senior management wants, thereby empowering the employee level by default. For example, a brilliant manager in one technical group would launch an important initiative and demand total support but two weeks later would launch a new initiative without indicating whether or not people were supposed to drop the old one. As subordinates two and three levels down observed this seemingly erratic behavior, they began to rely more and more on their own judgment of what they should actually be doing.

Some of the most important signals of what founders and leaders care about are sent during meetings and in other activities devoted to planning and budgeting, which is one reason why planning and budgeting are such important managerial processes. In questioning subordinates systematically on certain issues, leaders can transmit their own view of how to look at problems. The ultimate content of the plan may not be as important as the learning that goes on during the planning process.

For example, in his manner of planning, Smithfield made it clear to all his subordinates that he wanted them to be autonomous, completely responsible for their own operation, but financially accountable. He got this message across by focusing only on financial results. In contrast, both Jones and Murphy asked detailed questions about virtually everything during a planning processs. Jones's obsession with store cleanliness was clearly signaled by the fact that he always commented on it, always noticed deviations from his standards, and always asked what was being done to ensure it in the future. Murphy's assumption that a good manager is always in control of his own situation was clearly evident in his questions about future plans and his anger when plans did not reveal detailed knowledge of product or market issues.

Attention is focused in part by the kinds of questions that leaders ask and how they set the agendas for meetings. An even more powerful signal, however, is their emotional reactions, especially the emotional outbursts that occur when leaders feel that an important assumption is being violated. Such outbursts are not necessarily very overt because many managers believe that one should not allow one's emotions to become too involved in the decision process. On the other hand, some leaders allow themselves to get angry and upset and use those feelings as messages. Even for those leaders who attempt to suppress their emotions, subordinates generally know when they are upset.

Subordinates find emotional outbursts on the part of their bosses painful and try to avoid them. In the process they gradually come to adopt the assumptions of the leader. For example,

Murphy's concern that line managers stay on top of their jobs was originally signaled most clearly in an incident at an executive committee meeting when the company was still very young. A newly hired treasurer was asked to make his report on the state of the business. The treasurer had analyzed the three major product lines and brought his analysis to the meeting. He distributed the information and then pointed out that one product line in particular was in financial difficulty because of falling sales, excessive inventories, and rapidly rising manufacturing costs. It became evident in the meeting that the vice president in charge of the product line had not seen the treasurer's figures and was somewhat embarrassed by what was being revealed.

As the report progressed, the tension in the room rose because everyone sensed that a real confrontation was about to develop between the treasurer and the vice president. The treasurer finished and all eyes turned toward the VP. The VP said that he had not seen the figures and wished he had had a chance to look at them; since he had not seen them, however, he had no immediate answers to give. At this point Murphy blew up, but to the surprise of the whole group he blew up not at the treasurer but at the vice president. Several members of the group later revealed that they had expected the president to blow up at the treasurer for his obvious grandstanding in bringing in figures that were new to everyone. However, no one had expected Murphy to turn his wrath on the product line VP for not being prepared to deal with the treasurer's arguments and information. Protests that he had not seen the data fell on deaf ears. He was told that if he were running his business properly he would have known everything the treasurer knew, and he certainly should have had answers for what would now be done.

Suddenly everyone realized that there was a powerful message in Murphy's behavior. He clearly expected and assumed that a product line VP would always be totally on top of his own business and would never put himself in the position of being embarrassed by financial data. The fact that the vice president did not have his own numbers was a worse sin than being in trouble. The fact that he could not respond to the troublesome figures was also a worse sin than being in trouble. The blowup at the line manager was a far clearer message than any amount of rhetoric about delegation and the like would have been.

If a manager continued to display ignorance or lack of control of his own situation, Murphy would continue to get angry at him and accuse him of incompetence. If the manager attempted to defend himself by noting that his situation was the result of actions on the part of others over whom he had no control or resulted from prior agreements made by Murphy himself, he would be told emotionally that he should have brought the issue up right away to force a rethinking of the situation and a renegotiation of the prior decision. In other words, Murphy made it very clear, by the kinds of things to which he reacted emotionally, that poor ultimate performance could be excused but that not being on top of one's own situation and not informing others of what was going on could never be excused.

Murphy's deep assumption about the importance of always telling the truth was signaled most clearly on the occasion of another executive committee meeting when it was discovered that the company had excess inventory because each product line, in the process of protecting itself, had exaggerated its orders to manufacturing by a small percentage. The accumulation of these small percentages across all the product lines produced a massive excess inventory, which the manufacturing department disclaimed because it had only produced what the product lines had ordered. At the meeting where this situation was reviewed, Murphy indicated that he had rarely been as angry as he was then because the product lines had lied. He stated flatly that if he ever caught a manager exaggerating orders again, it would be grounds for instant dismissal no matter what the reasons. The suggestion that manufacturing could compensate for the sales exaggerations was dismissed out of hand because that would compound the problem. The prospect of one function lying while the other function tried to figure out how to compensate for it totally violated Murphy's assumptions about how an effective business should be run.

Both Jones and Murphy shared the assumption that meeting the customer's needs is one of the most important ways of ensuring business success, and their most emotional reactions consistently occurred whenever they learned that a customer had not been well treated. In this area the official messages, as embodied in company creeds and the formal reward system, were totally consistent with the implicit messages that could be inferred from founder reactions. In Jones's case, the needs of the customer were even put ahead of the needs of the family, and one way that a family member could get in trouble was by mistreating a customer.

Other powerful signals that subordinates interpret for evidence of the leader's assumptions are what leaders *do not react to*. For example, in the Action Company, managers were frequently in actual trouble with cost overruns, delayed schedules, and imperfect products, but such trouble rarely caused comment if the manager had displayed that he or she was in control of the situation. Trouble could be expected and was assumed to be a normal condition of doing business; only failure to cope and regain control was unacceptable. In Action's product design departments, one frequently found excess personnel, very high budgets, and lax management with regard to cost controls, none of which occasioned much comment. Subordinates correctly interpreted this to mean that it was far more important to come up with a good product than to control costs.

The combinations of what founder leaders do and do not pay attention to can create problems of deciphering because they reveal the areas where unconscious conflicts may exist. For example, at Action the clear concern for customers was signaled by outbursts if customers complained. But this attitude coexisted with an implicit arrogance toward certain classes of customers because the engineers often assumed that they knew what the customer would like in the way of product design and Murphy implicitly reinforced this attitude by not reacting in a corrective way when such attitudes were displayed. Murphy's own attitudes toward more or less technically sophisticated customers were not clear, but his silent condoning of his engineers' behavior made it possible for others to project that Murphy also believed deep down that he knew better what the less sophisticated customer really wanted.

The company's own history reinforced this latter set of assumptions because the original product designs were based on the principle that in this new technology the engineers were, in fact, a good surrogate of the ultimate customers: "If we like it, our customers will like it." As the market matured and the products became much more differentiated, however, managers began to notice that the original assumption no longer held and that a marketing orientation involving market research might be needed. As the conflicts between engineering and marketing increased, Murphy's own behavior became less consistent, leading subordinates to assume that he too was unsure of which assumption was correct.

In summary, what leaders consistently pay attention to communicates most clearly what their own priorities, goals, and assumptions are. If they pay attention to too many things or if their pattern of attention is inconsistent, subordinates will use other signals or their own experience to decide what is really important, leading to a much more diverse set of assumptions and many more subcultures. (The latter process is explored more fully in Chapter Thirteen.)

Leader Reactions to Critical Incidents and Organizational Crises

When an organization faces a crisis, the manner in which leaders and others deal with it creates new norms, values, and working procedures and reveals important underlying assumptions. Crises are especially significant in culture creation and transmission because the heightened emotional involvement during such periods increases the intensity of learning. Crises heighten anxiety, and anxiety reduction is a powerful motivator of new learning. If people share intense emotional experiences and collectively learn how to reduce anxiety, they are more likely to remember what they have learned.

What is defined as a crisis is, of course, partly a matter of perception. There may or may not be actual dangers in the external environment, and what is considered to be dangerous is itself often a reflection of the culture. For purposes of this analysis, a crisis is what is perceived to be a crisis and what is defined as a crisis by founders and leaders. Crises that arise around the major external survival issues are the most potent in revealing the deep assumptions of the leaders and therefore the most likely to be the occasions when those assumptions become the basis of shared learning and thus become embedded.

A story told about Tom Watson, Jr., in the context of IBM's concern for people and for management development has it that a young executive had made some bad decisions that cost the company several million dollars. He was summoned to Watson's office, fully expecting to be dismissed. As he entered the office, the young executive said, "I suppose after that set of mistakes you will be wanting to fire me." Watson was said to have replied, "Not at all, young man, we have just spent a couple of million dollars educating you."

Innumerable organizations have faced the crisis of shrinking sales, excess inventories, technological obsolescence, and the subsequent necessity of laying off employees in order to cut costs. How leaders deal with such a crisis reveals some of their assumptions about the importance of people and their view of human nature. Ouchi (1981) cites several dramatic examples in which U.S. companies faced with layoffs decided instead to go to short work weeks or to have all employees and managers take cuts in pay to manage the cost reduction without people reduction. At one such company, Hewlett-Packard, which survived a financial crisis early in its history without laying off anyone, many organizational stories are told and retold to show what kinds of values were operating in their leaders at the time.

The Action Company assumption that "we are a family who will take care of each other" came out most clearly during periods of crisis. When the company was doing well, Murphy often had emotional outbursts reflecting his concern that people were getting complacent. When the company was in difficulty, however, Murphy never punished anyone or displayed anger; instead, he became the strong and supportive father figure, pointing out to both the external world and the employees that things were not as bad as they seemed, that the company had great strengths that would ensure future success, and that people should not worry about layoffs because things would be controlled by slowing down hiring.

On the other hand, Jones displayed his lack of concern for his own young managers by being punitive under crisis conditions, sometimes impulsively firing people only to have to try to rehire them later because he realized how important they were to the operation of the company. This gradually created an organization built on distrust and low commitment, leading good people to leave when a better opportunity came along.

Crises around issues of internal integration can also reveal and embed leader assumptions. I have found that a good time to observe an organization very closely is when acts of insubordination take place. So much of an organization's culture is tied up with hierarchy, authority, power, and influence that the mechanisms of conflict resolution have to be constantly worked out and consensually validated. No better opportunity exists for leaders to send signals about their own assumptions about human nature and relationships than when they themselves are challenged.

For example, Murphy clearly and repeatedly revealed his assumption that he did not feel that he knew best through his tolerant and even encouraging behavior when subordinates argued with him or disobeyed him. He signaled that he was truly depending on his subordinates to know what was best and that they should be insubordinate if they felt they were right. In contrast, a bank president with whom I have worked, publicly insisted that he wanted his subordinates to think for themselves, but his behavior belied his overt claim. During an important meeting of the whole staff, one of these subordinates, in attempting to assert himself, made some silly errors in a presentation. The president laughed at him and ridiculed him. Though the president later apologized and said he did not mean it, the damage had been done. All the subordinates who witnessed the incident interpreted the outburst to mean that the president was not really serious about delegating to them and having them be more assertive. He was still sitting in judgment on them and was still operating on the assumption that he knew best.

Observed Criteria for Resource Allocation

How budgets are created in an organization is another process that reveals leader assumptions and beliefs. As Donaldson and

Lorsch (1983) show in their study of top-management decision making, leader beliefs about the distinctive competence of their organization, acceptable levels of financial risks, and the degree to which the organization must be financially self-sufficient strongly influence their choices of goals, the means to accomplish them, and the management processes to be used. Such beliefs not only function as criteria by which decisions are made but are constraints on decision making in that they limit the perception of alternatives.

Murphy's budgeting and resource allocation processes clearly revealed his belief in the entrepreneurial bottom-up system. He always resisted senior management's setting targets, formulating strategies, and setting goals, preferring instead to stimulate the managers below him to come up with business plans and budgets that he and other senior executives would approve if they made sense. He was convinced that people would only give their best ideas and maximum commitment to projects and programs that they themselves had invented, sold, and were accountable for.

This system created problems as the Action Company grew and found itself increasingly operating in a competitive environment where costs had to be controlled. In its early days the company could afford to invest in all kinds of projects whether they made sense or not. In today's environment one of the biggest and as yet unresolved issues is how to choose among projects that sound equally good when there are insufficient resources to fund them all. Strong pressures are building for a more centralized strategy and some broader criteria of what businesses the company wants to be in, but there is steadfast resistance to undermining in any way the entrepreneurial spirit that Murphy believes to be the strength of the company.

Deliberate Role Modeling, Teaching, and Coaching

Founders and new leaders of organizations generally seem to know that their own visible behavior has great value for communicating assumptions and values to other members, especially newcomers. At Action, Murphy and some other senior executives have made videotapes that outline their explicit philosophy, and these tapes are shown to new members of the organization as part of their initial training. However, there is a difference between the messages delivered from staged settings, such as when a leader gives a welcoming speech to newcomers, and the messages received when that leader is observed informally. The informal messages are the more powerful teaching and coaching mechanism.

Jones, for example, demonstrated his need to be involved in everything at a detailed level by his frequent visits to stores and minute inspections once he got there. When he went on vacation, he called the office every day at a set time and asked detailed questions about all aspects of the business. This behavior persisted into his semiretirement, when he would call every day from his retirement home thousands of miles away. Through his questions, his lectures, and his demonstration of personal concern for details, he hoped to show other managers what it meant to be highly visible and on top of one's job. Through his unwavering loyalty to family members, Jones also trained people in how to think about family members and the rights of owners.

Murphy made an explicit attempt to downplay status and hierarchy at Action because of his assumption that good ideas can come from anyone. He communicated this assumption in many formal and informal ways. For example, he drove a small car, had an unpretentious office, dressed informally, and spent many hours wandering among the employees at all levels, getting to know them personally. Stories developed around this informality, and such stories institutionalized his behavior.

An example of more explicit coaching occurred at the Jones Food Company when the Jones family brought back a former manager as the CEO after several other CEOs had failed. One of the first things he did as the new president was to display at a large meeting his own particular method of analyzing the performance of the company and planning its future. He said explicitly to the group: "Now that's an example of the kind of good planning and management I want in this organization." He then ordered his key executives to prepare a long-range planning process in the format in which he had just lectured and gave them a target time to be ready to present their own plans in the new format. At the presentation meeting he coached their presentations, commented on each one, corrected the approach where he felt it had missed the point, and gave them new deadlines for accomplishing their goals as spelled out in the plans. Privately, he told an observer of this meeting that the organization had done virtually no planning for decades and that he hoped to institute formal strategy planning as a way of reducing the massive deficits that the organization had been experiencing. From his point of view, he had to change the entire mentality of his subordinates, which he felt required him to instruct, model, correct, and coach.

Observed Criteria for Allocation of Rewards and Status

Members of any organization learn from their own experience with promotions, performance appraisals, and discussions with the boss what the organization values and what the organization punishes. Both the nature of the behavior rewarded and punished and the nature of the rewards and punishments themselves carry the messages. Leaders can quickly get across their own priorities, values, and assumptions by consistently linking rewards and punishments to the behavior they are concerned with.

What I am referring to here are actual practices, what really happens, not what is espoused, published, or preached. For example, as described in Chapter Five, the product managers in a large food company were each expected to develop a successful marketing program for their specific product and then were rewarded by being moved to a better product after about eighteen months. Since the results of a marketing program could not possibly be known in eighteen months, what was really rewarded was the performance of the product manager in creating a "good" marketing program, as measured by the ability to sell it to the senior managers who approved it, not the ultimate performance of the product in the marketplace.

The implicit assumption was that only senior managers

could be trusted to evaluate a marketing program accurately; therefore, even if a product manager was technically accountable for his product, it was, in fact, senior management that took the real responsibility for launching expensive marketing programs. What junior managers learned from this was how to develop programs that had the right characteristics and style from senior management's point of view. If a junior-level manager developed the illusion that she really had independence in making marketing decisions, she had only to look at the relative insignificance of the actual rewards given to successful managers; they received a better product to manage, they might get a slightly better office (which was graded according to a company manual specifying size, type of furniture, allowable wall decorations, and carpeting), and they received a good raise. But they still had to present their marketing programs to senior management for review, and the preparations for and dry runs of such presentations took four to five months of every year even for very senior product managers. An organization that seemingly delegated a great deal of power to its product managers was, in fact, limiting their autonomy very sharply and systematically training them to think like senior management thought.

To reiterate the basic point, if the founders or leaders are trying to ensure that their values and assumptions will be learned, they must create a reward, promotion, and status system that is consistent with those assumptions. Whereas the message initially gets across in the daily behavior of the leader, it is judged in the long run by whether the important rewards are allocated consistently with that daily behavior. If these levels of message transmission are inconsistent, one will find a highly conflicted organization without a clear culture or any culture at all at a total organizational level.

Observed Criteria for Recruitment, Selection, Promotion, Retirement, and Excommunication

One of the most subtle yet most potent ways through which cultural assumptions get embedded and perpetuated is the process of selecting new members. If a founder assumes that the best

way to build an organization is to hire very tough, independent people and then leave them alone and he is successful in
continuing to hire tough and independent people, he will create the kind of culture that he assumes will work best. He may
never realize that the success of the culture lies in the success
of the recruitment effort and that his beliefs about how to organize might become disconfirmed if he could no longer hire
the right kinds of people to fit his assumptions.

This cultural embedding mechanism is subtle because it
operates unconsciously in most organizations. Founder and
leaders tend to find attractive those candidates who resemble
present members in style, assumptions, values, and beliefs. They
are perceived to be the best people to hire and are assigned characteristics that will justify their being hired. Unless someone
outside the organization is explicitly involved in the hiring, there
is no way of knowing how much the current implicit assumptions are dominating recruiters' perceptions of the candidates.
(It would be interesting to study search firms from this perspective. Because they operate outside the cultural context of the
employing organization, do they become implicitly culture
reproducers or changers, and are they aware of their power in
this regard? Do organizations that employ outside search firms
do so in part to get away from their own biases in hiring? In
any case, it is clear that initial selection decisions for new members, followed by the criteria applied in the promotion system,
are powerful mechanisms for embedding and perpetuating the
culture, especially when combined with socialization tactics
designed to teach cultural assumptions.)

Basic assumptions are further reinforced through criteria
of who does or does not get promoted, who is retired early, and
who is in effect excommunicated by being actually fired or given
a job that is clearly perceived to be less important, even if at
a higher level (being kicked upstairs). At Action an employee
who was not bright enough or articulate enough to play the idea-
debating game and to stand up for his own ideas soon became
walled off and eventually was forced out through a process of
benign but consistent neglect. At Multi a similar kind of isolation occurred if an employee was not concerned about the com-

pany, the products, and senior management. Neither company fired people except for dishonesty or immoral behavior, but in both companies such isolation became the equivalent of excommunication.

The foregoing mechanisms all interact and tend to reinforce each other if the leader's own beliefs, values, and assumptions are consistent. By separating these categories I am trying to show in how many different ways leaders can and do communicate their assumptions. Most newcomers to an organization have a wealth of data available to them to decipher what the leader's assumptions really are. Much of the socialization process is, therefore, embedded in the organization's normal working routines. It is not necessary for newcomers to attend special training or indoctrination sessions to learn important cultural assumptions. They become quite evident through the behavior of leaders.

Secondary Articulation and Reinforcement Mechanisms

In a young organization, design, structure, architecture, rituals, stories, and formal statements are cultural reinforcers, not culture creators. Once an organization has matured and stabilized, these same mechanisms come to be primary culture-creating mechanisms that will constrain future leaders. I have labeled these mechanisms secondary because they work only if they are consistent with the primary mechanisms discussed above. When they are consistent, they begin to build organizational ideologies and thus to formalize much of what is informally learned at the outset. If they are inconsistent, they either will be ignored or will be a source of internal conflict.

All the items in this list can be thought of at this stage as cultural artifacts that are highly visible but may be difficult to interpret without insider knowledge obtained from observing leaders' actual behaviors. When an organization is in its developmental phase, the driving and controlling assumptions will always be manifested first and most clearly in what the leaders demonstrate in their own behavior, not in what is written down or inferred from visible designs, procedures, rituals, stories, and published philosophies. As we will see in Chapter Thirteen, however, these secondary mechanisms can become primary ones in perpetuating the assumptions even when new leaders in a mature organization would prefer to change them. Once again, the reader is reminded that here we are still talking of how cultures get built in a growing organization.

Organization Design and Structure

As I have observed executive groups in action, particularly first-generation groups led by their founder, I have noticed that the design of the organization—how product lines, market areas, functional responsibilities, and so on are divided up—elicits high degrees of passion but not too much clear logic. The requirements of the primary task—how to organize in order to survive in the external environment—seem to get mixed up with powerful assumptions about internal relationships and with theories of how to get things done that derive more from the founder's background than from current analysis. If it is a family business, the structure must make room for key family members or trusted colleagues, cofounders, and friends. Even in the first-generation publicly held company, the organization's design is often built around the talents of the individual managers rather than the external task requirements.

Founders often have strong theories about how to organize for maximum effectiveness. Some assume that only they can ultimately determine what is correct; therefore, they build a tight hierarchy and highly centralized controls. Others assume that the strength of their organization is in their people and therefore build a highly decentralized organization that pushes authority down as low as possible. Still others, like Murphy, believe that their strength is in negotiated solutions; therefore, they hire strong people but then create a structure that forces such people to negotiate their solutions with each other. Some leaders believe in minimizing interdependence in order to free each unit of the organization; others believe in creating checks and balances so that no one unit can ever function autonomously.

Beliefs also vary about how stable a given structure should

be, with some leaders seeking a solution and sticking with it, while others, like Murphy, are perpetually redesigning their organization in a search for solutions that better fit the perceived problems of the ever-changing external conditions. The initial design of the organization and the periodic reorganizations that companies go through thus provide ample opportunities for the founders and leaders to embed their deeply held assumptions about the task, the means to accomplish it, the nature of people, and the right kinds of relationships to foster among people. Some leaders are able to articulate why they have designed their organization the way they have; others appear to be rationalizing and are not really consciously aware of the assumptions they are making, even though such assumptions can sometimes be inferred from the results. In any case, the organization's structure and design can be used to reinforce leader assumptions but is rarely an accurate initial basis for embedding them because structure can usually be interpreted by the employees in a number of different ways.

Organizational Systems and Procedures

The most visible parts of life in any organization are the daily, weekly, monthly, quarterly, and annual cycles of routines, procedures, reports, forms, and other recurrent tasks that have to be performed. The origin of such routines is often not known to participants or sometimes even to senior management, but their existence lends structure and predictability to an otherwise vague and ambiguous organizational world. The systems and procedures thus serve a function quite similar to the formal structure in that they make life predictable and thereby reduce ambiguity and anxiety. Though employees often complain of stifling bureaucracy, they need some recurrent processes to avoid the anxiety of an uncertain and unpredictable world.

Given that group members seek this kind of stability and anxiety reduction, founders and leaders have the opportunity to reinforce their assumptions by building systems and routines around them. For example, Murphy reinforced his belief that truth is reached through debate by creating many different kinds of committees and attending their meetings. Jones reinforced his belief in absolute authority by creating review processes in which he would listen briefly and then issue peremptory orders. Multi reinforced its assumptions about truth deriving from science by creating formal research studies before making important decisions.

Systems and procedures can formalize the process of "paying attention" and thus reinforce the message that the leader really cares about certain things. This is why the president who wanted management development programs helped his cause immensely by formalizing his quarterly reviews of what each subordinate had done. Formal budgeting or planning routines are often adhered to less to produce plans and budgets and more to provide a vehicle to remind subordinates of what the leader considers to be important matters to pay attention to.

If founders or leaders do not design systems and procedures as reinforcement mechanisms, they open the door to historically evolved inconsistencies in the culture or weaken their own message from the outset. Thus, a strong president who believes, as Murphy did, that line managers should be in full control of their own operation must ensure that the organization's financial control procedures are consistent with that belief. If he allows a strong centralized corporate financial organization to evolve and if he pays attention to the data generated by this organization, he is sending a signal inconsistent with the assumption that managers should control their own finances. Then one subculture may evolve in the line organization and a different subculture in the corporate finance organization. If those groups end up fighting each other, it will be the direct result of the initial inconsistency in design logic, not the result of the personalities or the competitive drives of the managers of those functions.

Rites and Rituals of the Organization

Some students of culture would view the special organizational processes of rites and rituals as central to the deciphering as well as to the communicating of cultural assumptions (Deal and Kennedy, 1982; Trice and Beyer, 1984, 1985). I suspect that the centrality of rites in traditional anthropology has something to do with the difficulty of observing firsthand the primary embedding mechanisms described earlier in this chapter. When the only salient data we have are the rites and rituals that have survived over a period of time, we must, of course, use them as best we can; as with structure and processes, however, if we have only these data, it is difficult to decipher just what assumptions leaders have held that have led to the creation of particular rites and rituals. On the other hand, from the point of view of the leader, if one can ritualize certain behaviors that one considers important, that becomes a powerful reinforcer.

At Action, for example, the monthly meetings devoted to important long-range strategic issues were always held off-site in highly informal surroundings that strongly encouraged informality, status equality, and dialogue. The meetings usually lasted two or more days and involved some joint physical activity such as a hike or a mountain climb. Murphy strongly believed that people would learn to trust each other and be more open with each other if they did enjoyable things together in an informal setting. As the company grew, various functional groups adopted this style of meeting as well, to the point where periodic off-site meetings have become a corporate ritual with their own various names, locales, and informal procedures.

At Multi, the annual meeting always involved the surprise athletic event that no one was good at and would therefore equalize status. The participants would let their hair down, try their best, fail, and be laughed at in a good-humored fashion. It was as if the group were trying to say to itself, "We are serious scientists and businesspeople, but we also know how to play." And in the play, informal messages that would not be allowed in the formal work world could be conveyed, thus compensating somewhat for the strict hierarchy.

One can find examples of ritualized activities and formalized ritual events in most organizations, but they typically reveal only very small portions of the range of assumptions that make up the culture of an organization. Therein lies the danger of putting too much emphasis on the study of rituals. One can perhaps decipher one piece of the culture correctly, but one may have no basis for determining what else is going on and how important the ritualized activities are in the larger scheme of things.

Design of Physical Space, Facades, and Buildings

The physical design category is intended to encompass all the visible features of the organization that clients, customers, vendors, new employees, and visitors would encounter. The messages that can be inferred from the physical environment, as in the case of structure and procedures, potentially reinforce the leader's messages, but only if they are managed to do so (Steele, 1973). If they are not explicitly managed, they may reflect the assumptions of architects, the planning and facilities managers in the organization, local norms in the community, or other subcultural assumptions.

Leaders who have a clear philosophy and style often choose to embody that style in the visible manifestations of their organization. For example, Action, with its assumptions about truth through conflict and the importance of open communications, chose an open-office layout, as described earlier. This layout clearly articulates the emphasis on equality, ease of communication, and importance of relationships. What the visitor experiences visually in this organization is an accurate reflection of deeply held assumptions, and one indicator of this depth is that the effects are reproduced in the offices of this organization all over the world.

Multi also strongly values individual expertise and autonomy. But because of its assumption that an occupant of a given job becomes the ultimate expert on the area covered by that job, it physically symbolizes turf by giving people privacy. Managers at Multi spend much more time thinking things out alone, having individual conferences with others who are centrally involved, and protecting the privacy of individuals so that they can get their work done. At Multi, as at Action, these are not incidental or accidental physical artifacts. They reflect the basic assumptions of how work gets done, how relationships should be managed, how one arrives at truth. One can learn a great deal from such artifacts if one knows how to interpret them, and leaders can communicate a great deal if they know how to structure and create such settings.

Stories About Important Events and People

As a group develops and accumulates a history, some of this history becomes embodied in stories about events and leadership behavior (Martin and Powers, 1983; Wilkins, 1983). Thus, the story—whether it is in the form of a parable, legend, or even myth—reinforces assumptions and teaches assumptions to newcomers. However, since the message to be found in the story is often highly distilled or even ambiguous, this form of communication is somewhat unreliable. Leaders cannot always control what will be said about them in stories, though they can certainly reinforce stories that they feel good about and perhaps can even launch stories that carry desired messages. Leaders can make themselves highly visible to increase the likelihood that stories will be told about them, but sometimes attempts to manage the message in this manner backfire; that is, the story may focus more on the inconsistencies and conflicts that observers detect in the leader.

Efforts to decipher culture from collecting stories have the same problem as the deciphering of rituals. Unless one knows other facts about the leaders, one cannot always infer correctly what the point of the story is. If one understands the culture, then stories can be used to enhance that understanding and make it concrete, but it is dangerous to try to achieve that understanding in the first place from stories alone.

Formal Statements of Organizational Philosophy, Creeds, and Charters

The final mechanism of articulation and reinforcement to be mentioned is the formal statement, the attempt by the founders or leaders to state explicitly what their values or assumptions are. These statements typically highlight only a small portion of the assumption set that operates in the group and, most likely, will highlight only those aspects of the leader's philosophy or ideology that lend themselves to public articulation. Such public statements may have a value for the leader as a way of emphasizing special things to be attended to in the organization, as values around which to rally the troops, and as reminders of fundamental assumptions not to be forgotten. However, formal statements cannot be viewed as a way of defining the organization's culture. At best they cover a small, publicly relevant segment of the culture, those aspects that leaders find useful to publish as an ideology or focus for the organization.

Summary and Conclusions

The purpose of this chapter is to examine how leaders embed the assumptions that they hold and thereby create cultures. How do they get others to gradually share those assumptions? Culture embedding in a young organization is essentially a socialization process, but one in which most of the socialization mechanisms are in the hands of the leaders. In more mature organizations, the socialization process takes on a different shape (for example, Schein, 1978; Van Maanen and Schein, 1979), but in young organizations one must focus primarily on leadership behavior to understand cultural growth.

Six of the mechanisms discussed in this chapter are powerful primary means by which founders or leaders are able to embed their own assumptions in the ongoing daily life of their organizations. Through what they pay attention to and reward, through the ways they allocate resources, through the role modeling they do, through the manner in which they deal with critical incidents, and through the criteria they use for recruitment, selection, promotion, and excommunication, leaders communicate both explicitly and implicitly the assumptions they really hold. If they are conflicted, the conflicts and inconsistencies are also communicated and become a part of the culture or become the basis for subcultures and countercultures.

Less powerful, more ambiguous, and more difficult to control are the messages embedded in the organization's structure, its procedures and routines, its rituals, its physical layout, its stories and legends, and its formal statements about itself. Yet these secondary mechanisms can provide powerful reinforcement of the primary messages if the leader is able to control them. The important point to grasp is that all these mechanisms do communicate culture content to newcomers. Leaders do not have a choice about whether or not to communicate. They only have a choice about how much to manage what they communicate.

What are secondary mechanisms at the growth stage will, of course, to a large degree become primary maintenance mechanisms as the organization matures and stabilizes, what we ultimately call bureaucratization. The more the structure, procedures, rituals, and espoused values work in making the organization successful, the more they become the filter or criteria for the selection of new leaders. As a result, the likelihood of new leaders becoming cultural change agents declines as the organization matures. The socialization process then begins to reflect what has worked in the past, not what may be the primary agenda of the management of today. The dynamics of the "midlife" organization are therefore quite different from those of the young and emerging organization, as will be shown in Chapters Thirteen and Fourteen.

Though the leadership examples in this chapter come primarily from founders, any manager can begin to focus on these mechanisms when attempting to teach subordinates some new ways of perceiving, thinking, and feeling. What the manager must recognize is that all of the primary mechanisms must be used, and all of them must be consistent with each other. Many change programs fail because the manager who wants the change fails to use the entire set of mechanisms described. To put it positively, when a manager decides to change the assumptions of a work group by using all of these mechanisms, that manager is becoming a leader.

CHAPTER THIRTEEN

Organizational Midlife
Differentiation and the
Growth of Subcultures

To understand the dynamics of culture growth and change, we must first examine what happens in *any* group or organization as it grows and develops. Cultural dynamics are ultimately a reflection of group dynamics. As groups (organizations) mature, they develop subgroups, and as those subgroups share their own histories, they develop cultures of their own, which from the point of view of the larger organization are subcultures. The maturing process can be divided into three stages if one considers leadership and cultural dynamics: (1) the founding and development stage that has been illustrated in the last two chapters, (2) organizational midlife, and (3) organizational maturity and decline.

The founding and development stage can be thought of as the period of founder or family ownership. From this point of view, an organization can be quite large and quite old and yet still be culturally in the developmental stage. Examples of companies that fit this definition are Digital Equipment, Hewlett-Packard, and Microsoft, where the founder is either still in charge or close by on the board of directors.

One can identify a transitional stage in which ownership shifts away from the founder or owning family and a general manager is brought in as CEO. Such transitional companies include Apple and Polaroid, where the founders are no longer in the picture but only one generation of general management has been in place.

A midlife organization has had at least two generations of general managers and is publicly owned. Note again that this has nothing to do with age or size. It is a definition that highlights the importance of a diffusion of ownership feelings and a psychological distance from the original founder and family that allows cultural evolution to occur more broadly. In midlife organizations the leadership issue is more complex because general managers who have been promoted to be CEOs do not have the same leadership options as founders and owners (Schein, 1983). They are not as likely to have longer tenures and are always more vulnerable to removal by their boards of directors. Companies such as IBM, Kodak, and Citibank exemplify this stage.

Organizational maturity and decline is defined more by the interaction of the organization with its environment than by its internal dynamics alone. As the organization matures and remains successful for a period of time, its structures, processes, rituals, and norms come to be taken more and more for granted. At this stage the culture defines leadership more than leadership creates culture. A mature organization in this sense can function successfully for a long time as long as its cultural assumptions are in line with the realities of its environmental contexts. However, if the environment shifts and the organization is not ready to adapt rapidly, it enters a gradual period of decline such as we have seen in a number of large organizations in the steel and automobile industries.

To understand the cultural dynamics in each of these stages, we must first examine how an organization differentiates itself into subgroups that eventually become subcultures. What a *group* is and what a *subgroup* is are matters of one's initial definitions and purposes. From the point of view of society, all organizations are subgroups. From the point of view of organizations, departments or divisions are subgroups. From the point of view of departments, work units are subgroups. The definition only becomes meaningless when we get to the level

of the small face-to-face group in that further "subgroups" typically do not have stability or life cycles in the sense we are discussing here. Therefore, for purposes of this analysis I consider
the cultural unit to be an organization and the subcultures to
be whatever cultures arise in the divisions, departments, and
other fairly stable subgroups of that organization.

All organizations undergo a process of differentiation as
they grow. This is variously called division of labor, function-
alization, divisionalization, or diversification. The common element, however, is that as the number of people, customers,
goods, and services increases, it becomes less and less efficient
for the founder to coordinate everything. If the organization is
successful, it inevitably creates smaller units that begin the
process of culture formation on their own with their own leaders.
The major bases on which such differentiation occurs are as
follows:

1. Functional/occupational differentiation
2. Geographical decentralization
3. Differentiation by product, market, or technology
4. "Divisionalization"
5. Differentiation by hierarchical level
6. Mergers and acquisitions
7. Joint ventures, strategic alliances, multiorganizational units
8. Structural opposition groups

Functional Differentiation

The forces creating functional subcultures derive from the technology and occupational culture of the function. The production department hires people trained in manufacturing and engineering, the finance department hires economics and finance
types, the sales department hires sales types, research and development hires technical specialists, and so on. Even though
these newcomers to the organization will be strongly socialized
into the basic culture as described in Chapters Eleven and
Twelve, they will bring with them other assumptions derived
from their education and from association with their occupa-

tional community (Van Maanen and Barley, 1984). Such differences arise from initial personality differences in terms of what kind of person is attracted to a given field and from the occupational socialization that derives from particular properties of the core technology with which the occupation is concerned (Holland, 1985; Schein, 1978, 1990a). One will find in each functional area, therefore, a blend of the founder assumptions and the assumptions associated with that functional/occupational group.

Recall Dougherty's (1990) study of successful and unsuccessful new product introductions in which she found that all product development teams agreed that one needed to know as much as possible about one's potential customers, but subcultural assumptions about the customers biased what kind of information each functional group had. The problem was that these categories of information were couched in the language and concepts particular to that occupational subculture, and each member of the team was making assumptions about the other members based on information from his or her own subculture. Dougherty referred to these as "thought worlds," using the concept articulated by Douglas (1986) to describe cultures, and noted that if these thought worlds did not interpenetrate each other, the product development team would believe itself to be in consensus when in fact it was not.

With organizational growth and continued success, functional subcultures become stable and well articulated. Organizations acknowledge this most when they develop rotational programs for the training and development of future leaders. When a young manager is rotated through sales, marketing, finance, and production, she or he is learning not only the technical skills in each of these functions but the point of view, perspective, and underlying assumptions of that function, that is, its subculture. Such deeper understanding is thought to be necessary to do a good job as a general manager later in the career. One can find many examples where organizations complain that their general management has always come from just one function, leading to real misunderstanding of the other functions and consequently less effective decisions.

In some cases the communication barriers between functional subcultures are so powerful and chronic that organizations have had to invent new boundary-spanning functions or processes. The clearest case is production engineering, a function whose major purpose is to smooth the transition of a product from engineering into production. If one asks why this function is necessary, one finds that without it engineering often designs things that cannot be built or are too expensive to build and that the "normal" communication process between production and engineering is not sufficient to cure the problem. Engineering is likely to perceive production as lazy and unimaginative, while production perceives engineering to be unrealistic, lacking in cost consciousness, and too concerned with product elegance instead of the practicalities of how to build the product.

The subcultures of sales/marketing and R & D are often so out of line with each other that organizations have learned to create task forces or project teams that bring all the functions together in the initial product development process. But as Dougherty's (1990) research showed, even that is not by itself enough to guarantee understanding across the subcultural boundaries. Organizations must create processes that first of all acknowledge the problem of cross-functional communication and then facilitate a level of mutual understanding across subcultural boundaries.

In summary, functional subcultures bring in the diversity that is associated with the occupational communities and technologies that underlie the functions. This diversity creates the basic problem of integration and coordination that is often the most difficult part of general management in that one is attempting to bring into alignment organizational members who have genuinely different points of view based on their education and experience in the organization. Teaching the basic elements of the organization's overall culture to the new members then becomes one of the most important coordination and integration mechanisms available to leaders, but that itself must be supplemented by other structures and processes that acknowledge the difficulty of communicating across functional subcultures.

Geographical Differentiation

A second and equally powerful basis for the creation of subcultures is established when the organization grows to the point where it decides to break into several geographical units. The organizational logic for such differentiation usually has one of four bases: (1) the need to get closer to different customer bases and the discovery that geographically dispersed customers often require genuinely different goods and services, (2) the need to take advantage of local labor costs in some geographical areas, (3) the cost advantages of getting closer to where raw materials, sources of energy, or suppliers are located, or (4) the requirement by local customers that if products are to be sold in a local market, they must be produced in that market area as well (to protect local labor). The cultural consequences, however, are often unanticipated because the geographical units inevitably adopt some of the assumptions of the host culture in which they operate.

Even subsidiaries or sales units that operate in different countries are inevitably influenced by the cultures of those countries even if they are staffed primarily by employees and managers from the home country. If local nationals are hired, this influence, of course, becomes even greater. The process of local influence becomes most salient where business ethics are involved, as when giving money to suppliers or local government officials is defined as a bribe or kickback and is illegal and unethical in one country, while in another country the same act is not only legal but considered an essential and normal part of doing business.

The selection of people to run geographically dispersed units is itself a culturally related decision. If the organization feels strongly about perpetuating and extending its core assumptions, it tends to send senior managers from the home country into the regions, or if it selects local managers, to put them through an intensive socialization process. For example, I remember meeting in Singapore an Australian who had just been named head of Hewlett-Packard's local plant there. Though he had been hired in Australia and was to spend most of his career in Singapore, he was a dedicated HPer. When I asked him how come, he explained that shortly after being hired he had been flown to California, where he had immediately been met by Mr. Packard himself and then spent six hours with all the top managers. In the following two weeks he was given a thorough indoctrination in the "HP Way" and was encouraged to visit headquarters often. What impressed him most was how important his appointment was to senior management. Their willingness to spend time with him motivated him to really get to know and perpetuate the central values embodied in the HP Way.

At Action the senior managers responsible for large regions and countries are based in those countries, but they spend two to three days of every month in meetings with Murphy and other senior managers at headquarters, so the basic assumptions under which Action operates are constantly reinforced, even though most of the employees are locals.

I was once invited to address an American group of Multi managers and to tell them about the Multi culture as I had experienced it at the European headquarters. I had had no contact with the American subsidiary group at all up to that time. After I described the cultural paradigm to them as I saw it (as outlined in Chapter Three), there was a real sense of shock in the audience, articulated by one manager who said, "My God, you're describing us!" He was particularly shocked because he had believed that Multi's U.S. group, by virtue of the fact that most of the members were American, would be very different. Clearly, however, the company culture had asserted itself across national boundaries.

On the other hand, the local culture inevitably shapes the geographic subculture as well. One finds a different blend of assumptions in each geographical area, reflecting not only the local national culture but the business conditions, customer requirements, and the like. For example, I am familiar with several European pharmaceutical companies that operate in the United States. In each case the U.S. subsidiary mirrors many of the basic assumptions of the European parent (even if it has an American president), but its day-to-day practices in research and in clinical testing reflect the requirements of the U.S. Food and Drug Administration and the U.S. medical establishment. The U.S. pharmaceutical researcher will say that the European is much less thorough in his testing of compounds not because his research is inferior but because many European countries do not require the same amount of testing before a drug is approved. Over time, these testing methods become habits and become embedded, leading to real conflict between the research organizations in Europe and the United States.

In the case of Action, the geographic dispersion has led to a situation where organizational innovations are more likely to be created in Europe than in the United States, and so there is a cultural flow in that direction. The most likely explanation is that the diversity of national cultures within Europe has led to a wider examination of how to do things and the distance from headquarters has made it easier to try out innovations that are needed to meet local customer requirements. The diversity of approaches being used in Europe allows Action to single out those that it needs to move the main organization in what it considers a healthier direction, a process that has happened in several critical business areas over the years.

As organizations mature, the geographical units may take over more and more of the functions. Instead of being just local sales or production units, they may evolve into integrated divisions, including even engineering and R & D. What one then sees in those divisions is the additional subcultural difficulty of integrating across functional boundaries where the home functional culture is geographically distant. For example, Action's various European divisions, typically organized by country, have found that the customers in different countries want different versions of the basic products, leading to the question of where the engineering for the local needs should be done. On the one hand, it is very important to maintain common engineering standards worldwide, but on the other hand, those common standards make the product less attractive in a given geographical region. Engineering units that were placed in various countries then found themselves in conflict with local marketing and sales units about maintaining standards and in conflict with their home engineering department over the need to deviate from standards.

If a common culture and good understanding exist across the subcultural boundaries, this kind of problem can be resolved rationally in terms of the costs and benefits of different solutions. However, if there is misunderstanding because of a lack of common language and concepts in terms of which to communicate and state the problem, it is likely that the organization will generate conflict and ineffective solutions. In Multi I encountered one situation where the U.S. research and development group in one division totally mistrusted the research conducted in the headquarters labs and felt that it had to repeat everything at enormous cost to determine whether the results were usable in the U.S. market.

In summary, as geographical units mature and become divisions and integrated subsidiaries, one will find in them a number of cultural and subcultural phenomena: (1) a blend of the total organization's culture and the geographic host culture, (2) a local version of the functional subcultural issues that exist in the total organization, and (3) more complicated communication problems based on the fact that the functional subcultures will also take on a local character as they hire locals to perform tasks and thereby introduce host country assumptions.

Differentiation by Product, Market, or Technology

As organizations mature, they typically differentiate themselves in terms of the basic technologies they employ, the product sets this leads to, and/or the types of customers they ultimately deal with. The Multi Company started out as a dyestuffs company, but its research on chemical compounds led it into pharmaceuticals, agricultural chemicals, and industrial chemicals. Though the core culture was based on chemistry, as described previously, one could clearly observe subcultural differences that reflected the different product sets.

The forces that created such subcultural differences were of two kinds. First, different kinds of people with different educational and occupational origins were attracted into the different businesses; second, the interaction with the customer required a different mind-set and led to different kinds of shared experiences. I remember at one point suggesting a marketing program that would cut across the divisions and was told, "Professor Schein, what do you really think an educated salesman who deals all day with doctors and hospital administrators has in common with an ex–farm boy slogging around in manure talking farmers into buying the newest pesticide?"

One of the most innovative and countercultural steps Multi took in its efforts to become more of a marketing-based organization was to promote a manager who had grown up in the agricultural division to head of the U.S. pharmaceutical division. It happened that this man was such a good manager and such a good marketer that he overcame the stereotypes based on where he had grown up in the business. Although he was ultimately successful, he had a tough time winning the respect of the pharmaceutical managers when he first took over.

Contact with customers is a very powerful force in creating local subcultures that can appropriately interact with the customer's culture. A vivid example is provided by a large aerospace company that prided itself on its egalitarianism, high trust, and participative approach to its employees. An analysis of the company's artifacts revealed the headquarters organization was very hierarchical; even the architecture and office layout of the headquarters building strongly reflected hierarchy and status. The managers themselves felt this to be anomalous but upon reflection realized that they had built such a headquarters organization to make their primary customers, representatives of the U.S. Defense Department, feel comfortable. They pointed out that the Pentagon is highly structured in terms of hierarchy and that customer teams on their visits to this company were only comfortable if they felt they were talking to managers of an equivalent or higher status than themselves. To make this visible, the company introduced all kinds of status symbols such as graded office size, office amenities, office locations in the building, private dining rooms, and reserved parking spaces.

A trivial but amusing example of the same phenomenon occurred at Action, where a young employee who ordinarily drove vans to deliver mail or parts internally was assigned to drive board members and other outsiders with high status to special meetings. On such an occasion, he was allowed to drive the one fancy company car, and he dressed for the event by putting on a black pinstriped suit! Only if the passenger interrogated the driver would he or she discover that this was a special assignment, not a routine job.

One of the reasons that the marketing and sales departments of an organization often develop communication problems with each other is that the salespeople develop part of their culture from their constant interaction with the customer, while the marketing group is generally more immersed in the headquarters culture and its technical subculture. The salespeople deal in daily face-to-face contacts, while the marketing people deal with data, long-range strategy, broad concepts, and sales tools such as advertising and promotional programs. Often marketing sees itself as creating the strategies and tactics that sales must then implement, leading to potential status conflicts. The important point to recognize is that the difficulty often encountered between these functions can be seen to result from genuine subcultural differences that are predictable and that can be analyzed. To get marketing and sales to work together effectively requires more than a proper reward and incentive system. It requires the development of a common language and common shared experiences.

Divisionalization

As organizations grow and develop different markets, they often "divisionalize" in the sense of decentralizing most of the functions into the product or market units. This process has the advantage of bringing all the functions closer together around a given technology, product set, or customer set, allowing for more integration across the functional subculture boundaries. The forces driving subculture formation then begin to play out more at the divisional level. Typically, to run an integrated division requires a strong general manager, and that manager is likely to want a fair amount of autonomy in the running of his or her division. As that division develops its own history, it will begin to develop a divisional subculture that reflects its particular technology and market environment, even if it is geographically close to the parent company.

Strong divisional subcultures will not be a problem to the parent organization unless the parent wants to implement certain common practices and management processes. Two examples from my own experience highlight this issue. In the first case, I was asked to work with a large conglomerate organization in a European country to help headquarters decide whether or not it should work toward developing a common culture. We examined all of the pros and cons and finally decided that the only two activities that required a common perspective were financial controls and human resource development. In the financial area the headquarters staff had relatively little difficulty establishing common practices, but in the human resource area they ran into real difficulty. From the point of view of headquarters it was essential to develop a cadre of future general managers, requiring that divisions allow their high-potential young managers to be rotated across different divisions and headquarters functional units. But the division subcultures differed markedly in their assumptions about how to develop managers. One division considered it essential that all of its people be promoted from within because of their knowledge of the business, so its members rejected out of hand the idea of cross-divisional rotation of any sort. In another division, cost pressures were so severe that the idea of giving up a high-potential manager to a development program was unthinkable. A third division's norm was that one rose by staying in functional stove-pipes, and managers were rarely evaluated for their generalist potential. When the development program called for that division to accept a manager from another division in a rotational developmental move, it rejected the candidate outright as not knowing enough about the division's business to be acceptable at any level. In this total organization the divisional subcultures won out, and the development program was largely abandoned, to the possible detriment of the parent organization.

In the other case a similar phenomenon occurred in relation to the introduction of information technology. Interviews with a large number of CEOs in different kinds of industries revealed that one of the biggest problems of those who headed large multidivisional organizations was trying to introduce an electronic mail system across all the divisions (Buzzard, 1988). Typically, each division had developed its own system and become highly committed to it. When the corporate information technology department proposed a common system, it encountered strong resistance; when it imposed a common system, it encountered subversion and the system was not used. Several CEOs even commented that this was the single hardest thing to get implemented across autonomous divisions.

One of the remarkable phenomena in large multidivisional firms such as IBM, General Electric, Hewlett-Packard, General Motors, and so on is that they do preserve a strong organizational culture even though strong subcultures evolve in their divisions and geographical units.

Differentiation by Hierarchical Level

As the number of people in the organization increases, it becomes increasingly difficult to coordinate their activities. One of the simplest and most universal mechanisms that all groups, organizations, and societies use to deal with this problem is to create additional layers in the hierarchy so that the span of control of any given manager remains reasonable. Of course, what is defined as reasonable will itself vary from five to fifty; nevertheless, it is clear that every organization if it is successful and grows will sooner or later differentiate itself into more and more levels.

The interaction and shared experience among the members of a given level provide an opportunity for the formation of common assumptions. The strength of such shared assumptions will be a function of the relative amount of interaction and the intensity of the shared experience that the members of that level have with each other as contrasted with members of other levels. Thus a top-management team that functions in isolation at corporate headquarters is quite likely to form a subculture. Similarly, a group of supervisors in a large geographically isolated plant or a group of workers in a union will interact primarily with each other and therefore eventually form a subculture.

An excellent example of what might be called top-management culture is described by Donaldson and Lorsch (1983) in their study of how senior executive decision making is guided and constrained by what the authors describe as the "dominant belief systems" that such executives seem to share. For example, they all have strong beliefs about the necessity of balancing the requirements of their major constituencies — the capital markets from which they must borrow, the labor markets from which they must obtain their employees, the suppliers, and most important, the customers. Scarce resources must be allocated in such a way that the needs of each group are met to an optimal degree.

Senior managers have complex mental equations by which they make their decisions. Constraining such broad strategic decisions, Donaldson and Lorsch found, was a set of interrelated beliefs about (1) the distinctive competence of their organization, (2) the degree of financial risk that was appropriate for their organization, and (3) the degree to which they felt their organization should be financially self-sufficient. The specifics of such beliefs differed from industry to industry and company to company, but in each company studied senior management had strong beliefs in these three areas, and those beliefs guided specific decisions about goals, means, and management practices.

What we can say about the nature of top-management cultures, then, is that they are similar in *structure;* the basic assumptions are concerned with the same kinds of issues that all top managers face. How they resolve those issues, however, depends on other factors such as the technology, the maturity of the products and markets, and the unique historical experience of each company.

One could extrapolate further and hypothesize that the subculture at each level of the organization will over time structurally reflect the major issues and tasks that must be confronted at that level and that the resolution of those tasks will provide different kinds of cultural content in different industries and companies. Thus all first-line supervisors will develop assumptions about human nature and how to manage employees, but whether they develop idealistic assumptions or cynical assumptions will depend more on the industry and actual company experience. Similarly, all sales managers will develop assumptions about human motivation on the basis of their experience in managing salespeople, but whether they come to believe in salary plus commission, pure commission, bonus systems, or individual or team reward systems will again depend upon the industry and the company.

In other words, the structure of any given hierarchical level's culture will be primarily defined by the tasks that must be achieved at that level. One can also anticipate that the group will have only weak assumptions or no assumptions at all in other areas because its members have not faced tasks or had shared experiences in those areas. To use the first-line supervisor again as an example, she may have very strong assumptions about human nature and either weak assumptions or no assumptions about how much debt a company should carry. On the other hand, top management will have very strong assumptions about debt level and only weak ones about how to manage technology or specific customer sets.

Mergers and Acquisitions

The issue of culture and subculture arises whenever two companies merge or one company acquires another. In the former case one attempts to blend two cultures into one without necessarily treating one or the other as dominant. In the latter case the acquired organization automatically becomes a subculture in the larger culture of the acquiring company. In either case the problem of blending or assimilation is compounded by the fact that the total new unit will not have any shared history and one or the other subunit will feel inferior, threatened, angry, and defensive (Buono and Bowditch, 1989; Centre for Organizational Studies, 1990; McManus and Hergert, 1988).

When the management of a company decides to merge with or acquire another company, it usually carefully checks the financial strength, market position, management strength, and various other concrete aspects pertaining to the health of the other company. Rarely checked, however, are those aspects that might be considered cultural: the philosophy or style of the company; its technological origins, which might provide clues as to its basic assumptions; and its beliefs about its mission and its future. Yet a cultural mismatch in an acquisition or merger is as great a risk as a financial, product, or market mismatch.

For example, some years ago the large packaged-food company mentioned earlier purchased a successful chain of hamburger restaurants. Despite ten years of concerted effort, however, it could not make the acquisition profitable. First of all, the company did not anticipate that many of the best managers of the acquired company would leave because they did not like the philosophy of the new parent company. Instead of hiring new managers with experience in the fast-food business, the parent company assigned some of its own managers to run the new business. This was its second mistake because these managers did not understand the technology of the fast-food business and hence were unable to utilize many of the marketing techniques that had proved effective in the parent company. Third, the parent company imposed many of the control systems and procedures that had historically proved useful for it and consequently drove the operating costs of the chain up too high. The parent company's managers found that they could never completely understand franchise operations and hence could not get a feel for what it would take to run that kind of business profitably. Eventually, the company sold the restaurant chain, having lost many millions of dollars over a decade.

The lack of understanding of the cultural risks of buying a franchised business was brought out even more clearly in another case, where a very stuffy, traditional, moralistic company whose management prided itself on its high ethical standards bought a chain of fast-food restaurants that were locally franchised all around the country. The company's managers discovered, much to their chagrin, that one of the biggest of these restaurants in a nearby state had become the local brothel. The activities of the town in which it was located were so well integrated around this restaurant that the alternative of closing it down posed the risk of drawing precisely the kind of attention the parent company wanted at all costs to avoid. The managers asked themselves, after the fact, "Should we have known what our acquisition involved on this more subtle level? Should we have understood our own value system better to ensure compatibility?"

A third example highlights the clash of two sets of assumptions about authority. A first-generation company run by a founder who injected strong beliefs that one succeeds by stimulating initiative and egalitarianism was bought by another first-generation company, which was run by a strong autocratic entrepreneur who had trained his employees to be highly disciplined and formal. The purchasing company wanted and needed the new managerial talent it acquired, but within one year of the purchase, most of the best managers from the acquired company had left because they could not adapt to the formal autocratic style of the parent company. The autocratic entrepreneur could not understand why this had happened and had no sensitivity to the cultural differences between the two companies.

What is striking in each of these cases is the lack of insight on the part of the acquiring company into its own organizational culture, its own unconscious assumptions about how a business should be run. As one contemplates some relatively recent major cross-industry mergers, such as Du Pont with Conoco, U.S. Steel with Marathon Oil, and American Express with Shearson, one can only wonder how these corporate giants will mesh not only their businesses but their cultures. The histories of these companies, as well as their differing technologies, suggest that substantial cultural differences almost certainly exist between them.

Occasionally, one will find an acquisition or merger that is made in order to bring in new cultural elements that are seen as necessary to revitalize the older, more dominant culture. Thus Multi bought a consumer goods company to force itself to learn more about marketing. AT&T bought an aggressive high-tech company and merged some of its R & D people into it to revitalize some aspects of its R & D operation. American Express is said to have merged with Shearson in order to import some of the elements of the Shearson culture, and so on. These mergers or acquisitions often do not work because the dominant culture of one company is simply too strong.

Joint Ventures, Strategic Alliances, and Other Multiorganizational Enterprises

Cultural issues come into even sharper focus when one observes what a number of companies are trying to do today in their efforts to draw on each other's strengths and to break into new products and markets. Salk (1992) made detailed observations of three joint ventures in which the parent companies came from different countries — a Canadian-Italian joint venture based in Europe, a French-German joint venture based in France, and a German-U.S. joint venture based in the United States.

The culture issues played themselves out in three different ways. In the first case the Canadian company espoused cultural equality, but for "practical reasons" the joint venture was located near the Canadian parent's European headquarters and many of its office procedures were adopted from the headquarters. Early interactions led to mutually negative stereotypes, which still dominated interaction three years later. The Canadians liked to write things down and to make requests on paper; the Italians felt that things on paper were unimportant and that if something was needed, one had to go and personally ask for it. Therefore, they tended to ignore the memos, leading the Canadians to conclude that the Italians were unmotivated and uncooperative.

The Italian parent company functioned in terms of personal relationships and personal influence; the Canadian parent functioned in terms of formal roles, job descriptions, and procedures. This led the Italians to view the Canadians as hopelessly bureaucratic. The significant point is that each side felt it to be inappropriate to bring their feelings out into the open. Somehow culture at this level became something that could not be discussed because it might threaten face too much. So the group lived with its stereotypes, grumbled silently to the researcher in interviews, but did nothing to correct the situation. To date, business results have not forced the issue because of a favorable business climate, but if that changes, the organization will have to confront more directly the cultural gap it is living with.

In the French-German venture the direction of cultural domination is increasingly being determined by the actual ratio of French to German managers in the venture and the location of the business. In this case the Germans appear to be adapting to the French style.

In the German-U.S. venture the situation was more complicated. Each parent had decided to provide cross-cultural training on what the other culture was like, and the venture had budgeted for a one-week Outward Bound type of experience to help the two teams come together. The initial company training created strong stereotypes, and the joint training was unfortunately canceled for time and money reasons. As a result the early interactions were very much dominated by the learned stereotypes. This became evident, for example, when production targets were set and the Germans assumed that the U.S. numbers were always inflated because "Americans always expect budgets and targets to be cut by higher management." On the other hand, the Americans had been warned that Germans are always too conservative. Each side tried to give fairly accurate numbers but totally mistrusted the numbers from the other side. Again, they were unable to bring this out into open lest they offend each other.

In this case some cultural blending resulted from a business crisis. Production was well below what both the Germans and the Americans had anticipated, there were unanticipated labor problems, and the U.S. parent changed key managers after these problems arose. In order to correct the problems the group finally got together as a group and chose procedures on the basis of which cultural assumptions were best suited to each problem. In the labor relations area the Germans ended up leaning more on the Americans, but in the technical area the reverse happened. Gradually, a new culture was forged by taking some assumptions from each parent.

Salk (1992) makes the point that although these were cross-national joint ventures, the more decisive factors determining outcomes were specific company policies, especially those pertaining to the physical location of the venture and the defined career paths of the managers sent to the venture. If the managers saw their careers as still located in the parent company, it was much harder for the venture participants to become a team. This situation was especially problematic in the Canadian-Italian venture because the Italian managers had a much higher incentive to keep their relationships with the parent in good order than to learn to get along with the Canadians. What had initially been defined as a study across national cultural boundaries turned out to be as much a study of company cultures and their career development policies.

Structural Opposition Groups

As organizations grow and evolve, they sometimes develop groups that initially define themselves in terms of their opposition to other groups and form subcultures that are in some respects deliberately countercultural with respect to the main culture. The most typical examples are unions that form in opposition to management and base their ideology on the assumption that management and labor are structurally and permanently in conflict. The organization then consists of subcultures that cannot be integrated, and the leadership issue becomes one of how to create a climate of negotiation and conflict resolution in which organizational goals can be achieved. When such opposing subcultures have ties in other organizations, such as international unions or political parties, leaders must go outside their own organizations and negotiate with other organizations and government units.

Opposition-oriented subcultures can also arise from management philosophies that emphasize internal competition among individuals and groups. As noted earlier, in the Jones case Jones's bias in favor of family members created a managerial counterculture. When mature and declining organizations become too rigid they sometimes create countercultures organized around new products or process ideas such as DeLorean's attempt to build a different kind of car within General Motors (Martin and Siehl, 1983; Wright, 1979).

Shop floor culture is often alleged to be very different from the culture of the rest of the organization, as one would expect in terms of hierarchical differentiation and the different tasks of different levels. But one should not automatically assume that shop floor culture will be a counterculture. In any given organization that one studies one should empirically determine how the different-level subcultures relate to each other.

Finally, in U.S. organizations there is a growing issue surrounding diversity and the possibility that different racial groups and genders are forming subcultures around their particular career concerns. In each organization that one examines, one should treat this as an empirical issue to be studied in order to determine the particular assumptions about gender and diversity that may be operating.

Summary and Conclusions

As organizations grow and mature, they will inevitably have to differentiate themselves, and the basis on which they do that will determine what kinds of subcultures will eventually arise in them. Differentiation can take place along functional lines; in terms of geographies; in terms of products, markets, and technologies; in terms of hierarchical levels; in terms of integrated divisions; in terms of new kinds of arrangements involving more than one organization; or in terms of opposition to other groups. If any of these means of differentiation produce fairly stable groups that develop some history of their own, the groups will develop sets of shared assumptions that will coexist with whatever overall organizational assumptions are shared.

The content of these subcultures will reflect the basic external and internal tasks that the group must fulfill. To the extent that such tasks will differ in different subgroups, we will see different kinds of cultures arising in them. That, in turn, will make it harder for higher levels to integrate the efforts of different groups. This point applies especially to functional subcultures where the personalities and occupational backgrounds of members make it likely that they will come to organizational tasks with very different assumptions.

It is important to recognize that at some point the task of integrating an organization is a problem of how to integrate a variety of subcultures. The leader must therefore be sensitive to different subcultures and must develop the skills of working across cultural boundaries. This means that leaders have to be sufficiently outside their own organizational and occupational culture to be able to perceive subcultural differences and to be sympathetic to them. Perhaps the essence of what we call general management is this ability to bring together people from different subcultures and get them working well with each other.

Leaders should not be surprised when they find that different functions seem to be talking completely different languages or when geographically isolated managers do not interpret headquarters memos accurately or when the concerns of senior management about costs and productivity are not shared by employees. Building an effective organization is ultimately a matter of meshing the different subcultures by encouraging the evolution of common goals, common language, and common procedures for solving problems.

CHAPTER FOURTEEN

Management and Information Technology
Two Subcultures in Collision?

Here at our company the two cultures interact not
at all well. For example, Computing Culture people persuaded a few top managers to put terminals
on their desks for direct access to Mainframe information, but the language required to communicate with the Mainframe is so unpleasant that
these terminals, and the laboriously crafted software
behind them, are probably the least utilized capital investment in the Company.

    One of the unspoken assumptions of the
Computing Culture is that transistors are very expensive so one should minimize the demands put
on the electronics and let the people extend themselves to deal with crude languages, dull displays,
Rube Goldberg graphics, etc. etc. The Computing Culture people know how to do better, but they
are prisoners of their own version of the Puritan
Ethic, "if computing were fun, it would be sinful."

    Our general managers know perfectly well
that transistors are dirt cheap now and getting
cheaper, but the implications of these facts have not
assimilated into Assumptions of the Management

276

Culture. So the General Managers tolerate but re-
fuse to use what the Computing Culture provides.
[VP Planning, personal communication, 1987]

Subcultures can be completely congruent, can be supportive of each other, can stand in opposition to each other, and
can be independent of each other. How the dynamics of particular subcultures play themselves out will depend on many factors. The letter that opens this chapter was written after a presentation on corporate culture to the top-management group of a
medium-size high-tech company and illustrates the importance
of applying the culture concepts to subunits and occupational
communities within larger organizations. Given the situation
that most organizations face today, it is especially important
to determine whether unconscious assumptions operate in the
community of information technology (IT) because of the growing evidence that this technology has a tremendous potential
impact on the performance of organizations and that the problems of implementing this technology have been horrendous (for
example, Gibson and Ball, 1989; Markus, 1984; Rockart and
DeLong, 1988; Zuboff, 1988).

For an organization to cope effectively with a rapidly
changing environment of the sort we see increasingly in today's
global context, it must be able to (1) import information efficiently; (2) move that information to the right place in the organization, where it can be analyzed, digested, and acted upon;
(3) make the necessary internal transformations to take account
of the new information; and (4) get feedback on the impacts
of its new responses, which starts the whole coping cycle via
information gathering all over again (Schein, 1980). In this organizational coping cycle, the flow of information is critical to
the health and effectiveness of the organization. Therefore, any
evidence that improved information flows via IT are failing to
be adopted or implemented is potentially very serious.

Can the concept of cultural assumptions help us understand such problems of adoption and implementation? Are
taken-for-granted assumptions making it difficult for the technology to be understood and utilized? If so, what is their nature,

and what can be done to reduce cultural conflict within the organization if managerial assumptions clash with IT assumptions?

The following is based on twenty-five years of (1) general inquiry, (2) personal efforts to learn how to use some of the technology, (3) consulting work with computer companies, (4) observations of the interaction of IT workers with others in the organization, (5) systematic interviewing of IT workers to check some of my emerging conclusions, and (6) systematic interviewing of CEOs about their attitudes toward IT (Schein, 1992).

Information Technology as an Occupational Community

Let me begin by defining an occupational community (Van Maanen and Barley, 1984; Orlikowski, 1988). This concept denotes a group of practitioners, researchers, and teachers who have a common base of knowledge, a common jargon, similar background and training, and a sense of identifying with each other. An occupational community is not a profession in the sense of having genuine autonomy and review only by peers, but it is often on the way to becoming or attempting to become a profession in this more traditional sense (Schein, 1972). Whether or not the IT community qualifies as a profession today is debatable. However, those who have examined the question sociologically have concluded that, like engineers, members of the IT community are primarily employed by others and therefore do not have the autonomy that one associates with the traditional professions (Orlikowski, 1988).

An occupational community can, however, have enough of a history and enough interaction within itself to have developed a shared set of basic assumptions about itself, its work, its relationship to its environment, and its clients. I am, of course, assuming more homogeneity in the IT community than probably exists in reality, but I have noted in my encounters with IT professors, IT consultants, and IT practitioners at the management and worker levels, how consistently similar many of their assumptions are.

I do not claim that I can describe the total culture of either the IT community or the subculture of top management. Rather,

I am trying to decipher those elements of the culture that bear on the observed difficulty of implementing IT solutions in organizations. The cultural description that follows is presented as I have experienced it over the years. Many of the assumptions of the IT worker are stark and clear, and many managers share those same assumptions. However, when one analyzes cases where implementation has gone poorly, one notices that a substantial number of senior managers hold assumptions that are quite different and often opposed to the assumptions of IT. My observations are organized around three sets of assumptions—those about the nature of information (Exhibit 14.1), those about the nature of human nature (Exhibit 14.2), and those about the nature of organizations and managerial work (Exhibit 14.3).

IT Assumptions About Information

Immediately following each IT assumption about information presented in Exhibit 14.1, the alternative that many users and managers feel to be valid appears in parentheses.

Members of the IT community will, of course, point out that they are well aware of the complexities of information and that they do not have such a simplistic view of the universe as portrayed in Exhibit 14.1. Nevertheless, when one examines the artifacts of the occupation—the computers, the software, the keyboards, the jargon, and the kinds of problems typically addressed by IT systems—one is struck repeatedly by the degree to which IT workers idealize the assumptions noted, even if they acknowledge their occasional lack of validity.

The central issue these assumptions raise is highlighted by the reaction of CEOs when one analyzes their own use of IT. In a study of ninety CEOs from a broad range of large and small companies in a variety of industries, we found that only 15 percent or so personally used desktop terminals (Schein, 1992). The main objection of the nonusers was that the kind of information they deal with does not lend itself to the kind of packaging and transmission that IT makes possible. As noted below, many of them felt that they needed face-to-face contact

Exhibit 14.1. IT Assumptions About the Nature of Information.

---

1. It is possible to package and transmit information accurately in an electronic medium.
   (Alternative: One can only transmit raw data and that information must be extracted by other means as a separate task.)

2. Information can be validly divided into bits.
   (Alternative: Meaning derives from complex patterns or gestalts.)

   The best example of the implementation of these two assumptions is the tendency in many companies to convert their descriptive performance appraisals and job histories in the personnel records into quantitative indexes that can be electronically stored. Complex concepts such as "potential" for higher-level general management jobs are measured in terms of numerical ratings and rankings on the premise that people can then be compared in terms of their numerical standing.

3. Information can be frozen in time on a screen or on a printout.
   (Alternative: Information is always changing and dynamic.)

   The best example of this contrast was provided by an Israeli tank commander who noted that in the war against Syria, the Syrian tank commanders operated from a predetermined battle plan, while the Israeli tank commanders opened their hatches and looked around to see what was happening moment by moment, giving them a tremendous tactical advantage.

4. Faster transmission and computation are always better than slower.
   (Alternative: The costs associated with speed may not be worth it.)

   As described later in this chapter, for some purposes it may be actually dysfunctional for managers to see information as quickly as their subordinates, so the general value of speed has possibly to be modified in terms of who sees what at what time.

5. More information is always better than less.
   (Alternative: Managers often get too much information, and what they need is more of the right kind of information; IT produces information overload.)

   It is a real question, to be explored in the context of managerial control systems, whether it is better for higher levels to know everything for every level below them or whether the problem of increasing organizational effectiveness is really how to conduct complex analysis of who needs to know what.

6. The more quantifiable the information is, the better.
   (Alternative: Much qualitative information, such as performance appraisals, should be left in qualitative form rather than converted into numbers as a "convenience" to the system.)

   If all information is ultimately quantified, it makes possible even more than is possible today "management by the numbers," a concept that is increasingly being criticized because it depersonalizes the organization too much and leads to the use of indicators that may not be valid representatives of what is going on.

Exhibit 14.1. IT Assumptions About the Nature of Information, Cont'd.

---

7. Ultimately, a paperless environment is more efficient and desirable. (Alternative: The ability to see and manipulate paper is intrinsic to some kinds of tasks.)

   There seems to be a general goal or ideal in the IT community of the paperless office based on notions of reduced costs and greater accessibility of electronically stored data. However, some tasks may continue to require the ability to look at many more things simultaneously than electronic screens can provide, raising questions about the ultimate validity of this vision.

---

to calibrate what was being said to them and to determine how their own messages were being received and that even teleconferencing did not give enough cues. What was information for nonusers was something more holistic, complex, and dynamic than what they could get from their IT systems.

IT Assumptions About Human Nature and Learning

A second area of potentially conflicting assumptions concerns the perceptions of human nature, human abilities, and human motivations. These are presented again from the IT point of view, with alternative assumptions of some users and managers appearing in parentheses, in Exhibit 14.2.

It is in this general arena that the potentially most difficult issues arise around implementing the technology because of overly rationalistic assumptions about people and the failure to recognize how difficult, anxiety provoking, painful, and time consuming new learning can be. For many, the learning involved in IT use is humiliating and stressful; for some, the cognitive style involved in working with desktop terminals or other IT tools is totally alien. They cannot learn or remember commands, they are not accurate enough to execute the commands correctly, they are not used to keyboards and other electronic devices, and they cannot visualize in their heads the impact on remote machines of pushing buttons on a control panel or hitting keys on a keyboard (Zuboff, 1988).

In our study of CEO attitudes toward IT, we encountered

Exhibit 14.2. IT Assumptions About People and Learning.

---

1. Technology leads and people adapt.
   (Alternative: Technology should adapt to people.)

2. All people can and should learn whatever is required to use the technology.
   (Alternative: People are different and some have cognitive styles that are inherently unsuited to the kind of thinking IT requires.)

3. People can and should learn the language of IT (for example, hardware, software, RAM, ROM, cursor, bits, bytes, mips, storage, LAN, terminal, interface, E mail, and so on).
   (Alternative: The necessary IT concepts can be expressed in ordinary English.)

4. People can and should adapt to the IT "interface" in the form of keyboards, command languages, windows, mice, and the like.
   (Alternative: People should be able to write, point, or speak to the computer.)

   All four of these assumptions reflect a fundamental implementation mentality based on taking for granted that the technology is superior to what is being done today and that the solutions offered by the technology are basically the right ones. If users are to get involved, it is at the level of how to implement things, rarely at the level of basic design. And even then, for users to be involved, it is expected that they will learn enough of the language, the commands, and how to operate the interface to be able to communicate with the specialists. Rarely do IT projects start with genuinely ethnographic studies of users to determine how to design the technology for a particular set of users and uses.

5. People already know how to communicate and manage; therefore, IT needs only to enhance these processes.
   (Alternative: Many managers do not know how to communicate or manage in the first place, so handing them sophisticated communications technology is like handing a racing car to someone who does not know how to drive.)

6. If IT facilitates task performance and efficiency, people will adopt it.
   (Alternative: Many people have motives, feelings, and anxieties that make them complacent and unwilling to learn new things in the first place. And/or efficiency is not automatically a high value.)

---

a number who said that they would not implement some of the new systems because "the troops are not ready for it and would screw it up." They felt they had to first teach their organizations some simple principles of management and communication, and only when those were well embedded, would it even be timely to think about a more sophisticated approach using IT. A number of CEOs were reluctant to get involved with desktop terminals and electronic mail not because they would not or could not type but because they were concealing a more fundamental lack — they felt they could not spell or apply grammar correctly. Until the technology adapted to them, they would not use it.

These problems are exacerbated by the possibility that members of the IT community, especially those who design some of the more advanced systems, have a particular cognitive style that they project onto everyone else. They tend to be (1) convergent thinkers, oriented toward discovering optimal and final solutions to problems; (2) intolerant of ambiguity, high in need for clarity and unambiguous resolutions to problems; (3) precise and accurate, oriented toward perfection with little sympathy for satisficing; (4) logical and oriented toward clear rules and procedures; (5) concrete and oriented toward clear output and quick feedback; (6) task oriented more than people oriented; (7) long-range oriented, seeking final solutions to problems that will continue to work; (8) decisive in the task area in the sense of having to make decisions when writing a program or designing a system; (9) control oriented in that the purpose of most systems is to reduce and eliminate human error and irrationality; and (10) more interested in the hardware and systems problems of management than in the people problems because the systems are supposed to make management "people proof."

If others are not like themselves, then the systems must somehow compensate. But in making that assumption, IT designers often forget that the problem is to get the human with a different cognitive style to use the system in the first place. And the IT cognitive style often leads to impatience with "dumb users," to satisfaction with instruction sets written for people like themselves, and a tendency to rationalize that future generations who grow up with the computer will be better able to handle everything. The possibility that some people will *never* learn some of what is being made available is not examined.

An even deeper psychodynamic hypothesis about managerial use of IT could be suggested on the basis of Zuboff's (1988) analysis of the evolution of managerial work. She points out that historically the growth of middle management and white-collar clerical work is related to the rationalization and routinization of managerial work. As managerial tasks were routinized, they tended to be pushed down the hierarchy, always leaving top management with the tasks that depended more on intuition, judgment, wisdom, and experience. The use of IT once again forces rationalization of decisions, making explicit one's assumptions and premises, an activity that would be defensively resisted by those senior managers who had achieved their high positions by the use of intuition and judgment. Refusing to use IT could then be seen as a way of protecting their turf and the mystique of managerial decision making. Whether the resolution then would be to figure out how IT can model intuition or whether senior management has to learn to be more explicit about its intuitive style is not clear.

An interesting scenario along these lines played itself out in one of the clinical testing groups of the pharmaceutical division of Multi. A group of doctors who designed and evaluated clinical tests were encouraged to try to use some expert systems and statistical packages that were so routinized that their secretaries could enter and evaluate the data. This appealed to the doctors because it would free up some time for other conceptual activities. However, their boss, who observed this increased free time, gave them extra tasks that the doctors did not consider worthy of them. Instead of rebelling, the doctors took back the statistical work from their secretaries and told the boss that they did not have time for the new assignments. The manner in which the IT implementation was handled led, in the end, to less productivity and incorrect claims by the doctors that only they could do the complicated statistical evaluations. The fact that the secretaries had been doing them was suppressed to allow the doctors to protect their time.

It should be noted that occupational communities typically grow up around new technologies and that the characteristics of the information technology itself, computer hardware and software design, require certain kinds of people with certain kinds of skills and cognitive styles. As IT becomes differentiated — designing computers, designing applications, and designing complex systems — we will see more variations in the styles of the members of the community and, indeed, will see subcommunities spring up with their own subcultures.

IT Assumptions About Organization and Management

The IT assumptions articulated in Exhibit 14.3 about organization and management are more characteristic of that wing of the IT occupational community that could be called the visionaries, those who foresee more fundamental changes in organizations as an inevitable concomitant of what IT makes possible (for example, Davis and Davidson, 1991; Drucker, 1988; Hedberg and others, 1976; Malone and others, 1987; Rockart and DeLong, 1988; Rockart and Short, 1991; Scott-Morton, 1991).

A number of the assumptions outlined in Exhibit 14.3 concern the use of information for control purposes. There is ample evidence that if one gives senior managers more and better information about the performance of all parts of the organization, one makes it possible for those managers to "micromanage," to overcontrol the organization, and thereby to create dysfunctional consequences. Such managerial behavior generally has several undesirable consequences.

First of all, employees resent having the details of their performance monitored at higher levels of the organization. This leads them to distort the information input into the system to protect themselves. McGregor (1960) tells of a precomputerized version of his process that was operating in a large telephone company. The operation of each local unit was closely measured, and a performance index that allowed comparison of all the units in the organization was computed. The numbers were regularly collected and assembled for scrutiny by the company president in a large book that came to be called the green dragon. If any local unit's index fell a few points, the president would be on the phone to that unit demanding to know what was going on. This was so painful for the local employees that they devised ingenious ways of fudging the data so that the numbers that were entered ultimately had little to do with actual performance.

A similar situation arose more recently in a large international company that manufactures elevators. Instead of having each city handle the calls to do its own servicing, it was found

Exhibit 14.3. IT Assumptions About Organization and Management.

1. A flatter organization will be a better one.
   (Alternative: Hierarchy is a primary and necessary coordination mechanism, as well as an intrinsic way for groups to allocate status, responsibility, and privilege.)

   Getting rid of layers of management is assumed to be one of the great incentives for installing IT systems, but beyond presumed cost saving, the logic of fewer levels is not typically spelled out and little attention is given to the possible dysfunctional consequences of fewer levels (Schein, 1989).

2. Management can and will give up hierarchy if other coordination mechanisms become possible.
   (Alternative: Hierarchy is intrinsic to human systems and will always be necessary as a coordination mechanism.)

3. A leaner, more automated organization will be a better one.
   (Alternative: To retain organizational flexibility, one should have some excess resources and should not automate processes that may themselves become obsolete.)

4. A more fully connected organization with open channels in every direction will be a better one.
   (Alternative: Full circulation of information will slow down the decision process and invite more local innovation and creativity than may be desirable in some business circumstances, such as those requiring tight coordination and discipline.)

5. Managers want a more open networked organization in which information will be readily available to many more levels.
   (Alternative: Managers gain their power in part from controlling information and therefore are intrinsically opposed to opening the channels more widely.)

6. Managers know how to use information responsibly and appropriately.
   (Alternative: Many managers will mishandle the information made available to them, and it is therefore up to the IT community to figure out the correct uses of information, to educate management to those uses, and to prevent or even forbid certain uses that would be harmful to the organization.)

that a central service organization located in the company headquarters could not only provide more prompt and standardized responses to service calls but could also dispense service more quickly by then calling the local service organization from the center. This way information could also be gathered on which elevators needed unusual levels of service, suggesting a design or manufacturing problem that could be corrected in the next generation of the product. Having a completely centralized worldwide system enabled the company to provide much quicker and more reliable service because an operator was always on hand to call the local service people at any hour of the day.

Unfortunately, the president of the company noticed that this information base could also be used to monitor the performance of the local service units. If, in a given city, the service calls were unusually high and one could rule out technological problems, he would call that office and ask what was going on there. The result was the same as in the telephone company; that is, the local people figured out a way to subvert the system. They went to their major clients and convinced them that they would get even faster service if they ignored the worldwide 800 service number and called them directly. The result was that the central office now had a distorted picture of what was actually going on and, worse, was losing valuable information about the technical performance of the elevators.

A second undesirable consequence of management use of information for control purposes is that overmanagement and overcontrol can and will eventually lead to employee dependency. If an employee feels that she is accountable for her own performance, she will create whatever feedback mechanisms she needs to ensure the appropriate quality level. If the information system monitors her at higher levels of the organization, there is a geat temptation to abdicate self-measurement and self-control. Eventually, the employee develops the attitude that "if the system knows how I am doing, 'they' will let me know if my performance is below standard; I don't have to worry about it myself." Complacency and a dependence on the system results.

Third, giving senior management detailed information about lower parts of the organization disempowers the layers of management in between, leading those middle layers also to resist or subvert the system to protect their own power and position. If the organization then follows through with forced elimination of the middle levels, senior management may find itself managing at such a level of detail that it may cease to pay attention to other more important aspects of its role such as longer-range planning and designing the work organization and systems.

Members of the IT community sometimes collude here either by admitting outright that they are only technocrats who know relatively little about how business organizations should be run or by granting managers too much power by letting them define how a particular IT enhancement could or should work. Because of their subordinate position in most organizations, some IT workers take the attitude that the client is always right, and they will not challenge management even if the system is being misused. Or they collude with top management by promising that they can make the system cheat proof and, thereby, decrease even further the willingness of lower levels to monitor themselves.

Many of the CEOs in our interviews were sophisticated users of IT but said that when they became CEOs they stopped using their desktop terminals because they felt it would undermine their ability to do their job. They saw the job of CEO as being genuinely different and, as noted above, requiring the gathering and analysis of a different level of information than was made available in the IT systems. They encouraged their staffs to use the systems but refused to get directly involved themselves.

These issues highlight the importance of managerial assumptions and attitudes about people and resurrect McGregor's issue of whether an effective manager must have Theory Y attitudes (that is, a basic trust of people). One could speculate that sophisticated IT systems that operate from the assumptions that more and faster are better would, in the hands of a cynical Theory X manager, inevitably lead to overcontrol and micromanagement because the system makes them so easy and convenient. The same kind of system in the hands of a Theory Y manager would have different results because that manager would be conscious of the dangers of creating dependency and resentment, would want her employees to continue to control and monitor themselves, and would want her middle managers to continue to function in terms of their own levels of responsibility. She would use the data for control purposes only at the appropriate organizational level.

A good example of how this would work was provided

by the president of a large division of an aerospace company. He had developed a system that allowed him to monitor each of his many projects on a day-to-day basis. If costs or schedules fell off, he was instantly on the phone to the project managers several levels down in the organization to determine what was wrong. He felt he needed that information because his outside contractors would be calling him and wanting more information. Because the president was an open and trusting manager, the project managers came to him with their resentment before they started to subvert the system and asked him to "stop bugging them" with the phone calls because they could not answer the questions if they themselves did not have time to investigate what was going on. The whole group genuinely explored all the feelings involved, including the president's that he really needed the information for his outside reporting, and developed a workable resolution. They would introduce a delay of a day or two between the time the project managers received the information and the time the president received it. That way the project managers would retain their autonomy, have time to find out what was wrong, and be able to inform the president so that he could deal with the outside questions. But to make this work the president had to be able to trust the project managers and to be willing to tolerate the delay, something he was glad to do if it preserved the managers' commitment to monitor their own projects effectively.

Complete openness of information in the projected nonhierarchical, networked organization of the future would have the effect of empowering everyone in the organization by giving everyone access to everything. This condition is often resisted by higher levels because their power depends in part upon the information that is uniquely available to them. If the flat-networked organization is to work, everyone must have a higher level of trust and must be willing to accept power and status on bases other than control of information. Thus what is technologically possible and maybe even desirable from a pure efficiency point of view depends very much on the motivation and attitude structure of the people in the system, not merely on the technology.

These IT assumptions also force an examination of what managers' deep motivational structure really is. Are managers ultimately motivated to make the organization optimally effective, or are they only motivated to make it effective enough to preserve their own position and career? Management, of course, presents itself as ultimately committed to the welfare of the organization, but if a proposed IT system makes managers' own position vulnerable, their own priorities might lead them to avoid or subvert the system even though it might help the overall organization. Removing layers of middle management and developing nonhierarchical coordination mechanisms may destroy what is for many managers the essence of management: the ability to rise to a position of power and responsibility. Many managers might find it inconceivable to give up the prerogatives and perquisites that hierarchy provides (Schein, 1989). The assumption that flat organizations are better may, therefore, clash with one of the most central assumptions of the management culture, one that may take some time to change if the flat organization is to materialize at all.

Some Assumptions of Senior Management

Thus far I have tried to present some of the major assumptions of the IT community as I perceive them and have indicated in each case an alternative assumption that could be made. Many of these alternative assumptions are, in fact, made by senior executive management and can be summarized here.

1. Information is intrinsically dynamic, holistic, and imprecise; therefore, it cannot be packaged and transmitted electronically.
2. IT systems only deal with data, and it takes human thought to turn data into information and knowledge.
3. The computer limits and distorts thinking by focusing the user on only those kinds of data that can be packaged and transmitted.
4. Communication requires face-to-face contact so that one can, at any given moment, assess the full range of cues

such as tone of voice, timing, and body language to determine how one's message is being received.

5. Hierarchy is intrinsic to organizations and necessary for coordination.

6. Personal success and career security are measured by progress up the hierarchy.

7. Human beings are intrinsically necessary to the performance of organizations and must be developed and enhanced, not replaced.

8. IT is just another tool among many tools that managers need in order to run the business and must be evaluated accordingly.

9. IT is too expensive, too complicated, and too unreliable to be a useful tool in spite of its potential strategic advantage in many companies.

10. IT threatens the security and orderliness of the present organizational structures and processes and, thereby, the welfare of the present members.

Because the culture of senior management is probably not as integrated and coherent as the culture of IT, the assumptions stated above are clearly not held by all senior managers. However, if even some senior managers hold such assumptions, consider the implications for the effective utilization of IT. The following quotations from our CEO interviews will make these clearer.

"Personal interaction with a terminal or PC is not part of the CEO's job."

"Data from a terminal is not enough for the kinds of decisions CEOs face."

"It isn't worth the trouble to master the mechanics; a CEO's time is better spent in other ways."

"If you have found a person running a big company who has time to sit at a terminal, I'd really have to be suspicious of him."

"The role of the CEO is one of dealing with people and exercising judgment in decision making. The PC is a tool for fact-finding, not for dealing with people and making decisions. A CEO who uses a PC is not using his time wisely."

"Computing is a toy and does not befit the position."

"As a CEO you don't ask routine questions. I ask different questions all the time."

"Computer use can become a substitute for thinking."

"Computer-generated data come to be treated as if they represent reality and are not checked for accuracy."

"Computers are causing people to be lazy; the increasing reliance on computers is reducing our propensity to think."

"Business becomes too numbers oriented; people look at the trees not the forest and miss the global aspects of the problem."

"I saw the last company I worked for get ruined and damn near broken by its MIS group. They are great at creating solutions to nonproblems."

Many of these same executives will point out the strategic necessity and advantage of IT, and many of them will point to successful implementation of systems in their organizations. They are not intrinsically opposed to the use of IT, but they perceive a barrier between themselves and the IT proponents that can only be understood from the point of view that they are making different initial assumptions of the sort outlined above.

In effect, the introduction of IT systems into organizations creates for a time a clash between several subcultures. Once we recognize that we are dealing with an intercultural issue, we have a better understanding of why it is so difficult to get effective utilization and implementation. This is not merely a problem of teaching people to use a new tool; it is an issue of whose assumptions are going to bend and give way.

A good example of how the failure to recognize some of these assumptions slowed down the introduction of what may have been a potentially useful technology comes from the international division of a global bank. The department head wanted to design and install multiproduct workstations that would allow a clerk generalist to deal with a whole range of customer problems instead of having a host of specialists dealing with letters of credit, money transfer, and so on. The introduction of these workstations would have displaced a large number of people and required some of the present clerks to be retrained, something the bank was reluctant to do. However, the factor that finally prevented their installation was that the planners could not figure out what the career line would be for these clerk generalists and what their managers' roles would be. The hierarchical thinking was the greatest stumbling block to implementing a design that the members of this organization themselves wanted. The assumptions involved, however, could never be brought to the surface in a manner to permit an examination of how the IT assumptions and the managerial assumptions did or did not mesh because no one recognized that the implementation group consisted of representatives of two powerful subcultures.

Summary and Conclusions

Senior management and the information technology community can be viewed as two subcultures, each making a set of assumptions about the nature of information, the nature of people, the learning process, organizations, and management. An examination of those assumptions strongly suggests that they may be very different and that those differences account to a large degree for the problems of implementing IT solutions.

I am suggesting that the most important step in improving the utilization of IT is to recognize at the outset that the IT community is making certain assumptions that must be nonevaluatively examined in relation to the assumptions of management and of the eventual users of the technology. This is especially important because many of those assumptions concern the role of top management and thus involve leaders directly.

When a CEO asks to have an IT system installed in her company, is she aware of the degree to which the IT designers are making assumptions about what she wants in terms of an organization design and control system? The CEOs in our research were very conscious of the cost and efficiency implications of IT, but only a few of them were aware of the organizational implications of adopting an IT view of their organizations. A major implication for leadership, then, is to be very active in examining the assumptions of IT and for the leader to make her assumptions explicit so that if an intercultural issue is involved, it will be recognized early enough to be worked through.

To the extent that these assumptions differ and possibly conflict with each other, intercultural processes must be invented and designed to open up better communication between these two subgroups. If each group has developed its own assumptions, we cannot assume that one set can be imposed on the other set. The only solution is to generate enough joint activity so that new learning can take place to create a new set of assumptions that maximizes the best elements of each subculture.

Though this chapter has focused on the particular assumptions of the IT occupational community and of senior management, the same issues apply between other subcultures in organizations. As previously noted, the problems between functional, geographical, and divisional units are also likely to be the result of differences in shared unconscious assumptions built up in those subcultures. Leaders who wish to resolve those kinds of issues would be well advised to recognize from the outset that hierarchically imposed solutions do not work well when subcultural differences are involved. Rather, processes must be invented to allow the strengths of each subculture to interact to form integrative new solutions.

The Evolution of Culture and Leadership

In Part Five we tackle the difficult question of culture change. The most important groundwork for this analysis was laid in the previous discussion of evolutionary stages of organizations because the culture change issue is different in each stage. In Chapter Fifteen general change theory as it applies to culture change is reviewed and the matter of how culture evolves in organizations that are still under the influence of founders and owners is discussed. The mechanisms of managed change that are available to leaders at this stage are also outlined in this chapter. In Chapter Sixteen culture change in the midlife and mature organization is analyzed, and the change mechanisms available to leaders at these stages are reviewed. Special attention is also given to the problem of culture change in a declining organization. Chapter Seventeen illustrates some of these change mechanisms in a major turnaround effort launched by the Multi Company. This case also illustrates how organizational change and improvement can occur without the organization's having to change some of the deeper assumptions on which it is built. Leaders are often more successful building their changes on existing cultural assumptions, even though early in the change process it may appear that culture stands in the way of change.

For leaders to manage culture in any of these ways, they

must have the ability to perceive and evaluate elements of their own culture and to change those elements in the service of organizational survival and effectiveness. The more dynamic the external environment, the more likely it is that some elements of culture will become maladaptive, and the more necessary it will therefore be for leadership to actively hasten the process of cultural evolution and change. In every sense, then, as we discuss culture dynamics, leadership is now at center stage.

How one approaches the difficult and controversial topic of culture evolution and change depends very much on whether one is looking at it from the perspective of an outside observer, a member of the organization whose behavior and attitudes become a target of change, or a leader/change agent who is attempting to produce the change. What may be a constructive change imposed by a leader may seem like a terrible disruption of work routine to an employee and may hardly be noticed at all by the outsider. The focus of the chapters in Part Five, as well as those in the rest of this book, remains on the leader and how culture change appears from the leader's perspective.

CHAPTER FIFTEEN

The Dynamics of Culture Change and Leadership in Young Organizations

The way in which culture can and does change depends upon the stage at which the organization finds itself. For example, when a culture is in the growth stage, the ways to manipulate the mechanisms of embedding discussed in Chapter Twelve are the ways to change a culture as well. That is, leaders can manipulate what they pay attention to, control, and reward; their role modeling and coaching; how they allocate resources; how they select, promote, and "deselect" people; the organizational structures and processes they create; and so on. However, once the culture has stabilized in a mature organization because of a long history of success, leaders find that such manipulations are often limited or superficial in their effects. They discover that changing deeply embedded assumptions requires far more effort and time.

In this chapter I will begin by discussing some aspects of general change theory that one must understand if one is to make any sense of the culture change process as I will describe it. Next, I will review the different evolutionary stages that most organizations go through and analyze the deeper dynamics of culture at each of those stages. For each major stage I will then review the major culture change mechanisms that seem to be most relevant to that stage and highlight what the leader as a change manager can do—beyond manipulating the mechanisms already referred to—to change cultural assumptions in a desired direction.

The Dynamics of Change

The fundamental assumptions underlying any change in a human system are derived originally from Kurt Lewin (1947) and elaborated by me in studies of coercive persuasion, professional education, group dynamics training, and management development (Schein, 1961a, 1961b, 1964, 1972; Schein and Bennis, 1965). All human systems attempt to maintain equilibrium and to maximize their autonomy vis-à-vis their environment. Coping, growth, and survival all involve maintaining the integrity of the system in the face of a changing environment that is constantly causing various kinds of disequilibriums. The function of cognitive structures such as concepts, beliefs, attitudes, values, and assumptions is to organize the mass of environmental stimuli, to make sense of them, and to provide, thereby, a sense of predictability and meaning to the individual. The set of shared assumptions that develop over time in groups and organizations serves this stabilizing and meaning-providing function. The evolution of culture is therefore one of the ways in which a group or organization preserves its integrity and autonomy, differentiates itself from the environment and other groups, and provides itself an identity.

Unfreezing

If any part of the core structure is to change in more than minor incremental ways, the system must first experience enough disequilibrium to force a coping process that goes beyond just reinforcing the assumptions that are already in place. The creation of such a disequilibrium Lewin called unfreezing, or creating a motivation to change. In my subsequent research I found that unfreezing is, of necessity, composed of three very different processes, each of which must be present to a certain degree for the system to develop any motivation to change: (1) enough *dis-*

confirming data to cause serious discomfort and disequilibrium; (2) the connection of the disconfirming data to important goals and ideals causing *anxiety and/or guilt;* and (3) enough *psychological safety,* in the sense of seeing a possibility of solving the problem without loss of identity or integrity, thereby allowing members of the organization to admit the disconfirming data rather than defensively denying it.

Disconfirming data are any items of information that show the organization that some of its goals are not being met or that some of its processes are not accomplishing what they are supposed to. Sales are off, customer complaints are up, products with quality problems are returned more frequently, managers and employees are quitting in greater numbers than usual, employees are sick or absent more and more, and so on. The information is often only symptomatic; it does not automatically tell the organization what the underlying problem might be, but it creates disequilibrium in pointing up that something is wrong somewhere. It makes members of the organization uncomfortable.

By itself such disconfirmation does not produce a motivation to change because members of the organization can perceive the information as being basically irrelevant to important goals or ideals. In other words, if turnover of employees suddenly increases, it is still possible for leaders to say, "It is only the bad people who are leaving, the ones we don't want anyway." Or if sales are down, it is possible to say, "This is only a reflection of a minor recession." The organization will only feel anxious or guilty if the disconfirming information relates to important goals or ideals and it is cognitively impossible to deny such connections even if the information is threatening. But anxiety and guilt can be denied and repressed as well, so even if the disconfirming information registers, so to speak, that is still not enough to motivate change if the change implies some threat to the more basic sense of identity or integrity that the person or group feels.

It is not an uncommon situation, therefore, that disconfirming data have existed for a long time but because of a lack of psychological safety, the organization has avoided anxiety or guilt by repressing it or by denying the relevance, validity, or even the existence of the data. The essence of psychological safety, then, is that we can imagine a needed change without feeling a loss of integrity or identity. If the change I have to make threatens my whole self, I will deny the data and the need for change. Only if I can feel that I will retain my identity or my integrity as I learn something new or make a change, will I be able to even contemplate it.

The same phenomenon occurs at the organizational level. If to increase its sales, the organization must adopt a whole new architecture of how the components of its technology interrelate — what Henderson and Clark (1990) call a generational change, as contrasted with an incremental or radical change (where a whole new technology is involved) — members of the organization will not pay attention to the disconfirming data or will rationalize them away. As Henderson and Clark point out, under such conditions the organization will have learned to use filters and only to pay attention to data that allow it to make minor incremental changes. The identity that the organization has built up and that has been the source of its success must now be preserved, even if that means ultimate failure to adapt successfully to a changing environment.

Lorsch (1985) calls this same phenomenon strategic myopia and shows how organizational belief systems prevent leaders from contemplating strategies that do not fit the prior beliefs based on past success. Once a new leader provides a vision that permits the organization to see a way to solve the problem, to get back into equilibrium without losing its identity, the process of change can then proceed very rapidly because of the prior buildup of disconfirming data.

To understand this, one must recognize that psychologically we can simultaneously hear something and deny it. We have all had the experience in adulthood of finally changing some aspect of ourself and remembering that we had obtained feedback on the need for this change long before, sometimes even in childhood from our parents. However, because we did not see a way to make the change, we "stored" the disconfirming feedback in our unconscious until we felt safe enough to let it out. One essential component of this feeling of safety is that we finally see a way to work on the problem or see a direction of learning that we had not seen before.

Groups and organizations do the same thing. Economic data that indicate the organization's performance is flagging can for a long time be ignored, denied, and rationalized, but unconsciously they are stored. Once members find a direction for solving the problem, they will often say that they "knew" about the problem for months or years but could not figure out what to do so they "ignored" it.

The importance of visionary leadership can be understood in this context, in that the vision sometimes serves the function of providing the psychological safety that permits the organization to move forward. Without a period of prior disconfirmation it is not clear that a visionary leader would be given much attention. In other words, new visions are most important when people are ready to pay attention, and they are only ready to pay attention when they are consciously or unconsciously hurting because of an accumulation of disconfirming information. One might speculate that the reason why we have had so many books on transformational visionary leadership in the last decade is because as a society the United States is hurting and the need for some psychological safety via new visions is particularly acute (for example, Bass, 1981, 1985; Bennis and Nanus, 1985; Conger, 1989; Kotter, 1988; Leavitt, 1986; Tichy and Devanna, 1986).

Cognitive Restructuring

Once an organization has been unfrozen, the change process proceeds along a number of different lines that reflect either new learning through trial and error based on scanning the environment broadly or imitation of role models based on psychological identification with the role model. In either case, the essence of the new learning is usually some cognitive redefinition of some of the core concepts in the assumption set. For example, when companies that assume that they are lifetime employers who never lay anyone off are faced with the economic necessity to reduce payroll costs, they cognitively redefine layoffs as "transitions" or early retirements, make the transition packages very generous, provide long periods of time during which the employee can seek alternative employment, offer extensive counseling, provide outplacement services, and so on to preserve the assumption that "we treat our people fairly and well." This process is more than rationalization. It is a genuine cognitive redefinition on the part of the senior management of the organization.

Most change processes emphasize the need for behavior change. Such change is important in laying the groundwork for cognitive redefinition but is not sufficient unless such redefinition takes place. Behavior change can be coerced, but it will not last once the coercive force is lifted unless cognitive redefinition has preceded or accompanied it. Some change theories (for example, Festinger, 1957) argue that if behavior change is coerced for a long enough period of time, cognitive structures will adapt to rationalize the behavior change that is occurring. The evidence for this is not clear, however, as recent developments in former Communist countries reveal. People living under communism did not automatically become Communists even though they were coerced for fifty years or more.

Lorsch (1985), in his study of top management, shows how they attempted to make changes with small incremental adjustments to individual beliefs but that the kinds of changes that were necessary to improve adaptation to a rapidly changing environment really required more substantial restructuring of concepts such as risk and what was an acceptable level of debt that a company could carry. At both Action and Multi the concept of what "marketing" was underwent substantial cognitive redefinition as those companies attempted to cope with their changing environments.

Refreezing

The final step in any given change process is refreezing, which refers to the necessity for the new behavior and set of cognitions to be reinforced, to produce once again confirming data.

If such new confirmation is not forthcoming, the search and coping process continues. Once confirming data from important environmental sources, external stakeholders, or internal sources are produced, the new assumptions gradually stabilize until new disconfirmations start the change process all over again.

The foregoing model describes any change process, whether at the individual, group, or organizational level. The model identifies the necessary psychological conditions that must be present for any change to occur. When we look at organizational cultures and subcultures, we need in addition some broader categories of change that apply particularly to larger social systems, recognizing that what occurs within each of these broader categories is a multitude of specific processes of the kind described above.

Change Mechanisms and Stages of Culture Formation

At different stages in the evolution of a given organization's culture different possibilities for change arise because of the particular function that culture plays at each developmental stage. Exhibit 15.1 shows these stages and identifies the particular change mechanisms that are most relevant at each stage. These mechanisms are cumulative in the sense that at a later stage, all the prior change mechanisms are still operating but additional ones become relevant.

Founding and Early Growth

In the first stage, the founding and early growth of a new organization, the main cultural thrust comes from the founders and their assumptions. The cultural paradigm that becomes embedded if the organization succeeds in fulfilling its primary task and survives can then be viewed as that organization's distinctive competence, the basis for member identity, and the psychosocial "glue" that holds the organization together. The emphasis in this early stage will be on differentiating oneself from the environment and from other organizations. The organization will make its culture explicit, integrate it as much as possible, and

Exhibit 15.1. Cultural Change Mechanisms.

Organizational Stage	Change Mechanism
Founding and early growth	1. Incremental change through general and specific evolution
	2. Change through insight from organizational therapy
	3. Change through promotion of hybrids within the culture
Midlife	4. Change through systematic promotion from selected subcultures
	5. Planned change through organization development projects and the creation of parallel learning structures
	6. Unfreezing and change through technological seduction
Maturity and decline	7. Change through infusion of outsiders
	8. Unfreezing through scandal and myth explosion
	9. Change through turnarounds
	10. Change through coercive persuasion
	11. Destruction and rebirth

teach it firmly to newcomers (and/or select them for initial compatibility).

In terms of the concept of distinctive competence, one can see in young companies biases toward certain business functions. At Action the bias was clearly in favor of engineering and manufacturing. Not only was it difficult for the other functions to acquire status and prestige, but professionals in those functions such as professional marketers were often told by managers who had been with the company from its origin that "marketers never know what they are talking about." At Multi a similar bias still persists for science and research, even though the company is much older. Because R & D was historically the basis of Multi's success, science is still defined as the distinctive competence, even though more and more managers are admitting overtly that the future hinges more on marketing, tight financial controls, and efficient operations.

The implications for change at this stage are clear. The

culture in young and successfully growing companies is likely to be strongly adhered to because (1) the primary culture creators are still present, (2) the culture helps the organization define itself and make its way into a potentially hostile environment, and (3) many elements of the culture have been learned as defenses against anxiety as the organization struggles to build and maintain itself.

Proposals to *deliberately change* the culture from either inside or outside are therefore likely to be totally ignored or resisted. Instead, dominant members or coalitions will attempt to preserve and enhance the culture. The only force that might unfreeze such a situation is an external crisis of survival in the form of a sharp drop in growth rate, loss of sales or profit, a major product failure, or some other event that cannot be ignored. If such a crisis occurs, the next stage (transition) may automatically be launched in that the crisis may discredit the founder and bring a new senior manager into the picture. If the founding organization itself stays intact, so will the culture. How then does culture change in the growth phase of an organization? Several change mechanisms can be identified.

Incremental Change Through General and Specific Evolution

If the organization is not under too much external stress and if the founder or founding family is around for a long time, the culture evolves in small increments by continuing to assimilate what works best over the years. Such evolution involves two basic processes: general evolution and specific evolution (Sahlins and Service, 1960; Steward, 1955; McKelvey, 1982).

General Evolution. General evolution toward the next historical stage of development involves diversification, growing complexity, higher levels of differentiation and integration, and creative syntheses into new and higher-level forms. Implicit in this concept is the assumption that social systems do have an evolutionary dynamic. Just as groups go through logical stages, so organizations go through logical stages, especially with respect to their ownership structure, though it has not been unequivocally demonstrated what those stages are or what internal dynamic creates the evolutionary thrust. Moreover, if a crisis brings in new leadership, there is evidence to suggest that the new direction in which the culture will move is quite unpredictable (Gersick, 1991; Tushman and Anderson, 1986).

The elements of the culture that operate as defenses are likely to be retained and strengthened over the years, but they may be refined and developed into an integrated and more complex structure. Basic assumptions may be retained, but the form in which they appear may change, creating new behavior patterns that ultimately feed back into the basic assumptions. Not all systems have the capacity to evolve to greater levels of complexity, but the evidence that human systems are capable of such evolution is fairly strong. The best example of such evolution is the small adjustments that occur in the belief systems and assumptions of organization leaders as they cope with disequilibriums caused by changes in the external or internal stakeholders (that is, stockholders, suppliers, customers, employees, and so on) (Quinn, 1978; Donaldson and Lorsch, 1983).

Specific Evolution. Specific evolution involves the adaptation of specific parts of the organization to their particular environments and the impact of the subsequent cultural diversity on the core culture. This is the mechanism that causes organizations in different industries to develop different industry cultures and subgroups to develop different subcultures. Thus, a high-technology company will develop highly refined R & D skills, while a consumer products company in foods or cosmetics will develop highly refined marketing skills. In each case such differences will reflect important underlying assumptions about the nature of the world and the actual growth experience of the organization. In addition, because the different parts of the organization exist in different environments, each of those parts will evolve to adapt to its particular environment, as discussed in Chapter Thirteen. As subgroups differentiate and subcultures develop, the opportunity for more major culture change later arises, but in this early stage those differences will only be tolerated, and efforts will be made to minimize them.

Self-Guided Evolution Through Organizational Therapy

If one thinks of culture as in part a learned defense mechanism to avoid uncertainty and anxiety, then one should be able to help the organization assess for itself the strengths and weaknesses of its culture and to help it modify cultural assumptions if that becomes necessary for survival and effective functioning. Therapy that operates by creating self-insight permits cognitive redefinition to occur. Members of the organization can collectively achieve insight if they collectively examine their culture and redefine some of the cognitive elements. Such redefinition involves either changing some of the priorities within the core set of assumptions or abandoning one assumption that is a barrier by subordinating it to a higher-order assumption. The internal deciphering process described in Chapter Eight typically produces a level of cultural insight that allows a group to decide the direction of its future evolution. The key role of the leader in this process is to recognize the need for such an intervention and to manage the internal deciphering. Though leaders would not typically describe this as therapy, it is functionally the equivalent (for groups) of what individuals undergo when they seek therapeutic help when things are not working.

Many of the interventions that have occurred over the years in the Action Company can be viewed as therapeutic in that the goal was insight. For example, at an annual meeting where the company's poor performance was being discussed, a depressive mood overtook senior management and was articulated as "We could do better if only our president or one of his key lieutenants would decide on a direction and tell us which way to go." A number of us familiar with the culture heard this as a wish for a magic solution, not as a realistic request.

I was scheduled to give a short presentation on the company's culture at this meeting and used the opportunity to raise the following question: "Given the history of this company and the kinds of managers and people that you are, if Murphy marched in here right now and told everyone in what directions he wanted you to go, do you think you would follow?" There was a long silence, followed gradually by a few knowing smiles and ultimately by a more realistic discussion. In effect, the group reaffirmed and strengthened its assumptions about individual responsibility and autonomy but also recognized that its wish for marching orders was really a wish for more discipline in the organization and that this discipline could be achieved among the senior managers by tighter coordination at their level.

Defenses do not always have to be given up. Sometimes it is enough to recognize how they operate so that their consequences can be realistically assessed. If they are considered too costly, one can engage in compensatory behavior. For example, Action's commitment to checking all decisions laterally before moving ahead may be a defense against the anxiety of not knowing whether or not a given decision is correct. As the company has grown, the costs of such a defense have mounted because it not only takes longer and longer to make a decision but also checking with others who have not grown up in the company and whose opinions one cannot calibrate may not resolve issues.

The options are, then, to (1) give up the mechanism, which is difficult to do unless some way is found to contain the anxiety that would be unleashed in the short run (for example, find a strong leader who will absorb the anxiety), (2) design compensatory mechanisms (for example, have less frequent but longer meetings, classify decisions and seek consensus only on certain ones, or find ways to speed up meetings), or (3) break the company down into smaller units where the consensual process can work because people can know each other and build efficient consensual processes. In Action's evolution all of these mechanisms have been and are being used.

Managed Evolution Through Hybrids

The two mechanisms described above serve to preserve and enhance the culture as it exists, but changes in the environment often create disequilibriums that force real change. How can a young organization highly committed to its identity make such changes? What one observes in such an organization is a process of gradual and incremental change through systematic promotion of insiders whose own assumptions are better adapted to the new external realities. Because they are insiders, these individuals accept much of the cultural core and have credibility. However, because of their personalities or life experiences or the subculture in which their career developed, they also hold assumptions that are in varying degrees different from the core and thus can move the organization gradually into new ways of thinking and acting. When such managers are put in key positions, they often elicit the feeling from others: "We don't like what she is doing in the way of changing the place, but at least she is one of us."

For this mechanism to work, some of the most senior leaders of the company must have insight into what is missing. This implies that they first must get somewhat outside their own culture by means of a therapeutic process. They may obtain insight through the questions of board members, from consultants, or through educational programs where they meet other leaders. If the leaders then recognize the need for change, they can begin to select for key jobs those members of the old culture who best represent the new assumptions that they want to enhance.

For example, at one stage in its history, Action found itself increasingly losing the ability to coordinate the efforts of large numbers of units. Murphy and other senior managers knew that bringing an outsider into a key position would be rejected, so they gradually filled several of the key management positions with managers who had grown up in manufacturing and in field service, where more discipline and centralization had been the norm. These managers operated within the culture but gradually imposed more centralization and discipline. Similarly, when Multi recognized the need to become more marketing oriented, it began to appoint to more senior positions managers who had grown up in the pharmaceutical division, where the importance of marketing had been recognized earlier.

Transition to Midlife: Problems of Succession

How companies actually move from the founding and early stage dominated by a founder or owning family to the midlife stage managed by second-, third-, and fourth-generation general managers has so many variants that one can only identify some prototypical mechanisms and events.

The first and often most critical of these mechanisms is the shift from founder to a second-generation chief executive officer. Even if that person is the founder's son, daughter, or some other trusted family member, it is in the nature of founder entrepreneurs to have difficulty giving up what they have created (Dyer, 1986; Schein, 1978; Watson and Petre, 1990). In Chapter Eleven I cited the extreme example of Jones, an entrepreneur who was unconsciously willing to destroy his organization to prove to the world how indispensable he was. On the other hand, I also described Smithfield, an entrepreneur whose passion was to keep creating new ventures, which made it easy for him to turn successful ones over to friends and colleagues.

During the transition phase, conflicts over what elements of the culture employees like or do not like become surrogates for what they do or do not like about the founder because most of the culture is likely to be a reflection of the founder's personality. Battles develop between "conservatives," who like the founding culture, and "liberals" or "radicals," who want to change the culture, partly because they want to enhance their own power position. The danger in this situation is that feelings about the founder are projected onto the culture and that in the effort to displace the founder, much of the culture comes under challenge. If members of the organization forget that the culture is a set of learned solutions that have produced success, comfort, and identity, they may try to change the very things they value and need.

Often missing in this phase is an understanding of what the organizational culture is and what it is doing for the organization, regardless of how it came to be. The succession mechanism must therefore be designed to enhance those parts of the culture that provide identity, distinctive competence, and protection from anxiety. This can probably be managed only from within because an outsider could not possibly understand the subtleties of the cultural issues and the emotional relationships between founders and employees.

The preparation for succession is usually psychologically difficult both for the founder and for potential successors. For example, founder entrepreneurs may officially be grooming successors, but unconsciously they may be preventing powerful and competent people from functioning in the successor role. Or they may designate successors but prevent them from having enough responsibility to learn how to do the job, what we might call the Prince Albert syndrome, remembering that Queen Victoria did not permit her son (later King Edward VII) many opportunities to practice being king. This pattern is particularly likely to operate in a father-to-son transition (Watson and Petre, 1990).

When senior management or the founder confronts the criteria for a successor, cultural issues are forced into the open. It is now clear that much of the culture has become an attribute and property of the organization even though it may have started out as the property of the founder. If the founder or the founder's family is still dominant in the organization, one may expect little culture change but a great deal of effort to clarify, integrate, maintain, and develop the culture, primarily because it is identified with the founder.

Formal management succession when the founder or founding family finally relinquishes control provides an opportunity to change the direction of the culture if the successor is the right kind of hybrid, representing what is needed for the organization to survive, yet being seen as acceptable "because he is one of us" and therefore also a conserver of the old culture. As noted earlier, after several outsiders had failed as CEOs in the Jones Food Company, the Jones family found someone who had been with the company earlier and was therefore perceived by the family to understand the company even though he brought in many new assumptions about how to run the business.

Summary and Conclusions

Cultural change and the role of leadership in managing it will occur through different mechanisms at different developmental stages of an organization. However, all change occurs through the mechanisms of disconfirmation, the creation of guilt or anxiety, and the creation of psychological safety. When those three factors are in appropriate balance the system is unfrozen and becomes motivated to change. Change then occurs through cognitive redefinition of key concepts, and the resulting behavioral changes become refrozen in the personalities of the individuals and in the norms and routines of the group.

In the founding and early development stage cultural assumptions define the group's identity and distinctive competence and, hence, are strongly clung to. If leaders detect maladaptive assumptions, the only way they can change culture is to bias the normal evolutionary processes or to produce therapeutic interventions that give group members new insight and thereby allow them to develop their culture in a more managed fashion. The other major mechanism available to leaders in this stage is to locate and systematically promote hybrids in the organization who represent the main elements of the culture but who have learned some other assumptions that are considered more adaptive.

The transition to midlife is fraught with cultural issues because succession problems force cultural assumptions out into the open. Group members are likely to confuse elements of the culture with elements of the founder's personality, and subgroups that are for and against some of what the founder stands for are likely to form. Although cultural issues become more salient during the transition of succession, the change mechanisms are likely to be the same as the ones described above unless in the transition the company is sold or taken over by complete new management, in which case a new culture formation process begins.

The key issue for leaders is that they must become marginal in their own culture to a sufficient degree to recognize what may be its maladaptive assumptions and to learn some new ways of thinking themselves as a prelude to unfreezing and changing their organization. This process is especially difficult for entrepreneurial founders because the early success of their organization is likely to make them believe that their own assumptions are ultimately the correct ones.

CHAPTER SIXTEEN

The Leader's Role in Midlife, Mature, and Declining Organizations

In Chapter Fifteen we reviewed the change options that are available to leaders when their organizations are young and growing. These options are limited by the degree to which the culture is, at that stage, a central element of the organization's identity. As organizations become differentiated into multiple subcultures, the change options grow; and if an organization begins to go into decline, more drastic options become necessary. In this chapter we will look at change during the midlife stage and that of maturity and possible decline.

Organizational Midlife

As mentioned earlier, the midlife stage is not very precise in definition but has some defining characteristics. When the founding family is no longer in an ownership or dominant position, or after at least two generations of general management, or when the organization has grown in size to the point where the sheer number of nonfamily managers overweighs the family members, we are talking about midlife.

From a cultural perspective, the organization is now facing a very different situation. It is established and must maintain itself through some kind of continued growth and renewal

313

process. It now must decide whether to pursue such growth through further geographical expansion, development of new products, opening up of new markets, vertical integration to improve its cost and resource position, mergers and acquisitions, divisionalization, or spinoffs. The past history of the organization's growth and development is not necessarily a good guide to what will succeed in the future because the environment may have changed and, more important, internal changes may have altered its unique strengths and weaknesses.

Whereas culture was a necessary glue in the growth period, the most important elements of the culture have now become embedded in the organization's structure and major processes. Hence, consciousness of the culture and the deliberate attempt to build, integrate, or conserve the culture have become less important. The culture that the organization acquired during its early years now comes to be taken for granted. The only elements that are likely to be conscious are the credos, dominant espoused values, company slogans, written charters, and other public pronouncements of what the company wants to be and claims to stand for, its philosophy and ideology.

At this stage it is more difficult to decipher the culture and make people aware of it because it is so embedded in routines. It may even be counterproductive to make people aware of the culture unless there is some crisis or problem to be solved. Managers view culture discussions as boring and irrelevant, especially if the company is large and well established. On the other hand, geographical expansions, mergers and acquisitions, and introductions of new technologies require a careful self-assessment to determine whether the new cultural elements to be integrated or merged are, in fact, compatible.

Also at this stage there may be strong forces toward cultural diffusion, or loss of integration, because powerful subcultures will have developed and because a highly integrated culture is difficult to maintain in a large, differentiated, geographically dispersed organization. Furthermore, it is not clear whether or not all the cultural units of an organization must be uniform and integrated. Several conglomerates I have worked with have spent a good deal of time wrestling with the question of whether to attempt to preserve or, in some cases, build a common culture. Are the costs associated with such an effort worth it? Is there even a danger that one will impose assumptions on a subunit that might not fit its situation at all? On the other hand, if subunits are all allowed to develop their own cultures, what is the competitive advantage of being a single organization? At this stage it is less clear what functions are served by the total culture, and the problem of managing cultural change is therefore more complex and diverse.

Unfreezing forces at this stage can come either from the outside or from the inside, as in the first stage: (1) the entire organization or parts of it may experience economic difficulty or in some other way fail to achieve key goals because the environment has changed in a significant manner, or (2) the organization may develop destructive internal power struggles among subcultures. For example, prior to Multi's launching of the redirection project described in Chapter Seventeen, some of its divisions were consistently declining, to the point where the total organization's economic health was called into question. At the same time, the functional groups in the country companies were increasingly fighting the headquarters organization and complaining that profits were undermined by the heavy overhead burdens imposed on them by the "fat" headquarters.

The change mechanisms available to leaders at this stage must be considered in combination with the ones described in Chapter Fifteen. It is in the nature of culture change that multiple forces have to be used to manage the unfreezing and change process.

Change Through Systematic Promotion from Selected Subcultures

The strength of the midlife organization lies in the diversity of its subcultures. Whether leaders are conscious of it or not, the way they develop midlife organizations culturally is by assessing the strengths and weaknesses of different subcultures and then biasing the total culture in favor of one of the subcultures.

Leaders do this by systematically promoting people from that subculture into power positions in the total culture. This is an extension of the previously mentioned use of hybrids, but it has a more potent effect in midlife because preservation of the total culture is not as big an issue as it was in the young and growing organization. Also, the midlife organization is led by general managers who will not be as emotionally embedded in the original culture and will, therefore, be better able to assess needed future directions. Whereas the diversity of subcultures is a threat to the young organization, it can be seen as an advantage in midlife. The only disadvantage to this change mechanism is that it is very slow. If the pace of culture change is to be increased, systematic organization development projects must be launched.

Change Through Organization Development — The Creation of Parallel Learning Systems

Organization development (OD) can best be defined as a planned change process, managed from the top, taking into account both the technical and human sides of the organization and using inside or outside consultants in the planning and implementation of the changes to be made (for example, Beckhard and Harris, 1987; Burke, 1987). Much of the work of organization development practitioners deals with knitting together diverse and sometimes warring subcultures, helping leaders, the dominant coalition, or the whole managerial subculture client figure out how to integrate constructively the multiple agendas of different groups. The managerial subculture usually becomes the agent of change and the initial target of change, but the ultimate client system is the organization as a whole in that the interests of all the stakeholders must be considered. Though the projects may be initiated by individual leaders, it is essential in OD projects that the client system be broadened to at least the top-management subculture and preferably the other hierarchical subcultures as well.

Not all organization development projects involve culture change. Often the purpose is to build a more effective executive team or to reduce specific intergroup problems. If, however, senior management discovers that the implementation of a new strategy or structure is constrained by some cultural assumptions and if there is enough time, the organization development approach will be attempted. Note that this presumes some insight on the part of leaders into their own culture and the degree to which cultural assumptions aid or hinder what they are trying to do. Such insight results either from formal activities such as those described earlier as therapeutic interventions or from less formal learning processes that leaders have undergone.

Once a decision is made to manage change by means of organization development, the actual change activities will vary according to the situation. However, almost all such programs involve the creation of a temporary parallel learning system in which some new assumptions are learned and tested (Bushe and Shani, 1991). It is too painful to give up a shared assumption in favor of an unknown substitute. If some part of the organization can learn an alternate way to think and if that alternative can be shown to work, then there is less anxiety as the alternative is gradually introduced into the main part of the organization. The trial and error in the temporary parallel system can create some of the necessary psychological safety.

These kinds of changes require anywhere from five to fifteen or more years if basic assumptions are really to be changed without destroying and rebuilding the organization. It takes time to build the parallel system, to learn some new assumptions, and then to design mechanisms that will allow those assumptions to be introduced into the original organization. For example, when Procter & Gamble decided to change the way it manufactured various products, it started with a staff group that was empowered to design a whole new plant. The staff was even allowed to hire the plant manager so that they could ensure that he or she would be a person with genuinely different assumptions from those that had traditionally prevailed in the company. Such a manager was hired, and the new plant was successful. Now the problem was how to spread the innovation. The staff group decided to apprentice young high-potential plant managers to the new plant manager. After a few years these managers understood the new system well enough to be moved out

318 Organizational Culture and Leadership

into other new plants to introduce the new system. Only when a number of such new plants were working successfully were these managers, who were now experienced, moved into old unionized plants that would require a longer period of conversion. It took almost twenty years before the last of these plants was converted to the new system.

What these organization development programs have in common is that they are planned and consciously managed by the leaders of the organization so that periods of disequilibrium will be anticipated as a normal part of organizational evolution rather than as painful disruptions. Underlying such efforts is a philosophy that the whole system must be helped to become more effective in managing itself and that the change agent must therefore operate from a broad sociotechnical model and from a set of values that includes all of the organization's stakeholders. It is also assumed that the organization cannot learn anything new if the leaders themselves do not learn anything new. Hence the need for the leaders to become marginal, to have some new insights, and to create the parallel system to explore the new learning in a wider context.

Change Through Technological Seduction

One of the less obvious ways that the leaders of midlife organizations choose to change cultural assumptions is through the subtle, cumulative, and sometimes unintended impacts of new technology. At one extreme we can observe the gradual evolutionary diffusion of technological innovation where a new technology such as the automobile displaces not only the horse and buggy but eventually many of the assumptions and rituals that accompanied the old technology. At the other extreme, technological seduction involves the deliberate, managed introduction of specific technologies for the sake of seducing organization members into new behavior, which will in turn require them to reexamine their present assumptions and possibly adopt new values, beliefs, and assumptions.

The focus here is on situations where a leader consciously decides to introduce a new technology to initiate cultural change.

Sometimes the goal is to reduce what is perceived to be too much cultural diversity by deliberately introducing a seemingly neutral or so-called progressive technology that has the effect of getting people to think and behave in common terms. Sometimes the goal is to force assumptions out into the open in a neutral and ostensibly nonthreatening way. Sometimes the technology is physical, such as the introduction of robots into an assembly line or the automation of a chemical or nuclear plant, and sometimes it is a sociotechnical technology, such as the introduction of a formal total quality program.

Many companies have used educational interventions to introduce a new social technology as part of an organization development program with the avowed purpose of creating some common concepts and language in a situation where they have perceived a lack of shared assumptions—for example, Blake's managerial grid (Blake and Mouton, 1964). The most recent and increasingly popular versions of this type of intervention are systems dynamics, as presented in Senge's *The Fifth Discipline* (1990), and total quality management, as presented in a variety of books and programs (for example, Ciampa, 1992). The assumption underlying this strategy is that a new common language and common concepts in a given cultural area, such as how one relates to subordinates or how one defines reality in terms of one's mental models, will gradually force organization members to adopt a common frame of reference that will eventually lead to common assumptions. As the organization builds up experience and resolves crises successfully, new shared assumptions gradually come into being.

The current practice of introducing personal computers to several layers of management as a vehicle for networking the organization, mandating attendance at training courses, introducing expert systems to facilitate decision making, and using various kinds of "groupware" to facilitate meetings across time and space barriers is clearly another version of technological seduction, though perhaps unintended by the original architects (Gerstein, 1987; Grenier and Metes, 1992; Johansen and others, 1991; Savage, 1990; Schein, 1992).

Sometimes leaders perceive that there is too much diversity

in the assumptions governing management decisions and bring this issue into the open by introducing a technology that forces decision-making premises and styles into consciousness. Some leaders also see in the technology the opportunity to impose the assumptions that underlie the new technology itself, such as the importance of precision, measurement, quantification, and model building (see Chapter Fourteen). In some cases the effects are unintended, as when information technology is brought in to enable everyone to communicate more effectively with each other and to reduce the impact of formal hierarchy, but the CEO uses the information for control purposes and unwittingly increases the impact of hierarchy.

An unusual example of unfreezing through coercive technological seduction is provided by a manager who took over a transportation company that had grown up with a royal charter one hundred years earlier and had developed strong traditions around its blue trucks with the royal coat of arms painted on their sides (Lewis, 1988). The company was losing money because it was not aggressively seeking new concepts of how to sell transportation. After observing the company for a few months, the new chief executive officer abruptly and without giving reasons ordered that the entire fleet of trucks be painted solid white. Needless to say, there was consternation. Delegations urging the president to reconsider, protestations about loss of identity, predictions of total economic disaster, and other forms of resistance arose. The CEO listened patiently to all of these but simply reiterated that he wanted the painting done, and soon. He eroded the resistance by making the request nonnegotiable.

After the trucks were painted white, the drivers suddenly noticed that customers were curious about what had been done and asked what they would now put on the trucks in the way of a new logo. This got the employees at all levels thinking about what business they were in and initiated the market-oriented focus that the president had been trying to establish. Rightly or wrongly, he assumed that he could not get this focus just by requesting it. He had to seduce the employees into a situation where they had no choice but to rethink their identity. Employees are, of course, sensitive to how new technologies will force them to reexamine their own assumptions. If they want to hold onto their assumptions, they know enough to resist the technology in the first place.

In summary, cultural change in organizational midlife is primarily a matter of deliberately taking advantage of the diversity that the growth of subcultures makes possible. Unless the organization is in real difficulty, there will be enough time to use systematic promotion, organization development, and technological change as the main mechanisms in addition to normal evolution and organizational therapy. Next, we examine the more problematic area—what leaders can do if their organizations are stagnating or declining, if some cultural assumptions seem to be an obstacle, and if there is not enough time to use evolutionary methods.

Organizational Maturity and Potential Decline

Continued success creates strongly held shared assumptions and thus a strong culture. If the internal and external environments remain stable, this is an advantage. However, if there is a change in the environment, some of those shared assumptions can become a liability precisely because of their strength. The mature stage is sometimes reached when the organization is no longer able to grow because it has saturated its markets or become obsolete in its products. Maturity is not necessarily correlated with age, size, or number of managerial generations but rather reflects the interaction between the organization's output and the environmental opportunities and constraints.

Age does matter, however, if culture change is required. If an organization has had a long history of success with certain assumptions about itself and the environment, it is unlikely to want to challenge or reexamine those assumptions. Even if the assumptions are brought to consciousness, the members of the organization are likely to want to hold onto them because they justify the past and are the source of pride and self-esteem. Such assumptions now operate as filters that make it difficult for key managers to understand alternative strategies for survival and renewal (Donaldson and Lorsch, 1983; Lorsch, 1985).

Outside consultants can be brought in and clear alternatives can be identified. However, no matter how clear and persuasive a consultant tries to be, some alternatives will not even be understood if they do not fit the old culture, and some alternatives will be resisted even if understood because they create too much anxiety or guilt and sufficient psychological safety is lacking. Even if top management has insight, some new assumptions cannot be implemented down the organizational line because people simply will not comprehend or accept what the new strategy may require (Davis, 1984).

For example, several parts of the Multi Company had to confront the unpleasant reality that patents on some of their better products had run out; that younger, more flexible, and more aggressive competitors were threatening; that there was overcapacity in several of their major markets because the entire industry overestimated the market potential; and that it was not clear whether there was enough "left to be invented" to warrant the continued emphasis on research. The company needed to become more innovative in marketing and had to shift its creative energy from R & D to manufacturing process innovation to bring its costs down. Because the culture was built around research, however, the creative marketers and the innovative production engineers had a hard time getting attention from senior management. The research department itself needed to become more responsive to the marketplace, but it still believed that it knew best. Even senior managers who could see the dilemma were caught in their own shared assumptions because they could not challenge and overrule some of the powerful research people and the culture dictated that they stay off each other's turf.

In such a situation, the basic choices are between more rapid transformation of parts of the culture to permit the organization to become adaptive once again through some kind of turnaround and the destruction of the organization and its culture through a process of total reorganization via a merger, an acquisition, or bankruptcy proceedings. In either case, strong new change managers or "transformational leaders" are likely to be needed to unfreeze the organization and launch the change programs (Kotter and Heskett, 1992; Tichy and Devanna, 1986). As I have emphasized before, such unfreezing must not only involve the disconfirmation and induction of guilt or anxiety; it must also offer psychological safety by providing a new vision, a new set of alternatives, and a plan for how to get there that reassures members of the organization that change is possible.

Managed Change Through Infusion of Outsiders

Shared assumptions can be changed by changing the composition of the organization's dominant groups or coalitions. The most potent version of this change mechanism occurs when a board of directors brings in a new CEO or when a new CEO is brought in as a result of an acquisition, a merger, or a leveraged buyout. The new CEO usually brings in some of his or her own people and gets rid of people who are perceived to represent the old and increasingly ineffective way of doing things. In effect this destroys the group or hierarchical subculture that was the originator of the total culture and initiates a process of new culture formation. If there are strong functional, geographic, or divisional subcultures, the new leaders usually have to replace the leaders of those units as well.

Dyer (1985, 1986) has examined this change mechanism in several organizations and found that it follows certain patterns: (1) the organization develops a sense of crisis because of declining performance or some kind of failure in the marketplace and concludes that it needs new leadership; (2) simultaneously, there is a weakening of pattern maintenance in the sense that procedures, beliefs, and symbols that support the old culture break down; (3) a new leader with new assumptions is brought in from the outside to deal with the crisis; (4) conflict develops between the proponents of the old assumptions and the new leadership; and (5) if the crisis is eased and the new leader is given the credit, he or she wins out in the conflict and the new assumptions begin to be embedded and reinforced by a new set of pattern maintenance activities.

People may feel that they don't like the new approach but

can't argue with the fact that it made the company profitable once again, so maybe they have to try the new ways. Members who continue to cling to the old ways are either forced out or leave voluntarily because they no longer feel comfortable with the direction the organization is taking and how it does things. However, if improvement does not occur or the new leader is not given credit for the improvement that does occur or the new assumptions threaten too much of the core of the culture, the new leader will be discredited and forced out. (This situation occurs frequently when this mechanism is attempted in young companies where founders or owning families are still powerful. In such a situation the probabilities are high that the new leader will violate owner assumptions and be forced out by them.)

To understand fully the dynamics of the process described by Dyer (1985, 1986), one would, of course, need to know more about why and how the pattern maintenance mechanisms have become weakened. One common cause of such weakening is a change in ownership. For example, when founders or founding families give up ownership of the company or ownership changes as a result of merger, acquisition, or leveraged buyout, this structural change substantially reduces the supports to the present cultural assumptions and opens the door to power struggles among diverse elements. This further weakens whatever cultural assumptions were in place. If strong subcultures have formed and one or more of them are strongly tied to outside constituencies that hold different assumptions, the existing culture is further weakened. For example, when employees vote to join a union and that union is part of a strong international union, management loses some degrees of freedom and new assumptions are likely to be introduced in the internal integration area. A similar effect can occur when senior management is increasingly selected from one function such as finance and that function becomes more responsive to the stockholders, whose interests may not be the same as those of the marketing, manufacturing, or technical people inside the organization.

Culture change is sometimes stimulated by systematically bringing outsiders into jobs below the top-management level and allowing them gradually to educate and reshape top management's thinking. This is most likely to happen when the outsiders take over subgroups, reshape the cultures of those subgroups, become highly successful, and thereby create a new model of how the organization can work (Kuwada, 1991). Probably the most common version of this process occurs when a strong outsider or an innovative insider is brought in to manage one of the more autonomous divisions of a multidivisional organization. If that division becomes successful, it generates not only a new model for others to identify with but creates a cadre of managers who can be promoted into more senior positions and thereby influence the main part of the organization.

For example, the Saturn car division and the NUMI plant of General Motors were deliberately given freedom to develop new assumptions about how to involve employees in the design and production of cars and thus learned what amount to some new cultural assumptions about human relationships. This approach is a more drastic version of what was earlier described as creating a parallel organization as part of an organization development project. Similarly, GM also acquired Electronic Data Systems as a technological stimulus to organizational change. In each of these cases, however, we also see that having an innovative subculture within the larger culture does not guarantee that the larger culture will reexamine or change its culture. The innovative subculture helps in disconfirming some of the core assumptions, but again, unless there is sufficient anxiety, guilt, or psychological safety, the top-management culture may remain impervious to the very innovations it has created.

The infusion of outsiders inevitably brings various cultural assumptions into conflict, raising discomfort and anxiety levels. Leaders who use this change strategy must therefore also figure out how to manage the high levels of anxiety and conflict that they have wittingly or unwittingly unleashed. Here again, strong visions help provide alternative pathways to the ones that must be abandoned.

Change Through Scandal and Explosion of Myths

As a company matures, it develops a positive ideology and a set of myths about how it operates, what Argyris and Schön

(1974, 1978) have labeled "espoused theories." At the same time, the company continues to operate according to the assumptions that have worked in practice, which Argyris and Schön call "theories-in-use" and which more accurately reflect what actually goes on. Moreover, it is not unlikely that the espoused theories, the announced values of the organization, come to be in varying degrees out of line with the actual assumptions that govern daily practice.

For example, an organization's espoused theory may be that it takes individual needs into consideration in making geographical moves; yet its theory-in-use may be that anyone who refuses an assignment is taken off the promotional list. An organization's espoused theory may be that it uses rational decision-making techniques based on market research in introducing new products; yet its theory-in-use may be that it indulges the biases and pet projects of a certain key manager. An organization may espouse the value of teamwork, but all of its practices may be strongly individualistic and competitive. An organization may espouse concern for the safety of its employees, but its practices may be driven by assumptions that one must keep costs down to remain competitive, leading to unsafe practices. If in the history of the organization nothing happens to expose these incongruities, myths that support the espoused theories and values may grow up, thus even enhancing reputations that are out of line with realities. The most common example today is the myth in many companies that they never lay off anybody.

Where such incongruities between espoused values and actual assumptions exist, scandal and myth explosion become relevant as mechanisms of culture change. Nothing changes until the consequences of the actual operating assumptions create a public and visible scandal that cannot be hidden, avoided, or denied. For example, in the company that prided itself on taking individual feelings into account in overseas moves, a senior executive who had been posted to an overseas position that he did not want committed suicide. He left a note that was revealed to the newspapers in which he made it clear that he felt the company had forced him to take the undesirable assignment. This event suddenly exposed an element of the culture in such a way that it could not be denied or rationalized away. The company immediately instituted a new set of procedures built on the espoused values and began a painful process of reconstructing some elements of its career development philosophy.

In the case where one manager's biases dominated the decision-making process in regard to the introduction of new products, what eventually happened was that one of the products he had insisted on failed in such a dramatic way that a reconstruction of why it had been introduced had to be made public. The manager's role in the process was revealed by unhappy subordinates and was labeled as scandalous. He was moved out of his job, and a more formal product introduction process was immediately mandated.

Disasters such as those at the Chernobyl nuclear plant and the Bhopal chemical plant, the Alaskan oil spill, and the explosion of the *Challenger* space shuttle triggered a process in each of the organizations involved of forcefully reexamining practices in regard to safety. Disasters and scandals do not automatically cause culture *change,* but they are a powerful disconfirming force that cannot be denied and that therefore starts the process of unfreezing and thereby provides the organization an opportunity to launch a change process that brings its assumptions more in line with internal and external environmental realities.

Though rarely made public, insiders sometimes create or engineer scandals in order to induce some of the change they want by leaking information to the right place at the right time. Such leaks are sometimes defined as whistle-blowing in the sense of exposing internal inconsistencies. Since whistle-blowing has the potential for precipitating a crisis that may force some cultural assumptions to be reexamined, one can see why people are cautious about it and why the organization often punishes it.

Change Through Coercive Persuasion

The concept of coercive persuasion was originally derived from my studies of prisoners of war who had undergone major belief and attitude changes during their three to five years or more of captivity during and after the Korean War (Schein, 1961a).

The key to understanding some of the dramatic changes that the captives underwent is to realize that if one has no exit option, one is subject to strong unfreezing forces, which sooner or later will motivate one to find new information that will permit cognitive redefinition to occur. Prisoners at first vehemently denied their guilt, thought it was ridiculous to be accused of espionage and sabotage, offered to make false confessions—which only produced more severe punishment—and in other ways attempted to cope but did not question their own assumption base.

After months or years of harassment, interrogation, physical punishment, pressure from cell mates, indoctrination, and the threat that they would be in prison forever unless they saw the light and made an honest confession, the prisoners started to search for an answer. They found it when they began to realize that such terms as *guilt, crime, espionage,* and *sabotage* have different meanings in different cultures and political systems. They were able to make sincere confessions once they cognitively redefined concepts such as guilt and crime, thereby making some fundamental changes in their assumptions about themselves.

What does all this have to do with culture change? Situations where elements of the old culture are dysfunctional but strongly adhered to are comparable to what the captor was up against with prisoners who asserted their innocence. The key to producing change in such situations is first to prevent exit and then to escalate the disconfirming forces while providing psychological safety. Although this is difficult to execute, it is precisely what effective turnaround managers do. By using the right incentives, they make sure that the people whom they wish to retain in the organization find it difficult to leave. By consistently disconfirming the old behavior patterns or actually mandating new behavior patterns, as in the case of the CEO who insisted on painting company trucks white, they make it difficult for people to sustain the old assumptions. By consistently being supportive and rewarding any evidence of movement in the direction of new assumptions, effective managers provide some psychological safety. If psychological safety is sufficient, members of the organization can begin to examine and possibly give

up some of their cognitive defenses. If they cannot, the turnaround manager is faced with removing them. In any case, the
essence of this mechanism is that the turnaround manager re-
tains his or her power indefinitely, thus preventing members
of the organization from developing a strategy of just waiting
until he or she is gone.

Change Through Turnarounds

Turnaround as a mechanism is really more a combination of
many of the foregoing mechanisms fashioned into a single program by a talented change manager or team of change agents.
In turnaround situations I have observed or heard about, what
strikes me is that all the mechanisms previously described may
be used in the total change process. The first condition for change,
as always, is that the organization must be unfrozen. Either because of external realities that threaten organizational survival
or because of new insights and plans on the part of the board
of directors, the CEO, or the dominant management coalition,
the organization comes to recognize that some of its past ways
of thinking, feeling, and doing things are indeed obsolete. A new
CEO or a redefined turnaround role for the present leader is put
into place, and a change program is launched as a turnaround.

  Once the organization is unfrozen, change is possible if
there is a turnaround manager or team with a clear sense of
where the organization needs to go, a model of how to change
culture to get there, and the power to implement the model.
If any one of these elements is absent, the process will fail, and
in any case, the anxieties that arise from implied change must
be actively managed. For example, if major replacement of people in critical positions is involved, that process must be managed
in such a way that it is seen as necessary and carried out according to some of the deeper cultural assumptions that may
need to be preserved. Otherwise, the employees on whom the
organization is still counting will become too anxious and unproductive.

  Turnarounds usually require the involvement of all organization members so that the dysfunctional elements of the old culture become clearly visible to everyone. The process of developing new assumptions then becomes a process of cognitive redefinition through teaching, coaching, changing the structure and processes where necessary, consistently paying attention to and rewarding evidence of learning the new ways, creating new slogans, stories, myths, and rituals, and in other ways coercing people into at least new behavior. All the other mechanisms described earlier come into play, but the willingness to coerce is the key to turnarounds.

Two fundamentally different leadership models have been promulgated for managing turnarounds or, as they have come to be known more popularly, transformations. In the *strong vision model,* the leader has a clear vision of where the organization should end up, specifies the means by which to get there, and consistently rewards efforts to move in that direction (Tichy and Devanna, 1986; Bennis and Nanus, 1985; Leavitt, 1986). This model works well if the future is reasonably predictable and a visionary leader is available. If neither of these conditions can be met, organizations can use the *fuzzy vision model,* where the new leader states forcefully that the present is intolerable and that performance must improve within a certain time frame but then relies on the organization to develop visions of how actually to get there (Pava, 1983). The "we need to change" message is presented forcefully, repeatedly, and to all levels of the organization. As various proposals for solution are generated throughout the organization, the leader selects and reinforces the ones that seem to make most sense. This model is obviously more applicable in situations where the turnaround manager comes from the outside and therefore does not initially know what the organization is capable of. It is also more applicable when the future continues to be turbulent in that it begins to train the organization to become conscious of how to change its own assumptions as part of a continuous adaptive process.

Turnarounds must usually be supplemented with longer-range organization development programs to aid in new learning and to help embed new assumptions. It is not enough to have strong leaders to unfreeze the system and get the change started because change may have to be managed in all of the organization's subcultures, a process that takes a great deal of time. It is much more difficult to embed new assumptions in a mature organization than in a young and growing one because all of the organization structures and processes have to be rethought and, perhaps, rebuilt.

Change Through Reorganization and Rebirth

Little is known or understood about the process of reorganization and rebirth, so little will be said about it here. Suffice it to say that if one physically destroys the organization that is the carrier of a given culture, by definition that culture is destroyed and whatever new organization begins to function begins to build its own new culture. This process is traumatic and therefore not typically used as a deliberate strategy, but it may be relevant if economic survival is at stake.

Organizational changes that are true transformations, not merely incremental adaptations, probably reflect culture changes at this level. In the evolution of companies such transformations occur periodically, and at those times the direction of the changes is not always predictable (Tushman and Anderson, 1986; Gersick, 1991). Change at this level sometimes results from mergers, acquisitions, or leveraged buyouts if the new owners decide to completely restructure the organization and are willing to get rid of most of the key managers of the old culture in the process.

Summary and Conclusions

Chapters Fifteen and Sixteen have described various mechanisms and processes that leaders in their role as change agents use to change cultural assumptions. Different functions are served by culture at different organizational stages, and the change issues are therefore different at each stage. In the formative stage of an organization, the culture tends to be a positive growth force, which needs to be elaborated, developed, and articulated. In organizational midlife the culture becomes diverse in that many subcultures will have formed. Deciding what elements need to be changed then becomes one of the tougher strategic issues that leaders face. At this time, however, leaders also have more options to change assumptions by differentially rewarding different subcultures. In the maturity and decline situation, the culture often becomes partly dysfunctional and can only be changed through more drastic processes such as scandals and turnarounds.

The eleven different change mechanisms described in Chapters Fifteen and Sixteen are cumulative. That is, cultural evolution, the systematic promotion of hybrids, organizational therapy, and the systematic manipulation of subcultures are prerequisites to organization development, technological seduction, and the systematic infusion of outsiders. Myth explosion through scandals is geared more to initial unfreezing, but then change also requires at least the foregoing mechanisms and possibly coercive persuasion, turnarounds, and more severe destruction and rebirth as well.

In each case, the change process must be understood as involving some unfreezing forces, consisting of disconfirming information, the creation of guilt or anxiety, and the creation of psychological safety. Once unfrozen, the organization must have some mechanisms to permit cognitive redefinition as a way of developing new assumptions. The change process must also provide the opportunity for refreezing, which occurs when new cultural assumptions consistently solve problems or reduce anxieties.

The implications for leadership are multiple. The most important point is that leadership starts the change process in the first place. This involves a number of different functions that are often not well understood by leaders. First, they often have to provide the disconfirming information that initiates the change process, and they have to induce the anxiety and guilt to motivate change. Even more important, at the same time leaders must find a way to provide enough psychological safety to get the members of their organization to accept the need for change and begin the traumatic learning process that is typically involved. The tremendous emphasis that recent writers have put on leaders having visions, being able to communicate and articulate those visions, and having the skills to implement the visions is probably a reflection of the degree to which vision provides some of the key psychological functions of both disconfirming old assumptions and providing enough psychological safety to launch new learning. Visions do not have to be very clear or complete. They have to provide a path and a process of learning to assure the members of the organization that constructive change is possible.

The mechanisms of culture change described in Chapters Fifteen and Sixteen are presented from the leader's perspective. Culture change also occurs as a result of the entry of new people with new assumptions and the different experiences that different parts of the organization have. For purposes of this analysis, those changes are captured in the observation that organizations differentiate themselves over time into many subcultures. The important point to focus on, however, is that it is within the power of leaders to enhance diversity and encourage subculture formation or, through selection and promotion, to reduce diversity and thus manipulate the direction in which a given organization evolves culturally.

CHAPTER SEVENTEEN

Facing the Complexities
of Culture Change
A Case Study

[T]he social context from which a new setting emerges, as well as the thinking of those who create new settings, reflects what seems "natural" in the society. And what seems natural is almost always a function of the culture to a degree that usually renders us incapable of recognizing wherein we are prisoners of the culture. Those who create new settings always want to do something new, usually unaware that they are armed with, and will subsequently be disarmed by, categories of thought which help produce the conditions the new setting hopes to remedy. If we accept the proposition that the more things change the more they remain the same, it is not because people will it or because of the perversity of the human personality but primarily because of what we think to be "natural," that is, so a part of us that it is inconceivable that things could be otherwise. [Sarason, 1972, pp. xii–xiii]

The purpose of this chapter is to illustrate the complexity of culture and culture change when one applies it to a particular organization faced with particular problems. In practice, the drive for culture change derives from the need to solve organizational problems. It is only when cultural assumptions get in the way that the issue of culture change arises. We will examine the case of a major turnaround that was designed to solve a great many problems that the Multi Company had generated. This case illustrates many of the mechanisms discussed in Chapters Fifteen and Sixteen but also raises some fundamental questions about whether or not real culture change took place.

In the earlier description of the Multi paradigm I tried to show how certain deep shared assumptions related to each other and how that pattern of assumptions explained a great deal of the organization's day-to-day behavior. Here I also want to show how a change process revealed elements of Multi's culture and how it did and did not change, even as the organization changed.

As I lay out the case what I mean by a clinical approach to studying culture will become clearer. I will present data from Multi along with contrasting observations of the Action Company to illustrate through concrete events how the change process unfolds and how the consultant gets involved. The cultures of Action and Multi did not reveal themselves easily or automatically. Rather, with the help of members of the organization, I had to reconstruct why certain events that struck me as incongruent made sense when viewed from a cultural point of view. I will therefore interweave into the following account how I made some of the cultural inferences that have been reported in this book.

The information presented here is, of course, not complete, either historically or ethnographically. It is limited by the clinical perspective I am taking and is therefore biased by what the client's purpose was in talking with me. Nevertheless, culture is pervasive, and so the deeper assumptions of a cultural paradigm show through in any of the settings that can be observed. What is less clear is the structure and content of the various subcultures that may have existed, though the impact of some of those subcultures became quite visible during the change process.

Initial Contact and First Annual Meeting

My involvement with the Multi Company began in 1979 with a major "educational intervention" for the top-management group at its annual worldwide meeting. Dr. Peter Stern, Multi's director of management development, had heard me speak at a 1978 open seminar on career development and career anchors (Schein, 1978, 1990a). Dr. Stern suggested to his boss, Richard Maier, the chairman of the executive committee (the group accountable for the company's performance), that my material on career dynamics might be worth sharing with Multi's senior management.

Maier's goal for the annual meeting was to combine work on company problems with some stimulating input for the group, broadly in the area of leadership and creativity. He saw that the company was moving into a more turbulent economic, political, and technological environment that would require new kinds of responses. Maier was a descendant of one of the founding families of the company but had spent ten years of his career in Multi's U.S. subsidiary and had come to appreciate that the more dynamic U.S. environment stimulated a level of creativity that he saw as lacking in the home country. His own educational background was not in science but in law. He was a good example of the kind of marginal leader who could simultaneously be in his culture and yet perceive it somewhat objectively. His bringing various outside speakers into the annual meeting was a deliberate attempt to broaden the perception of his top management. My two days of lecturing were to be focused on leadership and creativity in the context of individual career development.

Both the topic of creativity and the approach of lecturing to the group were completely congruent with Multi's assumptions that (1) creativity is important in science, (2) knowledge is acquired through a scientific process, and (3) knowledge is communicated through experts in a didactic way. By way of contrast, in the pragmatic environment of the Action Company, it would have been inconceivable to devote two whole days of senior management's time to a seminar primarily involving outside lecturers. Similarly, the topic of creativity would not have interested the senior managers. It would have been viewed as much too abstract and as irrelevant to their work.

Whereas at Action much took place without preplanning, at Multi everything was planned to the smallest level of detail. After Maier and Stern had agreed on the general topic, it was necessary for me to meet Maier to see whether my general approach and personal style were compatible with what he was looking for. I was invited to spend a day and night at his house, where I met his wife as well. Maier and I got along well, so it was agreed that we would go ahead with my sessions at the 1979 annual meeting.

Some weeks later, a Mr. Kunz visited me at MIT to discuss the details. Kunz was the seminar administrator responsible for the detailed agenda of the three-day meeting and, as it turned out, also had to indoctrinate me on how to deal with this group. He had been a line manager who had moved into executive training but by virtue of his prior experience was familiar with the expectations of senior line management. Kunz met with me for many hours some months prior to the seminar to plan for the materials to be used, the exercise to be designed to involve the participants, the schedule, and so on.

In this process I observed firsthand how carefully Multi managers planned for every detail of any activity for which they were responsible. The company was clearly willing to commit all the time and energy it might take to design as nearly "perfect" a meeting as possible. Not only was Multi's high degree of commitment to structure revealed in this process, but in retrospect, the process also revealed how basic the assumption was about managerial turf. Kunz had clear responsibility for the conduct of the meeting, though hierarchically he was two levels below the participants. He had formed a review committee that included Maier and some members of the executive committee to review the seminar plan and to obtain their involvement. However, this group gave Kunz considerable freedom to make final decisions on seminar format. Thus, at both Action and Multi, each culture was displaying itself in the manner in which I encountered the organization, but I did not know this at the time.

The participants at the Multi annual meeting were Maier; the chairman of the board, Maier's boss; several board members who came as visitors; the nine-person executive committee; all the senior functional and divisional managers; and the most important country managers — some forty-five people in all.

Though I did not know it at the time, the meeting served a major integrative and communication function in that it legitimized during the three-day event what culturally did not occur in day-to-day operations — a high level of open and *lateral* communication. It also reflected the hierarchical emphasis, however, in that this sharing across units took place in public under the scrutiny of the executive committee and board members. Moreover, there was still a strong tendency to defer to others and to share ideas only when information was specifically requested. The meeting also provided an opportunity for senior management to send a major message quickly to the entire organization and, as we will see, to involve the entire organization in crisis management when that was needed.

The meeting took place at a pleasant mountain resort and included a special recreational event that helped the group to loosen up with each other. My talks were delivered on the second and third day and included a set of mutual interviews on career histories to help participants determine their "career anchors." I put creativity into the context of innovation, especially role innovation, to highlight that scientific creativity is by no means the only kind and that managers in any role can become more innovative in their approach. I asked people to pair themselves up in any way that seemed comfortable. The chairman of the board enthusiastically participated and thereby set a good tone for the meeting.

His enthusiasm was confirmed when, during the informal dinner following the recreational event on the third day, he spoke humorously and personally about his own career anchors thereby legitimating the previous day's input, and again illustrating how ready managers in this organization were to listen to authority and utilize academic inputs.

The major effects of the two days as I now reconstruct these events were as follows:

1. The group obtained new insights and information about creativity and innovation, especially the insight that innovation occurs within a variety of careers and organizational settings and should not be confused with the pure creative process in which scientists are engaged. The assumption that only scientists are creative had crept in, so those managers who had left their technical identities behind long ago were reassured by my message that managerial role innovations in all the functions of the business were much needed in a healthy organization. This legitimized as "creative" a great many activities that had previously not been perceived as such and liberated some problem-solving energy by linking innovation to day-to-day problem solving. This insight would not have been all that important but for the fact that the group held such strong assumptions about science and the creative process within science. I learned later that it was Maier's intention all along to broaden the group's perspective and to lay a groundwork for changes that he had in mind.

2. The group obtained new insights from the discussion of career anchors, which emphasized the variety of careers and the different things people are looking for in their careers. The effect was to unfreeze some of the monolithic notions about careers and the role of scientific backgrounds in careers. The board chairman's humorous talk legitimized the notion of individual differences in careers, particularly since the chairman also was a lawyer, not a scientist.

3. The group got to know me and my style as a responsive process consultant through several spontaneous interventions that I made during the two days. In particular, I was allowed to attend Kunz's planning committee meetings to review each day's activities and found in that context a number of occasions where my ideas for process and design facilitated the group's planning. In these meetings Maier and other members of the executive committee observed that a process consultant could be very helpful at a meeting.

During the informal times at meals and in the evening, my spontaneous responses were geared to getting out of the expert role. For example, if I was asked what companies were doing today in the field of participative management, I would give examples and highlight the diversity of what I observed rather than generalizing as I was expected to do. I had the sense that in this process I was disappointing some of the managers with whom I was speaking because I did not fit the stereotype of the scientist who is willing to summarize the state of knowledge in a field. On the other hand, my willingness to delve into Multi's problems appealed to some managers, and they accepted my self-definition as a process consultant rather than an expert consultant.

My participation in the meeting ended when my two days were finished, but plans were made to institute career planning and job/role planning in broader segments of the company. Specifically, Maier and the executive committee decided to ask all senior managers to do the "job/role planning exercise," which involves rethinking one's own job in the context of how it has changed and will continue to change as one projects ahead five years and analyzes the environment around the job (Schein, 1978). Maier also encouraged more managers to do the "career anchor interview exercise" as input to the annual management development process and authorized the development of an adaptation of the original interview questionnaire for use specifically in the company. I was asked to work with the headquarters management development group to help implement these two activities by spending roughly ten to fifteen days during the subsequent year as a consultant. My clients were to be Maier and Stern, the management development director; the broad mission was to increase the company's ability to innovate in all areas.

First Year's Work: Getting Acquainted with the Culture

I visited the company several times during the year, each time for two to three days. During these visits I learned more about the management development system, met some of the members of the executive committee, and gradually got involved in what I considered to be my most important activity, the planning of the next annual meeting. From my point of view, if innovation was to take hold, the relatively more open climate of the annual meeting was the most important thing to take advantage of. My goal was to be accepted as a process consultant to the entire meeting, not as an educator coming in with wisdom for one or two days.

However, the notion that I could help "on line" continued to be quite foreign to most of the managers. At Action I had learned the opposite lesson: unless I worked on line with real problems, the group considered me more or less useless. Initially, I thought that the reactions of Multi's managers were simply based on misunderstanding. It was only with repeated experiences of not being invited to working meetings at Multi, of always being put into an expert role, and of always having to plan my visits in great detail that I realized I was up against something that could be genuinely defined as cultural. The Multi managers' perception of what consultants do and how they work reflected their more general assumptions about what managers do and how they work.

For example, on several occasions I noticed that managers whom I had met on previous visits looked past me and ignored me when I encountered them in the public lobby or the executive dining room. As I later learned, to be seen with a consultant meant that one had problems and needed help — a position that these managers strongly avoided. I could only be accepted in a role that fitted Multi's model, that of educator and expert to management as a whole. The point is important because my request to attend the next annual meeting as a process consultant was, unbeknownst to me, strongly countercultural. But Maier was intrigued, and his own innovativeness swayed other members of the planning committee.

We compromised on the notion that I would give some lectures on relevant topics based on the events I observed at the meeting, thus legitimizing my attendance. My role as a consultant was further legitimized by my being cast as a scientist who had to be given an opportunity to get to know top management better so that I could be more helpful in the future. Maier and other senior managers had a specific view of what the total group needed, and they were prepared to introduce an outsider in the consultant role to facilitate this process. I came to realize that they wanted to unfreeze the group to get it to be more receptive to the crisis message they were preparing to deliver. An outsider with new ideas was seen as helpful in this process, both as a source of feedback to the group and as an expert on the change process that was about to be launched.

Another outsider, a professor of policy and strategy who also occupied a position on Multi's board, was invited as well. Our attendance at the meeting was related to a decision made by Maier and the executive committee that at the 1980 annual meeting a major review of company performance, division by division, would be undertaken. Such a review, they believed, would bring out the need for change and innovation and thereby reverse a slide into unprofitability that had been going on but was not clearly recognized or accepted. They also planned to introduce a program of change called the redirection project.

This business problem had been developing over several years but had not yet been identified as a crisis to be collectively shared with senior management worldwide. The major product divisions of the company were the primary profit centers but, as indicated earlier, were not likely to communicate much with each other, even though their various headquarters were all in the same city. These divisions knew what their individual situations were but seemed unaware of the impact of dropping profit levels in many areas on the company as a whole. Only the executive committee had the total picture.

This situation could easily arise because of the low amount of lateral communication, permitting the manager of a division that was losing money to rationalize that his loss was easily compensated for by other divisions and that things would soon improve. The culture encouraged each manager to worry only about his own piece of the organization, not to take a broad corporate view. Although communications that had gone out to the divisions over the year had suggested a total company problem, no one seemed to take the message very seriously. Therefore, much of the annual meeting was to be devoted to selling the idea that there was a total company problem and helping managers in small group meetings to accept and deal with those problems.

Given these goals, the planning committee saw the point of having me help in the design of the meeting and plan lectures as needed on how to initiate and manage various change projects. In other words, the economic and market environment was creating a financial crisis, top management decided it was time to deal with it, and the consultation process became one piece of management's more general process of launching the redirection project.

Unfreezing at the Second Annual Meeting

The first segment of the second annual meeting that I attended was devoted to presenting financial data, division by division, and then having small group meetings to digest and analyze the situation and formulate proposals for reversing the business decline. What made the situation complicated was that some of the divisions, those operating in mature markets, were losing money and needed major restructuring while other divisions were growing and making significant contributions to overall profit levels. The division managers from the problem divisions were embarrassed, apologetic, and overconfident that they could reverse the situation, while others said privately that the losing divisions could not possibly accomplish their goals, were not really committed to change, and would make only cosmetic alterations.

The division managers from the profitable divisions bragged, felt complacent, and wondered when top management would do something about the "losers" who were dragging others down with them. However, many people from the losing divisions and from top management said privately that even the profitable divisions, although they might look good relative to others inside the company, were not performing as well as they should in comparison to outside competitors in their own industrial market segment. Clearly, it was up to the hierarchy to solve the problem, as the divisions saw it.

During the division reviews and presentations, another important cultural assumption became evident. The company had been diversifying for a number of years and was attempting to enter the consumer goods market via a recent acquisition in the United States of a company that manufactured a line of air-freshening, deodorizing, and cleaning products. I was sitting next to a chemist, a member of the executive committee, when some of the consumer-oriented advertisements were shown on the screen as part of the division review. He was clearly upset by the "low" level of the message and whispered to me in an agitated tone, "Those things aren't even products; they don't do anything." His assumption seemed to be that a product had to be something useful, such as a cure for disease or a successful pesticide that reduces starvation. As I learned subsequently, managers took great pride in the important and useful products that were a current source of success. Selling something only because it made money did not fit some of their cultural assumptions about the nature of their business, and dealing with an organization whose processes were primarily geared to marketing made them uneasy. It was no surprise, therefore, when in 1987 this division was sold even though it was profitable.

The country managers, representing subsidiary companies in the major countries of the world, acknowledged the cross-divisional issues but were actually more upset by the fact that the headquarters organization—representing such functions as research and development, finance and control, personnel, and manufacturing—had become overgrown. These managers insisted that the headquarters functional staffs should be reduced because they were an unnecessary overhead and in many cases an active interference in running the businesses in the various countries. A high degree of centralization of research and development, manufacturing, and financial control had made sense while the company was young and small; but as it expanded and became a worldwide multinational, the small regional sales offices had gradually become large autonomous companies that managed all the functions.

Country heads needed their own staffs; but these staffs then came into conflict with the corporate staffs and the division staffs, who felt that they could communicate directly with their division people in each country. Because of the hierarchical nature of the organization, the headquarters groups asked for enormous amounts of information from the regions and frequently visited them. They felt that if they had worldwide responsibility for something, they had to be fully informed about everything at all times. Because of the lack of lateral communication, the functional staffs did not realize that their various inquiries and visits often paralyzed local operations because of the amount of time it took to answer questions, entertain visitors, get permission to act, and so on.

As the cost structure of the company came under increasing scrutiny, the country organizations were asked to reduce costs, while the headquarters organizations remained complacent, fat, and happy. The question that most worried the country managers was whether top management considered the profit erosion to be serious enough to warrant reductions in the headquarters functional staffs. If not, this must be only a fire-fighting drill, not a real crisis.

By the end of the first day of the meeting, the disconfirming financial data had been presented and groups had met to consider what should be done, but the feedback from the groups indicated neither a complete understanding nor a real acceptance of the problem. There was clearly insufficient anxiety or guilt. The planning committee met to consider what to do and decided that the other consultant could help the participants recognize the seriousness of the problem if he interrogated them in the style of a Harvard case discussion and led them to the inevitable conclusion that a crisis really existed. On the second day of the meeting he did this very effectively in a two-hour session that proved conclusively to all present that the organization could not remain profitable in the long run unless major changes were made. The result was a real sense of panic and depression. For the first time, the message had really been accepted collectively, setting the stage for the introduction of the redirection project.

Why did this work? I had the sense that in a culture where senior managers function symbolically as parent figures, it is difficult for the parents to tell the children that the family may fail if they don't shape up. The children find it too easy to blame each other and the parents and to collectively avoid feeling responsible. At Multi there was too much of a tradition that senior managers (the parents) would take care of things as they always had. The anxiety of facing up to the "family problem" was too overwhelming, so a great deal of denial had been operating.

The outside consultant could, in this case, take the same information but present it as a problem that the family as a whole owned and had to confront and handle as a total unit. He could be much more direct and confrontational than insiders could be with each other, and at the same time he could remind the total group that all the members were in this together—the executive committee as the symbolic parents along with all the children. This recognition did not reduce the resultant panic; however, it forced it out into the open because denial was no longer possible. The group had been genuinely disconfirmed and made anxious, but it did not feel psychologically safe and hence felt paralyzed.

The next problem, then, was how to deal with the current panic and discouragement. How could we provide some psychological safety that would permit the group to redefine the situation, to begin to feel capable of doing something constructive? The other consultant and I took a long walk to think this out and came up with the idea that now would be a good time to give some lectures on the nature of resistance to change and how to overcome it. He had been confrontational, so I should now come on as supportive and facilitative.

I hurriedly pulled together notes, made transparencies, and on the following morning gave lectures on (1) why healthy organizations need to be able to change, (2) why individuals and groups resist change, (3) how to analyze forces that facilitate and forces that constrain change, and (4) how to develop valid change targets for the coming year, in the context of the redirection project, with timetables, measurements of outcomes, and accountabilities. I emphasized a point that is central to change projects: the period of change must itself be defined as a stage to be managed, with transition managers specifically assigned (Beckhard and Harris, 1987).

These lectures had the desired effect of giving the group members a way of thinking positively so that when they were sent back into small groups to develop priority issues for making the redirection project a success, they were able to go off to these meetings with a sense of realism and optimism. The general results of the small group meetings were quite clear. The groups saw the need for the unprofitable divisions to shrink and restructure themselves and the need for profitable divisions to become more effective relative to the competition. However, they stated clearly that neither of these things could happen if the headquarters organization did not confront the excess of people in the headquarters and the style of management that was emanating from the functional groups. The ideas were not new, but they were now shared and with some conviction. The meeting ended with top management making a commitment to confront all of the issues identified and to create a set of task forces to deal with the problems.

Creating a Parallel Structure for the Redirection Project

The Multi managers were skillful at working in groups. Maier and the executive committee used this skill first by creating a steering committee to organize the redirection project into thirty or so separate manageable tasks. The steering committee met for several days following the annual meeting to think through the specific tasks to be accomplished in the redirection process and to design the entire parallel system that would implement it.

A separate steering committee was created for each task and one member of the executive committee was made accountable for the performance of that task group. In order to avoid asking some of the senior managers to downsize and restructure divisions for which they had previously been responsible, assignments were reshuffled so that no conflicts of interest would arise and so that each division would be looked at with fresh eyes.

In addition, each task group was assigned a senior manager to review and challenge the proposed solutions of that task group to ensure that they made sense and had been properly thought through. The steering committee defined the timetables, and the broad targets. Each team was also given the services of an internal organizational consultant to help with the organization of the team itself, and several of the teams asked for and obtained my help on how to structure their work.

All of this was communicated clearly by top management in written form, in meetings, and during visits to various parts of the company throughout the following year. Not only the process but the necessity for it and top management's commitment to it were highlighted. Great emphasis was given to the particular project that would reduce the number of people at headquarters by at least one-third, no small task since in many cases this involved laying off friends and relatives.

These structural changes in job responsibilities were major innovations implemented by the steering committee. The skillful use of groups both at the annual meeting and in the design of the projects struck me as paradoxical. How could a company that was so hierarchical and so concerned about individual turf be so effective in inventing groups and in operating within a group context? The answer appeared to lie in the fact that the top management of the company was itself a group of people who had worked together for a long time and felt jointly accountable. The broader culture in which the company functioned also represented this same paradox—strong individualism but at the same time a strong sense of community and a commitment to work together in groups to solve problems.

This respect for groups was confirmed in a meeting where I was advising two young managers of executive training programs on the design of a one-week middle-management course. I suggested the use of one of the group survival exercises that clearly illustrates how groups can solve some objective problems better than individuals can. These managers told me that they had used the exercise in the past but that participants routinely asked why their time was being wasted, because they were already convinced that groups could do better than individuals in problem solving.

One might also speculate that group work had such importance in Multi because it was virtually the only form of lateral communication available. The sensitivities that might be operating if managers from one division offered or asked for help from another division could be overcome, with faces saved, if a task force consisting of members of both divisions adopted a process of taking turns reporting to each other on the progress of effective and ineffective interventions. The listener could then learn and get new ideas without either identifying himself as having a problem or having others identify him as a target of their input. Group meetings thus preserved face all the way around.

It was also recognized that groups helped build commitment to projects even though the implementation system was essentially hierarchical. If groups had discussed the issue, the hierarchy worked more smoothly, as in the Japanese system, where consensus is sought before a decision is announced. In various ways the redirection project was using the cultural strengths of the company and was redefining its formal procedures in order to deal with the business problem without changing the culture overtly.

Second Year's Work: Consolidating the Redirection Project

During my several visits to Multi following the second annual meeting, I worked on three important areas. First, I made myself available to any project group or group members who wished to discuss any aspect of how to proceed, the appointment to be made at their initiative. If I learned something that would help other projects, I would summarize it and write it up for circulation to others. I was consulted by several managers on how best to think about early retirement, how to ease people out without them losing face in their home community, how to get managers to think about innovative restructuring, and so on. As already mentiond, I soon discovered that my memos pulling good ideas together died on the desks of the people to whom I gave those memos. That was my first encounter with the cultural norm that at Multi information does not circulate laterally. I also spent a good deal of time with the executive committee member who was responsible for the whole project, helping him keep his role and his leadership behavior in his project group clear and effective. He was the only member of the executive committee who consistently used me as a process consultant. Parenthetically, he was the chief financial officer and also a lawyer. Several project managers wanted help in thinking through their roles as project chairmen and solicited my reactions to proposals before running them by the challengers.

Second, I became more familiar with the management development inventory and planning system and began a series of meetings with Stern to see how it could be improved. Bringing in and developing better and more innovative managers was viewed as a high-priority longer-range goal of the redirection project. It was also widely known that Stern would retire within a year and his successor might need a consultant who had learned something about the company to help him think out his program.

Third, I was asked by Maier and the planning group to think about the cultural assumptions operating, to interview managers about the company culture, and to figure out how the culture was aiding or hindering the redirection project. The basic idea was to be prepared to comment on the role of the culture at the third annual meeting.

Third Annual Meeting: The Culture Lecture Disaster

I had made it clear that one should think of change as a stage to be managed, with targets and assigned change managers. From this point of view, the third annual meeting provided a natural opportunity to review progress, find out what problems had been encountered, share successes and good innovations, replan some projects if necessary, and most important, announce newly defined role relationships between executive committee members, division heads, and country heads. The headquarters organization realized that it was too involved in the day-to-day operation of the local businesses. So as the functions were shrunk and restructured, it also appeared desirable to redefine the corporate headquarters role as more strategic, while the operating units would do more of the day-to-day management. This was possible because country managers were now willing and able to assume more responsibilities and because the executive committee increasingly recognized the importance of its strategic role.

At the opening session I was asked to review the progress of the redirection project on the basis of interviews with a series of managers about their experiences with the project. This lecture was designed to remind the participants of change theory, to legitimize their individual experiences and frustrations by giving a wide range of examples, to illustrate how innovative managers had dealt with restraining forces, and to introduce the concept of corporate culture as a force to be analyzed. On the basis of my observations and systematic interviews, I was also to review some of the major cultural assumptions operating at Multi.

The reaction to the lecture produced an important insight. Many participants said that I had stated things more or less accurately, but they clearly were not pleased that I, as an outsider, had made portions of their culture public. Some of them insisted that I had made errors of misinterpretation, and one or two executive committee members subsequently decided that I was not a useful consultant. For me to discuss their cultural assumptions created a polarized situation. Some managers moved closer to me, while others moved farther away. I concluded that if one did not want that kind of polarization, one should help the group decipher its own culture rather than present one's own view of that culture in a didactic manner.

Following the general presentation on culture and change, each of the project groups was asked to give a brief review of its status, and small groups met to consider implications and make suggestions. The last part of the meeting and, from the point of view of the planning group, the most difficult part concerned the problem of how to inform everyone about the new roles of the executive committee, the division heads, and the country heads. The executive committee members were not sure that their planned effort to have headquarters become more strategic and to have individual operating units assume more of the day-to-day responsibilities would be understood and accepted.

We therefore planned a three-step process: (1) a formal announcement of the new roles; (2) a brief lecture by me on the implications of role realignment, emphasizing the systemic character of role networks and the need for each manager to renegotiate his role downward, upward, and laterally if the new system was to work; and (3) a powerful emotional speech by the chief financial officer on the effect of this new alignment in streamlining the company for the future. The meeting ended on a high note, based on a sense of what had already been accomplished in one year, what accomplishments were in the works, and what improvements could be expected from the new role that the executive committee had taken for itself.

The fact that the headquarters organization had begun to shrink through early retirements and had reduced some of its more bothersome control activities sent the clear message that top management was serious about its role in the redirection project even though the early retirement of headquarters people was an extremely painful process. The fact that people were being retired destroyed the taken-for-granted assumption that people had a guaranteed career in the company, but the highly individualized and financially generous manner in which retirements were handled reinforced another basic assumption: the company cared very much for its people and would not hurt them if there was any way to avoid it.

Third Year's Work: Assessing the Redirection Project

Most of my regular visits subsequent to the third annual meeting were devoted to working with John Lyons, the new director of management development. Stern had been asked to retire as part of the headquarters restructuring. Though I continued to meet with members of the executive committee on redirection matters, the priority shifted to helping Lyons think through his new role and reexamine how the entire process could be improved. Dr. Stern was offered, as part of his retirement package, a consultantship with the company provided he developed a research project that could be jointly conducted with me.

We proposed a study of the careers of the top two hundred managers in the company, with the purpose of identifying critical success factors or problems in those careers. The project was approved by the executive committee on condition that I was to act as technical supervisor of the project, reminding me once again that my credibility as a consultant rested heavily on my scientific reputation and that scientific validity was the ultimate decision criterion for the company. The study involved a detailed reconstruction of the careers and revealed surprisingly little geographical, cross-functional, and cross-divisional movement as those careers progressed.

Stern presented these and other results to the executive committee, and this led to a major discussion of how future general managers should be developed. The committee reached a consensus that there should be more early geographical rotation and movement into and out of headquarters, but cross-functional and cross-divisional movement remained a controversial issue. The executive committee members also realized that rotational moves, if they were to be useful, had to occur early in one's career. They decided that such early movement would occur only if a very clear message about the importance of career development went out to the entire organization.

This decision led to the design of a half-day session on management development, which was inserted into the management seminars that are periodically given to the top five hundred managers of the company. A new policy on early rotation was mandated, and the data from the project were used to justify the new policy. Once senior management accepted a conclusion as valid, it was able to move decisively and to impose a proposed solution on the entire company. The message was communicated by having executive committee members at each seminar, but implementation was left to local management.

During this year Maier relinquished the job of chairman of the executive committee for reasons of health, providing a potential succession problem. However, the executive committee had anticipated the problem and had a new chairman and vice-chairman ready. The new chairman was a scientist, but the new vice-chairman was the chief financial officer who had shown great leadership skills during the redirection project. Both of them strongly reaffirmed the scientific and technical assumptions underlying the success of Multi, as if to say, "We are making major changes, but we are the same kind of culture as we were before."

By the end of the third year, the financial results were much better, and the restructuring process in the unprofitable divisions was proceeding rapidly. Each unit learned how to manage early retirements, and a measure of interdivisional cooperation was achieved in the process of placing people who were redundant in one division into other divisions. Initial attitudes were negative, and I heard many complaints from managers that even their best people were not acceptable to other divisions; but this attitude was gradually eroded because the assumption that "we don't throw people out without maximum effort to find jobs for them" eventually overrode the provincialism of the divisions. Managers who were too committed to the old strategy of running those divisions were gradually replaced with managers who were deemed to be more innovative in their approach. One of the managers of a division that needed to make major reductions and redesign its entire product line was deemed so successful in this project that he was promoted to the executive committee and is today its chairman.

Because the redirection project had fulfilled its functions, it was officially terminated at the end of the third year. Relevant change projects would now be handled by the executive committee, and I was asked to be "on call" to line managers needing help. The new head of one of the previously unprofitable divisions, for example, wanted help in restoring the morale of those managers who remained after many of their colleagues were retired or transferred to other divisions. He sensed a level of fear and apathy that made it difficult to move forward positively. In true Multi fashion, he had tried to solve this problem on his own by bringing in an outside training program, but it had been unsuccessful. He then requested a meeting with me to seek alternative solutions. Given the Multi culture and this manager's own commitment, it was obvious that he should build his program internally and enlist the aid of the corporate training people, who would know how to design a program that would be culturally congruent. He had never considered using the corporate training group to help him, though he knew of it and liked some of the people in it. I found myself being the broker between two parts of the organization that could have been talking to each other directly. This individual followed up on my suggestion, and in the following year a successful in-house program was developed.

During the following two years my involvement at Multi declined gradually. The head of the redirection project on headquarters reduction has since become the chairman of the board and the former head of the division that needed the most downsizing has become the chairman of the executive committee. Both of these managers showed their talent in the way they handled their projects. All of the changes were accomplished without any outsiders being brought into Multi. I continued to work with Lyons on management development issues and helped him implement some of his programs. I also worked with the U.S. subsidiary on projects where my knowledge of the culture was considered an asset. Nevertheless, the assumption that one only uses consultants when one has serious problems prevailed. Since 1988 my involvement with Multi has been virtually zero.

Summary and Conclusions

Based on what I observed and have heard, Multi has successfully weathered a major organizational crisis involving many elements of its culture. Let us look at some specifics.

1. The financial trend toward nonprofitability was decisively reversed.

2. Two previously unprofitable divisions restructured themselves by drastically cutting products, facilities, and people and by reorganizing their production and marketing activities to fit the current market and economic realities. One of these divisions was considered a loser, but because of its successful restructuring under a dynamic manager, it is now considered the hero of the company.

3. The functions at corporate headquarters were reduced by 30 to 40 percent, and more line responsibility was delegated to the countries and divisions.

4. The functions in the divisions were also reassessed, and their role was changed in line with headquarters becoming more strategic.

5. The profitable divisions thoroughly reassessed themselves and initiated programs to become more competitive in their particular industries, particularly the pharmaceutical division.

6. Executive committee members restructured their own areas of accountability so that each division, country, and function now has a clear line boss but one whose focus is strategic. In the previous system, these organizational units had felt accountable to the entire executive committee.

7. A major management succession occurred and was negotiated successfully in that the new chairman and vice-chairman of the executive committee were perceived by senior management as good choices, and the two have been promoted further in recent years.

8. In the three-year change process, many managers who were considered less effective were weeded out through early retirement, permitting key jobs to be filled by managers considered more dynamic and effective.

9. Senior managers acquired insight into the ways in which their culture both constrains and helps them.

10. A major cultural assumption about career stability, particularly at headquarters, was reassessed and abandoned. In that process another major assumption about dealing with people on an individualized and humane basis was reaffirmed.

11. Managerial career development was redefined in terms of required rotation geographically and through headquarters.

12. The consumer goods acquisition that did not fit was reevaluated and the decision was made to sell it. At the same time the corporate acquisition policy was clarified to look only for companies based on technologies with which Multi felt comfortable.

Most managers in Multi undoubtedly would say that they had undergone some great changes and that many of their assumptions about the world and the company have changed.

However, when one looks closely, the cultural paradigm of the company has not really changed at all. There is the same bias toward scientific authority, the hierarchy functions as strongly as ever but with redefined roles, the assumption that managers do their best job when left alone to learn for themselves is still very strong, and lateral communication is still considered mostly irrelevant. For example, there is still no regular meeting of division heads except at the annual meeting, where they meet with everyone else, and there are no functional meetings across countries or divisions.

Various projects — for example, to bring in MBAs on a trial basis and to hold worldwide meetings of functional people, such as the management development coordinators from all the divisions and key countries — are being advocated, but one senses that they are only tolerated in the culture, not encouraged. On one of my visits, Lyons arranged for me to meet five of the MBAs who had been hired into different parts of Multi to see how they were reacting to their different situations. We had a productive and constructive meeting. A week later Lyons was criticized by several MBAs' bosses for organizing the meeting because he was stepping onto the turf of these other managers, who would not have given permission for such a cross-departmental group to meet.

I mention all this because when the redirection project began, we all talked of culture change. To label a change as culture change enhances the drama of what is happening, so it may have some motivational value even if it is inaccurate. At the same time, it focuses people on the culture so that they can identify both the constraints and the enhancing features of the culture. The important thing to note, however, is that considerable change can take place in an organization's operations without the basic cultural paradigm changing at all. In fact, some of the assumptions could not have changed but for the even stronger action of deeper assumptions. Thus, some parts of the culture helped many of the changes to happen in other parts of the culture. In a study of major changes in large corporations, Donaldson and Lorsch (1983) report something very similar. The basic deep beliefs of management did not change but actually were used to fuel the changes that the organizations needed to make to become more adaptive and effective.

This insight leads to a further point. Many assumptions surrounding mission, goals, means, measurement systems, roles, and relationships can be superficial within the total structure of the cultural paradigm yet be very important to the organization's day-to-day functioning. The assumption that the headquarters functional groups had worldwide responsibility for tracking everything was not a very deep assumption within the whole Multi culture, but it was having a major impact on business performance and managerial morale in the country companies. Changing some of these superficial assumptions was crucial to Multi's effective adaptation. The deeper assumptions may drive the whole process but may not have to change.

It should also be noted that the deeper assumptions are not necessarily functional. Multi's commitment to science continued to be manifested in commitment to scientists, especially some of the older ones who had helped the company become successful. In one extreme case such a person was a country manager who was performing poorly in that role. A more skillful general manager had been groomed to take over in this country, but the decision to give him authority was held up for two full years in order to let the scientist retire at his originally scheduled time. It was felt that to force him into early retirement would not only be destructive to him but would send an incorrect signal to the rest of the organization.

What, then, really happened in the redirection project and why? Many in the company have also asked this question in order to understand the reasons for the success of the change effort. My own observation is that the effort was successful because the executive committee (1) sent a clear message that a change was needed, (2) involved itself fully in the change process, (3) tackled the impossible job of reducing headquarters staff as well as the power of the functional groups, and (4) thereby not only created involvement and ownership down the line in the country groups but made it clear that operational problems would increasingly be delegated downward. Even though lateral communication is still minimal, the vertical channels were opened wider. Financial information was shared more than before, suggestions rising through the project structure were listened to, and proposals that were accepted were effectively implemented through the existing hierarchy as a result of clear top-down signals.

Two additional reasons why the redirection project was successful were that the project was designed with an externalized steering committee that created project groups with consultants and challenger managers and the design provided clear goals, timetables, and time off to work on the problem, reflecting skills embedded in the Multi culture. The organization knew very well how to design group projects and work in groups. In this sense Multi used its cultural strength to redirect itself more rapidly than might have been possible in a less structured organization or one less sensitive to group process issues.

On the original issue that Maier asked me to address, the stimulation of innovation, very little change has taken place from my point of view. However, the culture of Multi works, so one cannot readily assume that some other way would be better.

The driving force and many of the key insights behind this change effort came from Maier, who as mentioned before was the kind of leader who could step outside of his own culture and assess it realistically. The willingness of the chief financial officer and various division managers to step outside their own subcultures and learn some new approaches also played a key role. But in the end the culture changed only in peripheral ways by restructuring some key assumptions. Nevertheless, such peripheral culture change is often sufficient to solve major organizational problems.

PART SIX

Learning Cultures
and Learning Leaders

In Part Six the focus shifts from analysis to normative speculation. There is much speculation nowadays about the direction
in which the world is heading and what this means for organizations and leadership. My sense is that the various predictions
about globalism, knowledge-based organizations, the information age, the biotech age, the loosening of organizational boundaries, and so on have one theme in common — we basically do
not know what the world of tomorrow will really be like except
that it will be different (Davis and Davison, 1991; Hirschhorn,
1988; Michael, 1985, 1991). *That means that organizations and their
leaders will have to become perpetual learners.*

When we pose the issue of perpetual learning in the context of cultural analysis, we confront a paradox. Culture is a
stabilizer, a conservative force, a way of making things predictable. Does this mean, then, that culture itself is increasingly
dysfunctional, or is it possible to imagine a culture that by its
very nature is learning oriented, adaptive, and innovative? Can
one stabilize perpetual learning and change? What would a culture that favored learning look like?

In leadership terms, what is the direction in which leaders
should be pushing cultural change? Is it enough for leaders to
be aware of their own cultures, to learn what the present shared

361

assumptions are? Or must leaders look beyond that question and ask what those assumptions should be if their organizations are to remain viable in an ever-changing world of surprises? I do not have answers to these questions, but I do have some speculations and biases that the next two chapters will explore. First, in Chapter Eighteen I will briefly describe what I consider to be the characteristics of a learning culture and the implications of that for leadership. Then in Chapter Nineteen I will summarize and extrapolate from earlier chapters the issues that leaders must address and the implications of those issues for the selection of leaders.

The Learning Culture
Managing the Contradictions of Stability, Learning, and Change

The most intriguing leadership role in culture management is one in which the leader attempts to develop a learning organization that will be able to make its own perpetual diagnosis and self-manage whatever transformations are needed as the environment changes (Bushe and Shani, 1991; Hanna, 1988; Mohrman and Cummings, 1989). But can one imagine and attempt to develop a set of assumptions that can become stable and thus function as a culture and yet encourage and allow for perpetual learning and change? In a sense these appear to be contradictory requirements in that culture is by definition a stabilizing, conservative process. Nevertheless, some leaders are attempting to institutionalize and stabilize learning and innovation itself. We must therefore consider what a learning culture might look like, using some of the dimensions we have previously identified.

The hypotheses spelled out in this chapter have resulted from many conversations with Donald Michael (1985, 1991) and Tom Malone (1987) about the organization of the future. They reflect a bringing together of what Michael sees as the learning needs of the future, what Malone sees as the theory and practice of coordination in the information age, what Senge (1990) visualizes as the art and practice of the learning organi-

363

zation, and my own thoughts about culture and innovation (Schein, 1990b). Combining these ideas leads to a first attempt to describe the characteristics of a learning culture as shown in Table 18.1. A number of dimensions and characteristics of organizations that have been discussed in the text and are relevant to the capacity of a culture to learn are shown in this table. Along each dimension, an X indicates the hypothesized ideal location for learning to occur on a continuing basis. By implication, we can hypothesize that other positions on the dimension lead to cultural rigidity.

Organization-Environment Relationship

A learning culture must contain a core shared assumption that the environmental context in which the organization exists is to some degree manageable. An organization that assumes that it must symbiotically accept its niche will have more difficulty in learning as the environment becomes more turbulent. Adaptation to a slowly changing environment is also a viable learning process, but I am assuming that the way in which the world is changing will make that less and less possible.

   In other words, the more turbulent the environment, the more important it will be for leaders to argue for and show that some level of control over the environment is desirable and possible.

The Nature of Human Activity

A learning culture must contain a core shared assumption that the appropriate way for humans to behave is to be proactive problem solvers and learners. If the culture is built on fatalistic assumptions of passive acceptance, learning will be more and more difficult as the rate of change in the environment increases. It is not clear how this kind of assumption works out in Asian cultures, where fatalistic acceptance is a central assumption. My speculation would be that in those cultures a differentiation will take place between domains such as religion, where the old assumption will hold, and "business," where new assumptions concerning active problem solving will come to coexist with the old assumptions.

Table 18.1. Characteristics of a Learning Culture.

Organization-Environment Relationship

Environment dominant	Symbiotic	Organization dominant
		X

Nature of Human Activity

Reactive, fatalistic	Harmonizing	Proactive
		X

Nature of Reality and Truth

Moralistic authoritative		Pragmatic
		X

Nature of Human Nature

Humans basically evil		Humans basically good
		X

Human nature fixed		Human nature mutable
		X

Nature of Human Relationships

Groupism	X	Individualism

Authoritative/paternalistic	X	Collegial/participative

Nature of Time

Past oriented	Present oriented	Near-future oriented
		X

Short time units	Medium time units	Long time units
	X	

Information and Communication

Low level of connectivity		Fully connected
		X

Subcultural Uniformity Versus Diversity

High uniformity		High diversity
		X

Table 18.1. Characteristics of a Learning Culture, Cont'd.

Task Versus Relationship Orientation

Primarily task oriented	Task and relationship oriented	Primarily relationship oriented
	X	

Linear Versus Systemic Field Logic

Linear thinking	Systemic thinking
	X

The learning leader must portray confidence that active problem solving leads to learning and, thereby, set an appropriate example for other members of the organization. What is important is to portray and exemplify the conviction that active learning helps, not necessarily to have solutions. The *process* of learning must ultimately be made part of the culture, not any given solution to any given problem.

The Nature of Reality and Truth

A learning culture must contain the shared assumption that solutions to problems derive from a pragmatic search for truth and that truth can be found anywhere, depending on the nature of the problem. Although this is essentially the pragmatic position on the moralism-pragmatism dimension, one would assume that pragmatism itself sometimes dictates reliance on authority and wisdom. What must be avoided in the learning culture is the automatic assumption that wisdom and truth reside in any one source or method.

As the problems we encounter change, so will our learning method change. For some purposes we will have to rely heavily on normal science; for other purposes we will have to find truth in experienced practitioners because scientific proof will be impossible to obtain; for still other purposes we will collectively have to experiment and live with errors until a better solution is found. Knowledge and skill will be found in many forms, and what I am calling a clinical research process, in which helpers and clients work things out together, will become more and more important because no one will be "expert" enough to provide an answer.

The toughest problem for learning leaders here is to come to terms with their own lack of expertise and wisdom. Once we are in a leadership position, our own needs and the expectations of others dictate that we know the answer and be in control of the situation. Yet if we provide answers, we are creating a culture that will inevitably take a moralistic position in regard to reality and truth. The only way to build a learning culture that continues to learn is for leaders themselves to realize that they do not know and must teach others to accept that they do not know. The learning task is then a shared responsibility.

It is also worth noting that in many cultures, notably Western ones, the assumption that one knows and is in control is particularly associated with masculine roles. It is quite possible that women as leaders will find it easier to accept a whole range of methods for arriving at solutions and will therefore be more able in a learning role.

The Nature of Human Nature

Learning leaders must have faith in people and must believe that ultimately human nature is basically good and in any case mutable. Learning implies some desire for survival and improvement. If leaders start with assumptions that people are basically lazy and passive, that people have no concern for organizations or causes above and beyond themselves, they will inevitably create organizations that will become self-fulfilling prophecies. Such leaders will train their employees to be lazy, self-protective, and self-seeking, and then they will cite those characteristics as proof of their original assumption about human nature. The resulting control-oriented organizations may survive and even thrive in certain kinds of stable environments, but they are certain to fail as the environments become more turbulent and as technological and global trends cause problem solving to become increasingly more complex. Knowledge and skill are becoming more widely distributed, forcing leaders, whether they like it or not, to be more dependent on other people in their organizations. Under such circumstances a cynical attitude toward human nature is bound to create bureaucratic rigidity at the minimum and counterorganizational subgroups at the maximum. In either case, the learning process will be fatally undermined.

One might speculate here about why McGregor's (1960) insight into this problem in terms of Theory X and Theory Y still has not taken hold more than thirty years after it was first promulgated. One hypothesis is that he was proposing the more idealistic Theory Y at a time when control-oriented bureaucracies were still working fairly effectively. The real relevance of Theory Y may well be to the learning organization of the future. It is inconceivable to me how a learning-oriented leader could have anything other than Theory Y assumptions about human nature and how an organization in which knowledge and skill are widely distributed can work on any basis other than mutual trust.

The Nature of Human Relationships

Should the learning culture be based on assumptions of individualism or groupism? I would hypothesize that if creativity and innovation are central to learning, an individualistic culture will be more favorable. On the other hand, if the implementation of complex interdependent solutions is the key to learning and adaptation, then a groupist kind of organization will perform better. The learning organizations I have observed thus far, for example Action and Multi, have a complex blend of individualism and groupism, and therein probably lies the key. Neither extreme on this dimension is inherently favorable to learning.

In terms of assumptions about authority, is it better for a learning culture to be authoritarian/paternalistic or collegial/participative? Here too the answer turns out to be complex. The participative organization is clearly more likely to generate creative solutions because it will tap a wider range of resources. However, once a solution has been found, whether the participative organization is the better one to implement it seems to depend on the nature of the solution. If it is easily communicated and understood, then an authoritarian system will be more efficient; if the solution is complex and requires the cooperation of different elements of the organization, then a participative system works better. Here as in the case of individualism or groupism, the answer seems to be that one needs a set of assumptions that legitimizes both positions and also a pragmatic orientation that encourages leaders to vary their managerial style according to the nature of the task at hand.

The Nature of Time

The optimal time orientation for learning appears to be somewhere between far future and near future. One must think far enough ahead to be able to assess the systemic consequences of different courses of action, but one must also think in terms of the near future to assess whether or not one's solutions are working. The assumption that the best orientation is to live in the past or to live in the present clearly seems dysfunctional if the environment is becoming more turbulent.

A similar argument can be made about assumptions of what is a correct unit of time in terms of which to think — minutes, hours, days, months, quarters, years, decades? This will, of course, depend on the task and the kind of learning that is going on, but the optimal assumption would be that one should pick "medium-length" time units for assessment so that one allows enough time to test whether or not a proposed solution is working but not so much time that one persists with a proposed solution that is clearly not working.

For any given task, the learning leader will have to make the diagnosis of what a medium length of time is, and that will vary from situation to situation. As the world becomes more complex we will be less and less able to rely on standard time units such as quarters or years. Because time has so many symbolic meanings and is so central to our daily conduct, the learning leader must be very conscious of her or his own assumptions about time and make these explicit for others.

Information and Communication

The learning culture must be built on the assumption that communication and information are central to organizational well-being and must therefore create a multichannel communication system that allows everyone to connect to everyone else. This does not mean that all channels will be used or that any given channel will be used for all things. What it does mean is that anyone must be able to communicate with anyone else and that everyone assumes that telling the truth as best one can is positive and desirable. This does not mean that one suspends all the cultural rules pertaining to face and adopts a definition of openness as equivalent to the proverbial "letting it all hang out." There is ample evidence that such interpersonal openness can create severe problems across hierarchical boundaries and in intercultural settings. It does mean that one must become sensitive to task-relevant information and be as open as possible in sharing that. One of the important roles for the learning leader will be to specify in terms of any given task what the minimum communication system must be and what kind of information is critical to effective problem solving and learning.

Notice that a fully connected network can only work if high trust exists among all the participants and that high trust is partly a function of leader assumptions that people can be trusted and have constructive intent. If a fully connected network ends up overloading everyone with information, it can voluntarily close certain channels, but the assumption that it is in principle possible and all right for anyone in the system to communicate with anyone else must remain in place.

Uniformity Versus Diversity

The more turbulent the environment, the more likely it is that the diverse organization will have the resources to cope with unpredicted events. Therefore, the learning leader should stimulate diversity and promulgate the assumption that diversity is desirable at the individual and subgroup levels. Such diversity will inevitably create subcultures, and those subcultures will eventually be a necessary resource for learning and innovation.

For diversity to be a resource, however, the subcultures must be connected and must learn to value each other enough to learn something of each other's culture and language. A central task for the learning leader, then, is to ensure good cross-cultural communication and understanding throughout the organization.

Task Versus Relationship Orientation

The dimension of task versus relationship orientation is difficult to analyze because, as with some of the other dimensions, the assumption that seems to be most productive of learning is to believe that both orientations are equally important. In a stable environment it is safe to be completely task oriented. In a complex, turbulent environment in which technological and other forms of interdependence are high, however, one needs to value relationships in order to achieve the level of trust and communication that will make joint problem solving and solution implementation possible.

One must also be careful not to project one's own cultural assumptions here, since cultures differ in how they conceptualize tasks and relationships. In some cultures it would be assumed that unless relationships are built, one cannot accomplish the task and that, from a long-range point of view, it is more important to maintain relationships even if this means short-run task failure. In engineering organizations such as Action, there is a tendency to define formal design as "real engineering" work and committee meetings, in which decisions are made about which products to design, as less desirable work. In a learning culture one would be objective about this point, noting that sometimes the real work is the committee meetings, the politics, and the interpersonal negotiation, whereas at other times the real work is design.

Linear Versus Systemic Field Logic

As the world becomes more complex and interdependent, the ability to think systemically, to analyze fields of forces and understand their joint causal effects on each other, and to abandon simple linear causal logic in favor of complex mental models will become more critical to learning (Senge, 1990). The learning leader and the learning culture must therefore be built on the assumption that the world is intrinsically complex, nonlinear, and overdetermined.

Indeed, this condition of the world argues for the need for learning leaders in the first place. One of the first things that the members of any organization must learn along with their leaders is that the environment is intrinsically a complex system, difficult to predict and analyze. At the same time, one must be able to believe that efforts to analyze it, to discover one's own mental models, and to test these against discovered reality constitute a valuable process that improves one's ability to cope. The task of learning leaders is not only to gain their own personal insights along these lines but to help others achieve such insights as well.

I am not implying that these are the only or even the most relevant dimensions of a learning culture. These dimensions are a first approximation based on our understanding of culture thus far. As we do more research at the national, organizational, and subgroup levels, other dimensions will surface. It does seem obvious, however, that some conceptual clarity about how we get organizations to learn and to learn faster is becoming a priority issue, and that we cannot get such clarity without tackling the difficult conceptual problem of how a culture itself can be a perpetual learning system.

Summary and Conclusions

To summarize, the learning culture must assume that the world can be managed, that it is appropriate for humans to be proactive problem solvers, that reality and truth must be pragmatically discovered, that human nature is basically good and in any case mutable, that both individualism and groupism are appropriate, that both authoritarian and participative systems are appropriate provided they are based on trust, that the best kind of time horizon is somewhere between far and near future, that the best kinds of units of time are medium-length ones, that accurate and relevant information must be capable of flowing freely in a fully connected network, that diverse but connected units are desirable, that both task and relationship orientations are desirable, and that the world is intrinsically a complex field of interconnected forces in which multiple causation and over-determination are more likely than linear or simple causes.

The role of learning-oriented leadership in a turbulent world, then, is to promote these kinds of assumptions. Leaders themselves must first hold such assumptions and then be able to recognize and systematically reward behavior based on those assumptions in others. In mature organizations leaders have to find subcultures and pockets of learning and innovation and systematically reward the managers and employees who hold the assumptions that made the innovation possible. It then remains to determine whether or not such innovative behavior leads to success in the external environment and comfort in the internal environment. If it does, a new and innovative culture will gradually be formed.

Programs such as total quality management can be assessed in terms of whether or not they operate on the assumptions outlined above. The overt and espoused values that are stated for such solutions often hide assumptions that are not, in fact, favorable to the kind of learning I have described. If leaders are not aware of the cultural underpinnings of what they are doing or the assumptions of the group on which they are imposing new solutions, they are likely to fail. Learning leaders must be careful to look inside themselves to locate their own mental models and assumptions before they leap into action.

CHAPTER NINETEEN

The Learning Leader
as Culture Manager

Throughout this book I have argued that leadership and culture are closely connected by showing how leaders create, embed, develop, and sometimes deliberately attempt to change cultural assumptions. In this chapter I want to summarize and collect in one place many of the points about leadership that have been made. Some of this is repetitious, but it needs to be stated in one place for the reader who wants to focus specifically on what a cultural perspective means for leadership.

Though it has been typically exemplified in this book by the founder, owner, or professional manager who has been promoted to be CEO, leadership can occur anywhere in the organization. Leadership is the attitude and motivation to examine and manage culture. Accomplishing this goal is more difficult lower down in the organization but by no means impossible in that subcultures can be managed just as can overall organizational cultures.

The issues that make the most difference to the kind of leadership required are twofold. First, different stages of organizational development require different kinds of culture management. Second, different strategic issues require a focus on different kinds of cultural dimensions. Each of these points is briefly examined below.

Leadership in Culture Creation

In a growing organization leaders externalize their own assumptions and embed them gradually and consistently in the mission, goals, structures, and working procedures of the group. Whether we call these basic assumptions the guiding beliefs, the theories-in-use, the mental models, the basic principles, or the guiding visions on which founders operate, there is little question that they become major elements of the organization's emerging culture (for example, Argyris, 1976; Bennis, 1989; Davis, 1984; Donaldson and Lorsch, 1983; Dyer, 1986; Kotter and Heskett, 1992; Pettigrew, 1979; Schein, 1983).

In a rapidly changing world, the learning leader/founder must not only have vision but must be able to impose it and to develop it further as external circumstances change. Inasmuch as the new members of an organization arrive with prior organizational and cultural experiences, a common set of assumptions can only be forged by clear and consistent messages as the group encounters and survives its own crises. The culture creation leader therefore needs persistence and patience, yet as a learner must be flexible and ready to change.

As groups and organizations develop, certain key emotional issues arise. These have to do with dependence on the leader, with peer relationships, and with how to work effectively. Leadership is needed to help the group identify the issues and deal with them. During this process leaders must often absorb and contain the anxiety that is unleashed when things do not work as they should (Hirschhorn, 1988; Schein, 1983). Leaders may not have the answer, but they must provide temporary stability and emotional reassurance while the answer is being worked out. This anxiety-containing function is especially relevant during periods of learning, when old habits must be given up before new ones are learned. Moreover, if the world is increasingly changing, such anxiety may be perpetual, requiring learning leaders to assume a perpetual supportive role. The traumas of growth appear to be so constant and so powerful that unless a strong leader takes the role of anxiety and risk absorber, the group cannot get through its early stages of growth and fails. Being in an ownership position helps because everyone then realizes that the founder is in fact taking a greater personal financial risk; however, ownership does not automatically create the ability to absorb anxiety. For many leaders this is one of the most important things they have to learn.

When leaders launch new enterprises, they must be mindful of the power they have to impose on those enterprises their own assumptions about what is right and proper, how the world works, and how things should be done. Leaders should not apologize for or be cautious about their assumptions. Rather, it is intrinsic to the leadership role to create order out of chaos, and leaders are expected to provide their own assumptions as an initial road map into the uncertain future. The more aware leaders are of this process, the more consistent and effective they can be in implementing it.

The process of culture creation, embedding, and reinforcement brings with it problems as well as solutions. Many organizations survive and grow but at the same time operate inconsistently or do things that seem contradictory. One explanation of this phenomenon that has been pointed out repeatedly is that leaders not only embed in their organizations what they intend consciously to get across, but they also convey their own inner conflicts and the inconsistencies in their own personal makeup (Schein, 1983; Kets de Vries and Miller, 1984; Miller, 1990). The most powerful signal to which subordinates respond is what catches leaders' attention consistently, particularly what arouses them emotionally. But many of the things to which leaders respond emotionally reflect not so much their conscious intentions as their unconscious conflicts. The organization then either develops assumptions around these inconsistencies and conflicts and they become part of the culture, or the leader gradually loses a position of influence if the behavior begins to be seen as too disruptive or actually destructive. In extreme cases the organization isolates or ejects the founder. In doing so, however, it is not rejecting all of the founder's assumptions but only those that are inconsistent with the core assumptions on which the organization was built.

The period of culture creation, therefore, puts an additional burden on founders — to obtain enough self-insight to avoid unwittingly undermining their own creations. Founding leaders often find it difficult to recognize that the very qualities that made them successful initially, their strong convictions, can become sources of difficulty later on and that they also must learn and grow as their organizations grow. Such insights become especially important when organizations face issues of leadership succession because succession discussions force into the open aspects of the culture that may not have been previously recognized.

What all of this means for leaders of developing organizations is that they must have tremendous self-insight and recognize their own role not only in creating the culture but also their responsibility in embedding and developing culture. Inasmuch as the culture is the primary source of identity for young organizations, the culture creation and development process must be handled sensitively with full understanding of the anxieties that are unleashed when identity is challenged.

Leadership at Organizational Midlife

As the organization develops a substantial history of its own, its culture becomes more of a cause than an effect. As subgroups develop their own subcultures, the opportunities for constructive use of cultural diversity and the problems of integration both become greater. The leader must be able to pay attention to diversity and assess clearly how much of it is useful for further organizational development and how much of it is potentially dysfunctional. The culture is now much less tied to the leader's own personality, which makes it easier to assess objectively, though there are likely to be sacred cows, holdovers from the founding period, that have to be delicately handled.

The leader at this stage must be able to detect how the culture influences the strategy, structure, procedures, and ways in which the group members relate to one another. Culture is a powerful influence on members' perceptions, thinking, and feeling, and these predispositions, along with situational factors, influence members' behavior. Because culture serves an important anxiety-reducing function, members cling to it even if it becomes dysfunctional in relationship to environmental opportunities and constraints.

Leaders at this stage need dianostic skill to figure out not only what the cultural influences are, but also what their impact is on the organization's ability to change and learn. Whereas founding leaders most need self-insight, midlife leaders most need the ability to decipher the surrounding culture and subcultures. To help the organization evolve into whatever will make it most effective in the future, leaders must also have culture management skills. In some instances this may mean increasing cultural diversity, allowing some of the uniformity that may have been built up in the growth stage to erode. In other instances it may mean pulling together a culturally diverse set of organizational units and attempting to impose new common assumptions on them. In either case the leader needs (1) to be able to analyze the culture in sufficient detail to know which cultural assumptions can aid and which ones will hinder the fulfillment of the organizational mission and (2) to possess the intervention skills to make desired changes happen.

Most of the prescriptive analyses of how to maintain the organization's effectiveness through this period emphasize that the leader must have certain insights, clear vision, and the skills to articulate, communicate, and implement the vision, but these analyses say nothing about how a given organization can find and install such a leader. In U.S. organizations in particular, the outside board members probably play a critical role in this process. If the organization has had a strong founding culture, however, its board may be composed exclusively of people who share the founder's vision. Consequently, real changes in direction may not become possible until the organization experiences serious survival difficulties and begins to search for a person with different assumptions to lead it.

One area to explore further here is the CEO's own role in succession. Can the leader of a midlife organization perceive the potential dysfunctions of some aspects of the culture to a sufficient extent to ensure that his or her successor will be able to move the culture in an appropriate new direction? CEOs have a great deal of power to influence the choice of their successor.

Do they use that power wisely in terms of cultural issues? For example, it is alleged that one of the main reasons why Reginald Jones as CEO of General Electric "chose" Jack Welch to be his successor was because he recognized in Welch a person who would create the kinds of changes that were necessary for GE to remain viable. Similarly, Steve Jobs "chose" John Sculley to head Apple even though at some level he must have sensed that this choice might eventually lead to the kind of conflict that in the end forced Jobs to leave. The ultimate paradox here is that truly learning leaders may have to face the conclusion that they must replace themselves, that they do not have the vision needed to bring the midlife organization into alignment with a rapidly changing world.

Leadership in Mature and Potentially Declining Organizations

In the mature stage if the organization has developed a strong unifying culture, that culture now defines even what is to be thought of as leadership, what is heroic or sinful behavior, and how authority and power are to be allocated and managed. Thus, what leadership has created now either blindly perpetuates itself or creates new definitions of leadership, which may not even include the kinds of entrepreneurial assumptions that launched the organization in the first place. The first problem of the mature and possibly declining organization, then, is to find a process to empower a potential leader who may have enough insight to overcome some of the constraining cultural assumptions.

What the leader must do at this point in the organization's history depends on the degree to which the culture of the organization has, in fact, enabled the group to adapt to its environmental realities. If the culture has not facilitated adaptation, the organization either will not survive or will find a way to change its culture. If it is to change its culture, it must be led by someone who can, in effect, break the tyranny of the old culture. This requires not only the insight and diagnostic skill to determine what the old culture is, but to realize what alternative assumptions are available and how to start a change process toward their acceptance.

Leaders of mature organizations must, as has been argued repeatedly, make themselves sufficiently marginal in their own organization to be able to perceive its assumptions objectively and nondefensively. They must, therefore, find many ways to be exposed to their external environment and, thereby facilitate their own learning. If they cannot learn new assumptions themselves, they will not be able to perceive what is possible in their organizations. Even worse, they may destroy innovative efforts that arise within their organizations if those innovative efforts involve countercultural assumptions.

Leaders capable of such managed culture change can come from inside the organization if they have acquired objectivity and insight into elements of the culture. Such cultural objectivity appears to be related to having had a non-conventional career or exposure to many subcultures within the organization (Kotter and Heskett, 1992). However, the formally designated senior managers of a given organization may not be willing or able to provide such culture change leadership. Leadership then may have to come from other boundary spanners in the organization or from outsiders. It may even come from a number of people in the organization, in which case it makes sense to talk of turnaround teams or multiple leadership.

If a leader is imposed from the outside, she or he must have the skill to diagnose accurately what the culture of the organization is, what elements are well adapted and what elements are problematic for future adaptation, and how to change that which needs changing. In other words the leader must be a skilled change manager who first learns what the present state of the culture is, unfreezes it, redefines and changes it, and then refreezes the new assumptions. Talented turnaround managers seem to be able to manage all phases of such changes, but sometimes different leaders will be involved in the different steps over a considerable period of time. They will use all the mechanisms previously discussed in the appropriate combinations to get the job done provided that they have the authority and power to use extreme measures, such as replacing the people who perpetuate the old cultural assumptions.

In summary, leaders play a critical role at each developmental stage of an organization, but that role differs as a function of the stage. Much of what leaders do is to perpetually diagnose the particular assumptions of the culture and figure out how to use those assumptions constructively or to change them if they are constraints.

Leadership and Culture in Strategy Formulation

Many companies have found that they or their consultants can think of new strategies that make sense from a financial, product, or marketing point of view, yet they cannot implement those strategies because such implementation requires assumptions, values, and ways of working that are too far out of line with the organization's existing assumptions. In some cases, the organization cannot even conceive of certain strategic options because they are too out of line with shared assumptions about the mission of the organization and its way of working, what Lorsch (1985) has aptly called "strategic myopia."

The Multi Company built its businesses by capitalizing on the intensive efforts of its research labs to develop "important" products that were "useful to society." Members viewed themselves as a company that produced life-saving drugs, pesticides that enabled countries to improve their food crops, sophisticated chemicals that made other industries possible, and so on. The company's success was based on brilliant research work and the protection from competition that patents allowed.

When the company began to compete in more diversified and mature markets, where patent protection had run out and product utility was not nearly as important as product marketability, some senior managers argued for a more pragmatic marketing strategy. Those managers wanted to decrease the research and development budget, increase marketing expenditures, and teach their colleagues how to think like marketers. But they were unable to convince senior management as a whole, leaving parts of the company in a financially vulnerable position. Clearly, the traditions, values, self-concepts, and assumptions about the nature of Multi made some aspects of the proposed new marketing strategy unthinkable or unacceptable to senior management.

Another example is provided by the Action Company, which became successful by developing a very complex product marketed to very sophisticated customers. The company later developed some smaller, simpler, less expensive versions of this product, which could have been further developed and marketed to less sophisticated customers. Even senior management argued that such low-end products had to be developed, but the product designers and marketers could not deal with the new customer type. The sales and marketing people could not imagine what the concerns of the new, less knowledgeable customer might be, and the product designers continued to be convinced that they could judge product attractiveness themselves. Neither group was motivated to understand the new customer because, unconsciously, they tended to look down on such a customer. The assumption that "dumb users" were not worth designing for was, in fact, held throughout the company, even by senior managers who were advocating low-end products.

To put this in the proper perspective, we must remember that cultural assumptions are the product of past successes. As a result they are increasingly taken for granted and operate as silent filters on what is perceived and thought about. If the organization's environment changes and new responses are required, the danger is that the changes will not be noticed or, even if noticed, that the organization will not be able to adapt because of embedded routines based on past success. Culture constrains strategy by limiting what the CEO and other senior managers are able to think about and what they perceive in the first place.

One of the critical roles of learning leadership, then, is first of all to notice changes in the environment and then to figure out what needs to be done to remain adaptive. I am defining leadership in this context in terms of the role, not the position. The CEO or other senior managers may or may not be able to fulfill the leadership role, and leadership in the sense that I am defining it can occur anywhere in the organization. However, if real change and learning are to take place, it is probably necessary that the CEO or other very senior managers be able to be leaders in this sense.

Leaders must be somewhat marginal and must be somewhat embedded in the organization's external environment to fulfill this role adequately. At the same time, leaders must be well connected to those parts of the organization that are themselves well connected to the environment — sales, purchasing, marketing, public relations and legal, finance, and R & D. Leaders must be able to listen to disconfirming information coming from these sources and to assess the implications for the future of the organization. Only when they truly understand what is happening and what will be required in the way of organizational change can they begin to take action in initiating a learning process.

Much has been said about the need for vision in leaders, but too little has been said about their need to listen, to absorb, to search the environment for trends, and to build the organization's capacity to learn. Especially at the strategic level, the ability to see and acknowledge the full complexity of problems becomes critical. The ability to acknowledge complexity may also imply the willingness and emotional strength to admit uncertainty and to embrace experimentation and possible errors as the only way to learn. In our obsession with leadership vision, we may have made it possible for learning leaders to admit that their vision is not clear and that the whole organization will have to learn together. Moreover, as I have repeatedly argued, vision in a mature organization only helps when the organization has already been disconfirmed and members feel anxious and in need of a solution. Much of what learning leaders must do occurs before vision even becomes relevant.

To summarize, the critical roles of leadership in strategy formulation and implementation are (1) to perceive accurately and in depth what is happening in the environment, (2) to create enough disconfirming information to motivate the organization to change without creating too much anxiety, (3) to provide psychological safety by either providing a vision of how to change and in what direction or by creating a process of visioning that allows the organization itself to find a path, (4) to acknowledge uncertainty, (5) to embrace errors in the learning process as inevitable and desirable, and (6) to manage all phases of the change process, including especially the management of anxiety as some cultural assumptions are given up and new learning begins.

Leadership and Culture in Mergers and Acquisitions

Mergers and acquisitions are usually initiated by the leaders of organizations as ways of growing or becoming more competitive. There is a natural tendency to analyze the merger decision to consider only the primary issues of finance, product, and market mix. Culture may be loosely thought about, but it is only after the merger that it is taken seriously, suggesting that most leaders make the assumption that they can fix cultural problems after the fact. I would argue that leaders must make cultural analysis as central to the initial merger/acquisition decision as is the financial, product, or market analysis.

Mistakes in this area can be costly. A U.S. company realized that it was about to be acquired by a larger British firm. The company conducted an internal audit of its own culture and concluded that being taken over by the British company would be highly unpalatable. It therefore instituted a set of procedures that made the company unattractive (such as "poison pills") and waited for a situation that looked more promising. A French company became a potential buyer and was perceived to be a much better cultural match, so the U.S. company allowed itself to be bought. Six months later the French parent sent over a management team that decimated the U.S. company and imposed processes that were much less compatible than anything the U.S. company had imagined. But it was too late.

What, then, is the role of leadership in these situations? Several critical tasks can be identified. First, leaders must understand their own culture well enough to be able to detect where there are potential incompatibilities with the culture of the other organization. Second, leaders must be able to decipher the other culture, to engage in the kinds of activities that will reveal to them and to the other organization what some of its assumptions are. Third, leaders must be able to articulate the potential synergies or incompatibilities in such a way that others involved in the decision process can understand and deal with the cultural realities. Fourth, if the leader is not the CEO, he or she must be able to convince the CEO or the executive team to take the cultural issues seriously.

Members of planning groups or acquisition teams often develop the cross-cultural insights necessary to make good decisions about mergers and acquisitions but lack the skills to convince their own senior managers to take the cultural issues seriously. Or, alternatively, they get caught up in political processes that prevent the cultural realities from being addressed until after the key decisions have been made. In either case, cultural diagnosis based on marginality and the ability to surmount one's own culture is again revealed as the critical characteristic of leaders. The learning leader in these instances is the one who is able to learn from people in her or his own organization as well as from outsiders or consultants.

Leadership and Culture in Joint Ventures and Strategic Alliances

Joint ventures and strategic alliances require cultural analysis even more than mergers and acquisitions because cross-national boundaries are more often involved in today's rapidly globalizing world. Deciphering differences between two companies in the same national culture is not as difficult as deciphering both national and company differences when one engages in a joint venture across national boundaries, as the previously reported research by Salk (1992) shows (see page 271). One special difficulty is to determine whether the differences that we perceive are attributable to national or organizational cultures. Yet it is important to make this determination because one would have to assume that the likelihood of changing national characteristics is very low.

The role of leadership in these situations is much the same as in the foregoing scenarios, except here leaders must even surmount their national identities. The European subsidiary of a U.S. company that could never find local managers to put on its board because they were all "too emotional" never came to terms with its own stereotype of managers as intrinsically non-emotional people and never realized or accepted that this was based on their U.S. assumptions. Many organizations make international assignments a requirement for a developing general manager. The explicit notion here is that such experience is essential if potential leaders with broader outlooks are to emerge. In other words, the learning leader must become marginal not only with respect to the organizational culture, but even with respect to national and ethnic culture.

Implications for the Selection and Development of Leaders

A dynamic analysis of organizational culture makes it clear that leadership is intertwined with culture formation, evolution, transformation, and destruction. Culture is created in the first instance by the actions of leaders; culture is embedded and strengthened by leaders. When culture becomes dysfunctional, leadership is needed to help the group unlearn some of its cultural assumptions and learn new assumptions. Such transformations sometimes require what amounts to conscious and deliberate destruction of cultural elements. This in turn requires the ability to surmount one's own taken-for-granted assumptions, seeing what is needed to ensure the health and survival of the group, and orchestrating events and processes that enable the group to evolve toward new cultural assumptions. Without leadership in this sense, groups will not be able to adapt to changing environmental conditions. Let us summarize what is really needed to be a leader in this sense.

Perception and Insight

First, the leader must be able to perceive the problem, to have insight into himself or herself and into the culture and its dysfunctional elements. Such boundary-spanning perception can be difficult because it requires one to see one's own weaknesses, to perceive that one's own defenses not only help in managing anxiety but can also hinder one's efforts to be effective. Successful architects of change must have a high degree of objectivity about themselves and their own organizations, and such objectivity results from spending portions of their careers in diverse settings that permit them to compare and contrast different cultures. International experience is therefore one of the most powerful ways of learning.

Individuals often are aided in becoming objective about themselves through counseling and psychotherapy. One might conjecture that leaders can benefit from comparable processes such as training and development programs that emphasize experiential learning and self-assessment. From this perspective one of the most important functions of outside consultants or board members is to provide the kind of counseling that produces cultural insight. It is therefore far more important for the consultant to help the leader figure out for himself or herself what is going on and what to do than to provide recommendations on what the organization should do. The consultant also can serve as a "cultural therapist," helping the leader figure out what the culture is and what parts of it are more or less adaptive.

Motivation

Leadership requires not only insight into the dynamics of the culture but the motivation and skill to intervene in one's own cultural process. To change any elements of the culture, leaders must be willing to unfreeze their own organization. Unfreezing requires disconfirmation, a process that is inevitably painful for many. The leader must find a way to say to his or her own organization that things are not all right and, if necessary, must enlist the aid of outsiders in getting this message across. Such willingness requires a great ability to be concerned for the organization above and beyond the self, to communicate dedication or commitment to the group above and beyond self-interest.

If the boundaries of organization become looser, a further motivational issue arises in that it is less and less clear where a leader's ultimate loyalty should lie — with the organization, with industry, with country, or with some broader professional community whose ultimate responsibility is to the globe and to all of humanity.

Emotional Strength

Unfreezing an organization requires the creation of psychological safety, which means that the leader must have the emotional strength to absorb much of the anxiety that change brings with it and the ability to remain supportive to the organization through the transition phase even if group members become angry and obstructive. The leader is likely to be the target of anger and criticism because, by definition, he or she must challenge some of what the group has taken for granted. This may involve closing down the company division that was the original source of the company's growth and the basis of many employees' sense of pride and identity. It may involve laying off or retiring loyal, dedicated employees and old friends. Worst of all, it may involve the message that some of the founder's most cherished assumptions are wrong in the contemporary context. It is here that dedication and commitment are especially needed to demonstrate to the organization that the leader genuinely cares about the welfare of the total organization even as parts of it come under challenge. The leader must remember that giving up a cultural element requires one to take some risk, the risk that one will be very anxious and in the end worse off, and yet the leader must have the strength to forge the way into this unknown territory.

Ability to Change the Cultural Assumptions

If an assumption is to be given up, it must be replaced or redefined in another form, and it is the burden of leadership to make that happen. In other words, the leader must have the ability to induce cognitive redefinition by articulating and selling new visions and concepts. The leader must be able to bring to the surface, review, and change some of the group's basic assumptions.

At Multi this process had only begun in the change program described in Chapter Seventeen. Many managers were beginning to doubt that the organization's commitment to science-based technical products could sustain the company in the long run. However, to that point no strong leader had emerged to convince the organization that consumer goods marketing through strong customer-oriented organizations could be a source of pride for the company.

The situation in the Action Company is highly ambiguous and difficult at the present time because it is neither clear whether Murphy will be able to sustain some of the original assumptions that he still believes in as the company faces economic downturns and a mature market requiring much tighter cost controls, or whether Murphy's assumptions about what the company needs today are correct, given the rapidly changing environment. Many of the basic assumptions on which Action was built are less and less sustainable as the company finds itself levelling off in sales and shrinking in terms of people, which poses the serious question of whether or not the basic cultural paradigm must be deliberately changed. If Murphy's belief in internal entrepreneurship and empowerment of his organization is to be sustained, he has to find a leadership succession process that will ensure that his successor has assumptions similar to his own.

Ability to Create Involvement and Participation

A paradox of culture change leadership is that the leader must be able not only to lead but also to listen, to emotionally involve the group in achieving its own insights into its cultural dilemmas, and to be genuinely participative in his or her approach to learning and change. The leaders of social, religious, or political movements can rely on personal charisma and let the followers do what they will. In an organization, however, the leader has to work with the group that exists at the moment, because he or she is dependent on the group members to carry out the organization's mission. The leader must recognize that, in the end, cognitive redefinition must occur inside the heads of many members and that will happen only if they are actively involved in the process. The whole organization must achieve some degree of insight and develop motivation to change before any real change will occur, and the leader must create this involvement.

The ability to involve others and to listen to them also protects leaders from attempting to change things that should not be changed. When leaders are brought in from the outside this becomes especially important because some of the assumptions operating in the organization may not fit the leader's own assumptions yet be critical to the organization's success. To illustrate the kinds of mistakes that are possible, we need remember only the period in the Atari Company's history when Warner Communications, the parent company, decided to improve Atari's marketing by bringing in as president an experienced marketing executive from the food industry. This executive brought with him the assumption that the key to success is high motivation and high rewards based on individual performance. He created and imposed an incentive system designed to select the engineers who were doing the best job in inventing and designing new computer games and gave them large monetary rewards. Soon some of the best engineers were leaving, and the company was getting into technical difficulty. What was wrong?

The new executive had created and articulated clear symbols, and everyone had rallied around them. Apparently, what was wrong was the assumption that the incentives and rewards should be based on individual effort. What the president failed to understand, coming from the food industry with its individualistic product management orientation, was that the computer games were designed by groups and teams and that the engineers considered the assignment of individual responsibility to be neither possible nor necessary. They were happy being group members and would have responded to group incentives, but unfortunately, the symbol chosen was the wrong symbol from this point of view. The engineers also noted that the president, with his nontechnical background, was not adept at choosing the best engineers, because their key assumption was that "best" was the product of group effort, not individual brilliance. Given the incompatible assumptions, it is no surprise that the president did not last long. Unfortunately, damage in terms of the loss of employees and in esprit had been done.

Ability to Learn a New Culture

Culture change leaders often have to take over a company in which they did not previously have any experience. If they are to diagnose and possibly change the culture they have entered, it is, of course, mandatory that they first learn what the essence of that culture is. This point raises the question of how much an individual can learn that is totally new. My hypothesis, based on various streams of research on leadership and management, is that leaders can cross boundaries and enter new organizational cultures fairly easily if they stay within a given industry, as defined by a core technology. A manager growing up in one chemical company can probably become the successful CEO of another chemical company and can learn the culture of that company. What appears to be much more difficult is to cross industry or national boundaries, because cognitive frames that are built up early in the manager's career are fundamentally more embedded. The ability of a John Sculley to become a successful leader of Apple is unusual. More typical is the Atari Company story mentioned above. The Action Company has had a series of senior financial officers drawn from the auto industry, and, though they were effective in bringing some new financial methods to the company, one always heard many stories concerning their inability to understand the Action culture and, consequently, to be ultimately ineffective.

In any case, the leader coming into a new organization must be very sensitive to his or her own need to truly understand the culture before assessing it and possibly changing it. A period of learning lasting a year or more, if the situation allows that much time, is probably necessary. If the situation is more critical, the leader could speed up his or her own learning by systematically involving the layers of the organization below him or her in culture deciphering exercises of the sort described in Chapter Eight.

Summary and Conclusions

It seems clear that the leaders of the future will have to be perpetual learners. This will require (1) new levels of perception and insight into the realities of the world and also into themselves; (2) extraordinary levels of motivation to go through the inevitable pain of learning and change, especially in a world with looser boundaries in which one's own loyalties become more and more difficult to define; (3) the emotional strength to manage their own and others' anxiety as learning and change become more and more a way of life; (4) new skills in analyzing and changing cultural assumptions; (5) the willingness and ability to involve others and elicit their participation; and (6) the ability to learn the assumptions of a whole new organizational culture.

Learning and change cannot be imposed on people. Their involvement and participation are needed diagnosing what is going on, figuring out what to do, and actually doing it. The more turbulent, ambiguous, and out of control the world becomes, the more the learning process will have to be shared by all the members of the social unit doing the learning. If the leaders of today want to create organizational cultures that will themselves be more amenable to learning they will have to set the example by becoming learners themselves and involving others in the learning process.

The essence of that learning process will be to give organizational cuture its due. Can we as individual members of organizations and occupations, as managers, teachers, researchers, and, sometimes, leaders recognize how deeply our own perceptions, thoughts, and feelings are culturally determined? Ultimately, we cannot achieve the cultural humility required to live in a turbulent culturally diverse world unless we can see cultural assumptions within ourselves. In the end, cultural understanding and cultural learning start with self-insight.

References

Adorno, T., and others. *The Authoritarian Personality*. New York: Harper & Row, 1950.

Argyris, C. *Integrating the Individual and the Organization*. New York: Wiley, 1964.

Argyris, C. *Increasing Leadership Effectiveness*. New York: Wiley-Interscience, 1976.

Argyris, C., Putnam, R., and Smith, D. M. *Action Science*. San Francisco: Jossey-Bass, 1985.

Argyris, C., and Schön, D. A. *Theory in Practice: Increasing Professional Effectiveness*. San Francisco: Jossey-Bass, 1974.

Argyris, C., and Schön, D. A. *Organizational Learning*. Reading, Mass.: Addison-Wesley, 1978.

Bailyn, L. "Accommodation of Work to Family." In R. Rapoport and R. N. Rapoport (eds.), *Working Couples*. London: Routledge & Kegan Paul, 1978.

Bailyn, L. "The Apprenticeship Model of Organizational Careers: A Response to Changes in the Relationship Between Work and Family." In P. A. Wallace (ed.), *Women in the Workplace*. Boston: Auburn House, 1982.

Bailyn, L. "Autonomy in the Industrial R & D Lab." *Human Resource Management*, 1985, *24*, 129–146.

Bailyn, L. "Changing the Conditions of Work: Implications for Career Development." In D. H. Montross and C. J. Shinkman (eds.), *Career Development in the 1990's: Theory and Practice*. Springfield, Ill.: Thomas, 1992.

Barley, S. R. "The Professional, the Semi-Professional, and the Machine: The Social Implications of Computer Based Imaging in Radiology." Unpublished doctoral dissertation, Sloan

School of Management, Massachusetts Institute of Technology, 1984a.

Barley, S. R. *Technology as an Occasion for Structuration: Observations on CT Scanners and the Social Order of Radiology Departments.* Cambridge, Mass.: Sloan School of Management, Massachusetts Institute of Technology, 1984b.

Barley, S. R. "On Technology, Time, and Social Order." In F. A. Dubinskas (ed.), *Making Time.* Philadelphia: Temple University Press, 1988, p. 145.

Barley, S. R., Meyer, G. W., and Gash, D. "Cultures of Culture: Academics, Practitioners, and the Pragmatics of Normative Control." *Administrative Science Quarterly,* 1988, *33,* 24–60.

Bartunek, J., and Moch, M. K. "First Order, Second Order, and Third Order Change and Organization Development Interventions: A Cognitive Approach." *Journal of Applied Behavioral Science,* 1987, *23,* 483–500.

Bass, B. M. *Stogdill's Handbook of Leadership.* (Rev. ed.) New York: Free Press, 1981.

Bass, B. M. *Leadership and Performance Beyond Expectations.* New York: Free Press, 1985.

Beckhard, R., and Dyer, W. G., Jr. "Managing Continuity in the Family-Owned Business." *Organizational Dynamics,* Summer 1983a, 5–12.

Beckhard, R., and Dyer, W. G., Jr. "Managing Change in the Family Firm: Issues and Strategies." *Sloan Management Review,* 1983b, *24* (3), 59–65.

Beckhard, R., and Harris, R. T. *Organizational Transitions: Managing Complex Change.* Reading, Mass.: Addison-Wesley, 1987.

Bennis, W. *On Becoming a Leader.* Reading, Mass.: Addison-Wesley, 1989.

Bennis, W., and Nanus, B. *Leadership.* New York: Harper & Row, 1985.

Berg, P. O., and Kreiner, C. "Corporate Architecture: Turning Physical Settings into Symbolic Resources." In P. Gagliardi (ed.), *Symbols and Artifacts.* New York: de Gruyter, 1990.

Blake, R. R., and Mouton, J. S. *The Managerial Grid.* Houston, Tex.: Gulf, 1964.

Bohm, D. *On Dialogue.* Ojai, Calif.: David Bohm Seminars, 1990.

Buono, A. F., and Bowditch, J. L. *The Human Side of Mergers and Acquisitions.* San Francisco: Jossey-Bass, 1989.

Burke, W. W. *Organization Development: A Normative View.* Reading, Mass.: Addison-Wesley, 1987.

Bushe, G. R., and Shani, A. B. *Parallel Learning Structures: Increasing Innovation in Bureaucracies.* Reading, Mass.: Addison-Wesley, 1991.

Butterfield, F. *China, Alive in the Bitter Sea.* New York: Times Books, 1982.

Buzzard, S. H. "An Analysis of Factors That Influence Management Information Technology in Multidivisional Companies." Unpublished master's thesis, Sloan School of Management, Massachusetts Institute of Technology, 1988.

Castaneda, C. *The Teachings of Don Juan.* New York: Pocket Books, 1968.

Castaneda, C. *Journey to Ixtlan.* New York: Simon & Schuster, 1972.

Centre for Organizational Studies. *Mergers and Acquisitions: Organizational and Cultural Issues.* Barcelona, Spain: Centre for Organizational Studies/Foundation Jose M. de Anzizu, 1990.

Ciampa, D. *Total Quality: A User's Guide for Implementation.* Reading, Mass.: Addison-Wesley, 1992.

Conger, J. A. *The Charismatic Leader.* San Francisco: Jossey-Bass, 1989.

Cook, S.D.N. *Know-How, Technology, and Practice.* (In preparation), 1992.

Cook, S.D.N., and Yanow, D. "What Does It Mean for a Culture to Learn? Organizational Learning from a Culture Perspective." Paper presented at the third National Symposium of Public Administration Theory Network, Los Angeles, Calif., April 1990.

Dandridge, T. C., Mitroff, I. I., and Joyce, W. "Organizational Symbolism: A Topic to Expand Organizational Analysis." *Academy of Management Review,* 1980, *5* (1), 77–82.

Davis, S. M. *Managing Corporate Culture.* New York: Ballinger, 1984.

Davis, S. M., and Davidson, B. *2020 Vision.* New York: Simon & Schuster, 1991.

Deal, T. E., and Kennedy, A. A. *Corporate Cultures.* Reading, Mass.: Addison-Wesley, 1982.

Donaldson, G., and Lorsch, J. W. *Decision Making at the Top.* New York: Basic Books, 1983.

Dougherty, D. "Understanding New Markets for New Products." *Strategic Management Journal,* 1990, *11,* 59–78.

Douglas, M. *How Institutions Think.* Syracuse, N.Y.: Syracuse University Press, 1986.

Drucker, P. F. "The Coming of the New Organization." *Harvard Business Review,* Jan.–Feb. 1988, pp. 45–53.

Dubinskas, F. A. *Making Time: Ethnographies of High-Technology Organizations.* Philadelphia: Temple University Press, 1988.

Dyer, W. G., Jr. "The Cycle of Cultural Evolution in Organizations." In R. H. Kilmann, M. J. Saxton, R. Serpa, and Associates (eds.), *Gaining Control of the Corporate Climate.* San Francisco: Jossey-Bass, 1985.

Dyer, W. G., Jr. *Culture Change in Family Firms.* San Francisco: Jossey-Bass, 1986.

Dyer, W. G., Jr. "Integrating Professional Management into a Family-Owned Business." *Family Business Review,* 1989, *2* (3), 221–236.

England, G. *The Manager and His Values.* New York: Ballinger, 1975.

Etzioni, A. *A Comparative Analysis of Complex Organizations.* New York: Free Press, 1975.

Evered, R., and Louis, M. R. "Alternative Perspectives in the Organizational Sciences: 'Inquiry from the Inside' and 'Inquiry from the Outside.'" *Academy of Management Review,* 1981, *6,* 385–395.

Festinger, L. A. *Theory of Cognitive Dissonance.* New York: Harper & Row, 1957.

Gagliardi, P. (ed.). *Symbols and Artifacts: Views of the Corporate Landscape.* New York: de Gruyter, 1990.

Geertz, C. *The Interpretation of Cultures.* New York: Basic Books, 1973.

Gersick, C.J.C. "Revolutionary Change Theories: A Multilevel Exploration of the Punctuated Equilibrium Paradigm." *Academy of Management Review,* 1991, *16,* 10–36.

Gerstein, M. S. *The Technology Connection: Strategy and Change in the Information Age.* Reading, Mass.: Addison-Wesley, 1987.

Gibson, C. F., and Ball, L. D. "Executive Mindscapes and Information Technology." *Indications* (Index Group Inc.), 1989, *6* (6), entire issue.

Goffman, E. *The Presentation of Self in Everyday Life.* New York: Doubleday, 1959.

Goffman, E. *Interaction Ritual.* Hawthorne, N.Y.: Aldine, 1967.

Grenier, R., and Metes, G. *Enterprise Networking: Working Together Apart.* Maynard, Mass.: Digital Press, 1992.

Hall, E. T. *The Silent Language.* New York: Doubleday, 1959.

Hall, E. T. *The Hidden Dimension.* New York: Doubleday, 1966.

Hall, E. T. *Beyond Culture.* New York: Doubleday, 1977.

Handy, C. *The Gods of Management.* New York: Penguin Books, 1978.

Hanna, D. P. *Designing Organizations for High Performance.* Reading, Mass.: Addison-Wesley, 1988.

Harbison, F., and Myers, C. A. *Management in the Industrial World.* New York: McGraw-Hill, 1959.

Hatch, M. J. "The Symbolics of Office Design." In P. Gagliardi (ed.), *Symbols and Artifacts.* New York: de Gruyter, 1990.

Hatch, M. J. *The Dynamics of Organizational Culture.* Copenhagen Business School Paper in Organization, no. 4. Copenhagen, Denmark: Copenhagen Business School, 1991.

Havrylyshyn, B. *Road Maps to the Future.* Oxford, England: Pergamon Press, 1980.

Hedberg, B.L.T., and others. "Camping on See-Saws: Prescriptions for a Self-Designing Organization." *Administrative Science Quarterly,* 1976, *21,* 41–65.

Henderson, R. M., and Clark, K. B. "Architectural Innovation: The Reconfiguration of Existing Product Technologies and the Failure of Established Firms." *Administrative Science Quarterly,* 1990, *35,* 9–30.

Hirschhorn, L. *The Workplace Within: Psychodynamics of Organizational Life.* Cambridge, Mass.: MIT Press, 1988.

Hofstede, G. *Culture's Consequences.* Newbury Park, Calif.: Sage, 1980.

Hofstede, G., and Bond, M. H. "The Confucius Connection: From Cultural Roots to Economic Growth." *Organizational Dynamics,* 1988, *16* (4), 4–21.

Holland, J. L. *Making Vocational Choices.* (2nd ed.) Englewood Cliffs, N.J.: Prentice-Hall, 1985.

Homans, G. *The Human Group.* Orlando, Fla.: Harcourt Brace Jovanovich, 1950.

Jaques, E. *The Forms of Time.* London: Heinemann, 1982.

Johansen, R., and others. *Leading Business Teams.* Reading, Mass.: Addison-Wesley, 1991.

Jones, G. R. "Transaction Costs, Property Rights, and Organizational Culture: An Exchange Perspective." *Administrative Science Quarterly,* 1983, *28,* 454–467.

Jones, M. O., Moore, M. D., and Snyder, R. C. (eds.). *Inside Organizations.* Newbury Park, Calif.: Sage, 1988.

Kets de Vries, M.F.R., and Miller, D. *The Neurotic Organization: Diagnosing and Changing Counterproductive Styles of Management.* San Francisco: Jossey-Bass, 1984.

Kets de Vries, M.F.R., and Miller, D. *Unstable at the Top: Inside the Troubled Organization.* New York: New American Library, 1987.

Kilmann, R. H. *Beyond the Quick Fix: Managing Five Tracks to Organizational Success.* San Francisco: Jossey-Bass, 1984.

Kilmann, R. H., and Saxton, M. J. *The Kilmann-Saxton Culture Gap Survey.* Pittsburgh: Organizational Design Consultants, 1983.

Kluckhohn, F. R., and Strodtbeck, F. L. *Variations in Value Orientations.* New York: Harper & Row, 1961.

Koprowski, E. J. "Cultural Myths: Clues to Effective Management." *Organizational Dynamics,* Autumn 1983, pp. 39–51.

Kotter, J. P. *The Leadership Factor.* New York: Free Press, 1988.

Kotter, J. P., and Heskett, J. L. *Corporate Culture and Performance.* New York: Free Press, 1992.

Kunda, G. *Engineering Culture.* Philadelphia: Temple University Press, 1992.

Kuwada, K. *Strategic Learning.* Research Paper, no. 1121. Stanford, Calif.: Graduate School of Business, Stanford University, 1991.

Lawrence, P. R., and Lorsch, J. W. *Organization and Environment.* Boston: Harvard Graduate School of Business Administration, 1967.

Leavitt, H. J. *Corporate Pathfinders.* Homewood, Ill.: Dow Jones–Irwin, 1986.

Lewin, K. "Group Decision and Social Change." In T. N. Newcomb and E. L. Hartley (eds.), *Readings in Social Psychology.* Troy, Mo.: Holt, Rinehart & Winston, 1947.

Lewis, G. *Corporate Strategy in Action: The Strategy Process in British Road Services.* London: Routledge, 1988.

Likert, R. *The Human Organization.* New York: McGraw-Hill, 1967.

Lorsch, J. W. "Strategic Myopia: Culture as an Invisible Barrier to Change." In R. H. Kilmann, M. J. Saxton, R. Serpa, and others, *Gaining Control of the Corporate Culture.* San Francisco: Jossey-Bass, 1985.

Louis, M. R. "Surprise and Sense Making." *Administrative Science Quarterly,* 1980, *25,* 226–251.

Louis, M. R. "A Cultural Perspective on Organizations." *Human Systems Management,* 1981, *2,* 246–258.

Louis, M. R. "Organizations as Culture Bearing Milieux." In L. R. Pondy and others (eds.), *Organizational Symbolism.* Greenwich, Conn.: JAI Press, 1983.

Louis, M. R. "Newcomers as Lay Ethnographers: Acculturation During Organizational Socialization." In B. Schneider (ed.), *Organizational Climate and Culture.* San Francisco: Jossey-Bass, 1990.

McGregor, D. M. *The Human Side of Enterprise.* New York: McGraw-Hill, 1960.

McKelvey, W. *Organizational Systematics: Taxonomy, Evolution, Classification.* Berkeley: University of California Press, 1982.

McManus, M. L., and Hergert, M. L. *Surviving Merger and Acquisition.* Glenview, Ill.: Scott, Foresman, 1988.

Malone, T., and others. "Electronic Markets and Electronic Hierarchies." *Communications of the ACM,* 1987, *30,* 484–497.

Markus, M. L. *Systems in Organizations.* Boston: Pitman, 1984.

Martin, J. "Stories and Scripts in Organizational Settings." In A. Hastorf and A. Isen (eds.), *Cognitive Social Psychology.* New York: Elsevier, 1982.

Martin, J. "A Personal Journey: From Integration to Differentiation to Fragmentation to Feminism." In P. Frost and others (eds.), *Reframing Organizational Culture.* Newbury Park, Calif.: Sage, 1991.

Martin, J., and Meyerson, D. "Organizational Cultures and the Denial, Channeling and Acknowledgment of Ambiguity." In L. R. Pondy, R. J. Boland, Jr., and H. Thomas (eds.), *Managing Ambiguity and Change.* New York: Wiley, 1988.

Martin, J., and Powers, M. E. "Truth or Corporate Propaganda: The Value of a Good War Story." In L. R. Pondy and others (eds.), *Organizational Symbolism.* Greenwich, Conn.: JAI Press, 1983.

Martin, J., and Siehl, C. "Organizational Culture and Counter Culture: An Uneasy Symbiosis." *Organizational Dynamics,* Autumn 1983, pp. 52–64.

Maruyama, M. "Paradigmatology and Its Application to Cross-Disciplinary, Cross-Professional, and Cross-Cultural Communication." *Dialectica,* 1974, *28,* 135–196.

Maslow, A. *Motivation and Personality.* New York: Harper & Row, 1954.

Merton, R. K. *Social Theory and Social Structure.* (Rev. ed.) New York: Free Press, 1957.

Michael, D. N. *On Learning to Plan—And Planning to Learn.* San Francisco: Jossey-Bass, 1985.

Michael, D. N. "Leadership's Shadow: The Dilemma of Denial." *Futures,* Jan./Feb. 1991, pp. 69–79.

Miller, D. *The Icarus Paradox.* New York: Harper & Row, 1990.

Mitroff, I. I., and Kilmann, R. H. "Stories Managers Tell: A New Tool for Organizational Problem Solving." *Management Review,* 1975, *64* (7), 18–28.

Mitroff, I. I., and Kilmann, R. H. "On Organizational Stories: An Approach to the Design and Analysis of Organizations Through Myths and Stories." In R. H. Kilmann, L. R. Pondy, and L. Sleven (eds.), *The Management of Organization Design.* New York: Elsevier, 1976.

Mohrman, S. A., and Cummings, T. G. *Self-Designing Organizations: Learning How to Create High Performance.* Reading, Mass.: Addison-Wesley, 1989.

Morris, C. *Varieties of Human Value.* Chicago: University of Chicago Press, 1956.

Newman, W. "Cultural Assumptions Underlying U.S. Management Concepts." In J. L. Massie and J. Luytjes (eds.), *Management in an International Context.* New York: Harper & Row, 1972.

Orlikowski, W. J. "The Data Processing Occupation: Professionalization or Proletarianization?" *Research in the Sociology of Work,* 1988, *4,* 95–124.

Ott, J. S. *The Organizational Culture Perspective.* Belmont, Calif.: Dorsey Press, 1989.

Ouchi, W. G. *Theory Z.* Reading, Mass.: Addison-Wesley, 1981.

Parsons, T. *The Social System.* New York: Free Press, 1951.

Pascale, R. T., and Athos, A. G. *The Art of Japanese Management.* New York: Simon & Schuster, 1981.

Pasmore, W. A., and Sherwood, J. J. (eds.). *Sociotechnical Systems: A Sourcebook.* La Jolla, Calif.: University Associates, 1978.

Pava, C.H.P. *Managing New Office Technology.* New York: Free Press, 1983.

Pedersen, J. S., and Sorensen, J. S. *Organizational Cultures in Theory and Practice.* Aldershot, England: Gower, 1989.

Perin, C. "The Moral Fabric of the Office." In S. Bacharach, S. R. Barley, and P. S. Tolbert (eds.), *Research in the Sociology of Organizations* (special volume on the professions). Greenwich, Conn.: JAI Press, 1991.

Peters, T. J. "Management Systems: The Language of Organizational Character and Competence." *Organizational Dynamics,* Summer 1980, pp. 9–26.

Peters, T. J. *Thriving on Chaos.* New York: Knopf, 1987.

Peters, T. J., and Waterman, R. H., Jr. *In Search of Excellence.* New York: Harper & Row, 1982.

Pettigrew, A. M. "On Studying Organizational Cultures." *Administrative Science Quarterly,* 1979, *24,* 570–581.

Pondy, L. R., Frost, P. J., Morgan, G., and Dandridge, T.

(eds.). *Organizational Symbolism*. Greenwich, Conn.: JAI Press, 1983.

Quinn, J. B. "Strategic Change: 'Logical Incrementalism.'" *Sloan Management Review*, 1978, *20*, 7–21.

Redding, S. G., and Martyn-Johns, T. A. "Paradigm Differences and Their Relation to Management, with Reference to Southeast Asia." In G. W. England, A. R. Neghandi, and B. Wilpert (eds.), *Organizational Functioning in a Cross-Cultural Perspective*. Kent, Ohio: Comparative Administration Research Unit, Kent State University, 1979.

Rice, A. K. *The Enterprise and Its Environment*. London: Tavistock, 1963.

Ritti, R. R., and Funkhouser, G. R. *The Ropes to Skip and the Ropes to Know*. Columbus, Ohio: Grid, 1982.

Rockart, J. F., and DeLong, D. W. *Executive Support Systems*. Homewood, Ill.: Dow Jones-Irwin, 1988.

Rockart, J. F., and Short, J. E. "The Networked Organization and the Management of Interdependence." In M. S. Scott-Morton (ed.), *The Corporation of the 1990's*. New York: Oxford University Press, 1991.

Roethlisberger, F. J., and Dickson, W. J. *Management and the Worker*. Cambridge, Mass.: Harvard University Press, 1939.

Sahlins, M., and Service, E. R. (eds.). *Evolution and Culture*. Ann Arbor: University of Michigan Press, 1960.

Salk, J. E. "International Shared Management Joint Venture Teams: Their Development Patterns, Challenges, and Possibilities." Unpublished Ph.D. dissertation, Sloan School of Management, Massachusetts Institute of Technology, 1992.

Sarason, S. B. *The Creation of Settings and the Future Societies*. San Francisco: Jossey-Bass, 1972.

Savage, C. M. *Fifth Generation Management: Integrating Enterprises Through Human Networking*. Maynard, Mass.: Digital Press, 1990.

Schein, E. H. *Coercive Persuasion*. New York: Norton, 1961a.

Schein, E. H. "Management Development as a Process of Influence." *Industrial Management Review* (MIT), 1961b, *2*, 59–77.

Schein, E. H. "Personal Change Through Interpersonal Relationships." In W. G. Bennis, E. H. Schein, D. E. Berlew, and F. I. Steele (eds.), *Interpersonal Dynamics.* Belmont, Calif.: Dorsey Press, 1964, pp. 357–394.

Schein, E. H. "Organizational Socialization and the Profession of Management." *Industrial Management Review,* 1968, *9,* 1–15.

Schein, E. H. *Process Consultation: Its Role in Organization Development.* Reading, Mass.: Addison-Wesley, 1969.

Schein, E. H. *Professional Education: Some New Directions.* New York: McGraw-Hill, 1972.

Schein, E. H. *Career Dynamics: Matching Individual and Organizational Needs.* Reading, Mass.: Addison-Wesley, 1978.

Schein, E. H. *Organizational Psychology.* (3rd ed.) Englewood Cliffs, N.J.: Prentice-Hall, 1980. (First published 1965, 2nd ed. 1970.)

Schein, E. H. "The Role of the Founder in Creating Organizational Culture." *Organizational Dynamics,* Summer 1983, pp. 13–28.

Schein, E. H. *The Clinical Perspective in Fieldwork.* Newbury Park, Calif.: Sage, 1987a.

Schein, E. H. *Process Consultation.* Vol. 2: *Lessons for Managers and Consultants.* Reading, Mass.: Addison-Wesley, 1987b.

Schein, E. H. *Process Consultation.* Vol. 1: *Its Role in Organization Development.* (2nd ed.) Reading, Mass.: Addison-Wesley, 1988.

Schein, E. H. "Reassessing the 'Divine Rights' of Managers." *Sloan Management Review,* 1989, *30* (3), 63–68.

Schein, E. H. *Career Anchors (Revised).* San Diego, Calif.: University Associates, 1990a.

Schein, E. H. "Innovative Cultures and Adaptive Organizations." *Sri Lanka Journal of Development Administration,* 1990b, *7* (2), 9–39.

Schein, E. H. "Legitimating Clinical Research in the Study of Organizational Culture." Massachusetts Institute of Technology Sloan School of Management Working Paper, no. 3288–91, 1991.

Schein, E. H. "The Role of the CEO in the Management of Change." In T. A. Kochan and M. Useem (eds.), *Transforming Organizations.* New York: Oxford University Press, 1992.

Schein, E. H., and Bennis, W. G. *Personal and Organizational Change Through Group Methods.* New York: Wiley, 1965.

Schneider, B. (ed.). *Organizational Climate and Culture.* San Francisco: Jossey-Bass, 1990.

Schultz, M. *Transition Between Symbolic Domains in Organizations.* Copenhagen Business School Papers in Organization, no. 1. Copenhagen, Denmark: Copenhagen Business School, 1991.

Schwartz, H., and Davis, S. M. "Matching Corporate Culture and Business Strategy." *Organizational Dynamics,* Summer 1981, pp. 30–48.

Scott-Morton, M. S. (ed.). *The Corporation of the 1990's.* New York: Oxford University Press, 1991.

Senge, P. M. *The Fifth Discipline.* New York: Doubleday Currency, 1990.

Shrivastava, P. "A Typology of Organizational Learning Systems." *Journal of Management Studies,* 1983, *20,* 7–28.

Silverzweig, S., and Allen, R. F. "Changing the Corporate Culture." *Sloan Management Review,* 1976, *17,* 33–49.

Sithi-Amnuai, P. "The Asian Mind." *Asia,* Spring 1968, pp. 78–91.

Smircich, L. "Concepts of Culture and Organizational Analysis." *Administrative Science Quarterly,* 1983, *28,* 339–358.

Smircich, L., and Calas, M. B. "Organizational Culture: A Critical Assessment." In F. M. Jablin, L. L. Putnam, K. H. Roberts, and L. W. Porter (eds.), *Handbook of Organizational Communication.* Newbury Park, Calif.: Sage, 1987.

Smith, K. K., and Simmons, V. M. "A Rumpelstiltskin Organization: Metaphors on Metaphors in Field Research." *Administrative Science Quarterly,* 1983, *28,* 377–392.

Steele, F. I. *Physical Settings and Organization Development.* Reading, Mass.: Addison-Wesley, 1973.

Steele, F. I. *The Sense of Place.* Boston: CBI Publishing, 1981.

Steward, J. H. *Theory of Culture Change.* Urbana: University of Illinois Press, 1955.

Tagiuri, R., and Litwin, G. H. (eds.). *Organizational Climate: Exploration of a Concept.* Boston: Division of Research, Harvard Graduate School of Business, 1968.

Tannenbaum, R., and Schmidt, H. W. "How to Choose a Leadership Pattern." *Harvard Business Review,* Mar./Apr. 1958, p. 36.

Tichy, N. M. *Managing Strategic Change.* New York: Wiley, 1983.

Tichy, N. M., and Devanna, M. A. *The Transformational Leader.* New York: Wiley, 1986.

Trice, H. M., and Beyer, J. M. "Studying Organizational Cultures Through Rites and Ceremonials." *Academy of Management Review,* 1984, *9,* 653–669.

Trice, H. M., and Beyer, J. M. "Using Six Organizational Rites to Change Culture." In R. H. Kilmann, M. J. Saxton, R. Serpa, and Associates, *Gaining Control of the Corporate Culture.* San Francisco: Jossey-Bass, 1985, pp. 370–399.

Trist, E. L., and others. *Organizational Choice.* London: Tavistock, 1963.

Tucker, R. W., and McCoy, W. J. "Can Questionnaires Measure Organizational Culture: Five Extended Field Studies." Paper presented at the annual meeting of the American Psychological Association, Atlanta, Aug. 12–16, 1988.

Tucker, R. W., and McCoy, W. J. "Objective Assessment of Organizational Culture: Generalizations from 10 Validation Studies." Paper presented at the annual meeting of the Academy of Management, Washington, D.C., Aug. 13–16, 1989.

Tushman, M. L., and Anderson, P. "Technological Discontinuities and Organizational Environments." *Administrative Science Quarterly,* 1986, *31,* 439–465.

Van Maanen, J. "Breaking In: Socialization to Work." In R. Dubin (ed.), *Handbook of Work, Organization and Society.* Skokie, Ill.: Rand McNally, 1976.

Van Maanen, J. "Experiencing Organizations." In J. Van Maanen (ed.), *Organizational Careers: Some New Perspectives.* New York: Wiley, 1977.

Van Maanen, J. "The Fact of Fiction in Organizational Ethnography." *Administrative Science Quarterly,* 1979a, *24,* 539–550.

Van Maanen, J. "The Self, the Situation, and the Rules of Interpersonal Relations." In W. Bennis and others, *Essays in Interpersonal Dynamics.* Belmont, Calif.: Dorsey Press, 1979b.

Van Maanen, J. *Tales of the Field: On Writing Ethnography.* Chicago: University of Chicago Press, 1988.

Van Maanen, J., and Barley, S. R. "Occupational Communities: Culture and Control in Organizations." In B. M. Staw and L. L. Cummings (eds.), *Research in Organizational Behavior.* Vol. 6. Greenwich, Conn.: JAI Press, 1984.

Van Maanen, J., and Kunda, G. "'Real Feelings': Emotional Expression and Organizational Culture." In B. Staw (ed.), *Research in Organizational Behavior.* Vol. 11. Greenwich, Conn.: JAI Press, 1989.

Van Maanen, J., and Schein, E. H. "Toward a Theory of Organizational Socialization." In B. M. Staw and L. L. Cummings (eds.), *Research in Organizational Behavior.* Vol. 1. Greenwich, Conn.: JAI Press, 1979.

Vroom, V. H., and Yetton, P. W. *Leadership and Decision Making.* Pittsburgh, Pa.: University of Pittsburgh Press, 1973.

Watson, T. J., Jr., and Petre, P. *Father, Son & Co.: My Life at IBM and Beyond.* New York: Bantam Books, 1990.

Wilkins, A. L. "Organizational Stories as Symbols Which Control the Organization." In L. R. Pondy and others (eds.), *Organizational Symbolism.* Greenwich, Conn.: JAI Press, 1983.

Wright, J. P. *On a Clear Day You Can See General Motors.* New York: Wright Enterprises, 1979.

Zuboff, S. *In the Age of the Smart Machine.* New York: Basic Books, 1988.

Index

A

Accountability, 134

Action Company: artifacts in, 31–33; assumptions in, 7, 35–38; bias, 304; communication in, 6, 73–74, 121, 222; and differentiation, 260, 261, 263–264; discipline in, 223; external vulnerability for, 202–203; founder, 220–226, 233, 234–237, 238, 239, 240–241, 246–247, 248, 249, 389; goals, 56–57; hiring, 76, 77; human activity in, 127–128; human nature in, 126–127; human relationships in, 133, 134, 137; means, 59; measuring results in, 62, 64; mission, 56; myths and stories, 89–90, 91; organizational evolution at, 307–308, 309; paradigm, 36; peer relationships in, 83–85; power and status in, 81; reality and truth in, 7, 36, 37, 98, 100–101, 103; remedial strategies in, 65–66; rewards and punishment in, 86; socialization in, 96–97, 232–233, 234–237, 238, 239, 240–241, 244–245, 246–247, 248, 249, 250; space in, 118, 119; strategic myopia at, 382; subcultures, 38; teamwork in, 138–139; values in, 33–35

Action research, 147–148. *See also* Internal analysis

Activity, human, 96; being-in-becoming orientation, 128–129; being orientation, 128; doing orientation, 127–128; Handy's typology of, 128, 129; interaction with time and space, 120–121; in learning culture, 364, 366; and organization/environment relations, 131; and role definition, 130–131

Adaptation, 11, 12

Adorno, T., 102

Aggression, 80–81, 135

Aids, to change, 154–155, 156, 357–358

Allen, R. F., 171

Ambiguity, 11; tolerance for, 102–103, 283

American Express, 270

Anderson, P., 306, 331

Anxiety, 22–23, 237, 299, 325, 375

Apple Computer, 255

Architecture, 17, 118–119, 222, 250–251

Argyris, C., 9, 20, 22, 125, 325, 326, 375

Artifacts, 17–18; Action Company, 31–33; identifying, 151; Multi Company, 38–42

Assumptions, basic, 21–26; Action Company, 7, 35–38; about boundaries, 75–79; about communication, 370; about diversity, 370–371; vs. espoused values, 16, 326; evolution of, 11–12, 19–20, 21; about external environment, 364; as filters, 321, 382; about goals, 52, 56–58; about human

407